PRENTICE HALL
PORTFOLIO EDITIONS

Prentice Hall is pleased to introduce *The West: Culture and Ideas, Prentice Hall Portfolio Edition* by A. Daniel Frankforter of The Pennsylvania State University, and William M. Spellman of University of North Carolina at Asheville. Prentice Hall Portfolio Editions feature a collection of concise textbooks on a variety of subjects. Written in classic narrative form, these books allow for the flexibility to enjoy the use of other material such as primary source documents, readings, and technology resources. As you use *The West: Culture and Ideas, Prentice Hall Portfolio Edition*, complete your portfolio by selecting one of many Prentice Hall resources to enhance your course.

Included with *The West: Culture and Ideas, Prentice Hall Portfolio Edition*

The Western Civilizations Documents CD-ROM. Provided at no additional charge with this textbook, the Western Civilizations Documents CD-ROM enables one to access over 200 primary source documents. Essay questions that conclude each selection allow students to respond and submit answers online.

The Study Portfolio

Includes *Practice Tests* and *Evaluating Online Resources for History 2003 with Research Navigator*. Free when bundled with the text.

The Penguin Portfolio

Adopters of *The West: Culture and Ideas, Prentice Hall Portfolio Edition* can receive significant discounts when orders for the text are bundled with Penguin titles. As a special offer from Prentice Hall, *The Letters of Abelard and Heloise* and Voltaire's *Candide* are available for free when bundled with *The West: Culture and Ideas, Prentice Hall Portfolio Edition*.

Create your own portfolio. Customize any of these portfolio options to suit your specific needs and interests. For additional details on any single item or portfolio option, please visit www.prenhall.com or contact your local Prentice Hall representative.

PRAISE FOR THE WEST: CULTURE AND IDEAS

"The writing is the best I have seen in a textbook. One of the goals in my courses is to teach students how to write effectively, concisely, and forcefully. The authors' writing is simple, to the point, and utterly engaging. It is the way I want my students to write."

—Larissa J. Taylor, Colby College

"This text will serve me well. It is written clearly and compactly and does an admirable job of addressing some issues, such as race and feminist concerns, that are typically added onto other texts."

—Sean Moran, Oakland University

"What makes this text readable is the extent to which interpretive issues are interwoven with facts. Textbooks that are hard to read cram a lot of information into a condensed space without helping students think about what they are learning. This book avoids that problem and is a good match for my students."

—Laurel Carrington, St. Olaf College

"The Larger Issues are perhaps the most interesting way of beginning a text that I have ever seen."

—James Halverson, Judson College

The West

Culture and Ideas

Volume I

A. Daniel Frankforter
The Pennsylvania State University

William M. Spellman
University of North Carolina, Asheville

PEARSON
Prentice
Hall

Upper Saddle River, New Jersey 07458

Library of Congress Cataloging-in-Publication Data

Frankforter, A. Daniel.
    The west : culture and ideas / A. Daniel Frankforter, William M. Spellman.—
1st ed.
        p. cm.
    Includes bibliographical references and index.
    ISBN 0-13-098421-3
    1. Civilization, Western—History.   I. Spellman, W. M. II. Title.

CB245.F7 2003
909′09821—dc21

2003050443

VP, Editorial Director: Charlyce Jones Owen
Senior Acquisitions Editor: Charles Cavaliere
Associate Editor: Emsal Hasan
Editorial Assistant: Shannon Corliss
Editor-in-Chief for Development: Rochelle Diogenes
Senior Media Editor: Deborah O'Connell
Development Editor: Gerald Lombardi
Executive Marketing Manager: Heather Shelstaad
Senior Marketing Assistant: Jennifer Bryant
Manager Editor: Joanne Riker
Production Editor: Jan H. Schwartz
Manufacturing Buyer: Tricia Kenny
Creative Design Director: Leslie Osher
Interior Design: Kathy Mystkowska
Cover Design: Bruce Kenselaar
Cover Image: MS CCC 157 p. 383 The visions treamt by King Henry I in Normandy in 1130,
inserted c. 1140 by John of Worcester into the chronicle begun by Florence of Worcester (d. 1118)
c. 1130-40 (parchment). Corpus Christi College, Oxford, UK. The Bridgema Art Library
International, Ltd.
Photo Researcher: Kathy Ringrose
Composition: Pine Tree Composition, Inc.
Printer/Binder: RR Donnelley and Sons
Cover Printer: Phoenix Color Corporation

Credits and acknowledgments borrowed from other sources and reproduced, with permission, in this
textbook appear in the rear matter of this book.

Pearson Education LTD.
Pearson Education Australia PTY, Limited
Pearson Education Singapore, Pte. Ltd.
Pearson Education North Asia Ltd.
Pearson Education Canada, Ltd.
Pearson Educación de Mexico, S.A. de C.V.
Pearson Education—Japan
Pearson Education Malaysia, Pte. Ltd.

BRIEF CONTENTS

CONTENTS

PREFACE

Why another Western civilization textbook? Indeed, in recent years some educators have dismissed the teaching of Western civilization as an outmoded concept. They claim that the Western civilization course was invented to promote Euro-American triumphalism and it has perpetuated colonialist attitudes, cultural intolerance, and even racism. In some undergraduate curricula, the course has been replaced by one that offers a broader survey of world civilizations.

The critics of Western civilization courses make some valid points—at least with respect to the way some courses have been taught. But the fact that a subject can be badly taught does not suggest that it should never be taught. Any national history can degenerate into propaganda and promote jingoism. The fault is less with the subject than with a loss of historical objectivity in its presentation.

Students at American colleges and universities are—regardless of their distant ethnic backgrounds—immersed in a culture deeply indebted to Europe and the Mediterranean region. Other parts of the globe have made undoubted contributions to the culture of what is largely an immigrant nation, but these influences integrate with the values and institutions of what is invariably described as "the West." Despite this, most students begin their undergraduate careers with very little knowledge of the roots of their Western way of life. Those who come from American high schools have repeatedly been taught their national history, but they seldom have more than a brief, cursory exposure to its background. Their lack of understanding of the historical processes that shaped the West makes it difficult for them to situate the American experience in a global context (see the map insert, "The West and the World"). Far from narrowing their perspective, a course in Western civilization can help them understand the development of other cultures and sympathize with their struggles.

Approach

The West: Culture and Ideas defines *West* in the broadest terms as encompassing all the cultures that trace at least some of their ancestry to the ancient Mediterranean world. Many of the textbooks currently available for teaching courses in Western civilization begin with a brief treatment of ancient Mesopotamian and Egyptian civilizations and then largely abandon the Middle East for Europe. When they reach the medieval period, they mention the rise of Islam but leave students with the impression that Islam is an alien, non-Western phenomenon. This obscures the fact that both Christians and Muslims built on the same cultural foundations: Hebraic religious tradition and Hellenistic philosophy and science. It also minimizes the importance of the aid that the Muslim world gave medieval Europe in reclaiming the legacy both shared from the ancient era. With the rise of the Ottoman Empire, Islam often disappears from the narrative (except for brief references to later European encroachments on Ottoman territory). Such minimal treatment of Muslim history poorly prepares students to understand the current international political situation and to evaluate critically common "Western" assumptions about what is, with only partial accuracy, called "the East." The future of much more than the West may depend on Western civilization's Euro-American and Middle Eastern heirs re-examining their history of interaction and divergence.

Despite the fact that civilization is their subject, most textbooks pay little attention to defining the term and usually content themselves with listing a few of its common attributes (cities, literacy, etc.). *The West: Culture and Ideas* urges students to think more deeply about the nature of civilized life by investigating the function of civilization—the explanation for the institutions and technologies that a specific civilization may or may not evolve. It defines *civilization* as the survival strategy characteristic of the human species; a strategy that relies on learning more than instinct. This definition invites reflection on the traditional distinction between history and prehistory and prompts discussion of the effects that eons of prehistoric experience may or may not have on contemporary human behavior.

Defining *civilization* as a survival strategy raises another issue that helps students discover the relevance of history for their lives. It suggests that historical events should be understood as adaptations to environments. *The West: Culture and Ideas* consistently relates historical developments to environmental contexts. Environments are conceived broadly to include both natural ecologies and cultural legacies. An insert of color art ("A Sense of Place: The World through Human Eyes") graphically illustrates how views of the world change in tandem with the evolving interests and values of human communities. The intent is to help students improve perspectives on their personal points of view by reminding them that cultures train their members to perceive the world around them in specific ways. Judgments that seem obviously correct to some may, therefore, appear less so to others. The environmental theme that runs through the text is not meant to promote a particular environmental reform agenda, but it is intended to suggest that an understanding of history is essential for assessing the ecological challenges that face contemporary societies (and are of special concern to many youth).

Organization

The volume of tourist traffic flowing through historical sites and the existence of a History Channel prove that the public at large finds the past innately interesting for its own sake. Students, however, are often afflicted with "presentism," the assumption that the past is an alien land—a curious, but irrelevant, realm. To encourage them to relate the experiences of long-vanished peoples to their own lives, each chapter of the text begins by posing a "larger issue," a question of broad scope or general significance that is raised by something in the period the chapter treats. The chapter is not an essay on the question, and the chapter does not propose a definitive answer to the larger issue it asks students to consider. The larger-issue feature provides a springboard for wide-ranging class discussions of questions that have no simple answers. Debating the issues they raise helps students discover for themselves that the past is more intriguing (and knowledge of its history more useful) than they may have realized.

Each chapter is supplied with aids to assist the comprehension of its reader. A quotation from a primary source introduces the chapter's theme. The topics covered in the chapter are listed at its head. The text is divided into sections and subsections with headings that make its content easy to outline. It contains ample maps, illustrations, and timelines. Two special features help expand the coverage and add human interest to the narrative. Each chapter has two sidebar essays, one dealing with an individual whose life illustrates something about the era being described and another exploring one of the period's significant technological or cultural developments. The narrative unfolds chronologically and avoids shifting back and forth in time—something that many students claim makes a text confusing and difficult to understand. Politics often provides the skeleton of the story, but the traditional "names, dates, and battles" are fleshed out with materials from social, economic, and intellectual history. Attention is paid to segments of society (women, slaves, peasants, etc.) whose contributions sometimes receive insufficient recognition in survey courses. To help students grasp the overall outline of the book, related chapters are grouped together into parts. An image and short essay introduce each part and establish its themes.

A list of review questions that can be used either for class discussion or written assignments ends each chapter. A list of suggested resources can also be found in the back of the book. Additional exercises, documents, study guides, and other resources are provided on the Companion Website™ and on a CD-ROM bound with the text.

Supplements

Companion Website™ A powerful study tool, the Companion Website™ provides chapter summaries, study questions, map-labeling exercises, document-based exercises, and Web-based exercises tied specifically to *The West*. The Faculty Module provides useful classroom material for instructors. Interactive maps, designated by this icon and located on the book's Companion Website™, encourage students to further explore the relationship between geography and history.

Western Civilization Documents CD-ROM Included with every new copy of *The West*, the new Documents CD-ROM offers over 200 primary sources central to the history of the West in easy-to-navigate, print-enabled PDF files. Analytical questions located at the end of each primary source allow students to respond online. A correlation chart at the front of *The West* coordinates the chapters of the book with the documents on the CD-ROM. A two-volume print version of the documents is also available, which can be bundled with the text at no extra charge.

Instructor's Resource Manual and Test-Item File The Instructor's Resource Manual provides chapter outlines, detailed chapter overviews, discussion questions, lecture strategies, and essay topics. The Test-Item File contains over 1,000 multiple choice, true-false, essay, and map questions, organized by chapter.

Prentice Hall Custom Test

Available for Windows and Macintosh platforms, this computerized test-management program allows users to create and edit their own tests using items from the Test-Item File.

Practice Tests (Volumes I and II) Free when packaged with *The West*, Practice Tests provide students with chapter outlines, map questions, sample exam questions, analytical reading exercises, and essay questions tied to the text.

Lives and Legacies: Biographies in Western Civilization (Volumes I and II)   This two-volume collection provides brief, focused biographies of 60 individuals whose lives provide insight into the diversity of the West. Each biography includes an introduction, pre-reading questions, and suggested readings. Free when bundled with the text.

Penguin Classics   Prentice Hall is pleased to provide students with significant discounts when copies of *The West* are purchased together with titles from the acclaimed Penguin Classics series in Western Civilization. Contact your Prentice Hall representative for details.

Evaluating Online Resources, with Research Navigator   This brief guide focuses on developing the critical-thinking skills necessary to evaluate and use online resources. It also provides an access-code and instruction on using Research Navigator™, a powerful tool that streamlines the research process. Free to students when bundled with *The West*.

Understanding and Answering Essay Questions   This brief guide, available free to students when bundled with the text, provides helpful study techniques for understanding different types of essay questions and crafting effective essays.

Reading Critically About History: A Guide to Active Reading   This brief guide focuses on the skills needed to master the essential information presented in college history textbooks. Free when bundled with the text.

Prentice Hall Atlas of Western Civilization   This four-color historical atlas provides additional map resources to reinforce concepts in the text.

ACKNOWLEDGMENTS

Although textbooks usually bear the names of only one or two authors, they are, in reality, communal projects on which many people have labored. Space exists to acknowledge only a few of these talented individuals. Charles Cavaliere, senior acquisitions editor with Prentice Hall, has personally overseen the project and guided its development every step along the way. His suggestions for supplementing the text with Web materials have been invaluable. Gerald Lombardi, developmental editor, has faithfully combed through the text improving phrasing, correcting organizational problems, and saving its authors from blunders of various kinds. Any shortcomings that remain are evidence of authorial obtuseness in profiting from his experience, intelligence, and tactful guidance. Ms. Jennifer M. Markel offered numerous timely improvements to Chapters 14-26. In addition, many other gifted people contributed to the book's design and to the creation of its Web materials, and the entire project owes its completion to the herculean efforts of its meticulous production editor, Jan Schwartz.

Finally, the transformation of a manuscript into a useful, accurate textbook owes much to the scholars who review its initial drafts. Their willingness to take time from their own research and writing to evaluate proposed books from the perspectives of their fields of specialization is a service to their profession that rarely receives the respect it deserves. Their contributions to this project are hardly repaid by this brief expression of gratitude:

Thomas Behr, University of Houston

Beverly Blois, Northern Virginia Community College

April Brooks, South Dakota State University

Laurel Carrington, St. Olaf College

Sara Chapman, Oakland University

Peter L. DeRosa, Bridgewater State College

James Halverson, Judson College

Mark Herman, Edison Community College

L. Edward Hicks, Faulkner University

Charles Hilken, St. Mary's College of California

David Hudson, California State University, Fresno

Gary J. Johnson, University of Southern Maine

Christine J. Kooi, Louisiana State University

Jennifer M. Lloyd, State University of New York at Brockport

Sean Moran, Oakland University

Michael G. Paul, University of South Florida

Jonathan S. Perry, University of Central Florida

Mary Pickering, San Jose State University

Larissa J. Taylor, Colby College

William B. Whisenhunt, College of DuPage

Andrew D. Wilson, Keene State College

DOCUMENTS CD-ROM

CD-ROM Contents

Corresponding chapter
in *The West*

CD-ROM Contents

Corresponding chapter in *The West*

CD-ROM Contents

Corresponding chapter in *The West*

CD-ROM Contents

CD-ROM Contents

Corresponding chapter in *The West*

MAPS

ABOUT THE AUTHORS

Daniel Frankforter is Professor of Medieval History at the Pennsylvania State University. He holds a bachelor's degree (philosophy) from Franklin and Marshall College, a master of divinity degree from Drew University, and master's and doctoral degrees (in medieval history and religious studies) from Penn State. His research has focused on the medieval English church and on the evolving role of women in medieval society. Articles on these topics have appeared in *Manuscripta, Church History, The British Studies Monitor, The Catholic Historical Review, The American Benedictine Review, The International Journal of Women's Studies, Classical and Medieval Literature and Criticism, The Encyclopedia of Monasticism,* and *The Journal of Women's History.* His books include: *A History of the Christian Movement: An Essay on the Development of Christian Institutions, Civilization and Survival* (vol. I), *The Shakespeare Name Dictionary* (with J. Madison Davis), *The Medieval Millennium: An Introduction,* (2nd edition) *The Western Heritage, Brief Edition* (3rd edition, with Donald Kagan, Steven Ozment, and Frank Turner), an edition and translation of Poullain de la Barre's *De L'Égalité des deux Sexes,* and *Stones for Bread: A Critique of Contemporary Worship.* With over thirty years of teaching experience, he has developed fifteen courses focusing on aspects of the ancient and medieval periods of Western civilization, religious studies, and gender studies. His work in the classroom has been acknowledged by the Penn State Behrend Excellence in Teaching Award and the prestigious Amoco Foundation Award for Excellence in Teaching Performance.

William M. Spellman is Professor of History at the University of North Carolina, Asheville. He is a graduate of Suffolk University, Boston, and holds the Ph.D. from the Maxwell School of Citizenship and Public Affairs at Syracuse University. He is the author of *John Locke and the Problem of Depravity* (Oxford, 1988); *The Latitudinarians and the Church of England, 1660–1700* (Georgia, 1993); *John Locke* (Macmillan, 1995); *European Political Thought, 1600–1700* (Macmillan, 1997); *Monarchies, 1000–2000* (Reaktion, 2000); and *The Global Ccommunity: Migration and the Making of the Modern World, 1500–2000* (Sutton, 2002).

LARGER ISSUES

Each chapter in *The West: Culture and Ideas* begins by posing a Larger Issue—a question that is raised by, but has implications beyond, the subject of the chapter. The Larger Issue feature invites readers to explore the past and to form their own opinions about its meaning and significance. The questions raised are not intended to lead to definitive answers but to prompt thinking about issues that continue to impact societies today.

Chapter 1: To what extent are differences among human communities products of environmental factors?

Chapter 2: Is political stability compatible with cultural diversity?

Chapter 3: When does civilization in the West become Western civilization?

Chapter 4: What did the Greeks contribute to the development of modern civilization?

Chapter 5: Are popular governments always preferable to monarchies?

Chapter 6: Do people prefer order to liberty?

Chapter 7: What role should religion play in society?

Chapter 8: How did Europe adapt the civilization it inherited from the ancient world?

Chapter 9: Was conflict among the medieval civilizations inevitable?

Chapter 10: Why are some ages and cultures more optimistic and self-confident than others?

Chapter 11: What did the crises of the late medieval era reveal about the strengths and weaknesses of Europe's civilization?

Chapter 12: How should a society use its history?

Chapter 13: How do people justify and rally support for wars?

INTRODUCTION

What is civilization? The word's Latin root (*civis*) means "citizen," the resident of a city (*civitas*), and the common assumption is that civilization is an urban lifestyle. Civilizations are said to be characterized by bureaucratic governments, stratified social systems, long-distance trade, and specialized technologies such as metal working and writing. Descriptions of this kind are, however, not very informative, for they merely assert that civilization appears when people begin to do what are thought of as civilized things. They do not explain what makes a behavior civilized. The lists of civilized behaviors they offer are not definitive, and they beg the question of how many civilized attributes a people must manifest to be considered civilized. The Inca of ancient Peru, for example, had urban institutions, monumental architecture, and metal working, but no writing system. Were they civilized?

It is tempting to side-step the challenge of defining *civilization* and to proceed on the assumption that because we are civilized, we know civilization when we see it. But it is risky to neglect analyzing key terms at the outset of any investigation. If fundamental concepts contain hidden assumptions, a long, arduous examination ends by concluding what it unwittingly posited at the outset.

Civilization is a particularly tricky term, for it indicates more than the objective attributes of a society. There are ethical and aesthetic dimensions to civilized living. To be civilized is to be more advanced than (and, therefore, superior to) people who have not made the kind of progress civilization allegedly represents.

It seems absurd to question whether civilization is a sign of progress. No rational person with a toothache would choose to be treated by a primitive shaman rather than a modern dentist. But, on the other hand, without the civilized world's sweet-laden diet, there would be less need for dentistry. Civilization does not always enhance, lengthen, or improve life. It may, for example, poison environments, promote unsustainable rates of consumption that exhaust resources, and create generally unhealthy conditions for human organisms. A painful gap often yawns between the problems that civilization causes and the technologies it invents to deal with these things. Civilization has also never invented a technology that prevents civilized people from behaving barbarously. The Nazis had excellent scientists and technicians, but their society was morally inferior to many aboriginal cultures.

Mere information and elaborate social systems do not inevitably make people wise, self-controlled, and morally accountable. Civilization can (and has) helped human beings magnify their inhumanity. Its history, consequently, is something other than a report of successive triumphs over primitive simplicity. Students of civilization's development need to ponder the cost of its advantages and ask themselves whether fair value has always been received for the price paid.

Civilized living involves more than practicing certain technologies or living in a community arbitrarily defined as a city. Generations hence, our descendants might find ways to escape the inconveniences of crowding into cities and communicating with written symbols that are open to misinterpretation. By transcending these traditional hallmarks of civilization they might achieve a level of mutual understanding and a humane lifestyle that made them more, not less, civilized. Instead of equating civilization with a list of civilized attributes, therefore, perhaps we should think of it as the process that has created the attributes that have been—and someday will be—praised as hallmarks of human achievement.

Civilization is the uniquely human survival strategy. Every species of living thing on Earth has to compete for the resources it needs to survive, and each species develops specialized behaviors that enable it to carve out a niche in the world of nature. Each is better at doing something than its competitors, and each pins its survival on the repertoire of skills it has acquired. Few species have played this game as successfully as human beings. Our survival strategy has worked so well that we can cope with every environment on Earth, and we have multiplied to the point where we have crowded out and forced into extinction countless species of plants and animals.

Survival strategies fall into two categories: those that operate by instinct and those that rely on learning from experience. Each one represents a trade-off between strengths and weaknesses. Instincts are efficient and unerring. Members of species that rely on instincts do not have to be taught what to do to survive, for they are programed from birth to respond correctly to crucial stimuli. Instincts also do not necessarily limit the creatures who depend on them for simple behaviors. Human beings had to develop satellite guidance systems before they could equal the ease with which some birds, fish, and insects navigate immense distances.

The chief risk that a species runs when it pins its survival primarily on instincts is inflexibility. If its environment changes, it must evolve a new set of instincts in order to adapt. That requires a timely genetic mutation that redesigns the species by equipping some of its members with new and appropriate attributes. If no useful mutation appears, the species dies out. Charles Darwin (1809–1882), the pioneer of evolutionary theory, hypothesized that evolution proceeds by the random generation of mutations that are sorted out by the struggle to cope with nature's environments. That is, evolution is a process of sink or swim. Mutations are tossed into the world, and those that work survive to reproduce and their descendants redefine their species.

The survival strategy that relies on instincts works well for species that have rapid rates of reproduction and short life-spans. These attributes maximize the potential for the appearance of useful mutations. A capacity for rapid mutation has, for instance, enabled bacteria to fend off modern medicine's arsenal of antiseptics and antibiotics.

The long life-spans and low birthrates of human beings limit opportunities for genetic mutation but provide the time needed to pursue nature's alternative survival strategy: learning. Human babies are born with some instincts (sucking and grasping, for example), but the human species would not exist if it depended primarily on its limited repertoire of instincts for its survival. By opting to learn the behaviors it needs to survive, it gains the advantage of flexibility. To adapt to change, human beings need only alter their thoughts, not their genes. This, however, entails risks. Learners are vulnerable until they acquire survival skills, and their learning (and their applications of it) can be faulty.

The human species maximizes the efficiency of its learning-based survival strategy by ensuring that its individual members do not have to discover everything for themselves. Communities pool what they have learned and pass on their accumulated knowledge to their descendants. The collective plan that a group evolves for adapting to its environment is called its *culture*. Some cultural behaviors (food sharing and gender-assigned occupations, for instance) are widespread, but human beings are defined as a species less by specific cultural behaviors than by their unique capacity for cultural behavior. Different groups of human beings may invent different cultures to adapt to the same environment, for, as folk wisdom maintains, "there is more than one way to skin a cat."

Cultural behavior is not unique to the human species. Many animals depend to some extent on behaviors that are learned and taught, and within a single primate species some groups may evolve behaviors that distinguish them from others. But the human species exceeds all others in the scope and range of its cultural activity–the ultimate manifestation of which is the creation of a civilization.

In ordinary conversation, simple societies are called cultures and complex ones civilizations. This suggests that culture and civilization are the poles of a continuum–that is, that civilization is only cultural behavior on a grand scale. If this is so, the search for a definitive description that applies to all civilizations (and for the features that indicate when civilization first appears) may be a misdirected inquiry. It might be more productive to explore the continuity between culture and civilization. When we view civilization from this perspective, two things become apparent: 1) Prehistory and history appear more linked by bridges than separated by gulfs; and 2) analyses of environments (the physical and mental contexts for human lives) loom large in our efforts to comprehend the histories of civilizations.

Humanity's prehistory is vastly longer than its recorded history. The hominid family to which human beings belong may be 7,000,000 years old. The modern human species, *homo sapiens sapiens,* appeared at least 130,000 years ago, but materials that enable us to reconstruct a history of its activities have been accumulating for less than 5,000 years. The exploration of the millennia that human beings and their hominid ancestors spent as migratory hunters and gatherers is a task for archaeologists and anthropologists more than historians. These scientists have developed sophisticated research techniques, but information about the remote past is scanty. Long before *homo sapiens sapiens* evolved, hominids began to use some of the rocks, sticks, and bones they found as tools. Gradually, they learned to manufacture implements from stone and other materials. They organized themselves into communities that doubtless had distinctive customs and unique identities. We can only speculate about what went on in the minds of these people as their fund of information about the world increased. We should regret our ignorance, for it is unlikely that all this prehistoric experience has left no impression on us. We are the products of eons of prehistory and have not, after all, been exposed to the effects of civilized life for long.

The environments with which civilization helps people cope are more complex than those that faced their prehistoric ancestors. But the environment for a culture-creating being like *homo sapiens sapiens* has always consisted of more than nature's resources and climate. A culture constructs a mental environment that interposes itself between an intelligent creature and the physical world. It determines how people see the space they inhabit. It organizes the world and sets the stage for human activity. It predisposes people to some actions and blinds them to others. People live in environments composed both of ideas and physical conditions, and ideas can pose challenges that are as daunting as anything found in nature. They define what is believed to be possible and permissible.

The history of civilization is only a record of the latest phase in what has been a long struggle for survival by the human species. It is important to remember that civilization is a fragile human and relatively recent construct. It might even be considered an experiment that has yet to be put to a real test. Its success cannot be taken for granted, and its past cannot be explained as if it were somehow preordained or inevitable. Civilization is a hard won heritage, the legacy of a double-edged sword that needs careful handling.

The West
Culture and Ideas

PART ONE

DEPARTURE
PREHISTORY TO 1000 B.C.E.

The technology of the last half of the twentieth century gave Earth's inhabitants, their first opportunity literally to step back and view their home world objectively. What they saw was what may prove to be the universe's rarest treasure: a planet that sustains a complex of delicately modulated systems without which the fragile phenomenon known as life would not exist. Humanity has only begun to unravel the mysteries of the great "blue marble" that gave it birth. In fairness, however, it has had little time to explore its habitat. Earth is about 4.5 billion years old. The current human species appeared only about 160,000 years ago, and it began to forge the tools of civilization only about five thousand years ago. It is a species in its infancy and as such is characterized by energy more than wisdom. To thrive and mature, it must educate itself, but it has no teacher other than itself. Human beings learn from their experiences, and history is their classroom.

	CULTURE	ENVIRONMENT AND TECHNOLOGY	POLITICS
C. 4,500,000,000 B.C.E.		Earth's origin	
C. 4,000,000 B.C.E.		hominid evolution begins	
	Australopithecines		
C. 2,500,000 B.C.E.	Lower Paleolithic Era		
	Homo Habilis	pebble tools	
C. 1,600,000 B.C.E.	Homo Erectus	pressure-chip tools	hunter–gatherer tribes
C. 200,000 B.C.E.	Middle Paleolithic Era Neanderthal		
C. 130,000 B.C.E.	Homo Sapiens Sapiens Upper Paleolithic Era		
		first arts: cave painting, sculpture	
C. 20,000 B.C.E.	Mesolithic Era		
		composite tools	
C. 10,000 B.C.E.	Neolithic Era	agriculture	
		farming and herding	settled life: villages
C. 3500 B.C.E.	Bronze Age	centers of population density	
		irrigation agriculture metal working	city-states appear in Sumer
C. 3000 B.C.E.		writing	unification of Egypt (3100 B.C.E.)
			Sumerian monarchy (3000 B.C.E.)
			Egypt, Old Kingdom (2700 B.C.E.)
		salinization of the Sumerian region	Egypt, Middle Kingdom (2025 B.C.E.)
			Sumer's fall (2004 B.C.E.)
C. 2000 B.C.E.		domestication of the horse	Indo-European migration (2000 B.C.E.)
			Amoritic Babylon (1800 B.C.E.)
			Egypt, Hyksos invasion (1630 B.C.E.)
			Hittite Empire (1600 B.C.E.)
			Egypt, New Kingdom (1550 B.C.E.)
C. 1200 B.C.E.	Iron Age	smelting and forging of iron	Sea Peoples invasion (1230 B.C.E.)
		infantry warfare	Assyrian empire (1114 B.C.E.)
C. 1000 B.C.E.			Kingdom of Israel (1000 B.C.E.)

CHAPTER 1

THE BIRTH OF CIVILIZATION

> I will proclaim the deeds of King Gilgamesh. . . . No one could resist the strength of his arms. . . . But his people of Uruk said among themselves: "Gilgamesh is arrogant and leads us into battle for his own pleasure. Fathers lose their sons, for he takes them all—even the young ones—to serve in his armies. A king ought to be the shepherd of his people, but Gilgamesh's lust spares no virgin for her fiancé nor even the wives and daughters of his soldiers and nobles. He is, however, the city's defender. . . ."
>
> —The Epic of Gilgamesh

Larger Issue: *To what extent are differences among human communities products of environmental factors?*

For thousands of years human beings were a migratory species. They supported themselves by hunting and by gathering the foodstuffs that nature spontaneously provided. When supplies in one place were exhausted, they moved to a new region. About 10,000 years ago, the human species began what became a nearly universal shift to farming and herding. This forced groups to settle more or less permanently in one place and confront a host of challenges—from the construction of buildings to the engineering of new social relationships. In a few exceptionally fertile locales, population increased to the point where the informal, personal relationships that governed tribes and villages could no longer maintain order. As social life grew more complex, civilization appeared.

The world's first civilization flourished some 5,000 years ago on the plains of southern Iraq in a land called Sumer. It was characterized by city-states ruled by kings. *The Epic of Gilgamesh* (the ancient poem quoted above) reflects on the pros and cons of the kind of life it provided. Gilgamesh was the king of the city of Uruk. His subjects admired his strength, wisdom, and beauty. They boasted of the monsters he killed, the great walls and temples he built, his dangerous journeys, and the exotic treasures he brought home from foreign lands. However, his heroic vigor also fueled ambitions and appetites that oppressed his people and drove him to sacrifice their sons to his wars and their daughters to his lusts.

The Epic of Gilgamesh may be the world's oldest literary reflection on the human condition and the cost of the glories and comforts of civilization. Sumerian monarchies provided efficient leadership and many services, but they also curtailed freedoms. They subordinated ties of family and kinship to hierarchies of class and institutionalized authority. They confiscated wealth and labor, and they imposed laws and regulations. In these ways they marshaled resources that allowed them to carry out projects that literally redesigned their world. They altered landscapes and redefined humanity itself. The assumption of such power entailed responsibilities that people have been slow to comprehend. As you reflect on civilization's history, consider the implications of civilization's ability to alter the natural environments on which human beings rely for their survival.

TOPICS IN THIS CHAPTER

The Evolution of the Prehistoric Cultures • The Archaic States • The Origin of Civilization in Mesopotamia: Sumer • The Rise of Civilization in Egypt

The Evolution of Prehistoric Cultures

Western civilization emerged from the prehistoric cultures that flourished around the Mediterranean Sea. The prehistoric eras are called the Stone Ages because most of what we know about them has been inferred from the study of the stone implements that are their chief surviving artifacts. It is difficult to reconstruct an entire culture from only one of its products, particularly when that product may not reflect that culture's most sophisticated work. Stone is a difficult medium, and prehistoric people doubtless produced other—and likely more elaborate—objects from more tractable materials (such as wood, leather, and fibers). Had specimens of these crafts survived, we might have a greater appreciation for the achievements of prehistoric peoples.

The Paleolithic Era   The Paleolithic ("Old Stone") era begins whenever we think we see the earliest traces of human behavior and continues (in the West) to the retreat of Europe's last Ice Age (about 10,500 years ago). Paleolithic societies were supported by hunting and gathering nature's bounty. Hunting and gathering can be organized in different ways, and environmental conditions probably created great variety among prehistoric societies. Some locales would have favored gathering, which in modern aboriginal communities is usually a female specialization. Others (such as the Arctic) would have increased dependence on hunting, a largely male occupation. Scholars have speculated about the distribution of power between males and females in Paleolithic communities, but theories about prehistoric gender relations are more abundant than evidence for them.

About 31,000 years ago, an explosion of cultural activity occurred just as *Homo sapiens sapiens* (modern humanity) was emerging as Earth's sole surviving hominid species. What happened to the other hominids—particularly the Neanderthals with whom *Homo sapiens sapiens* had coexisted for a long time—is unknown.

The people who lived in Europe as the Paleolithic era drew to a close refined the production of stone tools, but the period's cultural breakthrough is signified by the appearance of something entirely new: art. Paleolithic sculptors and painters may have been motivated by magical or religious concerns more than aesthetic motives, but their intentions are uncertain. Scholars, for instance, have puzzled over the significance of the numerous female figurines that are found at Paleolithic sites from Europe to Siberia. Some authorities claim that they prove the existence of a prehistoric mother-goddess cult, but this may read too much into sparse, ambiguous evidence.

Even more puzzling than Paleolithic sculpture is the art of cave painting that began about 30,000 years ago and thrived for over 15,000 years. Cave paintings were not decorations for dwellings, for they are found in deep caverns that were difficult to access. They probably had some ritualistic significance. Scholars initially assumed that they were products of hunter magic—depictions of hunts that were intended to ensure kills. But animals that people ate were only one of their subjects. Some caves also seem to have thematic plans that assign different kinds of animals to different places. Abstract shapes, hand prints, patterns of dots, and

Figure 1–1 The Venus of Willendorf This famous statuette, found near Willendorf, Austria, in 1908, may be about 25,000 years old. Because it is only four and one-half inches tall, it was easily portable. The limestone from which it was made is not native to the region where it was discovered.

clusters of lines are also found, but human figures are rare. If the paintings were meant to illustrate myths and legends, their meaning has been lost.

The Paleolithic era phased into the Neolithic ("New Stone") at roughly the same time in perhaps seven different places around the world. The cultural innovations that marked the event reflect efforts to increase the food supply. As the last Ice Age's glaciers retreated, global climate became warmer and wetter, sea levels rose, the tundras favored by herd animals shrank and shifted northward, and plant and animal species redistributed themselves. Stressed communities that could not migrate to the shrinking regions where their old way of life was still

People in Context: The Iceman

Prehistory usually consists of generalizations about groups, whereas history describes particular events or individuals. In September 1991 hikers in the Alps, on the border between Austria and Italy, made a discovery that constitutes a rare exception to this rule. They stumbled across the corpse of the Iceman, a male from a prehistoric culture who died about 3300 B.C.E. The Iceman's remains had survived frozen inside a glacier along with his clothing and possessions: a copper axe-head, a flint-bladed dagger, a pouch filled with tiny flint and bone implements, a bow whose length equaled its owner's height, a quiver with fourteen arrows (two of which were finished with stone points and feathered shafts), and a bone and wood tool for sharpening flint blades. His garments of leather and fur were stitched together, and he wore boots and an ornament or talisman suspended on a leather thong—a doughnut-shaped disk of white marble.

   The Iceman probably lived in a nearby village whose inhabitants pastured cattle (as villagers there do today) by driving them to highland meadows in the summertime. The contents of his stomach suggest that he died in late spring when the Alpine passes were still deep in snow. He did not die from natural causes. A flint arrowhead about an inch long is lodged about three inches under his left shoulder near his lung. It traveled upward into his body, missing organs but severing blood vessels. His possessions were not looted, so he may have killed whoever shot him or managed to flee his enemy. If so, he slowly bled to death alone on a cold mountainside and was never buried. Perhaps he was an outcast or had friends and relatives who searched for him but never found him.

Question: What do the Iceman's possessions reveal about his environment and his cultural adaptations?

possible had to figure out how to wring more sustenance from their changing environment. This inched some of them toward the brink of civilization.

The Neolithic Revolution   The Neolithic era, as a Stone Age, is associated with a particular kind of stone tool. In earlier periods, tools were manufactured by pressure chipping—by nicking flakes from pieces of flint, quartz, or obsidian (a volcanic glass) to make instruments with sharp edges. Neolithic toolmakers worked tougher kinds of stone by grinding them into shape, but theirs was not the most important new technology of the Neolithic period.

   The Neolithic has been characterized as a revolutionary era because of the new way of life it introduced. Neolithic people shifted from passively harvesting what nature provided to compelling nature to produce what they wanted. They ceased to rely exclusively on hunting and gathering, and began to farm and herd. Herding and farming revolutionized lifestyles, but they were not revolutionary discoveries. They were applications of what Paleolithic people had long known. Gatherers were intimately acquainted with the life cycles of plants, and hunters, who often trapped animals before killing them, knew that some of the species they captured would domesticate.

   It did not take a stroke of genius to turn a hunter-gatherer into a farmer-herder, but it did take a powerful motivation. Farming did not make life easier. Farming probably required longer and more arduous labor than hunting and gathering. Farmers had a less varied and healthy diet. They staked their survival on fewer resources, and they ran a greater risk of disease from contact with domesticated animals and human waste. Anthropological evidence even suggests that the transition to farming reduced life spans. Why, then, was farming so widely adopted?

Farming offered one advantage: It increased the yield of food from a finite amount of land. If climate change or population growth was making it difficult for a people to feed themselves, they had to go on the offensive—that is, to force nature to yield more than it would on its own.

The survival strategy that the Neolithic era pioneered has worked extraordinarily well for the human species. Some 500,000 years ago, Earth's hominid population may have numbered no more than a million. At the start of the Neolithic era, about 6 million people were spread around the globe. Plagues, wars, and famines moderated growth rates, but by the eighteenth century C.E., the human population stood at 1 billion. Another two centuries brought it to 6 billion, and there may be 9 billion humans by the mid–twenty-first century. Humanity may well be undone by its own success.

Prelude to Civilization   Farming appeared first where nature made it easiest. Pioneer farmers looked for fields that they could clear of undesirable vegetation, soil that they could work with simple tools, and a climate in which grains flourished. The thick forests of central and northern Europe, with their damp, heavy soils, were too challenging. The semi-arid grasslands of the Middle East were, however, ideal, and many of the domesticated species on which Western agriculture came to depend (wheat, barley, pigs, sheep, goats, and cattle) were native to that region. (See Map 1–1.)

The earliest agricultural settlements appeared about 10,000 years ago. Most of them probably combined hunting and gathering with farming. (Some Native Americans were still pursuing this way of life in the nineteenth century C.E.) The biblical city of Jericho, which was founded about 8400 B.C.E., is the oldest known continuously inhabited settlement in the world. By 7300 B.C.E., its 2,000 residents must have been prosperous enough to attract unwelcome attention, for they had built a stone wall to defend their community.

Many early agricultural sites in Syria and Palestine were abandoned about 6000 B.C.E, just as new villages began to appear in neighboring Anatolia (Asia Minor or modern Turkey). The most remarkable of Anatolia's settlements was Çatal Hüyük. At its peak (6200–5400 B.C.E.), it sprawled over 32 acres and housed about 7,000 people. It probably looked like a single, huge adobe building. Its approximately 1,000 houses were one- or two-story timber and mud-brick affairs. They surrounded open courtyards, but no streets divided them. Each structure abutted against its neighbor's, and people traveled over, and accessed them through, their roofs.

Most houses at Çatal Hüyük consisted of a single, large living space attached to a small storage room. They were furnished with mud-brick benches or sleeping platforms, woven floor mats, baskets, and various wooden and pottery vessels. Tools were made from obsidian that was mined locally and exported. People clothed themselves with fur, leather, and cloth woven from plant fibers and animal hair. They wore jewelry made from seashells. When they died, their bodies were exposed until carrion birds picked their bones clean. The bones were then collected and buried beneath the floors of their relatives' homes.

Of the 158 buildings excavated at Çatal Hüyük, forty or more contain religious shrines, many of which have the horns and skulls of cattle and wild beasts mounted in clusters on their walls. Clay models of women's breasts are also molded around animal skulls. The dominant

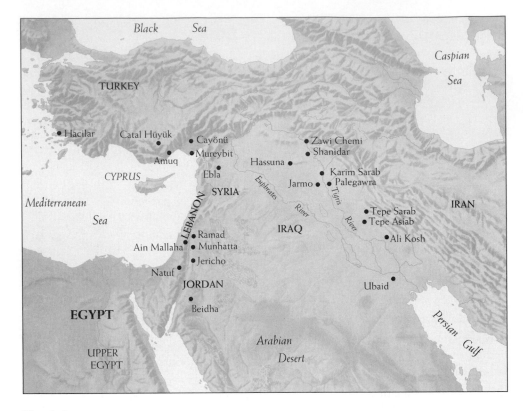

Map 1–1
Early Agricultural Settlements   The first civilizations arose along the Tigris, Euphrates, and Nile rivers, but that is not where the earliest farming communities were found. *Question:* Why did the places where agriculture was first practiced not produce the first civilizations?

images are of women, bulls, leopards, and vultures, and a common motif is a human female giving birth to a horned animal. All of this might suggest a religion preoccupied with fertility and death.

Men were buried with weapons and women with jewelry. Bone analysis suggests that men ate more meat than women, and the fact that some graves were more richly equipped than others implies that the community was socially stratified. Çatal Hüyük was a large, stable, long-lived community supported by a complex economy and amply indulging the human appetite for comfort, beauty, and meaning, but was it civilized?

The Archaic States

Societies that were undoubtedly elaborate enough to be classed as civilizations appeared in Sumer and Egypt well before 3000 B.C.E and somewhat later at other places around the globe. The Harappan civilization of the Indus River Valley emerged about 2500 B.C.E., and city-states ruled by the Shang Dynasty flourished along China's Yellow River sometime after 1800 B.C.E. A society capable of erecting monumental buildings flourished on the coast of Peru as early as 2000 B.C.E., and the Olmecs pioneered civilization in Mesoamerica about 1500 B.C.E.

Civilization dawned with the first of the metal ages: the Bronze Age. People were beating nuggets of copper into tools and ornaments as early as 7500 B.C.E., but it was not until about 5500 B.C.E. that they learned to smelt copper from its ores. The technique was developed in Anatolia, and by 4000 B.C.E., it had spread throughout the Middle East. Pure copper was too soft for use in tools, but when it was alloyed with tin or arsenic, it became the much more durable metal called bronze.

The Origin of Civilization in Mesopotamia: Sumer

At first glance, it seems surprising that the West's earliest civilization should have appeared in such a hostile environment. Average summer temperatures on the Mesopotamian plain hover around 104 degrees Fahrenheit and may reach 120 degrees Fahrenheit. There is little rainfall, and no natural barriers protect against the windstorms and floods that sweep the flat, open landscape. Resources are few: no stone, no metal ores, and no trees sturdy enough to provide lumber. There was, however, an abundance of deep, rich soil deposited over eons by the annual flooding of the Tigris and Euphrates rivers. Most of the primal civilizations (Sumer, Egypt, India, and China) sprang up along great rivers. Once the Sumerians developed irrigation systems, water from their rivers unleashed the unique fertility of their land. The Sumerian farmer may have got twenty seeds back for every one that he sowed—two to four times what a Roman or medieval farmer earned thousands of years later. (See Map 1–2.)

During the Neolithic era, farmers flourished in the Iranian highlands east of the Tigris River, but they were slow to conquer the Mesopotamian plain. The Tigris ran fast through a relatively deep channel that made its waters difficult to tap for purposes of irrigation. Early settlers preferred the banks of its partner, the shallower, slow-moving Euphrates. But it, too, presented them with problems. The Euphrates deposited silt that formed levees along its banks and raised its bed above the level of the surrounding countryside. The river sometimes broke through its levees to turn wide stretches of farmland into swamp, and it sometimes carved new channels that altered its course. It also flooded at an inconvenient time each year—in April, when grain crops were ripening. Skillful engineering and massive labor were needed to trap its waters in reservoirs and distribute them where needed in the appropriate seasons. Once the Sumerians managed this, however, their homeland could support a population of unprecedented density.

The Predynastic Era   We do not know where the Sumerian people originated or when they settled the lands north of the Persian Gulf. Language often provides a clue to a people's background, but it is of no help here. Sumerian is not related to any known tongue.

The Sumerians probably entered Mesopotamia from the east, from the Zagros Mountains. They were attracted to southern Mesopotamia because the marshes along the rivers and the coasts of the Persian Gulf provided sources of food. Pioneers in the region would have relied on a mixture of farming, herding, hunting, and gathering. Myths and archaeological evidence identify the town of Eridu near the later, more famous city of Ur, as one of the area's earliest settlements. It was inhabited by 5400 B.C.E.

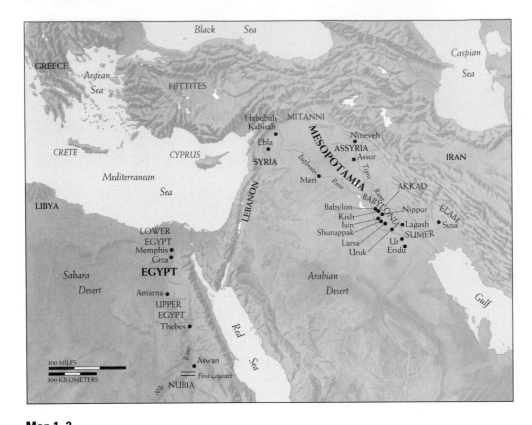

Map 1–2
The Fertile Crescent   The arc of agriculturally productive land where civilization first took root is called the Fertile Crescent. Farmers in its eastern portion (Mesopotamia— Greek for "between rivers") relied on irrigation and the annual floods of the Tigris and Euphrates rivers. Those inhabiting its center section (the Mediterranean coast) had enough rainfall to sustain their crops. The Nile's floods and irrigation ensured the productivity of the crescent's western segment. *Question:* Would geography have tied the West's two original civilizations together or encouraged them to develop separately?

During the first phase in Sumer's development, new kinds of settlements spread across the southern Mesopotamian plain. They were larger than Neolithic villages, and each boasted a major building, the construction and maintenance of which required a more sophisticated government than was characteristic of a simple village. Because all the dwellings in these communities were about the same size and there is little evidence of differences in wealth or of occupational specialization, privileged social classes may not yet have appeared. The investment that these communities made in their public buildings suggests, however, that this was changing. Their great buildings were probably temples, and temples create powerful priesthoods.

Sumerian city-states reached their full development between 3600 and 3000 B.C.E. Gilgamesh's Uruk (or Erech), for instance, grew by absorbing neighboring villages until it had about 50,000 inhabitants. Scholars have speculated about the motives for concentrating population in the dozen or so urban centers that sprang up in Sumer during the fourth millennium B.C.E. At one time, they assumed that the development of irrigation systems promoted the growth of cities, but archaeological evidence suggests that the expansion of irrigation systems followed the rise of cities. Legends describe this period as an era of warfare. This and archaeological evidence, such as the six miles of defensive walls that encircled Uruk, suggest that the Sumerians clustered together for protection.

The Dynastic Eras   Archaeology has provided most of what we know about the early phases in Sumer's development. Later eras are better documented, thanks to the Sumerian invention of writing toward the end of the fourth millennium B.C.E. Although buildings identifiable as palaces are not found much before 2500 B.C.E., kings appeared much earlier. About the year 2100 B.C.E., a scribe compiled a list of the names of all the kings who were believed to have reigned in Sumer. He claimed that monarchy was instituted by the gods in the wake of a great flood that nearly obliterated humanity about 3000 B.C.E. The Sumerian flood legend lies behind the Bible's account of Noah's ark, but no geological evidence confirms that there was ever a universal flood. When Sumerian myth-makers wanted an event to symbolize a break in history and a fresh start with new institutions, they naturally imagined a flood, for floods often forced Sumer's people to rebuild.

As villages grew into cities, monarchy most likely emerged of necessity. Sumer's early urban households continued, like those in villages, to be economically self-sufficient, and they may therefore, have been fairly autonomous. City life would, however, have eroded their independence. Informal meetings of heads of families suffice to run villages, but not cities—particularly when crises demand swift action. On such occasions, there is no time for large groups to meet and debate what to do. Survival necessitates submission to the authority of a single, all-powerful leader. After an emergency passes, he may surrender his powers and return to private life. But as crises become more frequent, people begin to depend on his services. The end result is the establishment of a monarchy and a dynasty, a family with a hereditary right to rule.

City Life   The security of a city required negotiation with heavenly as well as earthly powers. Powerful priesthoods probably appeared in Sumer's cities before kings were permanently established, and early researchers thought that Sumerian cities were religious communes in which everyone worked on temple estates and survived on rations doled out from temple granaries. This was an illusion created by the nature of the surviving documents, most of which come from temple archives. Sumerian cities were complex societies, not hives of temple slaves. Artisans, merchants, priests, and government officials lived in cities, and so did many farmers who commuted to the countryside to work their fields.

Temples and kings had large estates, but much property remained in private hands. Title to this private land was often held by kinship groups rather than individuals. It could be sold only with the consent of all the members of the family that worked it. The prejudice against selling land away from the family was so strong that sellers sometimes adopted buyers to make such transactions more acceptable. Personal property was passed down through the male line, and all a man's sons shared equally in his estate. Women could buy and sell land and testify in court cases. Monogamous marriage was the rule, but divorce and remarriage were possible. Women as well as men were impressed into labor gangs to work on communal projects such as clearing out irrigation ditches and building walls. Their rations were smaller than those of men at whose sides they toiled.

Urban economies were complex. They integrated the work of farmers, traders, artisans, and various kinds of professionals. Some families prospered more than others, and class divisions and social stratification became a fact of life. An aristocracy entrenched itself at the top of society, but there was some social mobility. A few men from obscure backgrounds even became kings. Captives taken in war kept slave markets supplied. Slavery was taken for granted, but it was not essential to the Sumerian economy. Slaves usually worked as household servants, for it was hard to prevent their running away if they were sent out into the fields to do agricultural work.

By our standards, Sumerian cities were uncomfortable. The thousands who sheltered behind the walls of a large town might be crammed into an area equivalent to about twenty football fields. Towns were unplanned. Space was at a premium, so streets were narrow (seldom more than nine feet wide) and plazas few. Everything was constructed of mud brick. Major public edifices were sometimes protected with expensive facings of fired brick or sheets of copper. Walls were decorated with mosaics made from cones of colored clay set in plaster. Most buildings were only one or two stories high. Houses fronted directly on the street, and they had few doors or windows on their outside walls. By depending on interior courtyards for light and air, they enhanced their security and cleanliness. The dust that was raised as the 50,000 or so residents of a city (and their animals) trod its unpaved streets must have been visible for miles. Homes were minimally furnished. Possessions were few and clothing simple. Men and women wore similar woolen skirts or kilts and cloaks.

Cities were unhealthy. They had no sewer systems. Wastes were dumped into streets for animals to scavenge, and drinking water was drawn from the same streams and canals into which sewage drained. One of the byproducts of civilization's urban lifestyle was epidemic disease. Dense human populations (particularly those that live in close association with domesticated animals) create ideal conditions for the spread of parasites and infectious agents.

The most imposing features of a Sumerian city were its fortifications and its temples. Mud-brick walls encircled the greater cities, and temples soared far above all other urban structures. Each city chose a deity to be its special patron and provided him or her with lavish accommodations. Sumerian gods were assumed to want the same things that human beings crave: shelter, food, and amusement. Temples were literally homes for gods. Sacred images were cared for like living things. They were provided with changes of clothing, meals, and entertainments.

The Sumerians believed that a god's residence should be elevated above the ordinary human plane. Before 3000 B.C.E., lofty terraces were being built to serve as foundations for temples. Builders then began to layer terraces on top of terraces to create pyramidal structures called ziggurats ("mountain tops"). A ziggurat was an artificial mountain, a solid structure on whose pinnacle a temple perched. The largest ziggurats covered about two acres and may have been as tall as a seven-story building. Given that they were made of fragile, sun-dried bricks, considerable engineering skill was needed to stabilize them. They also required constant maintenance, for they were huge piles of dirt that absorbed moisture and deteriorated at an alarming rate. Most are so badly ruined now that we can only speculate about their original appearance.

Sumerian Trade and Industry   Sumer produced surpluses of grain that it could trade for things that were not locally available. The merchants who procured goods from abroad did not necessarily make long journeys, for many items reached Sumer simply by passing from

Figure 1–2   The Ziggurat of Ur   This is an artist's recreation of a ziggurat built by the city of Ur about 2111 B.C.E. Only the lowest level of the building survives, so the sketch represents an archaeologist's informed guess at the appearance of the intact structure.

hand to hand. Lapis lazuli, a blue stone used for jewelry, came from northern Afghanistan some 1,500 miles from Sumer. Carnelian, a red stone, was mined in equally distant India.

Sumerian artisans made skillful use of the materials merchants imported. They created splendid jewelry from beaten gold and silver, and semiprecious gems. They carved statues from blocks of stone brought from distant mountains. They built furniture and musical instruments from rare woods and decorated these objects with subtle inlays. They wove garments from wool and linen for both domestic and foreign markets. (Cotton was not known to the Mediterranean world until the seventh century B.C.E., when an Assyrian king imported cotton plants from India to ornament his palace garden.) Sumerians knew how to make glass, and by 3000 B.C.E., their potters were using wheels to throw their vessels. (The Sumerians may have been the first to explore uses for the wheel; by 3500 B.C.E., they were replacing sledges with wheeled carts.) The most distinctive Sumerian artifact was an exquisite object called a cylinder seal. This was a small, engraved cylinder that was rolled across a clay tablet to imprint a design that served as a signature.

Writing, Religions, and Intellectual Life   The management of Sumer's cities and their economies prompted the most famous Sumerian invention: writing. Fortunately for us, the Sumerians wrote on tablets made from their country's most abundant and inexpensive resource: mud. Many of these, some sun-dried and others fired, have survived burial in the earth for thousands of years.

The earliest specimens of writing come from Uruk and may date as far back as 3500 B.C.E. No one has yet deciphered them, but they are consistent with the theory that writing was invented by accountants. As early as 8000 B.C.E., people began to make small clay tokens whose size, shape, or design represented quantities of various commodities. By assembling piles of these tokens, a merchant or warehouse manager could keep track of how many, and what kinds of items he or she had in stock. At some point, these accountants began to draw their tokens instead of modeling them. The early tablets from Uruk often display rows of lines that seem to indicate numbers. All the evidence suggests that writing was not invented to preserve the words of scholars and poets, but for more mundane, if vital, purposes. It was a long time before Sumerian scribes produced anything but business ledgers.

As busy scribes developed ways to speed up their work, writing systems became more efficient. Because it took a lot of time to draw realistic pictures of objects or tokens, scribes began to strip their images down to a few essential lines. This made writing easier to do but harder to learn. The meaning of simplified signs was not self-evident. People had to be taught what each one represented. The physical act of writing was also reformed to improve speed and clarity. Linear drawings were difficult to make on mud tablets. Inscribed lines gouged furrows that had jagged edges and ended in messy clumps. It was cleaner and faster to poke a stylus (a reed) into a clay tablet than to push or pull it across one. Poking produced a triangular indentation instead of a line, but a quick series of jabs could create a clump of wedge-shaped impressions that approximated one of the older linear symbols. The triangular indentations that cover Sumerian tablets constitute a script that modern scholars have named *cuneiform* (*cuneus,* Latin for "wedge").

The cuneiform writing system is complex. Its symbols can represent both objects and prominent sounds in the words for objects. The latter function allowed a scribe to record the sounds of speech. Once writing began to be thought of as a way to describe not what was seen but what was heard, a tablet could record anything that could be thought and said. Early cuneiform employed about 1,200 signs. Scribes steadily reduced their number, but the Sumerians never developed a true alphabet (a set of symbols for a language's elemental sounds). That was the achievement of Semitic-speaking Canaanites who lived in Palestine about 1600 B.C.E. The Phoenicians transmitted this invention to the Greeks and ultimately to us. The alphabet's short list of symbols "democratized" writing by making it much easier to learn. Cuneiform, however, was adapted to record many ancient tongues and remained in use until the end of the first century C.E.

Writing made history in every sense of the word. For the first time, thinking beings could leave an enduring, precise description of their thoughts. Most ancient cuneiform tablets are the by-products of mundane transactions, but some record myths, legends, laws, proverbs, medical texts, astronomical charts, mathematical calculations, scientific treatises, dictionaries, letters, poems, and prayers. The history of Western literature and thought begins with this legacy, and it has been particularly helpful to biblical scholars. Much of the material in the opening chapters of Genesis (the first book in the Bible) harks back to Sumerian sources.

The Sumerians worshiped gods who incarnated the powers of nature. They assumed that gods were analogous to human beings but were beyond human understanding. The wisest course, therefore, was to curry their favor by offering them gifts and praise. The Sumerian pantheon numbered about 3,600 gods and goddesses, but only a few were of major importancce: Anu, a remote high god; Inanna (also called Ninhursaga or Ishtar), a war and fertility goddess; Enlil, a storm god; and Enki, the god of the fresh waters that imparted life to Sumer's arid land. Sumerian gods were all too human. They schemed, lied, loved, formed alliances, sought revenge, and held grudges. The politics of heaven resembled those of a Sumerian city-state. Gods could be bribed, and they resorted to influence peddling. A god who did a favor for another god or a human being expected something in return. When struggles broke out among the gods, the fates of cities hung in the balance.

The major modern Western faiths all posit a connection between religion and ethics. They claim that people's treatment of one another has transcendent significance. The Sumerians did not share this conviction. They believed that gods were interested primarily in themselves and were restrained by neither reason nor morality. Gods might, however, be swayed by offerings and magic spells. To fend off disaster, therefore, it was important to anticipate their actions. The Sumerians saw the world as filled with omens. All kinds of things (the livers of sacrificial animals, flights of birds, patterns of smoke, deformed births, etc.) hinted at what the gods were about, and it was a priest's profession to interpret these coded messages.

Some Sumerian religious myths implied that people could not hope for much from life. The gods allegedly had created humanity for the sole purpose of working to keep their altars piled high with offerings. This meant that for the ordinary person, daily life was an unending struggle to win favor with both earthly and heavenly powers. Ultimately, everyone suffered the same fate: death followed by a lingering, shadowy existence in the underworld. In *The Epic of Gilgamesh*, Enkidu, Gilgamesh's friend, has a deathbed vision of the underworld. He describes it as a place of no return where even kings and priests "sit in darkness; dust is their food and clay their meat."

The Mesopotamian environment may explain this gloomy outlook. Sumer was wealthy but insecure. The rivers on which its life depended periodically threatened to destroy its civilization. Violent storms swept the countryside. Epidemics and plagues decimated cities. Nomads raided Sumer's fields. Power struggles raged within and between cities, and innocent people were caught up in tumultuous events that were beyond their control or understanding.

Sumer's History   Sumer's cities probably began as independent foundations, but as they grew, they came into conflict with one another. From time to time, one would subdue others, but Sumer was a difficult country to unify. Its featureless plain provided no natural boundaries for a state.

Sumer was eventually unified by a man named Sargon (2371–2316 B.C.E.), a native of Akkad, on Sumer's northern border. Sargon was a self-made man of obscure origin. He is said to have been abandoned as an infant and found floating in a basket on the Euphrates. (Similar stories were later told about the infancies of the Hebrews' Moses and Rome's Romulus and Remus.) Sargon's empire extended from the Persian Gulf up the Euphrates and across the caravan stations of northern Syria to the Mediterranean and Asia Minor. He could not have exercised much direct control over such a large area, for communication systems were primitive. If his major concern was continuously to police the trade routes that coursed through these territories, it is easy to see why he created history's first standing army. He doubtless hoped that family ties would foster loyalty, for he assigned key posts to relatives—some of whom were women. His daughter Enheduana was high priestess of the great temples of Ur and Uruk. She wrote hymns, and those that survive are the first works of literature whose author is known.

Sargon's empire fell about 2200 B.C.E. Leadership of Sumer eventually passed to the kings in the city of Ur, and they presided over the last phase in Sumer's history (2112–2004 B.C.E.).

By this time, the Sumerians had been a literate people for nearly a thousand years. Ur's kings tried to preserve the legacy of their civilization. They rebuilt temples, collected ancient documents for safekeeping in their archives, and sponsored a renaissance of Sumerian culture. However, in 2004 B.C.E. Elamite tribes invaded from southern Iran and overran Ur. The Amorites, nomadic tribes native to the deserts west of Sumer, then spread throughout Mesopotamia. They founded a city called Babylon (near Sargon's former capital), and its kings gradually restored order and rescued something from Sumer's fall.

The fall of a civilization that had perpetuated itself for nearly 2,000 years cries out for an explanation. Many things are possible. As governments age, they may develop rigid customs that make it hard for them to adapt to changing conditions. Bureaucracies become cumbersome. States also succumb if they do not find leaders whose talents are equal to their responsibilities. Divisions between rich and poor can undermine societies, or shifting trade routes and natural catastrophes can destroy their economies.

In addition to all these problems, Sumer may have been the victim of an environmental disaster of its own making. Sumer depended on irrigation, and irrigation can degrade farmland. The minerals dissolved in irrigation water are left behind in the soil when that water evaporates. Ground water also contains minerals that can rise to the surface. If these "salts" are not flushed out (which was hard to do on Sumer's flat, poorly drained terrain), the ground slowly becomes poisonous to plant life. The effect was mitigated by the new soil that the flooding rivers laid down, but as the years passed, the soil suffered. Farmers had to plant less wheat and more barley, for barley tolerates salted soil better than does wheat. But, ultimately, declining harvests would have encouraged people to move elsewhere. The fall of a civilization is not likely to have a single, simple explanation, but the site of humanity's first civilization may have been the scene of its first ecological disaster.

The Rise of Civilization in Egypt

The early years of the second millennium were a time of transition. Sumer disappeared. Urban settlements in Palestine declined, and the first phase in the history of the West's other premier civilization, Egypt, also came to an end.

The Egyptian Environment   Egypt coped with environmental conditions that were similar to Sumer's. It seldom rained in Egypt. Temperatures often hovered around 100 degrees Fahrenheit, and no civilization would have been possible without the water and fertile soil supplied by an annually flooding river. An ancient Greek historian aptly called Egypt "the gift of the Nile." Where the river's floods reached, Egypt was a fertile "black land" formed by deposits of rich silt. An utterly barren desert, the "red land," began at the edge of the river's floodplain and stretched out to the horizons.

The Nile's bounty was so generous that prehistoric Egyptians were slow to take up agriculture. Along the river's banks, where wildlife flourished, nature needed little encouragement to meet human needs. As early as 5000 B.C.E., Egyptians had domesticated sheep, cattle, goats, barley, and wheat. But for over a thousand years, herding and farming only supplemented hunting and gathering. Villages fully dependent on agriculture may not have appeared much before 3500 B.C.E., and no great feats of irrigation engineering were needed to support them. The Nile, unlike the Tigris and Euphrates, flooded predictably and at a convenient time for farmers. It rose in late summer following a harvest. Then it dropped a fresh layer of silt and saturated fields just in time for replanting. The Egyptians measured the flood's rise at their southern frontier, and the volume of water indicated how large the harvest would be. They were not afraid that the flood would disrupt their lives by erratic behavior, for Egypt occupied a valley that kept the Nile to its course.

The Nile rose in Uganda and flowed north toward the Mediterranean as if it were descending a huge staircase. When the river spilled over the edges of the higher steps, it created rapids or cataracts. Egypt's southern boundary was marked by what was, from the Egyptians' perspective, the First Cataract. From there to the Mediterranean—about 700 miles—there was no more white water. The Egyptians did not need roads to tie their country together. No one in Egypt was ever far from the river, for the Nile Valley is only about twelve miles across at its widest. The river provided all the transportation that was needed. Its current carried vessels north, and when boats raised their sails, prevailing winds pushed them south. The river offered such convenient transport that the Egyptians were slow to utilize wheeled vehicles.

Nature protected as well as provided for the Egyptians. Cliffs and deserts defended Egypt on both sides for most of its length. Egypt was a politically unified country for over 1,300 years before it suffered a major foreign invasion. Metal ores and good building stone were also to be found in Egypt's cliffs and deserts. The country's major material deficit was wood, but that was easy to import by sea from Palestine. Egypt's benign environment probably explains why its inhabitants felt more at peace with the human condition than did some Sumerians.

Egypt's Political Development   Nature divided Egypt into two distinct regions. The largest part of the country was Upper (up-river) Egypt, the long, narrow valley described above. Lower (down-river) Egypt was the broad delta that accumulated where the Nile emptied into the Mediterranean. Lower Egypt was a flat, swampy land much like Sumer, and it was the part of Egypt most exposed to the outside world. Mediterranean sailors used its ports, and coastal routes linked it by land with Libya in the west and the Sinai in the east.

Settlement patterns help to explain why Egypt became a politically unified country early in its development and enjoyed greater stability than did Sumer. On Sumer's open plain, people clustered in cities for protection, and their fields encircled their walled towns. This led to the rise of separate city-states that resisted unification. Egypt was settled differently, for the agriculturally productive floor of the Nile Valley was only about two miles wide in most places. Because lateral expansion was limited, Egyptians did not cluster together in large cities. That would have forced many of them to make long commutes to their fields. It made more sense for them to distribute themselves evenly in small villages throughout the valley.

The Nile Valley is a series of flood basins, and long before the dawn of history, each of these was claimed by a tribe. Struggles among these tribes gradually led to the formation of separate kingdoms in Upper and Lower Egypt, and about 3100 B.C.E. a king of Upper Egypt conquered the delta. Egypt became a unified country about the time that the first petty kings appeared in Sumer's city-states.

Greek historians were the first to try to impose order on the records of Egypt's past, and they concluded that thirty-one dynasties ruled Egypt between its unification in 3100 B.C.E. and its assimilation into the Roman Empire in 30 B.C.E. Greek scholars dated events by the reigns of the rulers in which they occurred, and modern researchers still use the numbers the Greeks assigned Egypt's dynasties.

Early Dynastic Period (3100–2700 B.C.E.)   An ancient stone palette honoring a certain Narmer, or Scorpion, may commemorate the wars that united Egypt. On one side the victorious Narmer wears the crown of Upper Egypt and on the other the crown of Lower Egypt.

◆ Chronology: Key Events in Sumerian and Egyptian History

MESOPOTAMIA	EGYPT
Predynastic Era (5300–3000 B.C.E.)	
earliest specimens of writing —	3500 B.C.E., agricultural villages appear
	3100 B.C.E., unification of Egypt
	Early Dynastic Period (3100–2700 B.C.E.)
Dynastic Era (3000–2004 B.C.E.)	
monarchy appears	Old Kingdom (2700–2200 B.C.E.)
	2550 B.C.E., pyramids at Giza
Sargon's empire (2371–2200 B.C.E.)	
	First Intermediate Period
	(2200–2025 B.C.E.)
Ur (2112–2004 B.C.E.)	
	Middle Kingdom (2025–1630 B.C.E.)

Narmer may have founded Egypt's first dynasty, but he was not a pharaoh. That title was not used until about 1400 B.C.E. Ancient peoples believed that naming something invoked its presence, and they preferred to refer to their god-king as *pharaoh* ("great house") rather than risk contact with his power.

The first dynasty established its seat at Memphis (on the border between Upper and Lower Egypt), and Egypt's rulers eventually adopted a double crown that symbolized the union of the country's two original kingdoms: the red circlet with a hooded cobra of the delta laid over the valley's white conical cap.

The institutions, artistic styles, and theologies that evolved early in Egypt's history set patterns that endured for 2,000 years. What had begun as a remarkably inventive society grew increasingly conservative as respect for tradition restrained the impulse to innovate. This may have been an effect of Egypt's rigorously centralized government. Egypt's pharaohs were worshiped as manifestations of an eternal god, and their court was the chief market for the products of artists and intellectuals. Court taste favored the repetition of traditional symbols and images—an inflexible orthodoxy consistent with the pharaoh's unchanging nature. Innovation may also have been inhibited, oddly enough, by the invention of writing. In modern societies writing stimulates development by facilitating communication and data collection. For ancient peoples, however, writing was an arcane skill that few possessed, and the mysterious markings that scribes made seemed magical. Many modern people share this primitive inclination to trust whatever is in print (or, worse, on the Web), and the word *scripture* ("writing") still connotes something holy—something that has authority and cannot be changed.

Archaeologists can trace the gradual development of Sumerian cuneiform, but Egypt's hieroglyphs ("sacred writings") have no comparable ancestry. They appear about 3100 B.C.E. and quickly become fully developed. Egypt had trade contacts with Sumer, and Sumerian experiments with writing may have given the Egyptians hints that speeded the development of hieroglyphs. Both the Sumerians and Egyptians based their writing systems on pictographs. As Sumerian scribes developed cuneiform's efficient clusters of wedge-shaped impressions, these became unrecognizable, but Egypt's hieroglyphs never lost their pictographic quality. Perhaps this was because Egyptian scribes did not inscribe clay tablets. They wrote with brushes and ink on a paperlike material made from the papyrus reeds that grew along the Nile. They had no difficulty making linear drawings. Hieroglyphs continued to be used for monuments and holy texts, but by 2000 B.C.E., a faster cursive script (called *demotic*) had been developed for writing mundane documents.

The Old Kingdom (2700–2200 B.C.E.)   The heart of ancient Egypt's civilization was its monarchy. The Egyptians believed that their pharaoh was their primary link with the supernatural powers on which all life depended. He was an incarnate god whose power was absolute (in theory, if not always in practice). Egypt and all its people belonged to him, but he was not supposed to be a whimsical tyrant. His task was to preserve *ma'at* ("justice"), a balance among nature's competing forces that guaranteed a stable world order. His authority was so sweeping that Egypt, unlike other ancient kingdoms, did not adopt a code of laws. Pharaoh's will was all the law that Egypt needed.

Pharaohs governed Egypt with the help of an elaborate bureaucracy. Some 2,000 titles have been identified for officials of the Old Kingdom. The pharaoh needed a horde of royal agents, for he had many functions. He was responsible for the religious ceremonies that placated the gods and sustained the order of nature. On a mundane level, he handled defense, dispensed justice, oversaw planning for the Nile's flood, coordinated food production and distribution, erected buildings, provided patronage for artisans, handled all long-distance trade, supervised public works projects, and employed an army of scribes to record and audit everything.

Egypt was highly centralized but minimally urbanized. Most Egyptians lived in small villages. For administrative purposes, the country was subdivided into units of local government called *nomes*. There were twenty-two of these in Upper Egypt and twenty in Lower Egypt. In theory, all the land belonged to the pharaoh, and he could compel all his subjects to work for him. Slavery may not, however, have been all that common in the Old Kingdom. In the ancient world, slaves were usually foreigners captured in wars, and the Old Kingdom was not very active militarily.

The tombs of the Old Kingdom's pharaohs are the best surviving testimonials to their power. The investment that the Egyptians made in tombs throughout their history can create the mistaken impression that they were a grim people preoccupied with death. In reality, their preparations for death attest to their love of life. Egyptian burial practices were meant to guarantee that the deceased would continue to enjoy life's pleasures beyond the grave. So similar and so close were the worlds of the living and the dead that the Egyptians believed that support from this side of the tomb was important for happiness on the other. The dead were assumed to need all kinds of things. Supplies were buried with them, and a steady stream of offerings was to flow in perpetuity across the altars of their funerary temples.

The Egyptian outlook on both life and death was more optimistic than the view described in some Sumerian texts. The Sumerians, on their exposed plain, were engaged in a constant struggle with one another and the seemingly arbitrary forces of nature. Life in the rich Nile Valley was easier and safer. The Sumerians conceived of the universe as a chaotic battleground for quarrelsome, incomprehensible gods, but the Egyptian universe was a stable

Culture in Context: How to Make a Mummy

Because a corpse buried in a tomb had no contact with the dry sand that would have naturally mummified it, it had to be preserved artificially. This was done by doing what nature did—that is, by drying out the decedent as quickly and thoroughly as possible.

To proceed:

1. Take one corpse.
2. Remove the brain by breaking the ethnoid bone, inserting a wire whisk up the nostrils and scrambling the brain tissue until it becomes fluid; turn the body over to drain the contents of the cranium out the nostrils; discard this material; then pour hot resin into the skull to destroy any remaining tissue.
3. Make an incision in the lower side of the abdomen; insert hands and pull out the stomach, liver, lungs, and intestines; leave the heart and kidneys in place.
4. Put each organ in a separate vessel; pickle with spices; seal the containers and place them in or near the coffin.
5. Cover the body with baking soda and salt; let it dry out for 35 days.
6. Stuff the body with dry rags to plump it out.
7. Carefully wrap each part of the body separately with strips of linen; then wrap the whole corpse in layers of bandages to hold it together.
8. Dip the wrapped body in pitch to encase it in a hard shell; place in a coffin.
9. Do not forget to recite the proper spells and incantations for each step in the process.

Question: Some cultures destroy the bodies of their dead (by cremation) and others go to great lengths to preserve them (by embalming). What might explain the different approaches to the rituals of death?

realm characterized by balance and order. The eternal, unchanging nature of things made it seem that death was an event in life rather than an end to life. Experience with the dead tended to confirm this. The Egyptians did not waste good agricultural land on cemeteries. They buried their dead in the deserts that bordered the Nile's floodplains. The desert's arid sands dehydrated corpses and shielded them from decay. Nature's reluctance to reclaim the physical remains of the departed suggested that their preservation was important.

It was more difficult to provide a secure grave for a corpse than to preserve it. Tomb construction evolved as the Egyptians experimented with ways to prevent bodies buried in the sand from being exposed by the wind or dug up by animals. Their earliest procedure was simply to heap sand over a grave. By the Dynastic era, brick masonry was being used to stabilize these mounds of dirt. This created a tomb called a *mastaba* ("bench"), a flat rectangular structure. At first, corpses were interred in the ground beneath mastabas, but eventually rooms were created within mastabas to house coffins and grave offerings.

Royal tombs conformed to this pattern until about 2650 B.C.E., when the pharaoh Djoser, the second king of the Old Kingdom, departed from tradition. The result was a monument so impressive that later generations assumed that its architect, Imhotep, was a god. Imhotep began by building a mastaba, but then he started to tinker with its design. First he enlarged it. Then he piled levels of masonry on top of it to create a building resembling a square, six-layered wedding cake. Imhotep's "step pyramid" (a pyramid whose layers are not angled to create smooth sides) is the world's first monumental stone building.

Djoser launched a fad for pyramid construction that lasted for centuries. The ruins of about 110 pyramids have been identified in Egypt, but the greatest are the earliest—those erected during the Old Kingdom. What pyramid builders strove to create was a soaring structure that rose at a steep angle. This was hard to do, for as any child who builds a sand castle at the beach discovers, the sides of a steep mound sheer off. But by 2550 B.C.E., the Egyptians had developed engineering techniques that enabled them to erect what is still the world's most massive stone structure: the Great Pyramid at Giza.

The Great Pyramid, which was probably built for the pharaoh Cheops (or Khufu), is the supreme example of its kind. It anchors a sprawling complex of smaller pyramids, tombs, temples, and other monuments on the western bank of the Nile near modern Cairo. Its statistics are staggering. It covers thirteen acres, rises to a height of 481 feet, and is constructed of 2,300,000 blocks of precisely cut and fitted stone. Some of the blocks of granite used for its interior chambers weigh fifty tons and were brought from quarries 500 miles away. Surveyors oriented the building precisely on a north-south axis and kept its sides in perfect alignment. When the Greek historian Herodotus visited the pyramid 2,000 years after it was built, he was told that it took only twenty years to complete. A modern authority has estimated that it might have been finished in as few as five.

Whatever the pyramids were built to contain was looted in antiquity, and what they symbolized for the ancient Egyptians is uncertain. Egyptian mythology envisioned the creation of the world as an island emerging from the waters of primal chaos. Pyramids may have represented this island, where life began, or their shape might have been inspired by the slanting rays of the sun, the path that the pharaoh's spirit took as it returned to the heavens after his death.

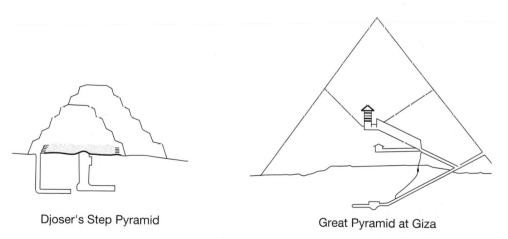

Djoser's Step Pyramid   Great Pyramid at Giza

Figure 1–3 The First Pyramid and the Greatest Pyramid   Most pyramids, like the first, were solid structures raised over subterranean tombs, or they had one small interior chamber. The Great Pyramid at Giza was not only the largest but it also had the most complex internal design. No one has a convincing explanation for its multiple chambers and passageways.

The most mysterious thing about the pyramids may be the motive that persuaded the Egyptians to undertake the physically and logistically daunting labor of constructing them. They are sometimes dismissed as the work of megalomaniacal tyrants who enslaved thousands to build monuments to their personal glory. Pyramids were, however, not the work of slaves, and they may have done more than exalt an individual. A pharaoh could use only one tomb, but some pharaohs built more than one pyramid. This suggests that the process of building was as important as the end product.

Early Egypt did not have to fend off many invaders, but its creation was not bloodless. Texts praise pharaohs for being great warriors. Some led armies into the deserts to discipline nomads or up the Nile to intimidate Egypt's Nubian neighbors. Some fought to maintain internal order. The Old Kingdom was a relatively new monarchy that was attempting to do something that had never been done before—to consolidate a huge territorial nation. Pyramid building might have contributed to this. Great projects demonstrate a leader's power, and their construction can distract his subjects from disruptive behavior. Agricultural work is seasonal, and during the months when Egypt's fields required little tending, its idle men probably had a tendency to brawl. Pharaohs may have forestalled this by occupying their subjects on great projects that were sources of both employment and national pride. Egypt built pyramids, and pyramids may have built Egypt.

First Intermediate Period (2200–2025 B.C.E.)   The Old Kingdom continued for about 500 years. No one is sure why its centralized government ultimately lost control and allowed regional governors to begin fighting among themselves. A severe drought afflicted much of the Middle East about the time that both the Old Kingdom and Sargon's Mesopotamian empire fell. The drought may have had some effect on Egypt's economy, but the pharaohs of the Old Kingdom may also have created the situation that ended their reign. Unless central governments move their regional governors from time to time, these officials build local power bases and become independent. But as governments take on greater responsibilities, a need for efficiency prompts them to leave experienced men at their posts indefinitely. The clever governor trains his son in the duties of his office and arranges for the boy to succeed him. If a family retains control of a post for several generations, it acquires a kind of hereditary right to its office and is tempted to assert its independence—particularly if its overlord shows signs of weakness. The last pharaoh of the Old Kingdom lived to a great age, and his failing powers may have given Egypt's governors the opportunity they were waiting for.

The collapse of the Old Kingdom was followed by a period of political upheaval, internal warfare, and economic hardship called the First Intermediate Period. Egypt did not function well when divided against itself, but the confusion was not entirely detrimental to Egypt's civilization. The destruction of the Old Kingdom's authoritarian government freed Egyptian society to evolve. When the country's unity was finally restored by the pharaohs of the Middle Kingdom, cultural creativity flourished with renewed vigor.

Larger Issue Revisited

The belief that primitive societies thrive without disturbing nature is a romantic fantasy. Any hiker who has tried to "tread lightly on the land" and visit the wilderness without altering it knows how difficult that is. Nature is constantly adjusting to what its resident species consume and produce. Prehistoric hunters and gatherers changed the world around them. They drove some species toward extinction and encouraged the proliferation of others. For eons, they struck a sustainable balance with nature, and then they turned to agriculture. Their interventions in nature's processes became more extreme as they consciously reconstructed the environments that supported them.

The West's early civilizations drastically altered humanity's physical and social environment. Sumer and Egypt did so in different ways, for they dealt with different challenges. But each struggled with a cycle that has continued throughout history. They changed the world as they interacted with it, and then the world forced them to adapt to its emerging conditions. The result was a race to rise to the ever more daunting challenges of an ever more complex environment. To be civilized is to grasp a tiger by the tail and live with the consequences.

Review Questions

1. How did Paleolithic and Neolithic societies differ?
2. How did the first civilizations differ from the prehistoric cultures that preceded them?
3. Do environmental resources explain why civilization appeared first in Sumer and Egypt?
4. How and why did Egypt's political evolution differ from Sumer's?
5. How and why did the Egyptian outlook on life differ from the Sumerian view?
6. Can civilizations be explained simply as adaptations to natural environments?

Refer to the front of the book for a list of chapter-relevant primary sources available on the CD-ROM.

THE WEST INTERACTIVE

For web-based activities, map explorations, and quizzes related to this chapter, go to *www.prenhall.com/frankforter.*

CHAPTER 2

THE RISE OF EMPIRES
AND THE BEGINNING OF THE IRON AGE

You march forth to take your enemy's land, and he comes to take yours.
—Mesopotamian proverb

Larger Issue: *Is political stability compatible with cultural diversity?*

The word *civilization* and its cognates (*civility,* for example) conjure thoughts of peaceful, or-derly behavior, but the history of civilization has been a history of war. People tend to view persons different from themselves with suspicion, contempt, and hostility, and they sometimes act as if the existence of alternative ways of life calls into question the validity of their own. These parochial attitudes may not have caused many problems for small, scattered hunter-gatherer bands and farming villages. But civilizations, the supreme products of the human ca-pacity for invention and imagination, maximized cultural differences and human contacts. They mobilized large populations by promoting values and institutions that set them apart from others.

Cities, city-states, and kingdoms had much more difficulty maintaining order—both in-ternally and externally—than simple rural villages. A city or city-state had to integrate differ-ent kinship groups, specialized workers, and distinct social classes. The greater political entities had to manage groups that spoke different dialects or languages, practiced numerous religions, and cherished their own customary laws. The large scale on which a civilization operated de-pended on people developing a shared identity that somehow accommodated their differences.

During the second millennium B.C.E., rulers in both Egypt and Mesopotamia began to use military force to build empires. This promoted a blending of cultures that produced so-phisticated, cosmopolitan societies. But it also raised questions about legitimate political au-thority and personal identity that created confusion and instability. Ancient empires were easier to create than to maintain.

The ancient world was hardly unique in wrestling with the problem of reconciling politi-cal stability with cultural diversity. The challenge is greater in our nuclear-armed age than ever before in history, for modern communications and economics are "shrinking" the globe and forcing peoples with very different values and lifestyles into ever closer contact. An examina-tion of the earlier phases in the struggle might help us as we go about the vitally important work of pursuing world peace.

TOPICS IN THIS CHAPTER

The Transition States • Imperial Egypt: The New Kingdom • The Indo-Europeans
and the Clash of Empires • The Bible and History

The Transition States

In 2004 B.C.E. the Third Dynasty of Ur was overthrown by the Elamites, tribesmen whose homelands lay east of the Tigris River. The Elamites were ill-equipped to maintain Sumer's urban institutions, and as the heartland of the West's first civilization declined, other groups took advantage of the political confusion. The Assyrians established the nucleus for a new state on the upper reaches of the Tigris River, but the immediate future lay with the Amorites. These nomadic tribes from the western deserts spread throughout Mesopotamia and Syria. Some of them settled in Akkad, north of Sumer, founded the city of Babylon, and gradually came to control much of the Middle East.

Babylon   The Babylonian empire was largely the work of the city's sixth king, Hammurabi (r. 1792–1750 B.C.E.). He was about twenty-five when he inherited his throne, and he devoted the first thirty years of his reign to wars of conquest. At its height, Hammurabi's Babylon held sway from the Persian Gulf to northern Assyria. This was not a large state in comparison with later empires, but its population was diverse and hard to pacify. Hammurabi is memorable for his novel approach to dealing with this problem. He imposed a common set of rules on all his subjects by publishing what is often said to be history's first code of laws. Fragments of earlier legal texts survive from the reign of the founder of Ur's third dynasty, Ur-Nammu, but they are probably records of decisions in particular court cases, not general principles meant to guide the administration of justice. Hammurabi's code, which contains almost 300 clauses, was much more ambitious and may have had a different purpose. Unlike modern legislation, it was not a set of statutes that lawyers cited when arguing cases. It was intended to provide judges with examples of the kinds of decisions the king wished them to make when dealing with various categories of disputes. By superseding local customs and establishing a common standard for justice throughout the empire, the king's law helped break down some of the cultural barriers that separated his subjects.

Hammurabi's laws provide historians with their first detailed description of an ancient Mesopotamian society. His subjects were divided into three classes: aristocrats, free commoners, and various categories of dependents and slaves. People's legal rights were determined by their class standing. An injury done to an important person was more harshly punished than the same injury done to a less significant individual. Because ancient societies were not equipped to maintain prisons, punishments took the form of fines, mutilations, and executions. Hammurabi's concept of justice was the biblical principal of "an eye for an eye, a tooth for a tooth." It was not always easy, however, to make "the punishment fit the crime," and Hammurabi's attempts to establish exact equivalencies sometimes enforced justice by inflicting what are, from the modern perspective, unjust punishments. For example, a builder who erected a house that fell down and killed its owner's son was punished by the execution of his own son. We might wonder what the boy thought of the justice of this decree, but in Hammurabi's world fathers owned their sons. They could sell them into slavery and lose them in property disputes.

Hammurabi's code gave significant space to property and family law. It spelled out principles governing land ownership, rights of renters and tenants, and responsibilities for the maintenance of communal facilities such as irrigation systems. It assumed that governments had some responsibility for protecting environmental resources. It regulated money lending, and it tried to set fair standards for wages and the quality of consumer goods.

Hammurabi's code is especially noteworthy for the protection it offered the poor and the weak. It forbade husbands to abandon wives who were barren or ill without providing for their support. It declared that women had rights to property of their own and could run businesses—so long as they did not neglect their domestic duties. It gave wives the power to initiate divorce and reclaim their doweries, but it enforced a sexual double standard. It allowed husbands to have sex outside of marriage, but it harshly punished adulterous wives. Babylonian society was patriarchal, and men were anxious to ensure that the children they raised were their own.

In addition to women, the law protected slaves, another vulnerable segment of the population. Some slaves were war captives, but some were members of citizen families. A man could discharge his debts by selling his wife, his children, and himself. Slavery was, however, not inevitably permanent. A slave could own property, go into business for himself, and earn the price of his freedom.

The rights Hammurabi's people had in theory no doubt exceeded those they had in practice, for it is unlikely that Hammurabi had the governmental machinery needed to enforce his laws and hold all his judges accountable. Public officials were legally liable for doing their duty, and they were even supposed to compensate victims if they failed to find and punish thieves and murderers. Given the difficulty modern governments have in meeting such high standards of justice, they may have been, for Hammurabi, little more than a pious hope.

In addition to progress in law and government, Babylonian intellectuals made significant advances in science—particularly astronomy and the mathematics needed to study the heavens. They used both decimal (base 10) and sexagesimal (base 60) systems. The latter survives in the conventional division of circles into 360 degrees and of hours into sixty-minute segments of sixty seconds each. Babylonians did not distinguish between astrology and astronomy, but that did not diminish the precision of their measurements of the movements of the heavenly bodies. The data they collected were used for centuries and greatly improved the accuracy of calendars.

Hammurabi's empire began to fall away shortly after his death, but his dynasty held on to Babylon for another 150 years. About 1595 B.C.E. the city fell to a group of northern raiders called the Hittites. They came to loot, not conquer. After they retreated to their base in Asia Minor, the Kassites moved down from the Zagros Mountains to occupy Babylon, Akkad, and Sumer. They ruled the lower Euphrates for the next 600 years and conscientiously guarded the region's cultural legacy. They restored temples, built libraries, and spread knowledge of cuneiform and its literary treasures.

Egypt's Middle Kingdom (2025–1630 B.C.E.)   Central government was reestablished in Egypt a few years before the fall of Ur's third dynasty and survived almost to the Hittite sack of Babylon. The pharaohs of this Middle Kingdom, contemporaries of Hammurabi's dynasty, presided over an era of prosperity and creativity. Their successors, the rulers of the New Kingdom, tore down most of their architectural monuments and replaced them with grander structures, but the Middle Kingdom's literary achievements were more enduring.

The Middle Kingdom was founded by a warrior from Thebes in Upper Egypt. The pharaohs of the Middle and New Kingdoms claimed descent from the sun god of Thebes, and they preferred Thebes to Memphis, the capital of the Old Kingdom. The pharaohs of the Middle Kingdom seem somewhat less remote than their predecessors. The literature of the period calls them the shepherds of their people and praises them for defending the poor and equitably enforcing justice. They invested less in grandiose tombs and more in what we think of as economic development. They extended their power up the Nile into Nubia. They sponsored trading expeditions to distant lands. They dug canals to improve transportation and created reservoirs and irrigation systems that greatly expanded the agricultural productivity of the Fayum, an oasis in northwestern Egypt.

Historians have learned less from the monuments of the Middle Kingdom's pharaohs than from the private tombs of their officials. These are fairly numerous, for wealth was more widely distributed during the Middle Kingdom than in earlier eras. More people could afford to invest in tombs, and they even appropriated funereal texts that had previously been reserved for pharaohs. The cult of Osiris, the god of the dead, and his wife Isis flourished during the Middle Kingdom and remained popular well into the Christian era. Osiris was a vegetation deity who, like the crops in Egypt's fields, died to be reborn. Each year, the innundation of the Nile restored life to Egypt, and Osiris promised his worshipers a similar victory over death.

Because the Egyptians believed that in death they would want and need everything they had enjoyed in life, they stocked their tombs with their favorite possessions. Tombs were also well supplied with pictures and sculptures, for these things were thought to have power to nurture the dead in their afterlives. Sometimes boxes filled with dolls representing servants at work were added to a tomb's equipment. They look like children's toys, but they had the serious adult purpose of supplying the deceased's needs for all eternity. They provide us with invaluable information about the kinds of ordinary daily activities that usually go unrecorded.

The Middle Kingdom was remarkable for its literary productivity. Mythological and theological works, administrative tracts, letters, medical and mathematical treatises, and a great deal of less formal material survive from the era. The Egyptians were fond of morally edifying tales, proverbs, and practical advice on how to get ahead in this world. The sages of the Middle Kingdom advised modesty, hard work, loyalty, and deference to superiors. They praised acts of charity and cursed officials who abused their offices and exploited the poor. They also warned young men to be especially careful in their dealings with women, but the love poetry that survives from the era suggests that such advice invariably was not heeded.

Second Intermediate Period (1630–1550 B.C.E.)   The Middle Kingdom had a strong government that cultivated a reputation for justice and shared its wealth. It gave Egypt about four centuries of peace and stability before it was undone by a development that it understandably failed to anticipate. For eons, Egypt's location and terrain had protected it from foreign invasion, but now these defenses were suddenly revealed to be inadequate. The delta was invaded and occupied by a people whom the Egyptians called Hyksos ("foreigners"). These were bands of Semitic warriors who may have had links with the Amorites. It was their military technology and not their political connections, however, that enabled them to rout the numerically superior Egyptians.

The Egyptians of the Middle Kingdom had fallen behind in the development of military technology—thanks in part to their environment. Egypt had little need for wheeled vehicles drawn by animals. Simple sledges sufficed for men to drag things to the banks of the Nile, and the river provided most of the transport the country required. As early as the Old Kingdom, Egyptian farmers were plowing with teams of oxen. Donkeys were domesticated to serve as pack animals, but horses may not have reached Egypt much before the end of the Middle Kingdom. (Horses had been domesticated in the Ukraine late in the fourth millennium, and they were not in widespread use in Mesopotamia until the second millennium.) The horse had greater speed and stamina than the ox or donkey, but it was more difficult to train and expensive to feed. By

Figure 2–1   Mortuary Temple of Hatshepsut The pharaohs of the eighteenth dynasty were buried in the Valley of the Kings in the desert west of their Theban capital. The female pharaoh, Hatshepsut, erected this unique temple of terraces and colonnades at the entrance to the valley.

1600, however, warriors from Asia Minor were demonstrating how useful horses could be on the battlefield. Archers who sped about in light, horse-drawn chariots could devastate companies of foot soldiers. The Hyksos taught the Egyptians this lesson—the hard way.

The Hyksos crossed the Sinai peninsula, occupied Lower Egypt, and established their capital at Avaris in the eastern Delta. Much of Upper Egypt remained in the hands of Egyptian chiefs who paid tribute to the Hyksos. Several generations passed before the Egyptians mastered the weapons and tactics of their invaders and began, under a leader who emerged from Thebes, to evict the Hyksos from their country (c. 1550 B.C.E.).

Newly liberated Egypt was ruled by the pharaohs of the famous eighteenth dynasty. The Hyksos interlude had taught them that isolationism was a luxury their country could no longer afford. Reasoning that the best defense is an offense, they dispatched armies into Nubia and Palestine and began to build an empire.

Imperial Egypt: The New Kingdom (1550–1075 B.C.E.)

With the return of independence and unity, Egypt entered the period in its history known as the New Kingdom. Many of the New Kingdom pharaohs were warlords, and their conquests brought ancient Egypt to the pinnacle of its wealth and power. Thutmose I (r. 1504–1492

B.C.E.), the third ruler of the eighteenth dynasty, led armies east to the Euphrates and farther south into Africa than Egyptians had ever before ventured.

The New Kingdom produced some pharaohs who were great generals and some who did not at all fit the military image of their office. One was a woman. Six women are believed to have governed ancient Egypt at some point in its long history. Some served as regents who ruled during the minority of a male heir. Others were the last surviving members of their dynasties. The most significant were Egypt's last pharaoh, the famous Cleopatra, and a woman of the eighteenth dynasty named Hatshepsut (r. 1478–1458 B.C.E.). The daughter of one pharaoh and the widow of another, Hatshepsut began her reign as regent for a stepson. She then shunted him aside, asserted her own hereditary right to the throne, and ruled Egypt for twenty years. Her chief ally was a man of obscure origin named Senenmut. He was her spokesman, the steward of her properties, and the supervisor of her many building projects. The most significant of the latter was her great mortuary temple at Deir el-Bahri, opposite Thebes, against the cliffs of the western Nile Valley. Egypt had never seen anything like it—a series of ascending colonnades and terraces on which gardens were planted. For her burial, the queen prepared several tombs in the valley behind her temple. Her father, Thutmose I, was the first of the sixty-two pharaohs who were ultimately interred in this Valley of the Kings. The location was probably chosen to provide greater security for royal tombs, the contents of which constituted an irresistible temptation for looters. Hatshepsut's multiple tombs were probably intended to throw grave robbers off the track. As it turned out, she had good reason to be concerned for the safety of her resting place. It is not clear how her reign ended, but following her death, an attempt was made to erase her name from her monuments—and thus deny her immortality.

Haptshepsut's successor, Thutmose III (r. 1458–1425 B.C.E.), was a vigorous military man. He fought seventeen campaigns to secure his hold on Palestine and Syria, and he brought all of Nubia under Egypt's control. The pharaoh was also something of a scholar. He collected plant specimens while on his military expeditions. He studied ancient literature, and he may have done some writing of his own. One of his strategies for consolidating his empire was to imbue the client kings who ruled its foreign provinces with enthusiasm for Egypt and its culture. The pharaoh took the sons of kings he conquered hostage and sent the boys to Egypt to be educated. By the time they returned home to inherit their fathers' thrones, they were thoroughly indoctrinated. Some of the New Kingdom's later pharaohs married foreign princesses to confirm treaties, and these women introduced alien cultural influences into Egyptian society at the highest level. Not until late in Egyptian history, however, did a pharaoh condescend to send an Egyptian princess abroad to marry a foreign ruler.

The Amarna Period   Egypt was managed by an army of bureaucrats that had to be closely supervised. Some reported to the pharaoh's chief wife, the high priestess of some of the state's most important temples, but most were under the pharaoh's watchful eye. Vigilant attention was also needed to preserve the empire. With the possible exception of Nubia, the Egyptians did not plant colonies abroad. They depended on military expeditions to maintain the loyalty of native princes who governed in Egypt's name.

The New Kingdom reached a pinnacle of power and prosperity during the reign of Thutmose III's son, Amenhotep III (r. 1390–1352 B.C.E.). He made major additions to ancient Egypt's most imposing temple complexes, the shrines of the Theban god Amun-Ra at Karnak and Luxor. Egypt's temples were not churches designed to accommodate congregations of worshipers. They were private residences for the gods whose statues were enshrined in their innermost chambers. The pharaoh delegated his responsibility to tend to the images of the gods to priests, who maintained an elaborate round of daily rituals. From time to time, a sacred idol was taken out of its temple and carried in procession so that it could be worshiped by the masses. Temples were branches of government, and their granaries provided a pharaoh with reserves of food for distribution to his subjects in time of need.

Pharaohs sometimes worried that certain priesthoods were becoming too strong. By the end of his reign, Amenhotep III appears to have had reservations about the growing power of the temple of Amun-Ra, which was endowed with about a quarter of Egypt's arable land. Amenhotep's son and successor, Amenhotep IV (r. 1352–1338 B.C.E.), took decisive action that may have been intended, among other things, to safeguard the absolute authority of Egypt's king. He closed many of the temples, confiscated their properties, and announced that henceforth Egypt would worship a new god—the Aten (the disk of the sun)—to whom only the pharaoh and his family had direct access. In 1348 B.C.E. the pharaoh changed his name to Akhenaten, "Beloved of the Sun," and began construction of a new capital called Akhetaten, "Horizon of the Sun." Akhetaten or Amarna (Tell el-Amarna, the modern name for its site) was situated between Thebes and Memphis on land that had no previous religious associations. It was strategically located opposite a cleft in the eastern walls of the Nile Valley through which the Aten's worshipers could glimpse the first signs of dawn, the daily rising of their god. The great temple at Amarna was not a dark sanctuary concealing a remote god. It was open to the heavens. Its god was depicted as a bright sun whose rays ended in open hands, a symbol of the blessings the sun generously bestowed on Egypt. The Aten was not a mysterious, hidden god but a power that everyone experienced.

Little is known about the theology of the Aten cult, for few of its monuments have survived. But given the unique spiritual powers it reserved to the pharaoh and his family, most scholars doubt that it was a true monotheism. It may have been an innovative attempt to revive the pharaoh-centered faith of the Old Kingdom.

Devotion to the Aten did not extend far beyond court circles, but it was sincere and powerful enough to inspire new artistic visions. One of the most famous of all Egyptian sculptures is a bust of Akhenaten's beautiful wife Nefertiti that was found in the ruins at Amarna. It realistically depicts the regal elegance of a queen, but much of the art of the Amarna period was expressionistic. Like some modern schools of art, it distorted forms to create graceful linear compositions. So odd are the jutting chins and protruding bellies that characterize the style's treatment of the human form that some people have speculated that it was intended to flatter a pharaoh whose body was misshapen by a glandular disease. It may be simplistic, however, to assume such a literal motive for the art of a faith that set out to overthrow so many of Egypt's traditions.

Akhenaten confined himself to his beautiful city, and his preoccupation with his new religion may have caused him to neglect the management of his empire. Some 350 clay tablets inscribed in cuneiform with the Akkadian language that was used for international diplomatic correspondence have been discovered at Amarna. Many contain appeals for help from client rulers, which suggests that trouble was developing in the eastern portion of Egypt's empire. The end of Akhenaten's reign is obscure, but it is likely that the old priesthoods joined forces with disgruntled military officers against their unconventional pharaoh. The identity of his immediate successor is uncertain. All the children of his chief wife, Nefertiti, were female. His male heirs may have been sons by minor wives who were wed to Nefertiti's daughters.

By 1336 B.C.E., a youth named Tutankhaten had become the pharaoh. He was controlled by a conservative political faction that was set on obliterating the cult of the Aten and returning

Figure 2–2   Akhenaten and Nefertiti Worship the Aten   This panel depicts the pharaoh Akhenaten and his wife Nefertiti worshiping the Aten. Note the sun disk of the Aten above them with its descending rays culminating in hands bestowing blessings. Note also the curiously shaped profiles of the figures.

Egypt to its traditions. The young pharaoh's name was changed to Tutankhamun (to honor Egypt's former high god), and the court returned to Thebes. Amarna was abandoned and dismantled. Fortunately for archaeologists, many of its inscribed stones were carted off for use in later buildings. Some 12,000 of them have been discovered at Karnak. They are pieces in what is doubtless the world's most unwieldy and historically important jigsaw puzzle.

People in Context: The Mysterious Death of King "Tut"

In1922 British archaeologist Howard Carter experienced the fulfillment of every Egyptologist's fantasy. He discovered the intact tomb of an Egyptian pharaoh—the only one known to have survived into the modern era. The richness and elegance of the tomb's furnishings, which include a 250-pound gold coffin, overwhelm visitors to the Cairo Museum where they are now housed. But the wealth and craftsmanship they represent only hint at the magnificence of other royal burials. The tomb Carter found was a small one that had been hastily furnished for a young and relatively unimportant king, Akhenaten's heir Tutankhamun. Its occupant's insignificance may explain why his grave survived. Shortly after his funeral, attempts were made to loot his tomb, but they were foiled before they did much damage. Its entrance was then covered by debris from the excavation of another, larger tomb, and it was forgotten until Carter stumbled across it.

Tutankhamun died at the young age of nineteen. It was far from unusual for a man to die young in the ancient world, but Tutankhamun's death is suspicious. Examination of his mummy reveals that he suffered a blow to the base of his skull, a fracture that is unlikely to have been caused by an accident. The events that unfolded following his funeral also suggest that he may have been assassinated to clear the way to the throne for one of his powerful officials. Tutankhamun had married Akhenaten's daughter, Ankhesenpaten. At the time of his death, she had suffered two miscarriages (which were buried with their father) and had not yet produced an heir for her dynasty. Ankhesenpaten knew that she would be forced to remarry quickly. Egypt's next pharaoh would bolster his legitimacy by wedding her, the last surviving member of the royal family. Some remarkable letters recovered from the archives of Suppiluliuma (ruler of the Hittites, a people based in Asia Minor) suggest that Ankhesen paten feared being forced into an unworthy marriage. Egypt's widowed queen wrote to ask for the hand of one of Suppiluliuma's sons and declared her determination never to wed one of her "servants." She urged the Hittite ruler to respond quickly, for she was afraid of what she might be forced to do. Suppiluliuma was understandably suspicious, but he eventually dispatched one of his sons. The prince and his entourage were killed before they arrived in Egypt, and its young queen married Aye, a man in his sixties who had been prominent in the governments of both her husband and Akhenaten. After she made her aged husband pharaoh, she disappeared from history. No further mention is made of her, and her tomb has never been found.

We can only speculate about what happened. Tutankhamun was about ten when he ascended the throne, and Aye's title, "God's Father," suggests that he was the boy pharaoh's regent. Having long held the power, if not the title, of pharaoh, Aye may have been reluctant to give it up as his charge came of age. Perhaps he took steps to assure that he was ultimately acknowledged for what he had long been: Egypt's true ruler.

Question: What does Tutankhamun's story reveal about the ways that legitimate authority could be passed from one person to another in ancient kingdoms like Egypt?

The three pharaohs who followed Tutankhamun were self-made men. Aye, the first of them, had been one of Akhenaten's most powerful officials. When he died without an heir, a general named Horemheb claimed the crown, and at his death another military man, Ramses, rose through the ranks to become pharaoh. Ramses's nineteenth dynasty restored the glory and stability of the New Kingdom and guided Egypt through its final years as a powerful, independent nation. Ramses I's son, Seti, was a vigorous campaigner, and Seti's son, Ramses II, was both a warrior and ancient Egypt's most prolific builder. About half of ancient Egypt's extant monuments were constructed during his reign (1279–1212 B.C.E.), one of the longest in Egypt's history. Ramses II did his best to ensure the future of his dynasty by fathering (with the aid of a large harem) about 160 children, but by the time he died, threats to the power of his successors had begun to materialize on the horizon.

Egyptian Society   No matter what happened abroad, Egypt's internal stability was rarely threatened. Life changed little from generation to generation. Security, a reliable economy, and the overwhelming authority of pharaohs moderated the development of the kinds of class differences that stressed societies in Mesopotamia and elsewhere. In theory, all Egyptians were on the same legal footing. They were the pharaoh's slaves. In practice, some families had opportunities for education and for government service that gave them advantages over others.

Most ancient Egyptians were peasants who lived in simple rural villages near the fields they farmed. Their ephemeral settlements have largely disappeared without a trace, making it difficult for archaeologists to find materials that illuminate the lives of ordinary people. Remains of villages that housed the artisans who worked on royal tombs have survived, for they were in arid regions close to desert cemeteries. Although these communities served a unique class of specialized laborers, they suggest how most Egyptians lived. Villages were laid out in an orderly fashion. Some had walls to protect their residents from robbers. Houses were flat-roofed, rectangular structures constructed of mud brick and coated with painted plaster. They clustered closely together to shade narrow streets from Egypt's glaring sun. They contained five or six rooms, and their flat roofs provided additional living space—a cool place to sit or sleep after the sun went down. Furnishings were few. Villages maintained community shrines and cemeteries, but each home also had an altar dedicated to the worship of its household gods. The great temples served the state's gods. Each locality had its own patron deities, and each family its own ancestral cult. Clothing was simple, and people sometimes dispensed with it entirely. The Egyptians valued bodily cleanliness. Soap had not yet been invented, but they scrubbed themselves with various compounds and applied unguents to protect their skin from the sun. They reduced its glare by outlining their eyes with dark makeup (like football players do today). They shaved or plucked most body hair and wore wigs that were easy to clean and keep free of vermin. Males were circumcised.

Warlike peoples tend to exalt the status of males and to value sons more highly than daughters, but thanks to the protection that nature provided, Egypt was a fairly secure place. This fostered a milder form of patriarchy than found in other ancient societies. Egyptian men and women of the same class had nearly identical legal rights. Both could inherit, purchase, and sell property. Both could enter into contracts, make wills, and bring suits in court. Pharaohs had harems, but ordinary people were monogamous. Marriage was a private arrangement. The state did not impose regulations, but couples sometimes drew up contracts to define the terms of their relationship. A household's possessions were considered communal property, and divorce could be initiated by either a husband or a wife. People traced their ancestry through both maternal and paternal lines and inherited estates from both parents. Some Egyptians may have practiced brother–sister marriages, but evidence for this is sparse. Most examples come from the royal family and were motivated by its unique concern for establishing clear hereditary rights to the throne. The princes and princesses who married were usually half siblings, a pharaoh's son and daughter by different wives.

Women were associated with domestic environments and occupations. Artists painted women white and men brown to indicate that the former led sheltered lives in the home, while the latter worked outside, exposed to the elements. Egyptians cherished their homes, and the home's female caretaker was highly respected. When Egyptian men composed epitaphs for their tombs, they often waxed sentimental about their mothers. The ancient Mediterranean world was, in general, not kind to women, but Egyptian women had a better lot in life than their sisters elsewhere.

The Indo-Europeans and the Clash of Empires

During Egypt's Second Intermediate Period (c. 1590 B.C.E.), new peoples migrated into the Middle East and caused considerable upheaval. They were part of a vast movement that spread the Indo-European family of languages from Ireland to Iran and India. The Indo-European mother tongue no longer exists, but the spread of its various offshoots suggests that it originated north of the Black Sea. People from this district began to migrate outward about 2000 B.C.E., and almost everywhere they went, their language dominated. It became the speech of the ancient Greeks, Romans, Persians, and Indians—and most modern Europeans and Americans. (See Map 2–1.)

The Hittites   An Indo-European people called the Hittites founded the most powerful of the Middle East's new states. Their base was in north-central Anatolia, but their influence was felt much farther afield. They sacked Babylon in 1595 B.C.E. but were prevented from immediately expanding into Syria and Mesopotamia by the Hurrians of Mitanni, a country north of Assyria. The Mitannians dominated Syria and northern Mesopotamia from about 1500 to 1360 B.C.E. and skirmished with the empire-building pharaohs of the early New Kingdom. About 1360 B.C.E. the Hittites defeated them and began to threaten Egypt's Middle-Eastern empire.

The contest between the Hittites and the Egyptians culminated in a battle that Ramses II fought in 1286 B.C.E. at a place called Qadesh. The pharaoh's monuments claim it as a great victory for Egypt, but it appears to have been a draw. At any rate, the rapprochement between the Egyptians and Hittites that followed Qadesh probably had little to do with the battle's outcome. The fall of the Mitannian Empire had liberated the Assyrians, a people who lived along the upper reaches of the Tigris River, and they had begun to pose a threat to the Hittites. The Hittites made peace with Egypt to avoid being caught between two enemies and dispatched a princess to Egypt to become one of Ramses's many wives.

The Hittites adapted cuneiform to write their language and assimilated the civilization they found already established in the Middle East. They lived in isolated, self-sufficient villages and established few cities apart from their heavily fortified capital, Hattusas. Theirs was a

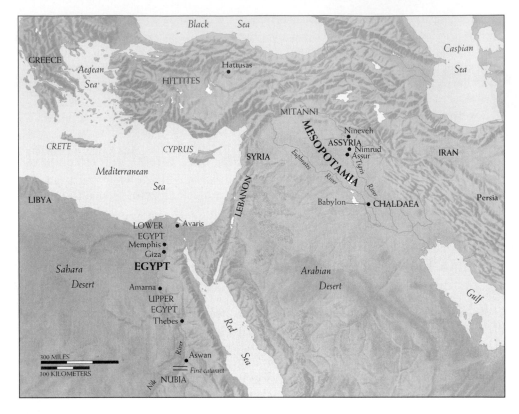

Map 2–1
The Seats of the Ancient Middle-Eastern Empires   Many states appeared in the Fertile Crescent, and from time to time one would attempt to bring the others under its control
and create an empire. ***Question:*** Are wars of conquest ever justified?

warlike society that was mobilized to support a large, expensively equipped army. Their king
shared power with a council consisting of the heads of the chief families, and their government
was plagued by coups, assassinations, and disputed successions.

The Invasion of the Sea Peoples   The Hittite empire collapsed about 1200 B.C.E. in the
wake of events that also forced Egypt to retreat from its empire. Seafaring raiders attacked the
coasts of the Mediterranean from Asia Minor to Libya. They were a polyglot band of pirates
whom the Egyptians lumped together as the Sea Peoples. The invasion of the Sea Peoples was
a mass migration that swept up different elements as it spread. It may have been triggered by
the collapse of some small states in Greece and expanded as a growing crowd of refugees undermined and overwhelmed one community after another. Incursions into the Egyptian delta
began in 1207 B.C.E. and continued for over twenty years. The Egyptians were not enthusiastic open-sea sailors nor adept at dealing with naval invasions. The Hittites were less exposed to
attack from the sea, but they failed to cope with the waves of dislocated peoples who flooded

across their borders. Famines may also have hampered the efforts of the established states to defend themselves. There is evidence that a prolonged drought afflicted much of the Mediterranean world at the end of the thirteenth century. Whatever the causes, the result was widespread disruption and resettlement.

Assyria's Opportunity   The Assyrians were a Semitic people who occupied the upper reaches of the Tigris River. Their homeland, on the fringes of Mesopotamian civilization, was a difficult, hilly country. It was under constant pressure from hostile tribes that dwelt in the mountains on its eastern and northern borders, and the threat these people posed may explain the militarism that took hold of Assyrian society.

The fall of the Mitannian Empire (c. 1360 B.C.E.) removed the chief obstacle to Assyria's expansion, but the Assyrians advanced slowly. To the south they confronted the powerful Kassites of Babylon. In the west they faced the Aramaeans, desert nomads who were seeking places to settle. Their old enemies in the northern and eastern mountains remained a problem. On top of all this, Assyria wrestled with internal political problems that finally caused its drive toward empire to falter late in the thirteenth century.

Assyria languished until Tiglath pileser I ascended the throne in 1114 B.C.E. He subdued Babylon and drove through northern Syria to the coast of the Mediterranean. After his death in 1076 B.C.E., Assyria entered another period of decline. Its march toward empire resumed in the ninth century B.C.E., when it won control of most of Mesopotamia and Syria. A glorious new city called Nimrud was built south of the old Assyrian capital at Nineveh, and the ruins of the palace that Ashurnasirpal II (r. 883–859) built in Nimrud were among the first sites to be explored by the European adventurers who pioneered the science of archaeology in the nineteenth century C.E. The great stone slabs covered with cuneiform inscriptions and bas-reliefs that formed the palace's walls were widely disbursed and can be seen in many European and American museums.

Disputed successions to the throne inaugurated another period of decline for Assyria in the late ninth century B.C.E. In 745 B.C.E. a general named Tiglathpileser III (r. 745–727 B.C.E.) seized power and built an empire that extended from the Persian Gulf north to Armenia and west to the Mediterranean coast and the borders of Egypt. In 722 B.C.E. the throne was usurped by Sargon II, who founded the last and greatest Assyrian dynasty. His grandson, Esarhaddon (r. 681–669 B.C.E.), brought the empire to its height in 671 B.C.E. by conquering Egypt.

Egypt's Fading Glory   Egypt's New Kingdom began to decline following the raids of the Sea Peoples, and it finally collapsed into a Third Intermediate Period (1069–702 B.C.E.) as local strongmen broke free of the central government and set up petty states. Their weakness tempted Nubia, which had so often been invaded by Egypt, to turn the tables on its old adversary. Nubian kings drove down the Nile, and by 727 they were the pharaohs of a reunited Egypt. The Nubians then overreached themselves by invading Palestine to regain Egypt's former empire. This prompted an Assyrian offensive that drove the Nubians from Egypt. The Assyrians then tried to govern Egypt with the help of native strongmen, but they were chronically unreliable. Esarhaddon and his successor, Assurbanipal (r. 668–630 B.C.E.), repeatedly sent armies into Egypt to reassert their authority. Their empire was, however, overextended militarily, and they had pressing problems elsewhere that prevented them from consolidating their hold on Egypt.

Figure 2–3 The Assyrian Army Besieges a City This bas-relief depicts Assyrian warriors battling their enemies, a task at which the Assyrians were notoriously adept. Note the weapons and shields.

By 655 B.C.E. the governors of Sais, a city in the delta, had restored Egypt's unity and independence. The Saite pharaohs sought allies and trading partners abroad and opened their country to the outside world. Foreigners established merchant colonies in Egypt and served the pharaohs as mercenary soldiers. The Saite dynasty tried to bolster its legitimacy (and maybe counter the influence of the alien cultures to which it had exposed its homeland) by restoring archaic Egyptian practices. Artists and architects resurrected the styles of the Old and Middle Kingdoms, and there was a literary renaissance. Egypt's destiny, however, was to be absorbed into a succession of empires: Persian, Greek, Roman, and finally Muslim.

Assyria's Culmination Assyria relied on brute force and psychological intimidation to build and hold its empire, and its most significant cultural contributions were to the field of military science. Assyria maintained a standing army composed of specialized units: infantry, cavalry, chariots, scouts, and engineers (to level roads, bridge rivers, and construct siege equipment). Progress in metallurgy made iron weapons and armor increasingly common, and breeders produced horses large enough to be ridden into battle. Most ancient armies were little

▶ Culture in Context: The Dawn of the Iron Age

The ancient Greeks were the first to divide history into eras defined by the use of different metals. They knew that their not-too-distant ancestors had lived in a world of bronze, whereas they had what the poet Homer described as swords of "blue iron." The Iron Age is said to begin about 1300 B.C.E., but the nature of iron makes it difficult to pin down when and where people learned to work it. Gold is an inert metal that survives burial in the earth. Bronze develops a surface corrosion that helps to preserve it, but because iron oxidizes, objects made from iron quickly rust and disintegrate. This makes it difficult for archaeologists to reconstruct the history of iron-working technology.

Meteors provided ancient peoples with a few specimens of iron, but the metal was so seldom found in a pure state in nature that it was treated as a precious commodity. Beads made of iron were sometimes used as jewelry and set in gold, the less valuable material. Iron is actually Earth's second most plentiful metal (after aluminum). The challenge early people faced was to discover how to extract it from ores and turn it into useful objects. The copper and tin from which bronze is made melt at relatively low temperatures. Ancient smiths could easily build fires hot enough to smelt their ores and turn them into liquids that could be poured into molds. To produce iron, however, air had to be forced into a furnace to create very high temperatures, and the metal that resulted was brittle. To make it durable enough for practical uses, it had to be forged into steel—a complicated process that involved rapid heating and cooling, and repeated hammering to combine iron with carbon.

The first ironworkers may have come from Armenia. The Hurrians of Mitanni were using some iron as early as 1500 B.C.E. After the Mitannian Empire fell, its Hittite successor became known for iron production. One of the treasures found in Pharaoh Tutankhamun's tomb was an iron-bladed dagger that was probably a gift from a Hittite king. Hittite iron production was, however, limited. Not until about 900 B.C.E. was iron plentiful and cheap enough to equip whole armies. The Assyrian military was the first to make extensive use of it, but soldiers were not the only people whose lives it affected. Unlike copper and (especially) tin, iron ore is widely distributed and abundant. That made iron implements relatively inexpensive compared to bronze. The Iron Age, therefore, opened the way for peasant farmers to acquire metal tools and explore what metals could do for their productivity.

Question: What sorts of things might have changed in the ancient world as a result of the increasing availability of iron?

more than armed mobs, but the units of the Assyrian army supported one another in the field and were trained to execute battle plans. Support structures were also devised to keep large armies well supplied during sieges and on the move.

Assyrian emperors resorted to terrorism to frighten their enemies into submission, and their monuments proudly listed their atrocities: heads lopped off, eyes gouged out, limbs severed, skin flayed from living bodies, and the mass slaughter of women and children. Such treatment was not designed to win the loyalty and love of the peoples whom the Assyrians conquered, and their empire was plagued by revolts and rebellions. Some regions were pacified by deporting and scattering entire populations, but garrisons had to be maintained throughout the empire to keep watch over hordes of resentful subjects. This imposed a fatal drain on the empire's manpower that led to its sudden collapse.

The creation and preservation of the Assyrian empire thoroughly militarized Assyrian society. Militarization sometimes promotes a kind of hyper-masculinization of a culture that makes life difficult for women. This is reflected in Assyrian law codes. They were preoccupied with property rights more than human freedoms and lavish in recommending mutilations and executions as punishment for all kinds of transgressions. The law declared wives to be the property of their fathers and husbands, and a woman who dishonored the man who was responsible for her was fortunate if she lost only ears, nose, or fingers. Some female offenders had their breasts ripped off. Because a man could get in serious trouble if he had contact with women belonging to another man, he needed to be able to recognize the status of every woman he met. Assyrian law ordered respectable women to veil their faces whenever they left their homes and punished any prostitute who tried to hide behind a veil. Among the legacies of Assyrian civilization are the restrictions that some Middle-Eastern cultures still place on the freedom of women.

Assyrian civilization reached its height under the warlike, but cultivated, Assurbanipal (r. 668–630 B.C.E.). Assurbanipal was a scholar and an aesthete as well as a general. He could read the long-dead Sumerian language and had a passion for collecting texts. He searched his empire for documents and created a huge library at Nineveh. Some 30,000 tablets have been recovered from its ruins.

Things deteriorated rapidly during the reigns of Assurbanipal's two sons. The Chaldaeans, an Aramaic-speaking tribe, seized Babylon, and war broke out with the Medes, an Indo-European people who had settled in Iran. In 612 B.C.E. the Chaldaeans and the Medes joined forces against Assyria and sacked Nineveh. By 610, the Assyrian empire was only a memory, and the Chaldaeans had become the rising power in the Middle East.

The Bible and History

No ancient peoples have had a greater influence on what Western civilization became than a tiny group to whom the great Mesopotamian and Egyptian empires paid scant attention. All three of the West's major religions (Judaism, Christianity, and Islam) trace their origins, at least in part, to the sacred literature of a people who are known variously as Hebrews (from a Semitic term for *nomad*), Israelites (from Israel, the northern part of their territory), and Jews (from Judah, the region around their sacred city, Jerusalem).

The ancient Israelites' concept of divine power contrasted with the views prevalent in the ancient world. The Israelites gradually developed a monotheistic faith, but more original than their belief in one god was how they conceived that god. Most ancient peoples equated gods with forces of nature and assumed that gods were simply part of the created order. The gods may have designed and constructed this world, but they did not create existence itself. The God of the ancient Hebrews was different. He was the transcendent Creator who was the source of everything that was. He was not subject to time and space, the dimensions of the reality He called into being. He was the Other, an omnipotence beyond mere existence.

The exalted nature of Israel's God removed Him from the realm of ordinary human experience. He could be known, therefore, only if and where He chose to manifest Himself. The Israelites reasoned that He was not revealed by the cycles of nature, for the things of nature follow fixed laws. They are not free, whereas the Creator is absolute freedom. He is nature's master, not its prisoner. The suitable place for Him to reveal Himself, therefore, was in the kinds of phenomena where free wills manifest themselves—in the events of history, not those of nature. Because God is beyond all compulsion, however, He is not required to appear in all history, but only in the history He chooses to use. The ancient Israelites believed that God had elected their history as the vehicle for His self-revelation. They were God's "Chosen People" not because He valued them more than others but because He chose them as His instruments.

Many ancient cultures thought of time as an eternal, repetitive cycle of days and seasons. They had little awareness of time as a sequence of unique, significant events—of time as history. The Israelite conception of God fostered a different view of life's temporal context. It implied that the passage of time was a kind of journey filled with adventures that were intended to bring people into relationship with their Creator.

This journey, the Israelites believed, did not truly get underway until long after the dawn of creation. They did not think of themselves as one of the world's ancient peoples. They traced their origin to a covenant (compact) that God made with a man named Abram (Abraham). They, the "children of Abraham," were descendants of a landless man who was born into a world that had already been parceled among various peoples.

The Bible's stories of Abraham and the creation of the Chosen People begin in the twelfth chapter of Genesis, its first book. To provide background for this event, the Israelites drew on the general religious mythology that circulated throughout the ancient Middle East. The opening chapters of Genesis, with their stories of gardens and snakes, floods and arks, and heaven-scaling towers, derive from the myths of the Sumerians and Babylonians. There was little history in this material, but the Israelites used it as a vehicle to explain their theory of history and their view of humanity's place in the world order.

Sacred Myth and History   The Bible purports to derive, at least in part, from the history of a real people, the ancient Israelites. Scholars have therefore sought to link its narrative with other ancient records. But because this undertaking has implications for the cherished convictions of both believers and nonbelievers, it excites endless controversy.

The Bible calls Abram a wandering Aramaean whose family came from "Ur of the Chaldaeans." Ur was gone long before the Chaldaeans appeared, but at the time when this text was written, the Chaldaeans ruled the Mesopotamian heartland where the Israelites believed their founding father's family had originated. There was significant migration of Aramaean tribes into northern Mesopotamia, where Abram is when the Bible picks up his story, following the collapse of the Third Dynasty of Ur in 2004 B.C.E.

Abram and his people began their history with nothing. They were Apiru (Hebrews), landless nomads, a people who "dwell in tents." A dynasty of patriarchs (Abraham, Isaac, Jacob, and Joseph) led them as they wandered about Syria, Palestine, and the Sinai. Archaeological evidence suggests that the Sinai was more hospitable to herders during parts of the second millennium than at other times, and Egyptian records from the fifteenth century B.C.E. document the presence of Apiru there.

Chronology: The Middle-Eastern Empires of the Iron Age

THE MIDDLE EAST	EGYPT	BIBLICAL NARRATIVE
2004, Ur falls	MIDDLE KINGDOM (2025–1630)	
BABYLONIAN EMPIRE {Indo–European migration} Hammurabi (1792–1750)		Abraham
	SECOND INTERMEDI-ATE PERIOD (1630–1550) Hyksos invasion of Egypt	
1595, Hittites sack Babylon Kassites occupy Babylon		sojourn of the Israelites in Egypt
MITANNIAN EMPIRE (–c. 1360) Hittite Kingdom	NEW KINGDOM (1550–1075) Thutmose I (1504–1492) Hatshepsut (1478–1458) Thutmose III (1458–1425) Amenhotep III (1390–1352) Akhenaten (1352–1338) {*The Amarna Period*} Tutankhamun (1336–1327)	
HITTITE EMPIRE (–c. 1200) 1286, Qadesh 1230, invasion of the Sea Peoples	Ramses II (1279–1212)	Exodus entrance into Canaan the Judges
ASSYRIAN EMPIRE (–612) Tiglath pileser I (1114–1076)		
	THIRD INTERMEDIATE PERIOD (1069–702) Nubian pharaohs (–c. 656) Saitic Dynasty (–c. 655–525)	The Kingdom Saul (1020–1000) David (1000–961) Solomon (961–922)
Ashurnasirpal (883–859) Tiglath pileser III (745–727) Esarhaddon (681–669) Assurbanipal (668–630) 612, Nineveh falls		ISRAEL and JUDAH 721, Israel falls
CHALDAEAN EMPIRE (612–538)		587, Judah falls The Exile
PERSIAN EMPIRE		

The Bible says that Joseph, the last of the patriarchs, persuaded a pharaoh to allow his people to settle in the "land of Goshen," a district on the border between Egypt's delta and the Sinai. If there is any truth to this, the Egyptian pharaohs who were most likely to welcome Apiru immigration were Hyksos. The Hyksos, like the Apiru, were Semites, and they may have wanted help with their occupation of Egypt. The Bible says that Joseph's people remained in Egypt for over 400 years, but it says nothing about these centuries.

Abraham's descendants became a distinct people with a unique identity, the Bible says, when a man called Moses (the root of Egyptian names such as Thut-moses, "Son of Thut") led them out of Egypt. This event, the Exodus, is described in some passages as a dramatic flight from a pursuing Egyptian army that drowned in the Sea of Reeds. There is no report of such a catastrophe in the Egyptian records. Some scholars have tried to connect Moses with the court of Akhnaten and to ground Hebrew monotheism in the cult of the Aten. Others favor a later date for the Exodus, during the reign of Ramses II (1279–1212 B.C.E.). All that the Bible says is that there was a change of dynasty that brought a new pharaoh to power, and he set the Hebrews to making bricks to build the cities of Pithom and Ramses. During the period of the New Kingdom, the residents of Egypt's eastern borderlands would have been impressed into service to construct the forts and depots (the Bible's "store cities") that were part of the empire's new military infrastructure.

The Hebrews who fled Egypt allegedly tried to break into the agricultural districts of southern Palestine, but were repulsed and forced to resume the nomadic life of their ancestors in the desert. Joshua, Moses's successor, finally led them across the Jordan River, past the city of Jericho, and into a land occupied by an urbanized people called the Canaanites. A likely time for desert tribes to breach Canaan's frontier defenses would be about 1230 B.C.E., when raids by the Sea Peoples were drawing defenders away from the inland borders to protect the coasts. The Egyptians paid close attention to events in Palestine, and the first extra-biblical reference to a people called Israel is found on a monument erected by the pharaoh Merneptah in 1207 B.C.E.

The Bible does not depict the Hebrew invasion of Canaan as a conquest. The Hebrews did not occupy any cities or claim the agriculturally rich Jordan Valley. They scattered into the mountains between the valley and the coast, and spent generations scratching out a precarious existence. They formed a loose federation of twelve tribes that was led, from time to time, by charismatic figures called judges. They survived but were no match for their more highly civilized neighbors.

Palestine   Urban settlement began very early (c. 7000 B.C.E.) along the eastern edge of the Mediterranean. The region had sufficient rainfall to support farming, and its rough terrain encouraged the formation of small city-states rather than large territorial kingdoms. The richest district was a strip of coast west of the Lebanese Mountains called Phoenicia. The Phoenicians, the West's first notable seafarers, derived their wealth from trade, for their ports (Tyre, Sidon, and Byblos) were ideally situated to mediate exchanges of goods between Mesopotamia and Egypt. Phoenicians were shipping wood from the Lebanese Mountains to treeless Egypt as early as the start of the Old Kingdom. They also trafficked in copper and manufactured a scarlet dye that was so costly that its color came to be identified with royalty. So many sheets of Egyptian papyrus passed through Byblos that the port's name became the Greek word for *book* (*biblos*) and ours for Bible.

The Phoenicians were explorers as well as traders. They traveled the length of the Mediterranean, colonized the coast of North Africa, and ventured onto the Atlantic. They may have reached Britain and, if a report in an ancient Greek history is accurate, circumnavigated Africa. They were the chief agents for diffusing the civilization that was evolving in the ancient Middle East throughout the Mediterranean world. Their influence lives on, for the Greeks adapted their letter forms and alphabet, and transmitted these things to the Romans and ultimately to us.

The primitive Israelites who settled in the mountains between the Jordan Valley and the Mediterranean coast were less concerned with the Phoenicians than with the Philistines (a Sea People who settled the coast west of Jerusalem) and the older residents of Palestine, the Canaanites. The Canaanites were related to the Amorites who founded Babylon, and their urbanized culture was much more advanced than that of the Israelites. The Bible says that the Israelites had to trade with them to obtain metal implements, for they did not know how to make these things for themselves. Disillusionment with their inferior status finally convinced the Israelites that they needed to make changes in their way of life so that they could "be like all the nations." This, they believed, required them to submit to the authority of a king.

Religious leaders appointed the Israelites' first king, a man named Saul (r. c. 1020–1000 B.C.E.). After Saul died in battle with the Philistines, his crown passed to an ambitious general named David (r. c. 1000–961 B.C.E.). David united the Israelite tribes, conquered Canaan, and created a state with its capital at Jerusalem. The new kingdom allegedly won international respect and grew very wealthy during the reign of David's son, Solomon (r. c. 961–922 B.C.E.). This was a time when small states like Solomon's might have flourished. The great empires of the Egyptians and Hittites had fallen, and no new superpower had yet appeared to threaten the independence of Palestine.

The Bible describes Solomon as a mighty ruler, but historians caution that no archaeological evidence confirms the Bible's picture of his or his father's kingdom. No inscriptions have been found verifying the existence of David and Solomon, and there is no trace of the great buildings that the latter is said to have erected.

According to the Bible, the ten northern tribes of Israelites refused to accept Solomon's heir and established a separate kingdom called Israel. Solomon's dynasty was left with a small, rural district known as Judah. Both states were caught up in the international conflicts that accompanied the rise of the Assyrian empire. In 721 B.C.E. Assyria overwhelmed Israel and deported its people. Israel's ten tribes were "lost" in that they were scattered throughout the Assyrian empire and absorbed into other cultures. The tiny kingdom of Judah managed to outlive the Assyrian Empire, but it succumbed to the Assyrians' successors, the Chaldaeans. In 587 B.C.E. the Chaldaeans destroyed Jerusalem and deported its people. This began the Exile, the period that was, after the Exodus, the most theologically significant in Hebrew history. (See Map 2–2.)

Exile was intended to extinguish a people's identity, but two things enabled the Jews to escape this fate. First was the fact that for some of them the Exile was relatively brief. In 539 B.C.E. Cyrus the Great conquered the Chaldaeans, established the Persian Empire, and permitted a few Jews to go back to Jerusalem to rebuild its temple. Jerusalem was rarely independent of the empires that subsequently rose and fell in the Mediterranean world, but its continuing existence provided an anchor for Jewish identity.

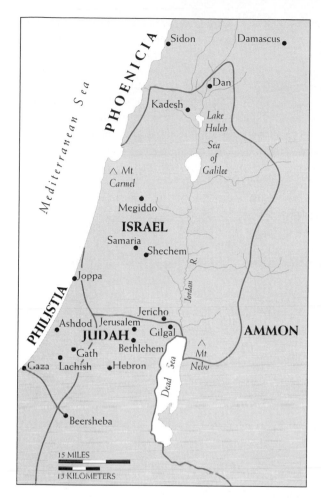

Map 2–2

Ancient Palestine The Bible credits the formation of the Israelite state to the second of Israel's kings, a man named David. He is said to have conquered and united the Canaanite city-states and linked the Jordan Valley with a strip of coast bordered by Phoenicia in the north and the territory of the Philistines in the south. Following the reign of his son and successor, Solomon, the state he had built split into rival kingdoms: Israel and Judah. *Question:* Which, would the map suggest, was the strongest of the two ancient Hebrew kingdoms?

The other thing that enabled the Jews to preserve their identity was the Bible, the first five books of which (the Torah) probably assumed their present form during the Exile. Court scholars, who worked for the kings of Israel and Judah, had recorded several versions of the ancient oral traditions of their people, and these were integrated into a single narrative by Jewish rabbis (teachers) working during the Exile. The Jews who returned to Jerusalem were the first to hear a reading of the Torah. Its stories of Abraham and his descendants reminded the Jews that it was a relationship with their God, not their land, that made them a people. This belief has helped them survive millennia of exile, diaspora (scattering), and persecution to become the only ancient people who have maintained their identity into the modern era.

The Biblical Faith The land of Israel did not make the Jews a people, but its loss was a challenge to their faith. They believed that David's kingdom had been given to them in fulfillment of the promises that God made to Abraham. The loss of this "Promised Land" might have been taken as a sign that God had abandoned them, or that He was too weak to keep his promises, or that He was untrustworthy. Meditating on the experience, however, helped religious leaders, whom the Jews called prophets, articulate some of the Bible's most profound insights into the human condition.

A twentieth-century philosopher has characterized the seventh and sixth centuries B.C.E. as the Axis Age, a crucial turning point for civilization. During these years, major religious leaders appeared in several parts of the world and changed how people thought about social relationships and the meaning of life. Greece produced the first philosophers. Zoroaster preached in Persia. Confucius and Lao-tzu appeared in China. Buddha emerged from India, and a number of Hebrew prophets added important books to the Bible.

The Hebrew prophets were not prophets in the sense of fortune tellers. They explained the religious significance of contemporary events, and their insights into the future were based on the lessons of history. For them, the loss of the Promised Land was part of a divine plan. God had given the Jews a law to explain how He wanted them to treat one another. They had tried to placate Him, like a pagan god, with ritual and sacrifice, but what He demanded was justice and concern for the poor and weak. The Jews had lost their land, the prophets claimed, because they had ceased to do God's will. But their situation was not hopeless, for God was more than a judge who punished transgressors. He was also a faithful and merciful Father who somehow reconciled the requirements of both justice and love. The Bible's claim that human communities are accountable to transcendent standards of justice and mercy sank deep into Western consciousness. Although Western societies have often fallen far short of the fulfillment of this vision, they have never lost some sense of obligation to it.

Larger Issue Revisited

Thanks to human ingenuity in finding multiple ways to adapt to environments of all kinds, human communities (and the cultural identities they create) are of nearly infinite variety. This poses a challenge to a government when it extends its authority over a large area and undertakes the management of a diverse population. The states that appeared in ancient Mesopotamia were the first to confront issues of this kind, and they developed a range of strategies for dealing with them—ranging from brute force to respect for transcendent principles of law and morality. The most common plan was to impose order from above. A need for efficiency in a world where means of travel and communication were still primitive encouraged concentration of power in the hands of a monarch. Such persons were so elevated above the common herd that their authority was usually assumed to have a divine mandate. But ideas about the accountability of monarchs to something beyond themselves also circulated as the West began to explore ways to maintain order in a world of increasing scale and complexity.

Review Questions

1. What strategies did Hammurabi employ to consolidate his empire?
2. What did religion and geography contribute to the construction of Egypt and its empire?
3. What strategies did the Assyrians employ to build and hold their empire?
4. What does the biblical history of the Jews contribute to the debate about how to create a stable society?

5. Which of the strategies employed by the ancient empire builders was most successful? Why?
6. Are there limits to how much cultural diversity a state can tolerate?

Refer to the front of the book for a list of chapter-relevant primary sources available on the CD-ROM.

THE WEST INTERACTIVE

For web-based activities, map explorations, and quizzes related to this chapter, go to *www.prenhall.com/frankforter.*

PART TWO

THE CLASSICAL ERA
2000 B.C.E. to 30 C.E.

Many of the characteristics that distinguish Western civilization first clearly emerged during the era when the Greeks and the Romans dominated the Mediterranean world. Their moment in history, therefore, became the West's classical period. Western peoples are not, and have never been, a homogenous group with a single outlook, and they do not honor, not have they ever honored, the same institutions or sets of values. But certain ideas or attitudes have repeatedly surfaced in their societies and provided continuity for their history. A major Greco-Roman legacy was a faith in humanity itself—in reason, science, and human intellect as adequate tools for understanding the world and coping with its challenges. Associated with this was the assumption that ethics and morality have a basis in nature—a belief that has inspired noble concepts of human rights and drives to organize just societies. Respect for the past has paralyzed some peoples, but the West's recurring bouts of enthusiasm for its classical period have encouraged it to change—and always for the better.

	CULTURE	ENVIRONMENT AND TECHNOLOGY	POLITICS
C. 2000 B.C.E.	Bronze Age	sea-faring ships	
	Minoan Crete	linear A script	merchant-princes
C. 1800 B.C.E.	Mycenaean Greeks	linear B script	bureaucratic administration
C. 1230 B.C.E.	Aegean Dark Age	geometric-style pottery	Sea Peoples
C. 1200 B.C.E.	Iron Age	warrior chiefdoms	
C. 750 B.C.E.	Greek Archaic Era	Phoenician alphabet	Greek colonization
	Etruscan expansion		
	Rome founded		
	Homer and Hesiod	hoplite infantry	*polis*
C. 500 B.C.E.	Hellenic Era	Ionian natural science	social engineering
	Spartan mobilization (650 B.C.E.)		
	Sophist philosophers	black-figure pottery	Athenian democracy (510 B.C.E.)
	Socrates	red-figure pottery	Persian Wars (492–479 B.C.E.)
	Athenian theater	Doric and Ionic architecture	Delian League (477 B.C.E.)
C. 400 B.C.E.	Herodotus	Peloponnesian War (432–404 B.C.E.)	
	Thucydides	Roman Republic founded (410 B.C.E.)	
	Plato	Philip of Macedon (359–336 B.C.E.)	
	Aristotle	Alexander (336–323 B.C.E.)	
C. 300 B.C.E.	Hellenistic Era	urban planning	Seleucid and Ptolemaic kingdoms
	pastoral and lyric poetry	Alexandrine science, museum	
	novels	Euclid	
C. 200 B.C.E.	New Comedy	Roman legion	Punic Wars (264–202 B.C.E.)
	Roman engineering: roads		
	Latifundia	Roman civil war (133-30 B.C.E.)	
C. 100 B.C.E.	Cicero	Julius Caesar (100–44 B.C.E.)	
	Jesus of Nazareth	Octavian Augustus (63 B.C.E.–14 C.E.)	
	Golden Age, Roman poetry	Roman Empire founded (30 B.C.E.)	
	Virgil, Horace, Ovid	Julio-Claudians (30 B.C.E.–68 C.E.)	
C. 100 C.E.	Silver Age, Roman poetry		Flavians (69–96 C.E.)
	"Good Emperors" (96–180 C.E.)		
C. 200 C.E.	Severans (193–235 C.E.)		
	"Barracks Emperors" (235–285 C.E.)		

CHAPTER 3

AEGEAN CIVILIZATIONS

I would rather be a humble servant plowing fields for the owner of a tiny farm than the greatest lord in the kingdom of the dead.

—**Achilles,** *The Odyssey*

Larger Issue: *When does civilization in the West become Western civilization?*

On his way home from the Trojan War, a Greek king named Odysseus paid a visit to the mouth of the underworld to consult the ghost of Achilles, a friend who died in the war. Achilles, who had been the greatest of Greece's heroes, used the occasion to explain the facts of death to Odysseus. He said that he would rather occupy the lowest station in the land of the living than the highest post in the world of the dead. The passion for life and the faith in the value of earthly existence implied by this remark help to explain the achievements of the Greeks. The civilization they founded on the shores of the Aegean Sea transformed the ancient world, and it continues to affect ours. We adapt the Greeks' architecture, imitate their sculpture, debate the theories of their philosophers, use their scientific vocabulary, and even go to the theater to be entertained by their playwrights.

The influence of the ancient Greek thinkers and artists has been so pervasive that some historians claim that the Greeks were the founders of Western civilization. Others caution that the Greeks did not develop in a vacuum—that they had close ties with Middle-Eastern states and borrowed much from them. A controversial school of contemporary scholars has gone so far as to claim that most of Greek civilization was derived from Egypt and Africa.

Advocates for all these positions make their cases by listing specific things that the Greeks are said either to have borrowed or to have originated. Arguments of this kind are not very persuasive, for a civilization is more than its component parts. The debate does, however, illustrate how difficult it is to draw hard and fast lines across the continuum of history.

The ancient Greeks' experience with civilization demonstrates how complex the interaction between people and environments can be. People inhabit two worlds simultaneously: one constructed by nature and one created in their minds. What they make of the former depends to a great extent on how they deal with the latter. Different people react differently to similar sets of challenges and opportunities, and explanations for their behavior are rooted in the mysteries of human psychology.

Greek history illustrates the role that imagination and creativity play in the human struggle for survival, for nature provided the Greeks with few resources. The Greek mainland was small (about the size of the state of Louisiana) and poor. It had no rivers like the Nile or Euphrates and no fields as productive as those of Egypt or Mesopotamia. Greek farmers could work only about eighteen percent of their country's mountainous terrain. Greece's forests were depleted in prehistory, and even the seas off its coasts were not particularly rich in fish. The success the Greeks had in building a civilization under such circumstances proves that environmental resources alone are not enough to explain the rise of a great culture. The Greeks made extraordinary use of what they were given by their homeland, but they also profited from contacts with older civilizations. The fame of Greek civilization should not obscure the fact that the role the Middle East played in the formation of "the West" did not end with the arrival of the Greeks.

TOPICS IN THIS CHAPTER

Minoan Mentors • The Mycenaeans, Greece's First Civilization • The Aegean Dark Age •
The Hellenic Era • The Rise of the Mainland Powers •
The Persian Wars: Catalyst of a Civilization

Minoan Mentors

What has long been regarded as the West's most influential ancient civilization appeared in the Aegean, the part of the Mediterranean that is bound by the island of Crete on the south, Asia Minor on the east, and the Greek peninsula on the west and north. It was the work of a people who called themselves Hellenes, but who are better known as Greeks, the name the Romans gave them.

The Greeks were introduced to civilization by the inhabitants of ancient Crete. We call them Minoans after Minos, a legendary king of Crete. We do not know what they called themselves, for the documents they left us have not yet been deciphered. Scholars speculate that their language was related to one of the Semitic tongues of the Middle East. If so, significant elements in their population may have migrated from that region.

Minoan Civilization Crete was inhabited as early as 7000 B.C.E., but the kind of monumental architecture that often signals the presence of a civilization did not appear until about 2000 B.C.E. Crete's great buildings, unlike those of Mesopotamia and Egypt, were not temples or tombs. They were palaces for *merchant-princes,* rulers whose major interest was trade, not conquest. Minoan civilization was forgotten until the largest of these structures, at a place called Knossos, was discovered in 1899. No one knows whether the ruler of Knossos presided over all of Crete or was only one of several Minoan princes. His court was certainly magnificent. The multistoried palace at Knossos had about 300 rooms arranged around its great courtyards—as well as lavishly decorated reception halls, ceremonial staircases, workshops, warehouses, and well-engineered ventilation, drainage, and sewage disposal systems. The fact that it was not fortified suggests that its owner enjoyed mastery of the sea and had no fear of invasion. (See Map 3–1.)

Seafaring funded Minoan civilization. Egypt had an insatiable appetite for northern products such as wood and olive oil (the all-purpose lubricant and the chief source of fat in the ancient world's grain-based diet). Peoples such as the Minoans and Phoenicians, whose island and coastal homes oriented them to the sea, were eager to serve the Egyptian market. Minoan merchants were active in Egypt as early as the Middle Kingdom (2100–1700 B.C.E.), and Egypt greatly influenced Minoan culture.

Map 3–1
The Bronze-Age Aegean World   Two distinct but related civilizations (the Minoan and the Mycenaean) arose in the Aegean region between 2000 and 1200 B.C.E. Both were maritime powers whose wealth derived from Mediterranean trade. *Question:* How would you expect Minoan civilization to differ from Mycenaean civilization given that the Minoans lived on an island and the Mycenaeans on the mainland?

Minoan trade supported the aristocrats who lived in palaces, such as Knossos on Crete's northern coast and Phaistos on its southern rim. It also enabled the residents of the towns scattered about Crete and on neighboring islands to erect comfortable homes. Little is known about its impact on the Minoan peasantry, for few traces of their villages survive.

Like other ancient peoples whose economic activities required them to maintain inventories of goods, the Minoans invented a system of writing. Crete's scribes may have been inspired by Egyptian hieroglyphs, but by 1800 B.C.E., they had evolved a distinctive script of their own. Scholars have named it Linear A to distinguish it from a later version, Linear B, that the early Greeks adapted for writing their language. Both scripts were drawn (rather than imprinted with cuneiform wedges) on clay tablets and both were probably used exclusively for the purpose of compiling economic records. Because Linear A cannot yet be read, most of what we know about Minoan civilization comes from the study of its ruined buildings.

The frescoes that decorated the walls of homes and palaces provide windows into the Minoan world, for Minoan art was realistic. It described plants, animals, landscapes, and a variety of human activities. The paucity of military scenes in paintings and of weapons in graves has led some scholars to conclude that the Minoans were a peace-loving people. No society that depended on the dangerous profession of long-distance trade could, however, have been indifferent to the martial arts.

Minoan frescoes depict a slender, graceful, and athletic people. The men of Crete, like those of Egypt, wore short kilts. Female court costume featured floor-length skirts and tight fitting bodices that left the breasts bare. Women are prominent subjects of a few frescoes, and Minoan religion featured a goddess, a young woman associated with snakes and birds. Some people claim that this is evidence that Minoan society was dominated by women, but many communities have honored a few privileged females and venerated goddesses while denigrating ordinary women. Minoan religious symbolism was also not exclusively female. Bulls represented the male element in what was doubtless a fertility cult. The horns of bulls decorated the walls of the palace at Knossos, and some frescoes depict young men and women engaged in a form of bull fighting that was probably a religious ritual. No Minoan temples have been discovered. The palace was a setting for religious ceremonies, and people also worshiped at sacred places under the open sky, in caves, and at shrines in their homes.

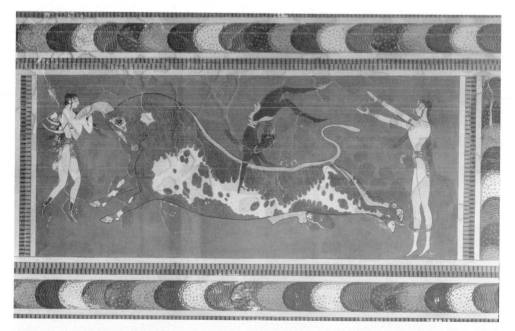

Figure 3–1 The Minoan Bull-Leapers This much-reconstructed fresco from the palace at Knossos illustrates what may have been both a sport and a religious ritual. The participants leaped at charging bulls, grabbed their horns, and somersaulted over their backs.

Minoan History   Minoan civilization belonged to the Bronze Age. During the Early Minoan Period (2600–2000 B.C.E.), Crete developed its trade. The Minoans clustered into urban settlements and built their first palaces during the Middle Minoan Period (2000–1600 B.C.E.). The Late Minoan Period (1600–1125 B.C.E.) emerged in the wake of a disaster that caused widespread destruction on the island. Because there was no change in Minoan culture, the damage was probably the result of a natural catastrophe and not a foreign invasion.

About 1450 B.C.E., the scribes working at Knossos switched from Linear A to Linear B. The significance of this change became clear in 1952, when a young British scholar proved that Linear B recorded an early form of Greek. The use of Greek at Knossos suggests that warriors from the mainland conquered and occupied Crete. About fifty years later the whole island was again devastated by the hand of either man or God, and Minoan civilization began to fade from memory. The Minoans may have sowed the seeds of their own destruction by introducing the Greeks of the mainland to seafaring, trade, and civilization.

The Mycenaeans, Greece's First Civilization

The Greeks created two quite different civilizations. The one for which they are famous is the second, their Hellenic or "classical" civilization. Their first, which flourished from about 1600 to 1200 B.C.E., modeled itself on the Minoan example. Historians have named it for Mycenae, a city in southeastern Greece that was ruled by Agamemnon, the king who appears in Homer's *Iliad* as the leader of the Greeks in their Trojan War.

Origin of the Greeks   The ancestors of the Greeks were part of the great wave of migration that spread Indo-European languages from the Atlantic Coast to the Indian Ocean. They entered the Greek peninsula from central Europe between 2100 and 1900 B.C.E. and displaced its earlier inhabitants, villagers with cultural ties to Asia Minor. They were a warlike people with strongly patriarchal customs, and as nomadic herders from the northern plains, they had no maritime experience. Their language even lacked a word for *sea*.

The Greeks' appearance in the Aegean world roughly coincided with the rise of Minoan civilization on Crete. There is no evidence that the Minoans ever ruled the Greek mainland, but mythology suggests that the early Greeks were overawed by Crete's superior culture. "Theseus and the Minotaur" narrates the adventures of a prince of Athens who was sent to Crete as human tribute. He negotiates a labyrinth, a maze that King Minos built to hold the Minotaur (Minos-bull), a beast born of a union between a bull and Minos's wife. Theseus kills the monster and escapes—with the help of Minos's daughter. The story suggests that the primitive Greeks knew that bulls were featured in Minoan religious sacrifices and that Minoans erected mysterious buildings, such as the labyrinth at Knossos, a structure decorated with a sacred symbol called a *labys* (a double-headed axe). Another Greek myth claimed that in infancy the god Zeus had been hidden on Crete to prevent his father from killing him. When he grew up, he overthrew the older deities and established the reign of the Greeks.

The Mycenaean Kingdoms   Mycenaean civilization was the invention of mainland kingdoms that were tiny versions of the great states of Egypt and Mesopotamia. Mycenaean kingdoms had centralized governments administered by elaborate bureaucracies, and they were intensely militaristic. Their palaces were citadels into which besieged populations could retreat. Their art featured battle scenes. Their leaders were buried with weapons, armor, and chariots, and their merchants trafficked in armaments. The Mycenaeans had inherited a warlike disposition from their nomadic Indo-European ancestors, and Greece's environment did little to moderate it. The country's mountainous terrain hampered political unification, and competition for its scarce resources and commercial opportunities sparked vicious rivalries among its inhabitants.

Mycenaean kings were, like the Minoan rulers, merchant-princes. The professions of merchant and warrior were closely allied in the ancient world, for traders who ventured far from home had no protection other than what they provided for themselves. They were heavily armed, and only opportunity distinguished them from pirates. When they encountered the strong, they traded. When they met the weak, they looted.

The earliest evidence for the wealth and power of Mycenaean kings comes from offerings found in *shaft-graves* dating from about 1600 to 1500 B.C.E. Later, the Mycenaeans constructed imposing *tholoi* to house their dead. *Tholoi* were vaulted masonry chambers (shaped like bee hives) that were mounded over with earth and used for multiple burials. The *tholos* at Mycenae is fifty feet in diameter and forty feet high. Young monarchies sometimes bolster their authority by acts of conspicuous consumption intended to overawe their subjects. *Tholoi* were probably shrines for the worship of royal ancestors. Like the Minoans (but unlike the later Greeks), the Mycenaeans did not construct temples. The fortress-palaces, which began to rise about 1400 B.C.E., were constructed of huge, irregularly shaped stone blocks that were fitted together like the pieces of a puzzle. So monumental were their remains that later Greeks concluded that these "cyclopean" structures were the work of the Cyclopes, an extinct race of giants.

Figure 3–2 The Lion-Gate at Mycenae The gate that provided entrance to the citadel at Mycenae was formed from huge blocks of stone and decorated with a tympanum depicting two lions guarding a pillar, a motif found in Middle-Eastern art.

The reception rooms of the Mycenaean fortresses were decorated with frescoes and tiled floors, and had furnishings made from exotic woods and precious metals. Like Minoan palaces, the Mycenaean royal residences housed the workshops, warehouses, and scribal offices essential to the livelihood of a merchant-prince. Mycenaean scribes developed Linear B, a writing system based on the Minoan's Linear A. Two major collections of their tablets have been found. One, as previously mentioned, is from Knossos. The other is from Pylos, a fortress on the southwestern coast of the Peloponnese (the mainland's southern peninsula). The 1,200 Linear B tablets from the archives of Pylos owe their survival to the destruction of the people who wrote them. Pylos fell to an attacker about 1200 B.C.E., and the flames that consumed the palace baked the fragile clay tablets in its scribes' offices and turned them into durable tiles.

The only things found on the Linear B tablets are inventories of supplies, but these reveal a great deal about Mycenaean life. Ration lists suggest that wheat and barley bread were the staples of the diet. Workers were also issued wine and figs. Meat is not often mentioned, but some must have been available. Many animals had to be slaughtered to produce the quantities of leather that palace artisans used to manufacture armor. Some agricultural products, particularly olive oil and honey, were cultivated for export. The 400 bronze smiths that Pylos's king employed would have turned out far more weapons than he needed, so he must have been an arms dealer. About 600 women were attached to the palace to weave linen and woolen cloth. The Pylos documents mention many specialized professions and list titles for numerous kinds of bureaucrats. The peasants who inhabited the kingdom's 200 villages may have been semifree laborers who were legally dependent on a military aristocracy. Slaves, a by-product of war, were plentiful. Most were female, for the males of defeated communities were usually slaughtered.

The Aegean Dark Age

Pylos was destroyed and abandoned about 1200 B.C.E., and within a few decades all the Mycenaean kingdoms had collapsed. Linear B, which was known only to the scribes who served the Mycenaean kings, was forgotten, and a Dark Age (an era without literacy) descended on the Aegean. Not until commerce revived in the eighth century B.C.E. did the Greeks again sense a need for writing. About 800 B.C.E. they adapted the Phoenician script for their own use.

Homer and the Fall of Mycenae   Although literacy disappeared from the Aegean with the Mycenaeans, an oral tradition preserved some memory of their existence and inspired the composition of the *Iliad* and the *Odyssey*, the first major pieces of Greek literature. Tradition attributes both these epic poems to a certain Homer, who supposedly flourished about 700 B.C.E., but it is doubtful that they were the work of one man. The *Iliad* is the story of a quarrel between two Greek kings, Agamemnon and Achilles, that took place in the tenth year of a Greek siege of Troy, a city in northwestern Asia Minor. The *Odyssey* catalogues the adventures of Odysseus, one of their companions, on his way home from the Trojan War. Both poems purport to narrate events from the Mycenaean era, but they read back into that period the conditions of the later and more primitive Dark Age.

It was once assumed that Homer's stories were entirely fictional, but in 1871 Heinrich Schliemann, a brilliant self-taught German archaeologist (who made a fortune in the California gold rush) discovered the site of Troy. His excavations uncovered evidence for several Trojan wars and for the great Greek kingdoms that could have fought them. Scholars dispute which of Troy's battles may have given rise to the tales collected in the *Iliad,* but Troy's location explains why the Greeks would have fought a Trojan war. Troy commanded the entrance to the Hellespont, the waterway by which Greeks imported grain from the Black Sea. If anything could have persuaded the Mycenaean kings to set aside their differences and wage a joint expedition against a foreign power, it was a threat to their food supply. Troy was sacked sometime after 1250 B.C.E., not long before the Mycenaean kingdoms themselves began to fall. If the destruction of Troy was the last proud achievement of the Mycenaean era, stories about it would have come, during the Dark Age, to represent the glories of an increasingly mythic past.

A spate of fortification building on the mainland of Greece suggests that around 1250 B.C.E. the Mycenaean governments sensed a need to strengthen their defenses. Historians once postulated that the Mycenaeans confronted a second wave of Indo-European migration from the north, an invasion by primitive tribes that spoke the Dorian dialect of Greek. But no archaeological evidence confirms a Dorian presence in Greece until after the Mycenaean decline. An attack from without is not the only explanation for a civilization's fall. Internal problems can also bring it down. By the thirteenth century the Mycenaeans were struggling with overpopulation, declining agricultural production, and costly, unwieldy bureaucratic administrations. Under these circumstances, the fall of one shaky kingdom could have initiated a domino effect that brought them all down. As refugees flooded from a collapsing state into the territory of its neighbor, that neighbor would be pushed over the edge and its people would join a swelling tide of refugees. Greeks seeking new homes probably triggered the invasions of the Sea Peoples who descended on the coasts of Egypt and Palestine in the late thirteenth century. At this time Greeks also occupied the Aegean islands and the coast of Asia Minor.

The Homeric Era   The Mycenaean collapse cleared the way for the Greeks to reinvent themselves, but almost five centuries passed before the outlines of their great Hellenic, or classical, civilization emerged. These transitional centuries were not devoid of achievement. Iron came into widespread use. Pottery painters began to develop a distinctive and historically informative art. Religious traditions changed. New weapons and battlefield strategies were introduced. Novel political and social institutions appeared, and colonization scattered Greek cities throughout the ancient world.

Mycenaean trade, industry, and agriculture had been centrally managed by royal agents. Once these officials passed from the scene, a much simpler economy emerged. It centered on the village and the household. This is the world that Homer (or the school of poets he represents) knew and projected onto the Mycenaean past. It was far less wealthy than its Mycenaean predecessor. Few of its settlements had as many as a thousand residents, and the decline of trade in the Aegean meant that each community had to produce almost everything it needed for itself.

Conditions were difficult during the Dark Ages but not unpromising. A reduced population lessened competition for farmland, and an economy of self-sufficiency minimized class differences based on wealth and access to imported luxuries. The collapse of centralized political authority allowed local governments to flourish. The chieftains who headed these were called kings, but they were far less powerful than Mycenaean royalty. The simple equipment they took to their graves suggests that the economic gap between them and their followers was not great. The Homeric king was a first-among-equals in a band of military companions. He fought at the side of his men and shared their way of life.

Homeric society was dominated by warrior bands that were only nominally subservient to a hierarchy of regional overlords. The leaders of these bands constituted a hereditary aristocracy, but it was a working aristocracy. A king and his nobles defended their people and enriched them by raiding their neighbors' territory. The monarch's office passed to his son, but only if his men considered the heir to be competent. A leader was accountable to a warrior code that demanded demonstrations of strength, courage, and honor. He was expected to inspire his men by his superior prowess in battle and in the hunts and athletic competitions that proved his readiness for the rigors of combat.

A Homeric king's income consisted of locally produced consumable items (olive oil, grain, and wine). It made no sense to hoard such things, for they deteriorated in storage. However, if they were invested as social capital—that is, distributed among his followers— they returned rewards in the form of increased loyalty. Noblemen were supposed to be open-handed and hospitable, and to strive to outdo one another in the giving of gifts. A chief had to be as generous with time and patience as with property. His men expected him to consult with them. They enjoyed freedom of speech in his councils, and they looked to him for eloquent oratory.

The works of Homer occupied a place in Greek society comparable to that of the Bible in the Christian communities of the medieval and early modern West. Most Greeks, regardless of their social status, identified with Homer's *aristoi* ("best men"), aristocrats. Lineage and famous ancestors were important, but good bloodlines were not enough. Individuals were expected to earn respect through their achievements. The ideal man had to be both competent and handsome—a harmony of muscle, bone, brain, and spirit that excited the envy of the gods. The greatest of men could, in myths at least, become deities themselves.

The Hellenic Era

As things settled down in the Aegean world, trade revived and population increased. The Dark Age drew to a close, and the vague outlines of a new Greek civilization appeared. Its fundamental institutions were quite different from those of the Mycenaean era.

The Archaic Period (750–500 B.C.E.)   Population did not have to increase much before pressures on the limited resources of the Aegean environment caused social problems. Division of land among heirs reduced many farms to tiny plots that could not support families. This forced their owners either to become dependents of more prosperous neighbors or to sell their land and relocate. Both options transformed Greek society by concentrating land in fewer and fewer hands and widening class divisions. This caused political unrest, and many Greeks chose to leave the Aegean for new homes elsewhere. Emigration expanded trade networks, and entrepreneurs began to venture forth looking for new markets. City-states in the homeland eased their population crunch by sponsoring colonies, but they did not exploit their colonies for their own benefit. Each colony was independent and self-governing, and many were in locations that gave them opportunities to grow larger and richer than their mother cities. (See Map 3–2.)

Between 750 and 500 B.C.E., Greeks scattered colonies around the Black Sea, across Sicily and southern Italy, and along the coasts of Asia Minor, France, Spain, and parts of North Africa. They preferred sites where they could maintain contact with the sea. Although they generally avoided places occupied by other maritime peoples, some long-established nations, such as Egypt, welcomed Greek merchants and gave them land on which to build.

People in Context: Hesiod, The Uncommon Common Man

Homer may not have been a real person, but the poet Hesiod, whose work dates from the same period as the *Iliad* and *Odyssey,* probably was. He is especially intriguing, for while Homer, like most ancient authors, concentrated on the aristocratic warrior class, Hesiod was a common man who used his uncommon gifts to describe the lives of people like himself.

Hesiod is credited with two major poems: *Theogony,* a history of the Greek gods, and *Works and Days,* a description of the annual round of labor on a Greek farm. In the latter, Hesiod speaks in the first person about what he alleges to be personal experiences. Some scholars think that this may have been a literary device, but, if so, that does not detract from the accuracy of the picture of rural life that Hesiod paints.

Works and Days takes the form of an open letter to Hesiod's brother Perses. The two men had fought over the division of their father's estate, and Hesiod claimed that Perses bribed the judges to obtain the larger share (which he then squandered by mismanagement). Hesiod's letter is a species of "wisdom literature," a version of the collections of proverbs and secular sermons that were popular throughout the ancient Middle East and that made their way into the Bible as the books of Proverbs and Ecclesiastes. *Works and Days* lectures farmers and the agents of government on their duties and singles judges out for special attention. Hesiod warns that authorities who take bribes risk divine punishment, for there is a moral order in the universe that holds rulers accountable—a natural standard of justice to which human laws must conform. This was a conviction he unknowingly shared with his contemporaries, the Hebrew prophets.

Hesiod believed that justice was simply common sense. People should pay their debts, honor their obligations, and deal fairly and generously with one another. He also insisted that there was no substitute for hard work, that idleness was a personal disgrace and an offense to the gods. The small-property-holders whom he addresses are assumed to have a few slaves or hired hands, but they sweat in their fields alongside their servants. Hesiod saw in the work of these ordinary men the kind of nobility that Homer praised in the feats of aristocratic warriors. His definition of the good man is the self-sufficient individual whose unrelenting labor keeps his barns filled. Such a man, the poet warned, chooses a wife with care. Hesiod valued women as resources, not companions. He claimed that females were by nature deceitful, lazy, wasteful, and the source of most of mankind's problems. A man had to take a wife, for he needed children to care for him in his old age. But Hesiod advised the potential bridegroom to choose his fiancee not for her sex appeal but for her ability to pull a plow.

Hesiod was, in short, the champion of the frugal householder who kept a constant eye on the bottom line. The poet accused the upper classes of living off the backs of men like himself, but he was blind to his own exploitation of slaves and hired men. He advised that they be fed only enough to enable them to do a day's work. Hesiod was the spokesman for an emerging yeoman class that was destined to play a major role in shaping Hellenic civilization.

Question: Why might Greece, at the start of the Classical era, have produced a poet with interests like Hesiod's when Egypt and the Middle East did not?

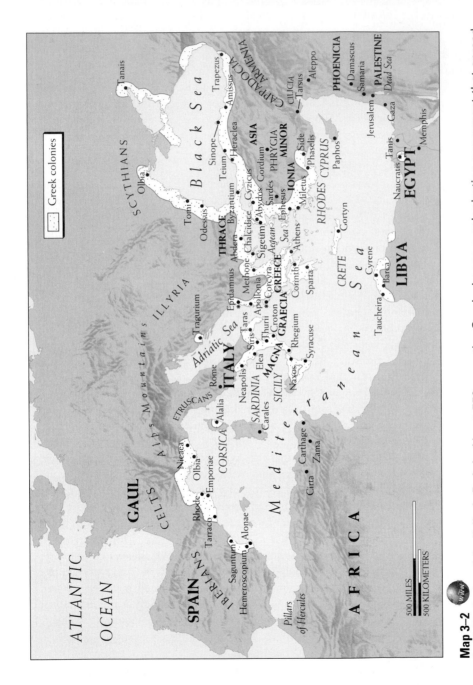

Map 3–2

Greek Territories of the Hellenic Period About 750 B.C.E. the Greeks began a colonization movement that spread them around the Black Sea and the Mediterranean. They looked for unoccupied harbors that could be developed as ports, and they prospered by trading with native peoples in the hinterlands. *Question:* Why were the Greeks able to create a coherent civilization, given that their cities were so widely scattered?

Greek colonists were exposed to alien cultural influences, but they resisted assimilation. The Greeks divided humanity into two categories: those who spoke Greek and "barbarians" whose unintelligible babble sounded like "bar-bar-bar." They saw themselves as scattered members of a single culture and jealously guarded their Greek identity. Pan-Hellenic ("all-Greek") religious shrines (e.g., Apollo's oracle at Delphi) and festivals (e.g., the Olympic Games) helped maintain ties among them and spread Hellenism (Greek culture) far beyond the Aegean. Many of classical civilization's major artists and intellectuals were citizens of the colonies, not the Greek mainland.

The Greeks who spread throughout the world during the Archaic era took with them a unique institution called the *polis* (plural: *poleis*). *Polis* is often translated as *city-state,* but that captures only part of the word's meaning. The *polis* created the environment that nurtured Hellenic civilization. *Polis* is the root of our word *politics,* but a *polis* was much more than a political entity. It was an experiment in social engineering that used art, religion, education, sport, and entertainment—as well as governmental authority—to create model citizens.

Classical civilization endorsed a philosophy called humanism. Humanism maintained that the world was a rational, humane place amenable to understanding and control. It taught that human beings were open-ended creatures who had the power and duty to invent themselves. The *polis* provided a means to this end. Most *poleis* were small states situated in sparse, competitive environments. Unlike the wealthy, populous kingdoms of the Middle East that could afford to squander manpower, *poleis* needed all their residents to contribute their best. Their small size also encouraged activism, for individuals were not lost in a mass of humanity. The impact they had on their communities was visible. This created a curious linkage in the Greek mind between individualism and community spirit.

The Hoplite Infantry   Military technology powerfully influenced the development of the *polis*. The dark-age battles that Homer describes were free-for-alls, simultaneous single combats fought by heavily armored champions who were carried about a battlefield in chariots. A horde of men from a chief's household accompanied him to war, but they did not fight in organized units. True infantry was an Assyrian invention of the eighth century. When it spread to Greece at the end of the Dark Age, it became uniquely lethal.

The Greek infantry soldier was called a hoplite—from his *hoplos,* a round, concave shield that was his most distinctive piece of equipment. A hoplite was a foot soldier who was laden with about seventy pounds of equipment (about half the body weight of an average male in the ancient world). He had a helmet and breast plate, was armed with a thrusting spear and a short sword, and carried his *hoplos* on his left arm. The *hoplos* was a shallow bowl of wood and leather about three feet in diameter. It protected its bearer's left side and sheltered his neighbor's right. Hoplites fought shoulder to shoulder in a tightly packed company called a phalanx. A phalanx was eight ranks deep, and only the men in the front lines could wield their weapons. Men in the rear ranks used their shields to push into the backs of the men in front of them. Their strategy was to pool their strength, weight, and the momentum of their charge so as to deal a crushing blow to their opponent's formation. Tactics were simple. Armies charged each other, smashed together, and the phalanx that broke exposed its scattered men to slaughter.

Hoplite battles were intended to be brief and murderous. They relied more on strength, endurance, and courage than on skill with weapons. There was no room for fancy sword play, but any man who hoped to survive had to stay in peak physical condition and learn to control himself. Sports and athletic activities were not mere entertainments for the Greeks. They provided the physical training that prepared a man for the duties of citizenship and preserved his life. The males of a *polis* were liable for military service from their teenage years until the age of sixty, and they could expect to be called into the field at frequent intervals. Because the strength of a *polis* literally depended on the physical condition of its men, the *polis* provided public facilities for training, made physical education part of their upbringing, and inspired them with art that celebrated the perfectly developed male body. The uniquely Greek custom of exercising in the nude spread after Homer's day and accompanied the rise of the *polis*. The Greeks themselves were not certain why this practice began, but it was consistent with the pressure the *polis* put on its men to demonstrate their readiness for combat.

Hoplite Culture   As the Greeks came to rely on their new infantries, the balance of power shifted in their communities. Infantry armies depend on numbers for their strength, and the small circle of aristocratic families that had traditionally monopolized military power and political leadership could not provide all the manpower that they required. A *polis* needed every

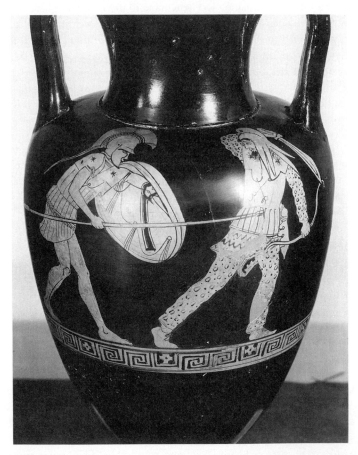

Figure 3–3 Warrior in Hoplite Armor This red-figure vase painting (c. 480–470 B.C.) of a duel between a greek warrior and a Persian soldier.

man who was competent to serve. Competence was determined by health, strength, and money. Simple governments were not equipped to collect taxes with which to finance armies. They expected their subjects to pay for their own arms and training. Only the rich could afford horses and chariots, but these were no longer all that important. Hoplite equipment was within the reach of men of moderate means, and they had good reason to invest in it. If their *polis* relied on them for its defense, it could not deny them some political recognition.

Service in the hoplite infantry enfranchised the male residents of a *polis*. Furthermore, because hoplite warfare put all soldiers on roughly the same footing, it promoted social egalitarianism. It turned the *polis* into a kind of military fraternity, a brotherhood of men who shared the bond of a common battlefield experience. The link the *polis* established between citizenship and soldiering also fueled intense patriotism and, like modern sports competitions, heightened rivalry among city-states. Greek *poleis* found it hard to coexist peacefully, and they often had more to fear from one another than from foreign invaders.

The militarized environment of the *polis* put women at a major disadvantage. The aristocratic women in Homer's epics are respected, influential people. There were some constraints on their activities, but they enjoyed freedoms that most *poleis* denied to women from their citizen families. Because women lacked the upper-body strength that would have enabled them to serve as hoplites (and earn citizenship), men regarded them as inferior creatures. They were declared unfit for public life and confined to their homes. A citizen woman had the same legal status as her children, but unlike her sons, she was a life-long dependent.

The legitimacy of children was extremely important, for citizenship in a *polis* was hereditary. They only way fathers could be sure that their offspring were their own was to limit the contact their wives had with other men. A woman's primary duty was to marry and produce the heirs that would perpetuate her husband's *oikos* (household). This was crucial, for a *polis*'s strength depended on preserving the *oikoi* that provided its fighting men. Poor women had no choice but to go about in public and work to earn money to support their families, but their better-off sisters were confined to special quarters in their homes and expected to be as invisible as possible. A woman could visit family members, go to the neighborhood well to draw water, and attend some religious festivals, but she did not take part in social gatherings with her husband and his friends. Indeed, her husband may not have thought of her as a companion. Men often delayed marriage until they were about thirty years old and financially established. Their brides were usually girls just past puberty who were half their ages.

Men were seldom at home and invested little in making their homes impressive or comfortable. They spent their time out of doors or in the public facilities that were a *polis*'s chief source of civic pride. A man had no opportunity to make female friends outside his family circle. When he desired female company, he turned to *hetairae*, professional entertainers who ranged from simple prostitutes to highly educated women who could engage a man in witty repartee and serious discussion. These women were usually slaves or foreigners.

The Rise of the Mainland Powers

There were hundreds of *poleis* scattered throughout the Mediterranean and along the shores of the Black Sea. It is difficult to generalize about them, but we can gain insight into how *poleis* operated by examining the two quite different city-states that dominated political life on the Greek mainland.

Culture in Context: The Olympic Games and Greek Unity

Greeks were scattered about the ancient world, but pride in language and culture gave them a kind of unity that transcended their territorial divisions. Allegiance to religious shrines, such as the god Apollo's oracle at Delphi, helped maintain their identity, as did a series of phenomenally popular pan-Hellenic religious festivals featuring athletic competitions. The Greek association of sport with worship was ancient. The *Iliad* ends with a description of the athletic contests that were part of the funeral rites for a Greek hero. These may have been tamed versions of bloody combats that were once staged as human sacrifices at the burials of important chiefs.

The most famous of the Greek games were the quadrennial celebrations held in honor of Zeus and his consort, Hera, at Olympia in southern Greece. No one knows when they began. The official list of Olympic victors reaches back to 776 B.C.E., but its accuracy is questionable. The reputation of the Olympic games was firmly established throughout the Greek world by the end of the seventh century B.C.E., and they proved so popular that similar competitions began to be held elsewhere to fill the years between Olympic contests. (The major meets were the Pythian games at Delphi, the Nemean at Argos, and the Isthmian at Corinth.) The Olympics flourished until 393 C.E., when a Christian emperor ended them because of their pagan associations.

The ancient Olympics had no team sports. All contests were designed to allow a single competitor to prove his superiority. Originally, there was only one Olympic event: a race of about 200 meters. (The marathon is a modern invention introduced when the Olympic Games were revived in 1896.) As more events were added, what had been a one-day festival extended to nearly a week. Many contests reflected combat training: races in armor, boxing and wrestling, javelin and discus tosses, and the extremely popular (and costly) chariot races. Events were scheduled for boys as well as men, but only Greeks could compete. Truces were proclaimed so that men from every part of the Greek world could safely gather at Olympia, but with the exception of a few priestesses, women were forbidden to watch, let alone participate.

The Olympics were the major world stage on which men could demonstrate their commitment to the Greek ideal: the realization of ultimate human potential. A victory in the Olympic games was the highest honor a Greek could earn. The official prizes were mere symbols (sprigs or wreathes of olive branches), but Greek cities lavishly rewarded native sons who brought these trophies home. Statues were raised to them. Famous poets, such as Pindar of Thebes (522–433 B.C.E.), commemorated their achievements, and some cities allegedly tore holes in their walls to provide their Olympian with a path into town that no lesser feet had trod.

Question: What was there about the Greek environment that caused the Greeks to put so much emphasis on sport and competition?

Sparta The Spartans possessed the most intimidating army in Greece. They created it by doing what the citizens of a *polis* were supposed to do. They decided what they wanted to be and then ruthlessly implemented a program of social engineering to achieve their goal.

The Spartans' ancestors were Dorian-speaking tribes that wandered into the Peloponnese during the Dark Age and settled along the Eurotas River. They expanded their territory by making war on their neighbors, and late in the eighth century they overran the plain of Messenia (the old Mycenaean kingdom of Pylos). This drastically changed the context for Spartan life. The war made Sparta the largest state on the mainland, but it left the Spartans outnumbered seven to one by people whom they had enslaved. The Spartans concluded that they would not survive unless they created a standing army that was so powerful it could frighten the *polis's* resentful *helot* (slave) population into submission. That meant that every male Spartan had to commit to becoming a superb, full-time soldier.

Legends claim that a sage named Lycurgos devised the system that kept Sparta in a state of permanent, total military mobilization. Sparta had to ensure that each of its citizens automatically accepted the lifetime of harsh discipline and regimentation that turned him into a professional soldier. It did so by making sure that it never entered his mind to be anything else. His training began at birth. State officials examined each newborn, and only those infants that were strong were allowed to live. Because all males were destined to serve the state as full-time soldiers, the state had to support them. Each boy was assigned a *kleros,* a farm worked by slaves, to maintain him, and the state did not invest in raising boys who could not fight.

At the age of six or seven, a boy left home and reported to a military camp. The army played a larger part in rearing him than did his family. He was taught basic literacy and subjected to trials that made him strong, courageous, and indifferent to hardship. At the age of twenty he saw front-line service. If he acquitted himself well in battle until the age of thirty, he was granted full citizenship. Those who failed to measure up were publically humiliated and shunned.

For most of his life, a Spartan lived in barracks as a member of a fifteen-man mess unit called a *susition.* A man's mess mates were closer to him than were his family numbers. He was expected to marry and sire children, but he could not set up a household and live openly with his wife until he received his full citizen privileges. This created unique opportunities for Spartan women. Because their husbands were rarely at home and men's time was taken up with military duties, women had both freedom and responsibility. Sparta could not afford, like other *poleis,* to confine women to their homes, and the interests of the state dictated that they be given much better treatment than most Greek women received. To ensure that they grew up to give birth to healthy children, Spartan girls were fed well, given physical training, and not married until they were fully mature at age eighteen.

The Spartan system produced the best army in Greece for the simple reason that the Spartans were the only Greeks who could devote all their time to training and physical conditioning. Most *poleis* were defended by part-time citizen militias, but the Spartans had a professional army. Sparta's primary weakness was the difficulty it had in maintaining its population. Birthrates were low, and the harsh conditions of Spartan life increased mortality.

The Spartans paid a high price for their system, but it gave them a tremendous sense of national pride. They did not marry foreigners and kept a careful eye on visitors to make sure that they did not spread alien ideas that caused citizens to question the Spartan way of life. The *polis's* economy ensured social stability by preventing the development of a gap between rich and poor. Some trade was necessary, but a primitive medium of exchange using iron bars kept it to a minimum. Each Spartan had his *kleros* to guarantee him a living wage. Private property existed, but the flaunting of wealth was discouraged. The Spartans boasted of their coarse food, rough attire, and indifference to comfort and luxury. Their educations taught them obedience to authority and tradition, and discouraged inquiry and speculation.

The Spartan *polis* had what the Greeks called a mixed constitution: that is, a government that combined aspects of different political systems. The monarchical element was represented by two royal families from whose princes the Spartans chose their kings. Spartan kings had little civil authority. Their chief function was to serve as commanders in the field. Sparta was a kind of all-inclusive aristocracy. Its chief organ of government was a council called the Gerousia. It was composed of twenty-eight men over the age of sixty who held office for life. The Gerousia set policies that were implemented by five executives called ephors. The democratic element in the system was represented by a popular assembly to which all full citizens belonged. It elected the members of the Gerousia and the ephors, but had very limited powers. It met primarily to be advised of government decisions. It could ratify or reject proposals put to it, but it could not debate or suggest alternatives. Sparta also had a *krypteia,* a secret police corps that terrorized the helots and eliminated potential troublemakers.

Sparta had reason to be proud of its achievements. It was more stable than most *poleis,* and the other Greeks were in awe of its military might. But Spartan success came at a cost. By refusing to evolve and by turning their backs on the outside world, the Spartans lived through one of the most creative periods in Western history without being touched by it. In an era of unprecedented artistic and intellectual activity, the Spartans produced no great thinkers, authors, or artists. They focused exclusively on military matters and prided themselves on ignoring most of the things for which Greek civilization became famous. Worse, their decision to halt development, ignore change, and pin their survival on a single strength ultimately proved fatal.

Athens   The *polis* that is most associated with the achievements of Hellenic civilization is Athens, an Ionian-speaking community on the plain of Attica in northern Greece. By the end of the Dark Age, its Mycenaean monarchy ("one-man rule") had been replaced by an aristocracy ("rule by the best," by those of elite lineage). Its chief organ of government was the Council of the Areopagus, a committee of leaders from aristocratic families. Its mandates were enforced by three officials called *archons,* and it occasionally convened a popular assembly to publicize its edicts. At this stage in its development Athens resembled Sparta, but the two *poleis* steadily diverged. Sparta halted its economic and social evolution at this point by absorbing all its men into a single class and training them for the same profession. Athens allowed an unregulated economy to create divisions and tensions within its society, and these propelled further political development.

Athens' citizens were not supported by the state. They had to earn their own livings. As trade began to revive in the eighth century, new sources of wealth enabled some commoners to prosper, and they forced the landed aristocracy to share its power with them. This delivered Athens into the hands of an oligarchy ("rule by the few"), a government dominated by the rich and the well born. Athenians who did not have large estates or commercial interests were at a serious disadvantage economically and politically. Each year, they had to raise enough grain on their small farms to feed their families and, if they hoped to accumulate any savings to fall back on, some surplus for sale. In years when harvests were poor, they could not make ends meet. They had to borrow from the rich and pledge to pay back their loans out of next year's crop. In effect, they mortgaged a portion of their labor for the following year and bound themselves to work their land for someone else's benefit. Over the long haul, the poor tended to dig themselves so deeply into debt that they were enslaved. Societies that allow wide gaps to develop between the few rich and the many poor flirt with disaster. The poor resent their condition, and when a leader appears to mobilize them, they have the strength of numbers to foment revolution. Revolutions are often begun by a member of the privileged class who rallies the people and uses them to drive his competitors from the city. This leads to a form of government the Greeks called tyranny ("rule by an individual who seizes power").

During the seventh century, many *poleis* passed into the hands of tyrants. The leading families in a *polis* were highly competitive and inclined to feud. When their fights threatened to destabilize a community, the lower classes often rallied behind a *tyrannos* ("a ruler who takes control by force") in an effort to restore order. Some tyrants abused their authority and oppressed their subjects. But if a tyrant was wise, he remembered the source of his power and courted the people by doing things that improved their lives. He funded buildings, festivals, and programs that provided jobs, promoted civic pride, and enhanced the reputation of his *polis*. In the process, he might encourage the growth of popular government. That, at least, was the Athenian experience.

In 632 B.C.E. Athens' aristocrats thwarted an attempted coup by a popular Olympic victor named Cylon. He raised a private army and seized the Acropolis, the citadel at the heart of Athens. He hoped that the Athenian masses would join him, but they were not ready. The aristocrats put Cylon down, but the crisis alerted them to the danger they faced.

In 620 B.C.E. the Council of the Areopagus asked an elderly aristocrat named Draco to improve the enforcement of justice in Athens. Athens was governed by vague oral traditions that were subject to manipulation by powerful individuals, and rather than looking to the state for help, men often waged vendettas to punish those who wronged them. These private wars could easily get out of hand, and Draco sought to create a credible alternative to them. His plan was to publish a code of law and make neutral state officials responsible for enforcing a standard of justice that applied equally to everyone. Our word *draconian* ("extreme severity") derives from the harsh punishments that Draco decreed for even minor offenses. He may have hoped that fear would inspire respect for the novel idea of rule by law.

Legal reforms were a good thing, but they did not address the economy—the chief source of discontent in Athens. In 594 B.C.E. Athens' politicians took the remarkable step of granting a man named Solon absolute authority to reorganize the *polis*. Solon began by abolishing the debts of the farmers who had become enslaved agricultural laborers. This got both the rich and the poor out of what had become a mutually unprofitable situation. By cancelling their debts, Solon freed poor peasants to sell the small farms that could not sustain them, and he provided them with alternative forms of employment. He promoted trade, made loans to small businesses, and invited foreign craftsmen with valuable skills to settle in Athens. The rich were compensated by the opportunity this gave them to increase their estates and turn the land to more profitable uses. Poor farmers grew grain. They needed it to feed themselves, and it was the only crop that brought them a rapid return on the little capital they had to invest. Grain did not grow all that well in Attica, but olives and grapes did. It made more sense to import grain and devote Athenian land to the production of olive oil and wine for export. These were, however, capital-intensive crops. Only the rich could afford the decades that it took to bring an olive grove or a vineyard into production. Solon's reforms cleared the way for wealthy investors to convert Attica from minimally profitable grain production to valuable export crops and for Athens to become a thriving manufacturing center.

Solon also implemented political reform. He reserved archonships, the *polis's* most prestigious offices, to candidates from the wealthiest strata of society. Men who could afford hoplite armor qualified for lesser offices, and the poor (who had no equipment but who rowed the city's warships) were allowed to vote in the popular assembly and serve on juries. To help the assembly assert its authority, Solon created the *boule,* a council of 400 representatives chosen from the four tribes into which the Athenian electorate was divided. It prepared the agenda for meetings of the assembly.

Solon's reforms were well conceived, but they did not improve people's lives quickly enough to head off support for tyranny. In 560 B.C.E. a well-known military hero named Peisistratus won control of Athens. He cultivated the masses who had lofted him to power by providing loans for the poor, promoting trade, commissioning public works, and sponsoring festivals. He commissioned a definitive edition of Homer's works for the city's archives, and his support for rites honoring the popular rural god Dionysus marked the dawn of one of the glories of Athenian civilization: the theater. (See Chapter 5, "The Hellenistic Era and The Rise of Rome.")

When Peisistratus died in 527 B.C.E., his sons Hippias and Hipparchus succeeded him. In 514 B.C.E. two men who had a personal grudge against Hipparchus tried to assassinate him and his brother. Hippias escaped, but fear turned him into a ruthless, suspicious dictator. In 510 B.C.E. the Alcmaeonids, an aristocratic family that Peisistratus had driven into exile, enlisted Spartan aid and forced Hippias to flee Athens. The Alcmaeonids' leader, Cleisthenes, became the city's next tyrant.

Cleisthenes set out to destroy the political machines on which the power of his aristocratic opponents was based by reforming Athens' electoral system. Each Athenian citizen inherited membership in a tribe through which he exercised his rights. These tribes were under the thumbs of the great families that had long dominated Athenian politics. Cleisthenes minimized their influence by limiting the four original tribes to religious functions and transferring their political duties to ten new and differently constituted tribes. Attica was divided into demes (counties or townships), and each of the new tribes was made up of demes from every region of the country. This meant that great landlords, who had always voted in tribes filled with their local dependents and retainers, now had to vote with strangers over whom they had no power. Cleisthenes may have gerrymandered the system for the benefit of his family, but it had the long-term effect of freeing up individuals to vote as they pleased. Aristocratic advantage was further diminished by the practice of filling many offices by casting lots. Each tribe chose fifty of its members by lot to serve on a new 500-member *boule* that led the assembly and oversaw state finances.

The assembly governed Athens, but it met only occasionally. When it or the *boule* was not in session, the aristocratic Council of the Areopagus was likely to assume power by default. Cleisthenes forestalled this by creating the *prytaneis* ("presider"). He divided the year into ten equal segments, each of which was assigned to one of the tribal committees that composed the *boule.* For the tenth of the year entrusted to it, each fifty-man committee met daily as the *prytaneis,* the body that "presided" over Athens. Each day during their term, the members of the *prytaneis* cast lots to determine which of them would serve as Athens' chief executive that day.

The army was also reorganized to reflect the principles by which the state was to be governed. Each tribe provided a company for the army, and the soldiers elected their own leader, their *strategos* ("general"). Because soldiers much prefer to follow officers who have earned their trust, generals, unlike civilian leaders, could serve consecutive terms. The board of ten *strategoi* was able, therefore, to provide some continuity for Athens' government.

Finally, according to tradition, Cleisthenes instituted a special vote called an ostracism to to prevent anyone from overthrowing the system he had established. From time to time the Athenian electorate was asked to take an *ostraca* (a fragment of pottery used as a ballot) and scratch on it the name of any man suspected of posing a danger to the city. No trial was held, but if an individual garnered 6,000 votes, he was immediately exiled for ten years.

Cleisthenes's reforms launched Athens on an experiment with a radical version of an untested form of government that the Greeks called "democracy" ("rule by the *demos*," the people). All laws and major policy decisions were made by the people themselves, not by a small group of their representatives. The use of lots to select men for office meant that any individual, regardless of his talents and experience, had a chance of finding himself charged, if only briefly, with major responsibilities. Small villages could operate informally on similar principles, but Athens was no village. History was to prove if the trust the Athenians placed in the masses was justified.

The Persian Wars: Catalyst of a Civilization

The larger world did not stand still while Greek civilization reorganized itself in the Aegean. In the wake of Mycenae's collapse and the invasions of the Sea Peoples, successive empires rose and fell in the Middle East. The Assyrians built on the ruins of the Hittite and Egyptian empires. In 614 B.C.E. the Assyrians fell to the Chaldaeans, and in 539 B.C.E. Chaldaean Babylon surrendered to Cyrus the Great (r. 559–530 B.C.E.), who founded a gigantic Persian Empire that ultimately stretched from Egypt to the borders of India and the Himalaya Mountains.

Ionia and Marathon   In 547 B.C.E. Cyrus conquered the wealthy kingdom of Lydia in central Asia Minor and pushed on to the Aegean to subdue Ionia, a coastal district occupied by Greek cities. More important campaigns elsewhere and palace coups subsequently distracted him and his immediate successors from further adventures in the Aegean. In 499 B.C.E. the Ionian city of Miletus organized a rebellion that prompted the Persian emperor, Darius I (r. 522–486 B.C.E.), to return to the Greek world. Miletus asked the *poleis* of the mainland for assistance. Sparta refused, but Athens sent help. Athens was dependent on imported grain, and it feared that Persian control of the Hellespont might endanger its access to supplies from the Black Sea. The Athenians also worried that Darius might restore their exiled tyrant Hippias, who had fled to his court. The Greek rebels had some initial successes, but after they drove the Persians from the former Lydian capital at Sardis, their alliance fell apart. Darius then counterattacked, recovered Ionia, and inflicted a horrible punishment on Miletus as a warning to the Greeks.

In 492 B.C.E. Darius decided to make sure that a hope of support from the mainland never again tempted the Ionian cities to rebel. He demanded that the Aegean submit to Persia. Many of the Greek *poleis,* mindful of Miletus's fate, yielded, but Athens and Sparta refused. In 490 B.C.E. Darius's fleet landed an army of 20,000 men on the plain of Marathon about twenty miles north of Athens. Some Athenians wanted to surrender, but the *strategos* Miltiades persuaded the assembly to fight. A champion runner was dispatched to Sparta to ask for help, but the Spartans claimed that a religious festival prevented them from offering immediate assistance. The tiny *polis* of Athens (led by its new, untested democratic government) was left almost entirely alone to confront the superpower of its day. (See Map 3–3.)

Miltiades's army may have been half the size of the Persian force, but the battle on the plain of Marathon gave his hoplites a chance to prove that Greek training and discipline could compensate for inferior numbers. Greek sources claim that 6,400 Persians, but only 192 Greeks, died at Marathon. Whatever the statistics, the losses persuaded the Persians to withdraw. The delighted, but stunned, Athenians credited their victory to the patriotic morale generated by democracy, and like the Spartans, their confidence in the program of their *polis* soared.

Thermopylae and Salamis   The loss at Marathon angered the Persians far more than it hurt them, but a rebellion in Egypt and other problems prevented Darius from continuing the war. It fell to his son and heir, Xerxes (r. 486–465 B.C.E.), to plan the Persian response. In 484 B.C.E. Xerxes began to make highly visible plans for a massive assault on the Aegean. This had the intended effect of persuading a number of *poleis* to submit voluntarily, but thirty-one states pledged to cooperate in defending the mainland. Prospects for their success were not good. The Persian army was huge—perhaps a quarter of a million men. Even the sacred oracles to whom the Greeks turned for advice were intimidated and did not offer much encouragement.

The Greeks wisely chose to take their stand at Thermopylae, a narrow strip of beach in northern Greece that had mountains on one side and the sea on the other. The Persians had to pass through Thermopylae to reach their targets in Greece, but its confines prevented their great army from spreading out and using the advantage of its numbers. If the Greeks' navy prevented Persia's ships from landing soldiers behind the Greek lines, the allies could halt Persia's advance, and this alone might have forced Xerxes to retreat. Sanitation problems spread disease in large armies unless they stayed on the move.

The Greek allies mustered a mere 7,000 men to face the Persians at Thermopylae, but with the help of their commander, the Spartan king Leonidas, they repelled Xerxes' assaults for three days. The battle was lost when a Greek traitor guided a troop of Persians through the mountains to a position behind Leonidas's lines. Realizing that his position was untenable, Leonidas dismissed most of his men. He, his 300 Spartans, and a handful of allies chose, however, to stay and fight to the death. Their willing self-sacrifice turned Thermopylae into a moral victory and made them the most celebrated heroes in Greek history.

The Greek army fell back to the Isthmus of Corinth, the land-bridge between northern and southern Greece. The plan was again to halt the Persian advance by blocking a narrow passage. This had failed at Thermopylae, but the Spartan generals who commanded the army saw no alternative. Athens, which lay north of the Isthmus, was abandoned to the enemy. Its women and children were ferried to various islands, and its men took to their ships and watched as the Persians burned their city.

In 482 B.C.E. the Athenian electorate had made a remarkably intelligent decision that now saved their homeland. A rich vein of silver was discovered in the state mines, and the assembly had to decide what to do with the profits. Some politicians courted popularity by proposing that the money be shared among the citizens, but Themistocles, the first non-aristocrat to rise to prominence in the young democracy, persuaded the voters to prefer their public to their private interest. He convinced them to use the money to expand their navy and make Athens a major sea power. The Spartans wanted the Athenians to use their navy to prevent the Persians from outflanking the Greek defenses on the Isthmus of Corinth, but Themistocles saw no advantage to Athens in sending its ships to protect the Peloponnese, Spartan territory. Because prospects for success on land were dismal, he decided to risk everything in a battle at sea. Themistocles lured the Persian navy into the straits between Attica and

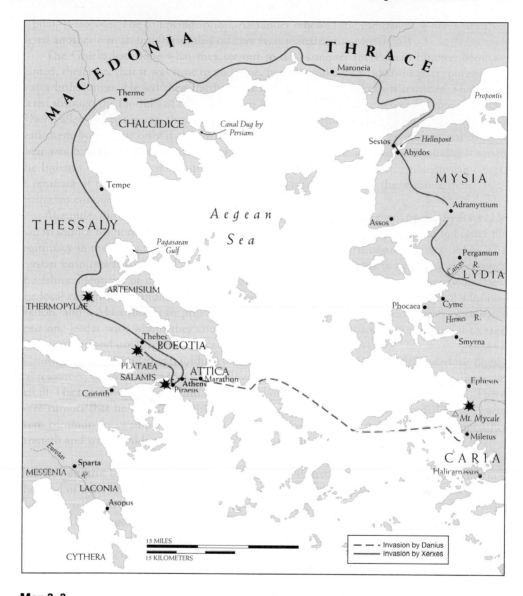

Map 3–3
The Persian Wars   The first of the Persian Wars was an attack from the sea on the plain of Marathon. The second involved a Persian army that was too large to be ferried across the Aegean. This map shows the routes taken by Xerxes' soldiers and the navy that accompanied them. (Stars mark the sites of major battles.) *Question*: Did the Aegean Sea provide protection for the Greek mainland?

Chronology: The Rise of Hellenic Civilization

Thirteenth century:

  1250 B.C.E., sack of Troy

  1200 B.C.E., fall of Mycenaean Civilization

  Dark Age

Eighth century:

  776 B.C.E., first Olympic victor

  750–700 B.C.E., Homer

  750 B.C.E., Greek colonization begins

  700 B.C.E., Hesiod

  hoplite warfare develops

  poleis appear

Seventh century:

  Spartan system established

  Athenian system evolves:

   632 B.C.E., Cylon's coup

   620 B.C.E., Draco's law   614 B.C.E., Assyrian Empire falls

Sixth century:

  594 B.C.E., Solon's constitution

  560–527 B.C.E., Peistratus tryanny 539 B.C.E., Chaldaean Empire falls

  510 B.C.E., Cleisthenes exiles Hippias Cyrus and the Persian Empire

   democracy established

Fifth century:

  499 B.C.E., Miletus rebels

  492 B.C.E., Persian Wars: Darius

  484–479 B.C.E., Persian Wars: Xerxes

the island of Salamis, and his smaller, faster ships, which were operating in familiar waters, outmaneuvered and sank many of the Persian transports. Xerxes could not afford to lose the navy that was his communications link with his empire. He chose to go home but to leave behind an army, under a general named Mardonius, to continue the fight.

Mardonius went into winter camp at Plataea, west of Attica, and prepared to resume the campaign the following spring. The Greeks used the time to amass the largest army they had ever assembled, and in the spring of 479 B.C.E. they took the offensive. Pausanias, the Spartan regent for the heroic Leonidas's infant heir, commanded the allied army. When he drove through the Persian line and killed Mardonius, the leaderless Persians scattered. The Greeks were again amazed to discover that they had succeeded against all odds. The conclusion seemed obvious: Their institutions were superior to all others. There was no limit to what they could do.

Larger Issue Revisited

The Greeks' victories over the Persians persuaded them that there was a wide gap between their civilization and that of their opponents. The Greek historian Herodotus (c. 484–425 B.C.E.), who wrote the first history of the Persian wars, claimed that the Greeks won because they were free men fighting for their homeland, while the Persians were the dispirited subjects of an autocrat. The war had been a contest between Western liberty and Eastern slavery, and the West had proved its superiority.

There were obvious contrasts between Persia's empire and Greece's city-states, but there were also ties between the Greek "West" and the Persian "East." The Mycenaean kingdoms had closely resembled and borrowed much from their Middle-Eastern neighbors. Many of the Greeks who fled their collapse settled in the Middle East, strengthened trade ties between the Aegean and the Middle East, and adapted Middle-Eastern technologies (such as writing and infantry warfare) as they emerged from their Dark Age. Trade with Egypt and the Middle East was extremely important to both the Mycenaean and the Hellenic civilizations, and Greek artists and intellectuals drew inspiration from, and had great respect for, the Middle East's older civilizations. There is no doubt that the Greeks were original and that they changed the course of civilization in the ancient world, but the assumption that they created a "West" that was independent of—and opposed to—an "East" deserves careful consideration.

Review Questions:

1. What were the similarities and differences between the Minoan and Mycenaean kingdoms and those of Egypt and the Middle East?
2. Might people who live in a Dark Age be more open to cultural innovation than those who inhabit a fully civilized period? Why?
3. How did the Hellenic *poleis* differ from the Mycenaean kingdoms?
4. What explains the differences between the *polis* systems of Athens and Sparta?
5. What impact did the military have on the development of Hellenic civilization?
6. Did the Persian Wars prove that Greece's civilization was superior to Persia's?

Refer to the front of the book for a list of chapter-relevant primary sources available on the CD-ROM.

THE WEST INTERACTIVE

For web-based activities, map explorations, and quizzes related to this chapter, go to *www.prenhall.com/frankforter.*

CHAPTER 4

THE HELLENIC ERA

Great are the works and monuments of the empire that we have created. Future generations will be in awe of us just as our contemporaries are.

—**Pericles**

Larger Issue: *What did the Greeks contribute to the development of modern civilization?*

In the winter of the year 431 B.C.E., an Athenian politician named Pericles delivered a speech in which he made the following points:

1. We Athenians owe our ancestors thanks for creating a free country and handing it down to us;
2. Our greatness lies in our unique form of government, a democracy in which everyone is equal before the law;
3. We respect people for their abilities, not their social class;
4. We do not look down on the poor, but only on those who do not try to better themselves;
5. We do not interfere in one another's personal affairs, but are tolerant and easy going;
6. We do not let our private interests keep us from our public duties;
7. We obey our elected officials, our laws, and the higher, unwritten standards that govern morality and human rights;
8. We have an abundance of good things and heartily enjoy our pleasures;
9. Our civilized lifestyle does not make us soft;
10. We are open to the world, for we entrust our defense to the loyalty and courage of our people and not to secret plots;
11. We make friends abroad by selfless acts of generosity; and
12. Each of us is free and independent.

This ancient speech could be delivered today in the United States Senate. Indeed, Pericles would find much that seems familiar were he to visit one of the modern Western capitals. Most are filled with buildings, monuments, and sculpture in a style he would recognize. He would not be surprised by the scientific orientation of the modern world, for he witnessed the rise of theoretical science. References to history would not confuse him, for the study of history was pioneered by men he knew personally. He might even attend a performance of a drama that he had previously seen in Athens.

Pericles' speech celebrated the virtues of what has come to be known as "classical" civilization. The adjective implies that his Hellenic (Greek) civilization set the standards for the West. Hellenic societies were, however, far from perfect. They were plagued by wars, internal conflicts, and injustices (particularly in their treatment of women and slaves). Despite their stated commitment to reason, moderation, and self-control, they were capable of senseless, self-destructive acts. Their moment of glory was brief, and the West may owe some of its weaknesses as well as its strengths to them.

TOPICS IN THIS CHAPTER

The Catalyst of the Persian Wars • The Peloponnesian War •
Intellectual and Artistic Life in the *Polis*

The Catalyst of the Persian Wars

The defeats the Persians suffered at Salamis and Plataea hardly crippled Xerxes' empire, and the Greeks assumed that Persia had by no means given up hope of conquering the Aegean. The most pressing business of the mid-fifth century, therefore, was to evict the remaining Persians from Greek territory and to organize a defense that would prevent their return.

Sparta's Retreat   The Greek *poleis* had worked together to repel Xerxes' invasion, and they could defend the Aegean only if they continued to cooperate. No one knew, however, how to structure a permanent alliance. The Spartans had the greatest land army, and the Athenians were the strongest naval power. The military resources of both cities were needed, but neither *polis* trusted the other.

The immediate advantage was with the Spartans, who had routed the last of Xerxes' forces at Plataea. The Athenians were temporarily homeless, for the Persians had burned Athens and leveled its walls. Sparta argued that Athens should not rebuild its defenses lest the Persians reoccupy the city and use it against the Greeks. They pointed out that Sparta's villages were unfortified, for Spartan men were all the "walls" they needed. Themistocles saw things differently. He dragged out discussions with the Spartans while the Athenians hastily rebuilt their ramparts.

Pausanias, the Spartan general who had triumphed at Plataea, commanded the allied forces as they pursued the retreating Persians. But power apparently went to his head. The allies accused him of behaving like a Persian despot, and Sparta recalled him and convicted him of treason. When he fled to a temple to avoid execution, the Spartan authorities—acting on a suggestion from his mother—bricked up the building's doors and windows and left him to starve.

The Spartans needed their men at home to guard against slave rebellions. As the Persian threat retreated, the Spartans returned to their accustomed isolation and left foreign affairs to Athens. Thanks to Solon's reforms, Athens had become a populous *polis* that was dependent on trade, and as a naval power, it was better equipped than Sparta to sweep the Persians from their outposts in the Aegean. Themistocles might have been the logical choice to be Pausanias's successor, but for some reason the Athenian electorate ostracized him in 471 B.C.E., and he fled to Persia—where he was appointed a provincial governor!

Athens' Advance   In 477 B.C.E. the *poleis* that believed that a permanent defense had to be organized to protect the Aegean from Persia sent delegates to a conference on the island of Delos. The result was the formation of the Delian League, an alliance that at its height numbered about 150 members. Athens dominated the league, but the league's treasury was headquartered on Delos, on neutral territory sacred to all the Ionian Greeks.

Cimon, son of the Miltiades who had won the battle of Marathon, assumed leadership of the league's navy and did such a good job of pushing the Persians back that by 468 B.C.E. some members of the Delian League concluded that the organization had served its purpose. Cimon, however, used force to prevent them from withdrawing. The league had become too important to Athens to be allowed to disband. Cimon had urged the allies to supply him with money rather than men and ships, and their contributions had built what was fundamentally an Athenian navy. The Delian League became an Athenian Empire, and in 454 B.C.E. its treasury was transferred to Athens. League money was used to fund the construction of Athens' famous temples.

Cimon fell from power in 462 B.C.E. He was an aristocrat, and Athens' aristocrats tended to be pro-Spartan. (They equated Spartan discipline with the Homeric virtues of their presumed ancestors.) When Sparta asked Athens for help in putting down a slave revolt, Cimon persuaded the reluctant assembly to allow him to lead four thousand Athenians into the Peloponnese. They no sooner arrived than the Spartans changed their minds and ordered them to leave. The offended electorate promptly ostracized Cimon and embraced radical democratization.

The hoplites, a relatively prosperous class, had been the original driving force behind the Athenian democracy. But the increasing prominence of the navy shifted power to the poorer element in the Athenian population, the men who rowed the state galleys. Athens' new generation of politicians, the most successful of whom was Pericles (c. 490–429 B.C.E.), cultivated this larger electorate. From 461 B.C.E. until his death, Pericles held the office of *strategos* and used his position to prod, manipulate, and lead his city first to the pinnacle of power and then to defeat.

The Peloponnesian War

Hellenic civilization was the product of a society that was almost constantly at war—more often with itself than with a foreign enemy. The Greeks' victory in the Persian Wars increased the threat of internal conflict by polarizing the Aegean world. Athens developed a maritime empire, and Sparta responded by expanding its league of Peloponnesian cities. This division of the Greeks into opposing armed camps set them up for civil war. (See Map 4–1.)

Precursor to Civil War   Great wars often begin with small quarrels. The first round in what was initially an undeclared war went to Athens. Corinth, the *polis* that occupied the narrow isthmus that connects northern and southern Greece, was Athens' major commercial competitor and Sparta's chief ally. Athens dominated the Aegean, but Corinth had access both to the Aegean and, through the Gulf of Corinth, to the Greek colonies in the western Mediterranean. About 460 B.C.E., Corinth's northern neighbor, the small *polis* of Megara, made a deal with Athens that allowed the Athenians to use Pegae, Megara's small port on the Gulf of Corinth. Corinth viewed this as a threat to its western trade.

Corinth invaded Attica in 459 B.C.E. The attack failed, but it prodded the Athenians into making an important addition to their city's fortifications. Athens had sprung up around the

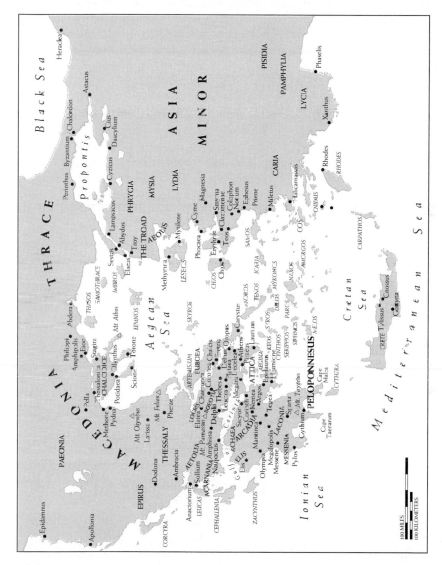

Map 4–1

The Hellenic Aegean The numerous poleis that sprang up in the Aegean during the Hellenic era (c. 500–338 B.C.E.) were so protective of their autonomy that the military alliances and leagues they occasionally formed tended to be unstable. *Question:* Did geography encourage or discourage the unification of the Aegean region?

Acropolis ("upper-town"), an outcropping of rock that served Attica as a natural citadel. The Acropolis was some four miles inland from the sea, and Athens' commerce passed through a small coastal port called the Piraeus. The obvious strategy for an invading army was to encircle Athens, cut its link to the sea, and starve it into submission. To prevent this, the Athenians built a fortified corridor (the Long Walls) to connect their capital with their port. So long as the Athenian navy ruled the sea and supplied the city through the Piraeus, land-based armies had little hope of taking Athens.

Athens' foreign policy in this era reflected the city's growing self-confidence and willingness to take risks. The most audacious decision the Athenian assembly made was to dispatch a fleet to Egypt to assist rebels who were trying to force the Persians out. The campaign bogged down, and in 453 B.C.E. the Persians cornered and obliterated the Athenian army.

The two hundred ships that Thucydides, an Athenian historian, says his city lost in Egypt sobered Athens, and in 451 B.C.E. the conservative politician Cimon returned to power and negotiated a five-year truce with the Peloponnesian League. At the same time, Callias, Cimon's former brother-in-law, seems to have come to an agreement with Persia. If so, it was not publicized, for a formal peace with Persia would have undercut the rationale for the Delian League. When the truce ended and a rebellion erupted among some of Athens' allies, Sparta seized the opportunity to invade Attica. Athens then abandoned most of its mainland holdings outside of Attica, and in 445 B.C.E. the two Greek superpowers signed the Thirty Years' Peace—a commitment that proved to be overly optimistic.

Figure 4–1   The Acropolis   The heart of Athens was the natural fortress provided by the Acropolis. By Pericles' day, it was more a religious than a military center, and he oversaw the building program that made it one of the wonders of the Hellenic world.

✳ People in Context: Aspasia, the Woman Behind the Great Man

The love of Pericles' life was his mistress, Aspasia, one of the few women who seem to have influenced Athenian politics. Unlike Sparta, Athens encouraged immigration to promote economic development, and it allowed its population to explode. However, as the city grew richer, more powerful, and more democratic, its citizens grew jealous and protective of their privileges. In Pericles' day, about fifty thousand of Attica's free male residents were citizens and about twenty-five thousand were classed as *metics* (resident aliens). Metics could not own land, but many of them prospered as craftsmen and merchants. Their families lived in Athens for generations without acquiring citizenship. The sons of metic women who married Athenian citizens had always inherited citizenship from their fathers. But in 451 B.C.E. Pericles persuaded the assembly to limit citizenship to men whose mothers and fathers both came from citizen families. Pericles' motive probably had less to do with Athens' metics than with the dangerous alliances that were created by intermarriage among the aristocratic families of various *poleis*. Whatever the law's purpose, it made Athens a more closed society and backfired on Pericles.

Pericles married a close relative who bore him two sons, but the union did not last. He divorced his wife and, a few years later (c. 445 B.C.E.), took up with Aspasia, a *hetaira* from Miletus. She lived with him for well over a decade (possibly until his death). After plague carried off Pericles' two older boys, his only surviving male child was a son that Aspasia bore him. To save his *oikos* (his lineage), Pericles had to plead with the assembly to make an exemption from the law he had sponsored and to grant citizenship to his heir.

Pericles' bond with Aspasia was (or became in legend) a love match. Athenian gossips circulated the shocking rumor that he kissed her each morning when he left for work and again at evening when he came home. Such affection was considered a sign of an unmanly passion that made him vulnerable to manipulation by his foreign lover. She was even blamed for pushing him to take the actions that caused the tragic Peloponnesian War.

Aspasia was a convenient target for Pericles' opponents, and accurate information about her is difficult to disentangle from their xenophobic and misogynistic propaganda. She was born in Miletus about 470 B.C.E. and may have come to Athens about 450 B.C.E. with an older sister who had married an exiled Athenian aristocrat. Pericles' decree doomed any hope she may have had for a marriage that would have placed her on the same footing as a citizen-wife. Some sources refer to her as Pericles' concubine. Some maintain that she was a *hetaira,* a professional entertainer, and some simply call her a whore.

In comic plays from the period, Aspasia is a vamp, a seductress who uses sex to manipulate men. But elsewhere she is described as a highly educated, intelligent woman who taught rhetoric and held her own in debates with the city's philosophers. Several of Socrates' students remarked on his friendship with her and testified to her skill as a conversationalist and speech writer. If she was Pericles' most influential advisor, he might have done worse.

After Pericles' death, Aspasia was taken up by another of Athens' leaders, whose political career was advanced by her advice and connections. No one knows when or where she died, but unlike most Greek women of her generation, she was not forgotten. For good or ill, she—a foreigner and a woman—had helped to shape Athens' destiny.

Question: What does the career of a woman like Aspasia imply about attitudes toward women in Pericles' Athens?

The Peloponnesian War   The Thirty Years' Peace gave the Athenians an opportunity to concentrate on trade contacts with the *poleis* of Italy and Sicily. This worried Corinth and Syracuse, a Corinthian colony that was the largest of the Sicilian *poleis*. Tensions increased in 433 B.C.E. when Corcyra, a Corinthian colony on an island off the western coast of Greece, quarreled with Corinth and asked for Athenian help. The ships Athens sent to observe developments intervened in a battle between Corinth and Corcyra, and this prompted Corinth to charge that Athens had committed an act of war. Athens exacerbated the situation by ordering Potidaea, a *polis* in Chalcidice (the northern Aegean) to dismantle its defenses. Potidaea was a Corinthian colony, and Athens feared that if war broke out, it might provide an enemy with a base for attacking the Hellespont and cutting off supplies of grain to Athens. Potidaea resisted Athens' order (with Corinthian help), and Athens had to undertake a lengthy, expensive siege.

As the international situation heated up, the Athenians concluded that they had two options. They could back down, or they could mount a show of force that frightened their enemies into retreating. Pericles preferred the latter strategy and persuaded the assembly to take an action that some of his contemporaries later claimed caused the Peloponnesian War. As a warning to others, Athens closed the ports of its empire to merchants from Megara. This devastated Megara, for it cut off most of its trade.

Corinth appealed to Sparta, and Sparta summoned a meeting of the Peloponnesian League. Fighting did not immediately break out, for factions in both Sparta and Athens were opposed to war. The decision, however, was not left to the superpowers. Sparta's ally Thebes attacked Athens' ally Plataea, and that forced the two great cities to act.

Civil wars are among the most senseless of conflicts, for by squandering the resources of a country, they undermine both victor and vanquished. The Peloponnesian War was a particularly hopeless struggle, for neither combatant knew how to deal with the military strength of the other. The Athenian navy could not harm the Spartan infantry, and the Spartan army could not attack Athens' ships. Pericles assumed that once Sparta understood that it could not deal Athens a lethal blow, Sparta would give up. His trust in the fundamental rationality of human conduct proved to be misplaced.

Pericles' strategy for winning the war was to refuse to fight it on the enemy's terms. He talked the Athenians into abandoning the defense of Attica and retreating behind the walls of their city. Thanks to the Long Walls and Athens' control of the sea, Athens could outlast any Spartan siege. Initially, things played out as Pericles predicted. Sparta led an army into Attica and found nothing for it to do but chop down olive trees and uproot vineyards. Sparta's army was shown to be impotent against Athens, but instead of concluding what Pericles took to be self-evident (that the war was unwinnable), Sparta refused to give up.

Pericles' strategy severely tested the discipline of the democracy, for it was as costly to individual citizens as it was to the state. Men were asked to stand idly by while an enemy torched their farms and taunted them with charges of cowardice. The resolve of the Athenian electorate was further tested in the second year of the war when plague spread through the crowded city. About a third of its inhabitants died. Among them were Pericles' elder sons and then Pericles himself.

As time passed and sacrifices mounted, emotion replaced reason in the deliberations of the Athenian assembly, and Athens' democracy began to deteriorate into demagogy (mob rule). Calls for restraint were equated with treason as politicians fanned the flames of jingoism in their attempts to sway the voters. Still, the city was slow to lose its moral compass. In 428 B.C.E. four *poleis* on the island of Lesbos declared their intention to secede from Athens' empire. Athens' refusal to engage the Spartans might have led them to conclude that Athens would not fight. If so, they seriously miscalculated. Athens descended on Lesbos in force and quickly retook the island. In a fit of vindictive passion the assembly then dispatched a ship with an order directing the commander on Lesbos to slaughter his captives. Overnight, Athenian tempers cooled, and consciences awoke. The assembly reconvened the next day, rescinded its decree, and managed to get word to Lesbos just in time to prevent genocide. The event provides a marker for measuring the effects of prolonged war on the ethics of a democracy. At the time of the Lesbos revolt, the Peloponnesian War was young, and its brutality had not yet lessened the Athenians' respect for the value of human life. Twelve years later, the situation was different. In 416 B.C.E. Athens ordered the tiny island of Melos to join its alliance. When Melos refused, Athens invaded, slaughtered the men, and enslaved the women and children. This time there were no second thoughts and no last-minute reprieves.

In 425 B.C.E. Athens scored a coup. A storm forced an Athenian fleet into the bay at Pylos, which had been abandoned since the fall of its Mycenaean kingdom over seven centuries earlier. Demosthenes, the admiral in charge, recognized the strategic importance of the site and decided to occupy it. The Spartans eventually noticed his presence and sent an army to evict him. However, relief forces arrived from Athens and surprised and trapped 420 Spartans on an island in the bay. Sparta, fearing the loss of so many men, promptly sued for peace. But no Athenian politician was willing to urge moderation on an assembly that had a taste of victory. Athens sent enough men to Pylos to overwhelm the blockaded Spartans, and 292 of them were taken alive.

The taking of Spartan hostages at Pylos emboldened the Athenians to abandon Pericles's strategy and pursue the war on land. They attacked Thebes, Sparta's major ally in northern Greece, and were soundly trounced. An even greater loss followed in the Chalcidice, where a Spartan general organized an uprising that cost Athens control of key ports on the crucial Hellespont grain route. The panicky assembly blamed the loss on an Athenian admiral named Thucydides and banished him. Posterity is grateful, for Thucydides devoted his enforced leisure to writing an extraordinary history of the war that was consuming his generation.

Athens' ardor for war cooled. In the spring of 423 B.C.E. it endorsed a temporary cessation of hostilities, and two years later, Nicias, an Athenian general, negotiated a treaty that was supposed to end the war. Athens promised to withdraw from Pylos and Sparta from the Chalcidice. Both states pledged to maintain the peace for fifty years. The treaty was a de facto defeat for Sparta, and several of its allies refused to sign. When the Chalcidice declined to submit to Athens, Athens refused to give up Pylos.

The treaty did not resolve the issues that had caused the war, so it was not likely to hold. Athens should therefore have proceeded with caution. Instead, it committed itself to a campaign on the distant island of Sicily. The chief advocate for the ill-advised expedition was Alcibiades (c. 450–404 B.C.E.), Pericles' nephew. Nicias, the elder statesman who had negotiated peace with Sparta, opposed it, but Alcibiades was the more appealing politician. Young, rich, handsome, intelligent, and totally unprincipled, he carried the day. The best that cooler heads could do was to persuade the assembly to split command of the expedition among Alcibiades and two older generals, one of whom was Nicias. The night before the fleet sailed, many sacred images were vandalized in Athens. This blasphemy had to be punished lest the gods turn against the city, and the finger of suspicion pointed at a group of young rowdies led by Alcibiades. A ship was sent to Sicily to bring him home for trial. Rather than risk conviction, Alcibiades chose to defect to Sparta. Nicias was left with responsibility for a campaign he had opposed, and the project's sponsor, Alcibiades, began to plot with the Spartans to bring about its failure.

Athens had committed about twenty-five thousand men and 250 ships to the invasion of Sicily, but this was not enough. Nicias claimed that twice as many were needed, and he urged the assembly to allow him to withdraw. It chose instead to send him more troops. The Spartans countered by dispatching a general to organize the defense of Syracuse, the great Sicilian city that Nicias was besieging. Syracuse's navy first trapped the Athenian fleet in its harbor. Then the Syracusan army outflanked and began to encircle the Greek camp. Seeing that the situation was hopeless, Nicias ordered his men to scatter and try to save themselves. All of them (some forty thousand) were captured. Nicias was executed, and his men were either enslaved or herded into a quarry and left to die from thirst and exposure. The loss of the army rendered Athens defenseless, but the city was unaware of that fact until a visitor in the port of the Piraeus casually mentioned the disaster to his barber.

Sparta could not pass up the opportunity presented by Athens' vulnerability. While Alcibiades moved through the Aegean urging members of the Athenian empire to revolt, Sparta established a fort on the edge of Attica as a retreat for runaway Athenian slaves. Some twenty thousand defected and helped the Spartans lay Attica under permanent siege.

Athens' fortunes had sunk suddenly and dramatically, but the city refused to give in. The war dragged on for another eight years and was finally ended by the intervention of Persia. The Spartans decided that they had to meet the Athenians on their own turf (metaphorically) by taking to the sea, and Persia financed the fleets with which Sparta pursued Athens' navy. Alcibiades may have arranged this, but when news of the hyperactive young man's affair with the Spartan king's wife leaked out, he fled Sparta for Persian territory. There he tried to make a deal that would allow him to return to Athens. The Persians were willing to offer Athens assistance, for it was to their advantage to help the Greeks destroy one another. All that was needed, Alcibiades said, was for Athens to replace democracy with a more reliable government. The Athenian elite promptly staged a coup that disenfranchised most of the *polis*'s citizens. But when news of this reached the sailors of the fleet, they threatened to mutiny and elected new generals—one of whom was Alcibiades! Democracy was restored, and under Alcibiades's leadership the Athenians won several victories. Suspicion of further double dealing prompted Athens to exile Alcibiades in 406 B.C.E. They replaced him with incompetent admirals whose blunders assured Athens' defeat.

In 404 B.C.E. Lysander, the Spartan admiral, destroyed the Athenian navy, blockaded Athens, and starved it into submission. Sparta allowed Athens to survive, for it wanted to block the expansion of Athens' ambitious neighbor, Thebes. But Sparta ordered the Athenians to tear down the Long Walls and limit their fleet to a mere dozen ships. Athens' days of military glory were over, but the city's fame as an intellectual center endured.

Sparta profited little from its victory, for it was poorly equipped by tradition, experience, and manpower to lead the Aegean world. It also alienated the Greeks by ceding Ionia to Persia as repayment for its war debt. Persia, for its part, continued to fund the Greeks' internecine quarrels. Rebellions erupted against Sparta, and in 371 B.C.E. Thebes, led by a brilliant general named Epaminondas, defeated Sparta and ended its hegemony. Thebes declined following Epaminondas's death a few years later, and without a dominant *polis* to maintain order, local wars proliferated. The Greeks continued to tear at the fabric of their civilization.

Only a little more than a century separated the victory at Marathon (490 B.C.E.) from the confusion that attended Sparta's fall (371 B.C.E.). From the military perspective, that century

Culture in Context: A Democratic Slave State

Given the role that debates about slavery have played in American history, it seems odd to us that the Athenians, who were so proud of their democratic freedoms, never questioned the institution of slavery. Slavery was so common, so universal, and so long-established that most people in the ancient world accepted it as part of the natural order. For most of human history, societies without slavery have been the exception.

Slaves may have outnumbered the free residents of Attica. Even poor families owned at least one, and large estates were worked with armies of them (as were state industries, such as Athens' silver mines). Slaves, the ancient equivalent of household appliances, provided the necessities and comforts of the Athenians' domestic lives and gave citizens the free time they needed to take part in the city's political and cultural activities.

Curiously, no jobs (except the worst in the mines) were exclusively reserved for slaves. In most occupations, free men and slaves worked side by side. Some slaves were skilled craftsmen or highly educated professionals who were entrusted with major responsibilities. A *polis* might even staff its police force with slaves. Many slaves (called "pay-bringers") lived and worked on their own and simply gave a percentage of what they earned to their owners. They had property rights and could save money to buy their freedom. Slavery and freedom were not totally distinct conditions, for there were degrees of enslavement. A slave might, for instance, have the right to live where he wanted but not the right to contract for his own labor. A poor citizen might be regarded as "enslaved" by poverty if he were working off a debt or lacked the capital needed to exercise his freedoms.

For all its horrors, slavery in the ancient world was not a permanent status based on race as it was in America before the Civil War. Emancipation was common, and freed slaves had little difficulty integrating into their communities. This and the universal acceptance of slavery may explain why servitude attracted so little attention from ancient moralists and social theorists.

Question: Was slavery inconsistent with the Athenian democracy, or would the democracy have been impossible without it?

was bloody, wasteful, and disastrous. Surprisingly, however, the carnage did not impede the work of artists and intellectuals. In the midst of the tumult, they created the artistic and literary monuments that made these years a classic era in Western civilization.

Intellectual and Artistic Life in the *Polis*

Traditional wisdom held that the world was a product of divine forces and that the causes of things were mysteries hidden in the minds of gods. The explanation for earthly phenomena lay, therefore, in a realm that human beings could not explore. During the sixth century B.C.E. some Greek thinkers from Ionia began to question such beliefs. They demystified the world and conceived of it as an orderly place governed by intelligible principles that could be discovered by observation and rational analysis. For centuries people had collected data about the world in order to refine their ability to manipulate things, but the Greeks went further. They invented science, the disinterested search for an understanding of how things worked.

The rationality of the Greek mind should not be overemphasized, for Greek culture had its dark side. The Greeks believed that there were mysteries and truths that could be grasped only through intuition, feeling, or divine revelation. They invented potent myths and symbols that still engage our imaginations. They were capable of bloody deeds. They cultivated irrational states of mind, and they thrilled at stories of mutilation, incest, and cannibalism. They believed in magic, rituals, spells, visions, dreams, omens, and oracles, and they bowed before inexplicable forces they called fate. Classical civilization was not a simple or even self-consistent phenomenon.

From Myth to Philosophy and Science   The *Iliad* and the *Odyssey,* which were composed in Ionia in the mid-eighth century, belong to the most ancient of literary genres—the hero epic, the story of people who are larger than life. During the seventh and sixth centuries, the Greeks began to produce poetry of a different kind—lyrics, short songs inspired by the private feelings of real individuals. These personal, intimate, and sometimes confessional poems mark a shift of interest among the Greeks from fantasies about the past to the real situations people face in the present. The greatest lyric poet of the archaic period (750–500 B.C.E.) was an aristocratic woman named Sappho (fl. c. 600 B.C.E.), a native of the island of Lesbos. Her passionate love songs were so exquisite that they joined Homer's epics as standard texts in Greece's schools.

The lyric poets' interest in the real world was shared by their contemporaries, the first thinkers to seek rational alternatives to the mythic view of nature. Greeks called these people *philosophers,* "lovers of wisdom." They set aside stories about the gods and proposed natural explanations for natural phenomena.

Thales (fl. c. 550 B.C.E.), from the Ionian city of Miletus, pioneered the field of metaphysics, the search for the fundamental principles of existence. He was fascinated by the fact that things around us are constantly changing, yet the world remains a stable, permanent place. How, he wondered, could change and permanence, which are opposites, coexist in the same system? That the world maintains a balance between them suggested to Thales that there was a more fundamental reality, a "substance" ("something standing under"), that controlled them. Such a substance had to be able to exist as a solid, a liquid, and a gas, for all these states are found in nature. Thales knew only one thing that fit the bill: water. He concluded, therefore, that everything that exists is a form of water. Things hold together because their contrasts are more apparent than real. Ultimately, only one thing exists, a watery substance that naturally assumes different states of being.

Thales' followers, the Monist ("one thing") philosophers, taught that change was only a shift among the states that are natural to a single, eternal substance. They disagreed, however, about the identity of that substance. Anaximander (c. 611–546 B.C.E.) objected that nothing we could experience with our senses (such as water) was complex enough to account for the variety of things found in nature. He postulated, therefore, that the ultimate substance was "the indefinite," a material that is never directly perceived in its pure essence, but only as it manifests aspects of itself in particular things. His successor, Anaximenes (d. c. 500 B.C.E.), was not convinced. He pointed out that an unknowable substance offered no better explanation for the world than an unknowable god. To explain anything, Anaximenes said, the ultimate substance had to be something identifiable. He proposed air. Just as the "breath of life" sustains the human body, air, he theorized, maintains and activates the universe.

Chronology: The Classical Era

POLITICS	ARTISTS AND INTELLECTUALS
[600–500 B.C.E.]	
Solon (c. 638–c. 559)	Sappho (fl. c. 600)
Peisistratus (fl. c. 560)	
	Thales (c. 640 546)
Cyrus The Great (c. 600–530)	
	Anaximander (611–547)
Cleisthenes (fl. c. 507)	Pythagoras (d. c. 497)
	Anaximenes (d. c. 528)
	Aeschylus (525–456)
[500–400 B.C.E.]	
Miletus revolt (499–494)	
	Heracelitus (fl. c. 500)
	Parmenides (fl. c. 500)
	Hecataeus (fl. c. 550–480)
	Sophocles (496–406)
Darius invades Greece (492)	
	Empedocles (493–433)
Xerxes' campaign (484–479)	Protagorus (d. c. 421)
Pericles (490 429)	
	Aristophanes (488–380)
	Euripides (485–406)
	Herodotus (480–425)
	Socrates (469–399)
	Democritus (460–347)
	Hippocrates (460–377)
	Thucydides (460 399)
Peloponnesian War (432–404)	Plato (429–347)
[400–300 B.C.E.]	
	Aristotle (384–322)
Thebes defeats Sparta (371)	
Philip of Macedon (r. 359–336)	
Alexander the Great (r. 336–323)	

The problem with these theories was that they were unverifiable. This led some thinkers to suspect that their premise was incorrect. The Monists had begun by asking how opposites like change and permanence coexist, but what if change and permanence do not exist? What if only one of them is real and the other is an illusion?

Heracleitus of Ephesus (fl. c. 500 B.C.E.) argued that permanence was the illusion. Things that change more slowly than we do appear permanent to us, but in actuality everything is constantly changing. Being is analogous to a flowing river, and no one, he pointed out, can step into the same river twice. If we need to imagine a primal substance for the world, we should envision it as fire, pure energy. Parmenides of Elea (fl. fifth century B.C.E.) came to the opposite conclusion, for he regarded change as an illogical concept. Change implies that something new has come into being. There are only two ways this could happen, and neither is possible. If a change comes from what already exists, there is nothing new and therefore no change. If a change comes from something that does not exist, then nothing has created something, which is absurd. Nothing is the negation of being, not a kind of being with the power to create. Therefore, the universe must, Parmenides insisted, be an inert solid. Empty space in which movement might take place cannot exist. Emptiness is nothingness, and nothingness means nonexistence.

The rigorous logic of Heracleitus and Parmenides led to dead-end conclusions and a description of the world that defied common sense. The Pluralist ("multiple things") philosophers therefore hoped that by reconciling them, they might find a logically coherent explanation for the natural world that was consistent with ordinary experience. The Pluralists claimed that changing configurations of a number of different, but permanent, components create the world we experience. Empedocles of Agrigentum (f. c. 450 B.C.E.) suggested that everything that exists is a product of the interaction of four fundamental *elements* ("irreducibles"): earth, air, fire, and water. The elements themselves never change, but their combinations do. Democritus of Abdera (c. 460–370 B.C.E.) felt that a few elements were insufficient to explain the incredible variety of human experience. Like the Monists, he believed that only one substance existed, but that it existed in the form of discrete *atoms* ("indivisibles"). These were innumerable, eternal bits of a material that had only primary characteristics (size, shape, and location). All secondary attributes (such as color and odor) were mere impressions created by interactions among the atoms.

Democritus reduced the universe to a mechanism: a swirl of physical objects that randomly come together and split apart. This implied that existence had no meaning, but it encouraged the development of science by suggesting that physical measurements might suffice to explain everything. A century earlier, Pythagoras, a contemporary of the Ionian Monists, had proposed something similar. Pythagoras concluded from the mathematical relationships that exist between sounds (pitches) and physical objects (lengths of plucked string) that mathematics was the key to unlocking the mysteries of the universe.

Greek science developed these portentous theories largely by intuition and imagination, but speculation alone could carry science no further. Unless hard data could be found to confirm the existence of Empedocles' elements and Democritus's atoms, they were no more helpful in explaining the universe than were the gods. Two thousand years passed before the West invented instruments that could gather the information needed to test the ancient Greek hypotheses.

Medicine   Greek science tended to trust rational argument more than observation and to be abstract and theoretical, but it also made advances in applied fields—particularly medicine. Hippocrates of Cos (c. 460–377 B.C.E.), Democritus's contemporary, acquired such a reputation as a healer that modern physicians take a vow to honor the principles he allegedly established for the conduct of their profession. Almost no dependable information survives about him, but about 300 B.C.E. Greek scholars collected a body of medical literature that they claimed stemmed from his school. It influenced the practice of medicine for over two millennia.

Much ancient healing relied on spells and charms, but the Hippocratic tradition was relatively free of superstition. It sought natural causes for physical problems, relied on observation to diagnose them, and sought to cure them with drugs, surgery, and changes in diet and regimen. Many of its analyses went astray, but its method had merit. Medicine did not make much more progress until the early modern era, when the microscope and advances in chemistry began to provide new clues to the mechanisms of disease and human physiology.

History   The invention of history was another sign of the Greek's preoccupation with science. The word *historia* ("inquiry") originally meant an inquiry by a judge (a *histor*) into the facts of a dispute. A *histor* became a historian when he broadened his inquiry and searched for explanations for larger events.

It may seem odd to speak of the invention of something like history. Because human beings have memories, it is obvious that they have always been aware of the past. Early civilizations even compiled annals and lists of the names of kings or other officials and dated events by assigning them to years in the reigns of certain rulers or priests. The peoples of Egypt and the Middle East accumulated much more of this material than the Greeks, whose civilization was comparatively young. But it was the Greeks who turned records of this kind into history by looking for patterns that made the past meaningful. Most of their neighbors dismissed history's panorama as transitory and meaningless or as a by-product of mysterious struggles among the gods. Parts of the Hebrew Bible foreshadow history, but there, too, the past was of interest primarily as a revelation of God's will. Greece's historians, like its philosophers, were curious to see how far they could go in explaining the world in purely human terms.

History developed from geography. The Greeks of the archaic era were traders and colonizers who needed accurate information about foreign lands. Anaximenes was a cartographer as well as a Monist philosopher. He produced a map of the world, and one of his contemporaries was ancient Greece's first great cultural geographer, Hecataeus of Miletus (fl. c. 500 B.C.E.). Hecataeus believed that information of all kinds (topography, climate, plants, animals, religions, customs, and institutions) was needed to make foreign lands intelligible. (Hippocratic physicians agreed—maintaining that hard environments produced hardy people and that rich lands undermined both strength and character.) Herodotus of Halicarnassus (480–425 B.C.E.), the "father of history," began as a geographer building on the work of Hecataeus.

At a time when literate people were few and manuscripts rare, authors like Herodotus made their livings by giving lectures and public readings. They resembled Homeric bards and were regarded as entertainers. But what Herodotus offered his audiences was something different from Homer's epics. Poetry was the traditional medium for sacred myth and serious literature. Even secular leaders like Athens' Solon wrote poems to explain their political agenda. But Herodotus composed prose. Anaximenes was the first major thinker from whom we have a few lines of prose. Prose signaled science's break with sacred myths and legends. Herodotus learned much about storytelling from Homer, but his use of prose declared his intention to depart from the epic tradition and view the past from the perspective of the new secular science.

Herodotus began by writing ethnographical studies in the style of Hecataeus—sketches of life in exotic locales like Egypt and Babylon. But when he visited Athens, he found the theme that transformed geography into history. The Athens Herodotus experienced was fresh from its victories over the Persians and riding the crest of a wave of self-confidence. The city's heady environment persuaded Herodotus that, thanks to the Greeks and particularly the Athenians, the world was on the brink of a glorious new age. He decided to try to explain how this had come about and suspected that the answer was to be found in a study of the Persian War. The war had pitted the might of a despotic empire against the will of a free people, and freedom had proved invincible. The Greek victory had changed the world by revealing for the first time what a free society could achieve.

The generation that had fought the Persian War was dying out by the time Herodotus arrived in Athens, and his history of it appeared during the early years of the Peloponnesian War. He may have wanted to remind his readers of what their ancestors had achieved by working together, but he probably did not expect this to divert them from their current path. Herodotus suspected that events were not entirely under human control. Individuals certainly affected what happened, but chance played a role, as did a mysterious force that maintained a cosmic balance in the universe. Some outcomes seemed fated no matter what people did: Wealth and power undermined themselves; fortune and happiness did not last forever.

The era that invented history also produced two of the West's greatest historians. Herodotus was about twenty years old when his future Athenian colleague, Thucydides (460–399 B.C.E.), was born. The two men not only worked in the same field; they treated complementary subjects. Herodotus told the story of the "good" war that launched Greece's Golden Age, and Thucydides narrated the sad tale of the willful conflict that frittered away Greece's opportunities. There were differences in their approaches to their common subject. Herodotus was not overly credulous. He went out of his way to check information and find reliable sources. Sometimes he warned his readers that they should not assume that he believed every story that he felt obliged to tell. He was, however, a religious man who trusted in omens and who felt that human agency alone could not explain history. For Thucydides, history was simply an account of human decisions and their consequences.

Thucydides was an aristocratic Athenian who was deeply immersed in his city's political and intellectual life. An intuitive sense of the importance of the time and place in which he found himself inspired him to do something that had never been done before: to record history as it unfolded. He had time and opportunity, for a few years after the Peloponnesian War began, the Athenians blamed him for losing a battle and exiled him for twenty years.

Thucydides claimed that the proper subjects for the historian were politics and war, and he rigorously excluded everything else from his narrative. He believed that events could be explained as the outcomes of decisions that individuals made and that these decisions were rooted in the intelligence and character of their authors. No gods or mysterious powers intervened. An element of chance affected how situations played out, but chance was not a mystical force (a providence, fate, or destiny). Chance entered in because the human ability to anticipate developments and plan for every possible contingency is limited. Thucydides viewed human beings as fundamentally rational agents who are motivated by self-interest. Pursuit of power is part of their nature, and the strong always dominate the weak. The study of history has much to teach, he insisted, because human nature does not change. We learn about ourselves by analyzing the motives of our predecessors and the consequences of their actions. What ultimately counts is developing the skill we need to bring about the outcomes we want.

Philosophy, Psychology, and Politics   Natural scientists and physicians work by observing phenomena and collecting and rationally analyzing data, but Greek thinkers of Thucydides's generation wrestled with the troubling discovery that what is observed depends, in part, on the observer. They knew that the unaided human senses (their primary scientific instruments) could deceive them. They concluded, therefore, that to learn more about the world, they had to learn more about themselves. In the interim between the Persian and Peloponnesian Wars (the 470s and 460s B.C.E.), Greek philosophers shifted their attention from the external world of the senses to the internal world of the human psyche. They began to analyze thought itself—to work out the mechanics of logic, explore the emotions, and ask themselves what "truth" meant. Some wondered if such a thing existed.

The earlier Greek philosophers are lumped together as "pre-Socratics." This suggests that the Athenian thinker Socrates (469–439 B.C.E.) was responsible for a major shift in philosophy's focus, but philosophy's reorientation actually began with his teachers, professional educators called Sophists. Sophists taught public speaking and the arts of persuasion, valuable skills in a democracy. Their study of the uses of language led them to explore how the mind forms concepts and opinions and caused them to wonder what words like *justice, virtue,* and *truth* really signify.

Relativism was in the air that Socrates breathed. Colonization and trade had brought the Greeks into contact with all kinds of people, and the knowledge that alternative cultures existed was causing some Greeks to question their traditional values and institutions. Furthermore, the Sophist sellers of oratorical training claimed that truth, if it was even knowable, was irrelevant. A skillful speaker could make weak causes appear strong and black look white. There were no absolute standards or values, for as Protagoras (493–421 B.C.E.), one of the leading Sophists, succinctly put it, "Man is the measure of all things." One person sees things one way, and another sees them differently. Both are "right," for no one can rise above his or her individual perspective and grasp pure, objective truth. We might prefer one opinion to another, but only because it is useful or consistent with our preconceptions, not because it is true.

This radical skepticism had alarming implications. It undercut the possibility of shared values and objective standards and justified selfish individualism. If everything is simply a matter of personal opinion, how can people justify the laws and values that make it possible for them to form communities? How can they maintain a *polis*? The Greeks valued the individual, but believed that individuals were formed by community life. Citizenship in a *polis* made them what they were, and citizenship implied a duty to subordinate self-interest to the common good.

Socrates devoted himself to the search for an alternative to the relativism and skepticism of the Sophists. Because he never wrote anything, we know him today only through the reports of others—and those reports differ significantly. The most elaborate descriptions of his conversations (he would not have said "teachings") are dialogues penned by his devoted pupil Plato (c. 429–347 B.C.E.). These are imaginative recreations, not verbatim reports, and it is likely that they tell us more about Plato than Socrates.

In Plato's dialogues, Socrates is an ingenious debater who spends his life forcing people to justify their beliefs. He delights in revealing the absurd and contradictory implications of the commonsense opinions held by his fellow Athenians. He is adept at demolishing belief systems and unwilling to propose anything to take their place. Some people, like Plato himself, were devoted to Socrates for liberating them from sterile complacency and teaching them how to think; others considered him a nuisance or a threat to the beliefs on which the *polis* was based.

In the wake of the Peloponnesian War, the Athenians struggled with humiliation and self-doubt, and they had little tolerance for intellectual gadflies. Citizens of a democracy are responsible for what their government does. When it flourishes, they congratulate themselves; but when it blunders, they look for scapegoats on whom to place the blame. Socrates' habit of questioning the legitimacy of traditional values made him a convenient target. He may indeed have had little respect for democracy, a form of government guided by the kinds of commonly held opinions he delighted in demolishing. Socrates was indicted, tried, and convicted on a charge of corrupting the youth of Athens by undercutting their faith in the gods and the wisdom of their elders. This was a capital offense, but Athens, having made its point, was not eager to put a defenseless old man to death. Socrates was given an opportunity to flee, but he insisted on being executed. He told his friends that having been protected by Athens' laws all his life, he could not reject the authority of those laws just because they were now inconvenient. His death was perhaps his ultimate attempt to refute the relativists and skeptics.

Plato, Socrates' ardent disciple, was determined to justify belief in the existence of truth, and he thought he found the evidence he needed in the way our minds organize the things we perceive. When we encounter a thing, we assign it to a class of objects. A collie does not look much like a dachshund, but somehow when we see either of these animals (even the first time), we know that it is a dog. Plato believed that this was only possible if all the members of a class had something in common that our minds recognize—a defining reality that he called a form or an idea. This makes them what they are even if it manifests itself somewhat differently in each individual. Plato claimed that the forms are eternal and exist apart from the particular things that we experience. We recognize dogs because our minds are born with some previous experience of "dogness," of the pure ideal that makes a dog a dog. Plato noted that our knowledge becomes more accurate as we study more individuals. By combining multiple examples, we discover the higher category of being that each individual only partially represents. What is true of individual objects is also true of individual ideas. They fit into categories, and those categories compose a hierarchy of increasingly abstract ideas: The class of dogs is subsumed in the class of animals, and the class of animals, in higher and higher classes until we arrive at the ultimate idea—all-encompassing Truth. Plato's theory that the world of sense experience is less real than a realm of pure intelligibility (which is accessible only to the mind) has a mystical aspect that appeals to religious thinkers. The ultimate form, which contains all things, resembles a divine creator.

Plato was born after the Peloponnesian War began, and the Athens he knew was a *polis* that labored, and finally broke, under the strains of that campaign. The great experiment with democracy that Athens had conducted was not an unqualified success. In the opinion of scholarly aristocrats, such as Plato and Thucydides, democracy tended to degenerate into mob rule. The ideal state that Plato conceived in his youth, therefore, was not a democracy. He claimed that power ought to be entrusted only to persons who had the knowledge and self-control to use it wisely. The best form of government was one that vested all authority in individuals whom nature had especially equipped to rule. When democratic societies lose confidence in themselves, they tend to look for a savior, a person with extraordinary gifts that will supposedly enable him or her to do for the people what the people have failed to do for themselves. The young Plato pinned his hope for the future on such saviors, but as he aged, he came to doubt their existence.

The Arts and Politics   The Greeks practiced all the arts known to us and some that we no longer regard as fine arts. The influence of the remnants of their architecture and sculpture has been and remains incalculable, but their achievements in other media are harder to assess. We know that they produced skilled painters. Athens had a state art collection, which it displayed in a public gallery. Fragmentary mosaic copies of a few paintings exist. But because none of the original work has survived, no one knows what it was like. Greek music and dance are also lost. The Greeks experimented with musical notation systems, but did not have much success. Sculptors and vase painters depicted dancers, but it is difficult to infer choreography from frozen images. The texts of some ancient tragedies and comedies have survived, but words were only part of the experience of Greek theater. It was a multifaceted art that combined dance, music, costuming, and conventions of acting that are hard for us now to imagine.

Much Hellenic art was public art. That is, it was meant to educate and inspire citizens, to impress a *polis*'s allies, and to intimidate its enemies. There was, however, an art that served private collectors: pottery painting. The Greeks turned the decoration of pottery into high art. Their jars, bowls, and cups were in demand throughout the ancient world, and they provide us with invaluable pictorial documentation of Hellenic society.

The Minoans and Mycenaeans produced sophisticated pottery decorated in multiple colors with naturalistic figures, but it was replaced during the Aegean Dark Age by a novel "geometric" style. Geometric pottery, as its name implies, featured bands of repetitive, abstract figures. It was an art that celebrated order and control, the preoccupations of a world struggling to rebuild. About 700 B.C.E., black-figure pottery appeared. Its images were painted in black glaze against a red background of fired, unglazed clay. Red-figure ware, the pinnacle of the Greek potter's art, emerged in the second half of the sixth century B.C.E. Its practitioners achieved greater realism by painting backgrounds in black glaze and letting the color of unglazed pottery represent the ruddy skin tones of their human figures. The drafting skills of the great pottery painters were extraordinary. Although they worked on curved surfaces, they were able to give figures volume, substance, and convincing proportions. They provide us with more intimate knowledge of the lives of the Greeks than we have for most other ancient people.

Greek sculptors worked in wood, stone, and bronze, and also assembled monumental figures from sheets of ivory and gold. Much of what they made survives today only in Roman copies. The principles of classicism (balance, restraint, simplicity, and harmony of proportions) are clearly apparent in their work (particularly in their treatment of their favorite subject, the human form). They did not record the idiosyncrasies of their models but eliminated oddities and imperfections to create visions of the human ideal. Males were more commonly represented than females. Greek science maintained that the perfect human form was male and that females were born when something went wrong with the process of gestation. Female figures were usually clothed, but males were nude. Perfection required no decoration or concealment.

The consummate examples of Greek architecture are temples. Greek temples were not analogous to modern churches, synagogues, or mosques, for they were not built to house worshiping congregations. They sheltered images of gods and goddesses and provided storage space for sacred treasures. Public religious ceremonies were held at outdoor altars, for which a temple's facade provided a backdrop.

Greeks practiced multiple religions simultaneously. Families maintained household shrines and venerated sacred objects inherited from their ancestors. Many individuals sought

Figure 4–2   Black-Figure and Red-Figure Pottery   The Hellenic era produced two styles of pottery painting. Both the first, black-figure ware (left), and the second, red-figure ware (right), are historical documents as well as works of art.

initiation into mystery cults whose secret rituals and teachings provided them with spiritual support. Magicians cast spells to promote fertility or to curse enemies. Trust in omens and oracles was widespread. Greece's official pantheon consisted of relatives and courtiers of Zeus, an Indo-European sky-deity associated with Olympus, a mountain on Greece's northeastern frontier. The "Olympians" were the household gods of the state, the guardians of the *polis,* and their temples celebrated the humanistic principles on which it was founded.

Unlike the soaring complexity of a Gothic cathedral, a Greek temple was not meant to inspire a sense of transcendent mystery. Its purpose was to confirm the Greeks' humanistic belief that the world was fundamentally intelligible. The principles of a temple's construction—its stout pillars supporting horizontal lintels and a low-pitched roof—were meant to be immediately obvious and reassuring. Its symmetry, balance, and proportion reflected the stability and rationality that was fundamental to the order of nature.

Hellenic architects created three styles. The earliest, the Doric, featured sturdy, fluted pillars with plain, flat capitals and no bases. The pediments on the facades of its temples were filled with statuary. The second style, the Ionic, was inspired by the elegant arts of the Middle East. It was light, refined, and highly decorated. Its pillars were slender columns with bases and capitals sculpted to resemble curved rams' horns. The third style, the Corinthian, spread in the wake of the Peloponnesian War and reflected values associated with the decline of *poleis* and the rise of empires. Corinthian buildings were imposing and florid. Their pillars had capitals resembling sheaves of acanthus leaves (a plant common to the Mediterranean region).

Some Greek temples had no roofs or pillared facades. They were amphitheaters. Drama (comedy as well as tragedy) was a sacred ceremony, and actors had the status of priests. The Greek plays were staged to honor Dionysus, the inebriated god of the vineyard. His intoxication represented the power of the irrational—of ecstasy, inspiration, and feeling.

Theater's conventions evolved from rural holidays that featured dancing and singing. The tyrant Peisistratus may have introduced these celebrations to Athens. He is alleged to have established the Great Dionysia, a spring festival for which the plays that survive were written. The theater was not a mere entertainment. It was a civic duty. Everyone was expected to attend. Wealthy citizens were honored publically for funding productions. Thousands of men and boys took part as singers and dancers, and prestigious prizes were awarded to the playwrights who won the audience's favor. Theater-going was serious, arduous business. During the four days of the Great Dionysia, Athenians sat through seventeen plays. Each playwright who won a slot at the festival had to create enough plays to fill the bill for an entire day.

Because Dionysus was attended by satyrs (men with the loins and legs of goats), hymns to him were called tragedies ("goat songs"). Originally, these took the form of dithyrambs, anthems sung and danced by choruses. Drama, as we know it, was allegedly born in the sixth century when a poet named Thespis made dialogue possible by separating a soloist from the chorus. (The modern term for actor, *thespian*, honors his memory.) Early Greek plays devoted a great deal of space to choruses and were written so that one or two actors could perform all the parts. Later plays reduced the role of the chorus, but authors of tragedies never employed more than three actors. The rules governing comedy were less strict. All performers were male, and men could play women and take multiple roles as different characters because actors were costumed and masked. Masks were functional as well as traditional. Plays were staged in huge amphitheaters that seated thousands. Superb acoustical design meant that a trained actor's voice could be heard without difficulty, but many in the audience were seated so far from the stage that they could not have seen facial expressions and subtle gestures. Actors had to be magnified to make them visible. They performed on elevated stages above the level where the chorus danced and sang. Padded costumes, elevator shoes, and large masks enhanced their stature, but these ponderous outfits forced them to move carefully and to use choreographed, stylized gestures. They could not stage convincing fights or engage in violent action. Incidents of this kind took place offstage and were described to the audience by speeches from the actors or chorus. Scenery and props were limited, and Greek audiences (like Shakespeare's) were expected to use their imaginations to supply what was missing.

The oldest complete plays we have from the ancient Greek theater are those of Aeschylus (525–456 B.C.E.), a veteran of the battle at Marathon. (It was this service to his *polis* and not his literary achievement that he ordered recorded on his tombstone.) Aeschylus was twenty-six when his first tragedy was produced. He continued to write throughout his long life, creating a total of eighty or ninety plays. Among the seven that survive is our only complete bill for a day in the Athenian theater, the *Oresteia*, a trilogy (cycle of three plays) staged at the Great Dionysia in the year 458 B.C.E. Aeschylus's earliest extant play is unusual in that it treats a historical event (the Persian War). Playwrights customarily chose themes from sacred mythology. Aeschylus's dramas have long choruses, and his characters and plots deal with clashes of ideas

Figure 4–3 The Parthenon The Parthenon, the chief temple that the Athenians raised to their patron goddess, Athena, superbly illustrates the Doric style. Its seemingly straight lines have been subtly curved to compensate for the tricks of vision that distort our perceptions. The Greeks often painted their temples and statues in vivid colors, so the Parthenon may originally have made a very different impression than it does now.

more than with the behavior of realistic people. His gods harshly punish men who overstep human bounds, and the society he describes is preoccupied with codes of honor and duty to blood kin.

Sophocles (496–406 B.C.E.), Aeschylus's younger contemporary, was a member of the Athenian democracy's second generation, and his was a different mental universe. He was a politically active aristocrat, a friend of Pericles, who served as treasurer of the Delian League. Despite a busy public life, he found time to write 123 plays. Seven survive, some of which (particularly *Oedipus Rex* and *Antigone*) are perennial favorites with modern audiences. Sophocles reduced the role of the chorus, wrote compelling dialogue, and created characters who undergo psychological transformations. He was intrigued by competing moral obligations and by the fact that people never have enough information to know how the decisions they make will turn out. He pondered the relationship of society's laws to the higher obligations intuited by ethically sensitive individuals. He claimed that the moral order of the universe holds us accountable for the consequences of our actions—whether they are intended or not.

Euripides (485–406 B.C.E.), the youngest of Athens' three great tragedians, was socially and intellectually an outsider. His family was not prominent, and he did not hold major public offices. The Athenians also had a love-hate relationship with his work. He wrote ninety-two

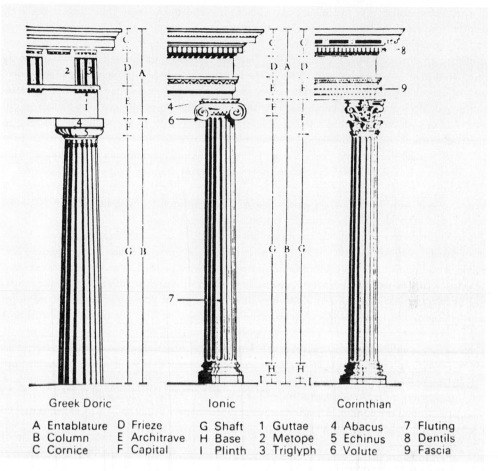

Greek Doric	Ionic	Corinthian

A Entablature	D Frieze	G Shaft	1 Guttae	4 Abacus	7 Fluting
B Column	E Architrave	H Base	2 Metope	5 Echinus	8 Dentils
C Cornice	F Capital	I Plinth	3 Triglyph	6 Volute	9 Fascia

Figure 4–4 The Greek Architectural Orders   The templates for the three styles of classical Greek architecture (Doric, Ionic, and Corinthian) extend to every detail of a building, but they are most easily distinguished by their treatment of pillars.

plays, but won only five first prizes. The Greeks admired his poetry but found his plays troubling. Euripides' characters are psychologically complex, and his plots explore, but do not resolve, morally ambiguous situations. In the year in which the Athenians voted to slaughter the people of Melos, for instance, Euripides produced a play about the Trojan War that described the brutalization of Troy's women by Greece's "heroes."

Euripides' work highlights the function of theater in the life of the Athenian *polis*. No modern state periodically suspends its activities and gathers all its citizens together for a week of theater. Why did Athens? Perhaps the answer lies in the importance of education to a democracy. Popular government requires an informed electorate—voters who are trained to think about serious issues and make sound judgments. Modern democracies use free public schools, newspapers, and electronic media to equip their citizens to govern themselves. None of these was available to the ancient Athenians, but the theater was. The theater regularly brought the Athenians together for a crash course in the problems posed by ethical dilemmas and the complexity of decision making. It created safe opportunities for the masses to vent— and learn to deal with—passionate feelings. Because each play was intended to be staged only once, its author wrote with the concerns of the moment in mind. Although most dramas were set in Greece's mythic past, playwrights chose stories with themes that had contemporary relevance and often made their connections with living issues pointedly obvious. Actors might wear masks with the faces of prominent politicians, name people in the audience, and refer to current events.

The topical relevance of Greek theater is most obvious in comedies, for the rules governing comedy were much more liberal than those surrounding tragedy. Comedy was, however, as serious in its intent and function as tragedy. The only plays that survive to give us a sense of what comedy was like during the golden age of Greek theater are by Aristophanes (488–380 B.C.E.). He wrote about forty comedies, eleven of which are extant.

Comedy derives from a word meaning "phallic song," a clear indication of its roots in fertility rituals. Not surprisingly, therefore, Aristophanes' plays feature broad humor, parody, and crude sexual references. His actors wore costumes that were padded to accentuate sexual characteristics, and what they did on stage would shock most modern audiences. While provoking hilarity, Aristophanes also prodded his audiences to think about serious issues, the most compelling of which for his generation was the Peloponnesian War. The hero of *The Acharnians* is a country bumpkin who, disgusted by the war, makes a separate peace with Sparta. In *Peace* the gods are asked why they inflict war on mankind, and they claim that they have nothing to do with it—that men make war and can stop whenever they want to. *Lysistrata,* a romping farce, proposed that the women of Athens and Sparta force their men to stop fighting by staging a sexual strike. Aristophanes ended the play with a serious proposal for an exchange of territories to end the conflict. He also warned the Athenians of the continuing threat posed by Persia and reminded them of their cultural solidarity with other Greeks.

Larger Issue Revisited

The Peloponnesian War brought the Hellenic phase in Greek civilization to an end. The era's contributions to science, literature, politics, history, and art were of major significance. They transformed the Mediterranean world and radically altered the course of Western history. The Greeks did not, however, do everything on their own. They built on legacies from the older cultures of the Middle East and were stimulated by contact with them. They were also not solely responsible for what the West has become. Most obviously, the West's religions, which originated in the Middle East, challenge the values of Greek humanism. The unresolved tensions between these legacies may help to explain the West's dynamism and creativity.

Review Questions

1. Was civilization invented by the Greeks or passed to them?
2. How did Mycenaean Greek civilization differ from Hellenic civilization?
3. What contributed to the development of the *polis*?
4. Was Athens' experiment with democracy a success or a failure?

5. What does Greek history suggest about the influence of wars on civilization?
6. How did humanism manifest itself in the science, art, and literature of the Hellenic era?

Refer to the front of the book for a list of chapter-relevant primary sources available on the CD-ROM.

THE WEST INTERACTIVE

For web-based activities, map explorations, and quizzes related to this chapter, go to *www.prenhall.com/frankforter.*

CHAPTER 5

THE HELLENISTIC ERA
AND THE RISE OF ROME

No one is so intellectually sluggish or indifferent as not to want to understand how the Romans (in less than fifty-three years) conquered, and how they now govern, practically the whole inhabited world—an accomplishment that has no historical precedent.

—**Polybius**

Larger Issue: *Are popular governments always preferable to monarchies?*

Greek intellectuals tended to feel superior to non-Greeks, but Polybius (c. 201–120 B.C.E.) was an exception. He admired the Romans even though they repeatedly invaded his homeland, defeated its armies, and in 168 B.C.E. carted him and a thousand of his fellows off to Rome as hostages. In Rome he was treated more as a guest than a prisoner and was admitted to the highest levels of Roman society. Publius Cornelius Scipio Aemilianus Africanus Numantinus (185–129 B.C.E.), whose imposing name catalogued his aristocratic connections and professional achievements, became his friend, and for sixteen years Polybius enjoyed an insider's view of the workings of the Roman Republic.

Polybius's acute awareness of Greece's political problems contributed to his respect for his captor-hosts. The Greeks were better at the arts of war than those of peace. About 130 years before Polybius's birth, Alexander the Great had distracted the Greeks from fighting among themselves by turning their attention to the conquest of the Persian Empire. He led them on a triumphant march from the Aegean to Egypt and east to the Indus River Valley. At Alexander's death, his great empire came apart, and the Greeks returned to making war on one another.

The Romans shared Indo-European ancestry and many other things with the Greeks. Their civilization developed more slowly, but Polybius believed that they would ultimately solve problems that had defeated the Greeks. Romans did not just conquer lands; they held on to them. In Polybius's day, they had no philosophy, science, art, or literature that compared to the products of Greek civilization (which they were eagerly assimilating), but Polybius thought that the world had much to learn from the Roman Republic's political and military achievements. Time has vindicated his faith. Rome created the largest and most long-lived empire the West has yet seen, and centuries after its fall, its memory continued to influence the course of Western societies. Leaders as different as feudal kings, medieval popes, French philosophers, Russian czars, German kaisers, and American revolutionaries all laid claim to Rome's legacy.

The stability and longevity of Rome's empire was a hard-won prize for which the Romans paid dearly. The Roman Republic acquired a territorial empire long before it developed a viable imperial government. As the Republic struggled to manage the lands it conquered, it degenerated into civil war. Peace was not achieved until the Romans jettisoned their republican traditions and submitted to monarchy. As you study their history, reflect on the problems all forms of popular government face as they try to reconcile their inherent inefficiency with their need for a strong executive.

TOPICS IN THIS CHAPTER

The Hellenistic Era • The Origin of Rome • The Roman Republic • Rome's Civil War

The Hellenistic Era

The Peloponnesian War (432–404 B.C.E.) had no winner. Athens yielded to Sparta, but Sparta collapsed under the burdens of victory. Sparta owed its military preeminence to a unique social system that enabled it to field the only full-time professional army in Greece. The lengthy Peloponnesian conflict neutralized that advantage by professionalizing the armies of many Greek *poleis*. Thebes finally dispelled the myth of Spartan invincibility by routing Sparta's armies in fair fights, but Thebes failed to fill the leadership vacuum left by Sparta's decline. Greece's *poleis* formed leagues and alliances, and fell to fighting among themselves. War became a major Greek industry—producing hordes of mercenaries who found employment at home and abroad.

This dismal situation convinced some Greeks that their compatriots were incapable of self-government. Men as different as the philosopher Plato (c. 429–347 B.C.E.), the soldier-historian Xenophon (c. 435–354 B.C.E.), and the Athenian orator Isocrates (436–338 B.C.E.) advocated some form of monarchy. Their hope was that an individual with a unique genius for leadership would unite the Greeks and protect them from their ancient enemy, Persia.

Macedonia Takes Control   When people decide that they need a savior, candidates for the job appear. Greece's savior emerged from an unexpected quarter, from the semibarbarous kingdom of Macedonia on the northern rim of the Greek mainland. The Macedonians were a tribal people who had not taken to life in *poleis* and who had even backed the Persians against their fellow Greeks in the Persian Wars. In the mid-fifth century B.C.E., however, Macedonian kings decided to Hellenize their subjects. They established a capital at Pella and ornamented their court with artists, craftsmen, and intellectuals imported from the more advanced Greek states. Men as distinguished as Athens' tragic playwright Euripides and the philosopher-scientist Aristotle entered their service. Despite this, Macedonia remained a rough, politically volatile country. The hereditary chiefs of its tribes were powerful, and coups and battles shortened the lives of its kings. Eight men ascended Macedonia's throne during the first four decades of the fourth century B.C.E.

In 360 B.C.E. King Perdiccas III died in battle, and his brother, Philip II (r. 360–336 B.C.E.), won the ensuing struggle for the crown. Philip had spent two or three years of his youth as a hostage in Thebes. This had given him a chance to observe Greek politics at close hand and to acquire training in the best Greek military techniques. Philip used what he had learned to transform the Macedonian army and unite his kingdom's tribal factions.

During the 350s B.C.E. some *poleis* sought Philip's help in their wars with their neighbors, and this gave him an excuse to intervene in the affairs of the Greek states. As one war led to another, the Athenian orator Demosthenes (384–322 B.C.E.) tried to rally opposition to Philip in the name of defending democracy, but in 338 B.C.E. the Macedonian army won a decisive victory over Athens and Thebes at Chaeronea. Further resistance seemed futile, so most of the mainland states accepted Philip's invitation to a peace conference to be held at Corinth in 337 B.C.E. At the meeting, Philip persuaded the Greeks to join him in an attack on Persia, but on the eve of this campaign he was assassinated. His son, Alexander (who may have been implicated in his murder) seized the Macedonian throne.

Alexander (III) the Great   Alexander was not cast in the mold of his father. Philip was a brute of a man who enjoyed physically and psychologically intimidating others. Alexander, who had the slight build of a runner, was distinguished by will and nervous energy more than muscle. His youthful appearance was enhanced by his habit of shaving, a custom that spread as his reputation grew. Alexander (r. 336–323 B.C.E.) was only twenty years old when his father died, but he had considerable military experience. He commanded the elite cavalry unit in Philip's army that carried the day for the Macedonians at the crucial battle of Chaeronea.

Alexander assured the Greeks that he was going to lead them in the Persian War his father had proposed, but he had to delay its start. He was not the only man with a claim to Philip's throne, and his survival was uncertain. Young, untried rulers face tests to their authority, and Alexander spent the first year of his reign eliminating potential rivals and fighting for control of his kingdom. Anti-Macedonian Greeks confidently anticipated his failure and began to scheme against him. This ended when he suddenly descended on Thebes, the plot's ringleader, and destroyed the city. Similar acts of terrorism might have forced the Greeks to cooperate temporarily, but Alexander knew that he could not hold them against their will while trying to conquer Persia. After he departed for Persia, they would inevitably have rebelled and isolated him in enemy territory. His survival depended on inspiring them with genuine enthusiasm for him and his campaign.

Alexander left Greece, never to return, in the spring of 334 B.C.E. His army was ludicrously small for the task he set it. He had about thirty-seven thousand men, but over twenty-three thousand of these were Greek allies whose loyalty was doubtful. The core of Alexander's army consisted of twelve thousand Macedonian infantrymen and eighteen hundred cavalry, most of whom were more closely tied to their hereditary chiefs (Philip's contemporaries) than to their young king.

Alexander was ahead of his time in understanding what good public relations can do for a ruler. At the campaign's start, he made a side trip to Troy to sacrifice at what was said to be the grave of Achilles, the hero of the *Iliad*. He wanted the Greeks to link the war on which they were embarking with the epic victory their Homeric ancestors had won over Greece's first eastern enemy. Alexander may also have begun the development of something like the modern press corps. It was a troop of scholars, headed by Calisthenes (the nephew of Alexander's boyhood tutor, Aristotle). Its job was to build enthusiasm for the campaign by providing the homeland with reports of its progress and descriptions of the exotic lands it conquered.

Alexander desperately needed a quick victory that would assure his men that he could deliver what he promised. The Persians might have defeated him by retreating. As they drew him deep into their territory, his soldiers would have grown increasingly fearful until they turned against him and fled home. The Persians chose instead to give Alexander exactly what he had to have. They made a stand at the Granikos River in western Asia Minor (334 B.C.E.).

Figure 5–1   Portrait of Alexander   No one can be certain of the accuracy of ancient portraits, which were usually idealized for purposes of propaganda. Alexander was always depicted as a beardless youth.

Alexander understood that he would have no second chances in this war. Only by appearing utterly self-confident and invincible could he distract his men from the odds they faced. At the first hint of failure, they were likely to panic and desert him. Therefore, he threw everything he had into every engagement. He commanded the most dangerous positions and performed heroic acts that inspired his men to comparable feats. The strategy worked, but it placed an all but unbearable burden on Alexander. The king's injuries mounted as the war progressed. He was often ill. The hardships of the march sapped his strength, and the stress of command tested his will.

At Granikos the ferocity of Alexander's attack swept the Persians from the field, but Alexander resisted the temptation to pursue them. He slowed the pace of the march and spent a year exploiting his victory, building the morale of his men, and picking up allies. It was the spring of 333 B.C.E. before he reached the Taurus Mountains and crossed from Asia Minor into Syria. The Persian emperor, Darius III (r. 336–330 B.C.E.) was eager to confront him, but faulty intelligence led the Persian army astray. By the time Darius found Alexander, impatience may have been clouding the emperor's judgment. At the Issos River on the Syrian coast he committed himself to a battle on a narrow field where he could not deploy his superior numbers. Alexander struck the center of the Persian line, and when Darius pulled back, his men panicked and fled. (See Map 5–1.)

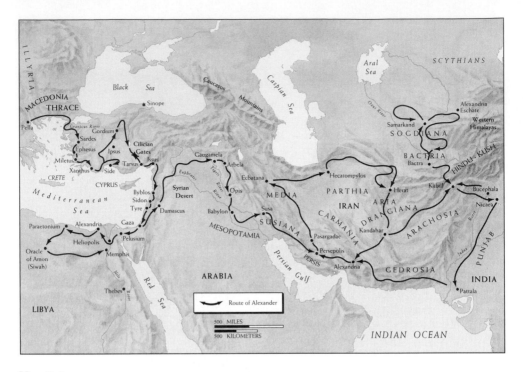

Map 5–1

Alexander's Adventure   Alexander executed one of history's most extraordinary military campaigns. After winning the Persian Empire, the prize for which his men had signed on, Alexander persuaded them to march farther and farther east into territory unknown to the Greeks. He was preparing to invade China when he died and was rumored to have had a plan for the conquest of the western Mediterranean. **Question:** Does Alexander's route suggest that he had a rational plan for conquering an empire?

Darius retreated from Issos in disarray, but Alexander did not go after him. Alexander could not risk proceeding inland, for the Persians controlled the sea. If Darius's navy had invaded the Aegean, Alexander would have had to go home to defend Greece. Because Alexander had no ships with which to challenge the Persians at sea, the only way he could neutralize their fleet was to take all of the ports from which it operated. This required arduous sieges of city after city until the whole coast as far as Egypt was in Greek hands.

By July 331 B.C.E., Alexander was finally free to leave Egypt and strike inland to challenge Darius. Darius wisely waited for Alexander to come to him and chose a battlefield that gave him all the advantages. The Persians dug in at Gaugamela, an arid plain north of Babylon. It provided ample space for them to maneuver and forced the Greeks to camp in a place that had no water. Despite the Persians' superior numbers and position, the Greeks triumphed at Gaugamela, but they were never entirely sure how. Dust and poor communications prevented anyone from having an overview of the battle.

Darius's army may have been too large for its own good. At any rate, it was thrown into confusion by Alexander's attacks, and Darius had to flee once again. Babylon submitted. The Greeks claimed the imperial treasury at Susa and made their winter camp at the Persian capital, Persepolis. The following spring, Alexander renewed the campaign. When Darius ordered another retreat, his disgruntled officers assassinated him.

The Greeks had done what they set out to do—conquer the Persian Empire. Most assumed, therefore, that it was time to go home, but Alexander persuaded them to continue the war a little longer. He led them farther and farther east into unknown territory. They wandered through the foothills of the Himalayan Mountains and finally descended into the Indus River Valley. At that point, they dug in their heels and refused to go on. Alexander agreed to lead them home, but only if they vowed to return and resume their conquests and to fight their way back through new territory. The Greeks battled their way down the Indus River to the Indian Ocean and then endured a brutal march across the wastes of the Gedrosian desert. A remnant of the army staggered back to Babylon, where Alexander threw himself into organizing his conquests and planning future campaigns.

Alexander did not have the manpower to occupy his huge empire and hold it by force. He had to induce his non-Greek subjects to submit to him voluntarily. His plan was to bolster his legitimacy in their eyes by interfering as little as possible with their customary way of life. The Persian Empire was composed of districts called *satrapies*. Their borders were drawn to respect the ethnic identities of their inhabitants. Alexander appointed a native governor (who knew the local customs) to handle each satrapy's civil affairs, a Greek to deal with its fiscal administration, and a Macedonian to provide for its defense. This gave the residents of a satrapy at least one leader with whom they could identify and made it difficult for any official to take over a satrapy and use it against the central government.

Alexander demanded extraordinary things of himself, and he finally exhausted his physical resources. On May 29, 323 B.C.E., following an all-night drinking bout with his officers, he fell ill. His fever rose. He sank into a coma, and on June 10, 323 B.C.E., he quietly died. There were rumors that he had been poisoned, but no evidence of foul play was uncovered. Fevers were common in swampy Babylon, and Alexander's arduous lifestyle must have sapped his strength and weakened his resistance.

The Hellenistic Environment   Alexander was only thirty-two when he died, and he was not the kind of man who cared to think about mortality. Death surprised him before he had provided himself with a successor. Alexander's primary emotional attachments were homosexual. He delayed marriage, and he had no children by mistresses. In 327 B.C.E. he had wed an Iranian princess named Roxane, and after returning to Babylon, he had also married one of Darius's daughters. Both women may have been pregnant at the time of his death. The Persian princess did not long outlive Alexander, but Roxane made him the posthumous father of a son, Alexander IV. Alexander's generals declared themselves regents for the infant, sent him to Macedonia to be raised, and set about carving up his empire. This inaugurated a period of shifting alliances and bloody conflicts. By 317 B.C.E. the surviving generals had disposed of Alexander's son, wife, and mother, and the outlines for a lasting division of his empire had emerged. The Aegean and the Macedonian throne went to Antigonus the One-Eyed (d. 301 B.C.E.). Seleukos (c. 358–280 B.C.E.), governor of Babylon, claimed the Persian heartland, and Ptolemy (d. 285 B.C.E.), one of Alexander's boyhood friends, made himself pharaoh of Egypt. Ptolemy also highjacked Alexander's body and enshrined it in a mausoleum in Alexandria, a great port in the Egyptian delta that Alexander had founded.

Alexander's empire did not survive, but his imperial conquests had lasting significance. They marked the end of the Hellenic (Greek) period and the beginning of the Hellenistic

(Greek-like) phase in Western civilization (c. 336 B.C.E. to 14 C.E.). Greeks had always avoided mixing with "barbarians" (non-Greeks), but Alexander believed that a blending of peoples and cultures was essential for the survival of his empire. He promoted intermarriage and adopted Persian customs at his court.

The garrisons that were posted throughout Alexander's empire grew into Greek towns that spread Hellenic culture as far east as India. It is debatable how much influence the Greeks had on indigenous peoples, but these peoples clearly influenced the Greeks. As thousands of Greeks migrated to the new towns that had been founded in the wake of Alexander's armies, they became a more cosmopolitan people. Their widening view of the world even affected their language. Its grammar and syntax simplified, and its vocabulary grew much richer as it assimilated words from other tongues. This new *koine* ("common") Greek became the international medium of communication. When the Romans added the eastern rim of the Mediterranean to their empire in the first century B.C.E., they found Greek so well established that they used it rather than imposing Latin. Many Romans were bilingual, and the early Christians (even those who were born Jews) wrote their New Testament in *koine* Greek instead of the language of the Hebrew scriptures.

The Hellenistic era witnessed the decline of the *polis,* the institution that had nurtured Hellenism. This signaled a significant change in the context for civilized life in the Mediterranean world. Small, self-governing city-states had failed to maintain order in the Greek world. As they succumbed to the builders of empires, political power shifted from their citizens to the bureaucrats who administered those empires. The Hellenistic era exalted professionals over citizen-volunteers. This was not necessarily bad, for the highly trained specialists who served Hellenistic rulers were extremely competent and able to do great things. They laid out orderly cities and equipped them with magnificent temples, monuments, baths, theaters, and arenas. They built sewage systems. They constructed aqueducts to convey fresh water over great distances. They organized police forces, regulated commerce and food supplies, and generally made urban life far more comfortable, clean, and secure than it had ever been.

Hellenistic communities were as prosperous as they were well run. Alexander returned to circulation a great deal of gold that had been sealed away in Persia's coffers, and the consolidation of large territorial states by his successors made trade easier and promoted economic growth.

There was, of course, a cost for the comforts of the new societies. As governments grew larger and specialists assumed responsibility for more of their functions, the power of popular assemblies and elected officials declined. A citizen's vote meant little to a huge, centrally managed state, and it had no use for his amateur military service or advice. Even his labor was not all that important, for wars kept up the supply of inexpensive slaves who did much of society's essential work.

Hellenistic Civilization   The subjects of the Hellenistic states were prosperous and well cared for, but they were pawns of forces beyond their control. For those who came from *poleis* proud of their democratic traditions, this required some adjustment. The Hellenic *polis* affirmed the worth of the individual by demanding much from him, but a Hellenistic empire reduced the individual to a replaceable cog in the machinery of a great state. The world of the *polis* was human in scale and amenable to control, but empires rendered their subjects small and impotent.

The art and literature of the Hellenistic era reflect the period's new sociopolitical environment. Theater flourished, but playwrights steered clear of political issues and focused on

Culture in Context: History's First Research Institute

Greeks had confidence in the superiority of their civilization, but they were willing to learn from other peoples. The Hellenistic empires broadened their horizons and stimulated their intellectual curiosity. There was both public and private sponsorship for cultural activities in most *poleis*, and Hellenistic monarchs offered patronage on a regal scale. The Egyptian dynasty founded by Alexander's friend, Ptolemy I (r. 323–285 B.C.E.), was particularly generous to scholars. The Ptolemaic pharaohs established a library in Alexandria and set themselves the goal of obtaining a copy of every important book. They dispatched agents abroad in search of rare volumes. They funded translations (including one of the Hebrew scriptures), and they even searched the baggage of travelers entering Egypt, hoping to find interesting texts. The result was a collection that may have numbered almost a million items.

A research institute was attached to Alexandria's library. It was called the Museum, the home of the Muses (the nine female deities who, according to Hesiod, preside over the arts). Some of the Museum's scholars devoted their lives to refining the library's collection. They compiled dictionaries and catalogues, and wrote commentaries on classic texts. What their work lacked in originality, it made up for in quantity. A certain Didymus of Alexandria is said to have written thirty-five hundred books—not one of which survives!

Pedantry did not characterize all the work at the Museum. Some of its scholars pioneered new literary genres. The most popular of these was a sophisticated pastoral poetry that romanticized rural life and reveled in obscure, learned references. The Museum was especially noted for encouraging progress in the sciences and mathematics. Euclid (fl. c. 300 B.C.E.) wrote the text that made his name synonymous with geometry, and Archimedes of Syracuse (c. 287–212 B.C.E.) laid the groundwork for calculus. Eratosthenes of Cyrene (c. 270–194 B.C.E.) calculated Earth's circumference with remarkable accuracy. Hipparchus of Nicaea (fl. 160–125 B.C.E.) made precise calendar calculations. Aristarchus of Samos (fl. c. 275 B.C.E.) advanced the theory that Earth was a globe that rotated on an axis and revolved around the sun, but for the next fifteen hundred years, most astronomers supported the contention of a non-royal Ptolemy of Alexandria (fl. c. 130 C.E.) that the sun revolves around Earth. The Hippocratic medical texts were edited at the Museum, and some of its physicians conducted important anatomical research. Herophilius of Chalcedon (fl. c. 270 B.C.E.) mapped the sensory nerves and identified the brain as the center of a nervous system. Although capillaries were too small to be seen by the naked eye, Erasistratus of Ceos (fl. c. 260 B.C.E.) hypothesized that veins and arteries were connected, a prelude to the discovery of blood circulation and the function of the heart.

Alexandrian technicians and engineers produced marvelous gadgets that ranged from useful pumps and astronomical instruments to amusing toys (one of which was a working model of a steam turbine). To the modern mind, the most puzzling thing about all of this activity is that so little of it found practical application. Hellenistic society was slave-based. Its educated classes were not motivated to think of ways to make work easier, and its workers had little freedom to innovate.

Question: How was scientific work encouraged as well as discouraged in the environment of the Hellenistic empires?

entertainment. Aristophanes, the master of Hellenic Old Comedy, used laughter to make people think, but Hellenistic New Comedy was the ancient world's equivalent of a television "sitcom." It relied on stock characters and plots that were as silly as they were predictable. Persons who wanted comparable entertainment at home turned to the era's new literary genre, the novel. The most popular novels were erotic romances set in exotic places or idealized bucolic locales. They conjured up fantasy worlds and provided escapist entertainment for literate urbanites.

Hellenistic architecture and visual arts, like the era's literature, appealed to emotion more than to intellect. Buildings grew large and imposing. The first skyscraper (a 400-foot tall lighthouse) was erected on an island in the harbor of Alexandria. The city of Ephesus on the coast of Asia Minor built a temple to Diana that was almost five times the size of Athens' Parthenon, the largest of the mainland's Hellenic temples. The port of Rhodes erected a bronze statue of the sun god that was 130 feet taller than America's Statue of Liberty. Sculptors developed incredible technique that imparted stunning realism to their work, and they expanded their range far beyond the Hellenic era's idealized male athletes. They sought out subjects that were novel and emotionally stirring: portraits of individuals, erotic female nudes, cute children and animals, persons suffering the ravages of age and poverty, and men and women in the throes of death or extreme passions. The human ideal, the art of the democratic *polis*, lost some of its relevance for the subjects of the Hellenistic empires. They lacked the political freedoms that gave dignity and meaning to *polis* citizenship and made Hellenic ideals worth striving for. What they wanted was art that dispelled boredom and affirmed the values of uniqueness and individuality that the imperial context diminished.

Hellenistic philosophy was largely consistent with the escapism of Hellenistic art and literature—with some major exceptions. Aristotle, Alexander's tutor, was one of the greatest minds the ancient world produced. Plato trained him, but he did not share Plato's belief that knowledge of truth came from the contemplation of abstract ideas. Aristotle was devoted to the study of the concrete and particular. He collected great amounts of information about all kinds of things and developed theories spanning an incredible range of subjects: animal and plant species, sexual reproduction, gendered behaviors, political systems, poetry, mathematics, logic, and metaphysics. His work was comprehensive, and his influence was enormous. But in a way he belonged to the era that was ending rather than to the one that was beginning.

Aristotle shared the Hellenic philosophers' curiosity about the natural world and the human community. But the new schools of Hellenistic philosophy were less interested in scientific research than in developing "philosophies of life." All of them urged people to distance themselves in some way from the world around them. Zeno (335–263 B.C.E.), the founder of the Stoics, preached acceptance of the inevitable. He maintained that everyone had a preordained place in the universe's unalterable, rational system. Fulfillment lay in doing the duties of one's station while cultivating an emotional detachment that preserved inner peace. Stoics warned that people could not control what happened to them but claimed that they could control their emotional responses to life's vicissitudes. Zeno's contemporary, Epicurus (341–270 B.C.E.), also taught in Athens. Epicureans believed that everything that existed (including the human soul) was the result of random, temporary conjunctions of atoms and that nothing, therefore, had meaning or permanence. Because lasting achievements were impossible, life's only purpose was the enjoyment of pleasure. True pleasure was tranquility, a state undisturbed by extreme emotions of any kind. Individuals who retreated from the world to "cultivate their gardens" had the best chance of achieving happiness, for they avoided

Figure 5-2   The Celtic Chieftain   This copy of a third century B.C.E. statue illustrates the dramatic nature of Hellenistic art. It depicts a barbarian chief who prefers to slaughter his wife and himself (note the bleeding wound at the point of his sword's entry) rather than surrender.

situations that might stir the emotions. The followers of Diogenes of Sinope (c. 400–325 B.C.E.) were called Cynics ("dogs"). Diogenes claimed that fulfillment derived from self-sufficiency, and self-sufficiency was achieved by minimizing one's needs and obligations. The Cynics were likened to dogs because, like animals, they spurned all social conventions and freely and openly did whatever came naturally. Diogenes lived in the street, expressed contempt for authority, and performed intimate bodily functions in public. The Cynics, Epicureans, and Stoics all agreed that individuals had no mastery over the world; the best they could do was to master themselves. This was a far less optimistic assessment of human potential than the visions that had inspired the social engineers of the Hellenic *poleis*.

The Origin of Rome

Hellenistic civilization spread to, and was spread by, the Romans. The Latins (Rome's founders) took to it readily, for they had much in common with the Greeks. Both peoples had Indo-European ancestry, and their languages were closely related. They settled in their respective homelands at about the same time (c. 1900 B.C.E.), and their cultures evolved in similar environments. The early Greeks, however, had the advantage of close contacts with the civilizations of the Middle East.

The Italian Environment   The Aegean Sea and its many islands facilitated communication between Greece and the Middle East, but Italy faced west. Like the Greek mainland, Italy is a mountainous peninsula. All its major agricultural plains and most of its natural harbors are on its western coast, and the Apennine mountain chain forms a spine along its eastern edge that makes access from the Adriatic Sea difficult.

The Greeks planted Naples (Nea-polis, "New Town") and other colonies on Campania, Italy's southwestern plain, in the mid-eighth century B.C.E. At the same time, the Etruscans, a people whose origin remains a mystery, built prosperous city-states on the plain of Etruria (Tuscany) north of the Tiber River. The Latins took their name from the small plain of Latium ("flat land") that lay between Campania and Etruria. North of Etruria and the Apennines lay the great basin of the Po River. It was inhabited by Celtic tribes and considered by the Romans to belong to Gaul more than Italy. (See Map 5–2.)

The Kingdom of Rome   The Romans were aware that their Latin ancestors had lived in Latium for a long time before they established Rome, but they knew little about them. Homer's epics provided the classical world with what it thought of as its earliest history, so the Romans looked to Homer to supply them with a past. Because Romans were not Greeks, they assumed that they had a connection with the *Iliad*'s other nation, the Trojans. Their myths claimed that a Trojan prince named Aeneas escaped Troy's fall and emigrated to Latium, where he married Lavinia, daughter of the native king, Latinus. Thirteen generations of their descendants reigned over Latium before Rome's founders, the twins Romulus and Remus, were born to a Latin princess and Mars, the Latin god of war. The city that Romulus founded (and that bore his name) began as a rough frontier post populated by outcasts and women abducted from the surrounding region. Although this Roman myth of national origin was fanciful, it contained some truth.

The traditional date for Rome's founding was April 21, 753 B.C.E. Archaeological evidence confirms the existence of primitive villages on the hills next to the Tiber in the mid-eighth century and suggests why the Latins might have planted them there at that time. Rome commanded the first spot inland from the coast (about twenty miles) where the Tiber River narrowed enough to be bridged. When the Greek and Etruscan civilizations that were flourishing on either side of Latium in the mid-eighth century began to take an interest in the trade routes that converged at Rome's site, the Latins hastened to occupy this corner of their territory.

Seven kings are said to have reigned over Rome from 753 B.C.E. to 509 B.C.E. They ruled in tandem with an aristocratic council called the Senate (*senex*, "elder"). Most of the stories told about the monarchy are legends, but some historical information can be gleaned from them. Etruscan names are recorded for two of Rome's kings, and it is unlikely that the Romans

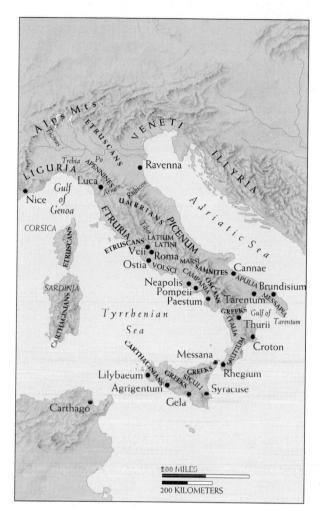

Map 5–2
The Rise of Rome The Apennine Mountains create a crescent-shaped wall that impedes access to Italy from the east and cradles the three western plains (Campania, Latium, and Etruria) where ancient Italy's urban communities developed. *Question:* Did Rome's location destine it to become the seat of a great empire?

would have invented a memory of a time when outsiders ruled their city if this had not been the case. There is ample evidence of Etruscan influence on Roman institutions and customs, but this does not necessarily imply Etruscan occupation of Rome. The Romans may have chosen Etruscan leaders to strengthen commercial or political ties with Etruria.

The Etruscans   Much that was unique about Rome can be traced to the Etruscans, but the Etruscans themselves remain something of a mystery. Their language does not appear to be related to any known tongue and has yet to be translated. Their cities developed very quickly (possibly in response to the trade that was increasing between Italy and the eastern Mediterranean in the eighth century B.C.E.). Etruria had a benign climate, fertile fields, and accessible deposits of metal ores. The skills of its gold and bronze workers were second to none. Etruscan traders had much to offer, and they took to the sea to compete with Greek and Phoenician merchants.

Stories circulated in the Greek and Latin worlds about the luxury and permissiveness of Etruscan society. The Greeks were shocked by the freedom enjoyed by Etruscan women, and the Romans, who wrested austere livings from small plots of poor land, insisted that the Etruscans' self-indulgent custom of feasting twice a day was evidence of their moral laxity. Some Etruscans were rich, for they built expensive subterranean chamber-tombs that replicated their lavishly furnished homes and banqueting halls. The favorite design for a sarcophagus was a dining couch with an effigy of the deceased reclining on its lid—at ease in festive clothes, wine cup in hand. Etruscan graves have yielded some of the finest specimens of pottery, jewelry, and bronze work to survive from the classical era.

The Etruscans may have been connoisseurs of life's pleasures, but wealth did not make them soft. They dominated Italy until the mid-fifth century. Their decline was caused, at least in part, by the failure of their independent city-states to cooperate in meeting the challenge posed by the Greeks. The Greeks planted colonies on both sides of Etruria and battled the Etruscans for control of the sea.

The Romans owed many of their political and social customs to the Etruscans, but it was in the area of religion that they were most aware of their debt. Numerous colleges of priests perpetuated ancient rituals and sacrifices of Etruscan origin, and the Romans were especially in awe of Etruscan diviners and soothsayers. Romans saw omens everywhere and studied them before undertaking any project. Long after the Etruscans disappeared, the Romans preserved their language for use by the priests who conducted arcane religious rites. A similar fate was, of course, one day to befall Latin.

The Roman Republic

Rome made significant progress under the leadership of its later kings, one or more of whom had ties with the Etruscan city of Tarquini. The Romans drained the swampy lowland that separated the hills on which they lived to create the Forum, a place for markets and assemblies. They built the largest temple in Italy on the Capitoline hill, and archaeological evidence suggests that they enjoyed a rising standard of living.

Kings may not deserve all the credit for early Rome's progress, for they operated under the watchful eye of the city's Senate. Relations between the monarch and the aristocratic families represented in the Senate must often have been strained. Few of Rome's kings (including the city's founder) were said to have died peacefully in their beds, and eventually the Senators decided to dispense with kings and govern the city themselves.

The Roman Revolution   Legends blame Sextus, the aptly named son of King Tarquinius Superbus (Tarquin the Proud), for the fall of his father's throne. In 509 B.C.E. Sextus supposedly raped a virtuous Roman matron named Lucretia, a deed that so infuriated the Romans that they drove out the Tarquins and vowed never again to submit to a king. The story is probably fanciful, but the revolution was real.

The republic that the revolutionaries established to govern Rome was not a democracy. It limited political privileges to the male members of the city's "patrician" families. Early Rome was a federation of extended families, and for reasons that even the Romans could not explain, citizen families were divided into two classes: the noble patricians and the common plebeians. In the republic, only the former could hold political offices and priesthoods.

Table 5–1 The Greek and Roman Pantheons

Greek Gods	Roman Equivalents	
Zeus	Jupiter	*The Greeks and Romans both were Indo-European people, so it is*
Hera	Juno	*not surprising that their state religions were similar. However, few*
Athena	Minerva	*of their gods and goddesses had Indo-European ancestry. Zeus or*
Apollo	[Apollo]	*Jupiter (Deiw-pitar, "Father of the Bright Sky") had impeccable*
Artemis	Diana	*Indo-European credentials, but some of his children (Apollo, for*
Hephaestus	Vulcan	*instance) had Middle-Eastern origins.*
Aphrodite	Venus	*Comparable gods did not always have the same significance*
Ares	Mars	*for Greeks and Romans. Mars, for example, loomed large*
Demeter	Ceres	*in the Roman pantheon as the god who brought victory*
Poseidon	Neptune	*in war. Ares, his Greek double, was a far less respected deity,*
Hades	Pluto	*symbol of the negative passions that spark conflict.*
Hestia	Vesta	
Hermes	Mercury	
Dionysus	Bacchus	

Family was such an important indicator of status that each Roman male needed three names to indicate the place he occupied in the social order. The first was one of a few common names used only by close friends. The second identified his *gens*, the great clan to which his paternal ancestors belonged. The third indicated his birth family. If his achievements were notable, the city might commemorate them by granting him a fourth name. The winner of a war in Africa, for example, bore the ponderous name Publius Cornelius Scipio Africanus Major.

A Roman *familia* included not only immediate blood kin but all the dependents of the household—including slaves. The male head of a *familia*, the *paterfamilias*, had absolute authority over all its members. His sons never outgrew his power, and he could, if he wished, order their execution.

Some of Rome's plebeian families were as ancient as (and richer than) their patrician superiors. The Senate expected them to contribute their men to its army, but it refused to allow them any role in government. Not surprisingly, they refused to accept this, and the challenges they mounted to the patrician monopoly of political power (the "struggle of the orders") dominated the early history of the republic. The plebeians were able to force concessions from the Senate, because the patricians needed their help to defend the city. Whenever the Senate balked at their demands, they threatened a military strike. These confrontations often ended in compromises that, over the course of two centuries, forged a complex constitution for the republic.

In 471 B.C.E. the plebeians set up an assembly of their own headed by ten magistrates called tribunes. In 451 B.C.E. they won acceptance of the Twelve Tables, a law code establishing a common standard of justice for all citizens. In 445 B.C.E. marriage between patrician and plebeian families was legalized, and elective offices began to be opened to plebeian candidates. In 287 B.C.E. the Hortensian Law made plebiscites (votes by the people) binding on all Romans. This granted legislative authority to the people, but the result was hardly a triumph for democracy. The end product of the struggle of the orders was a complicated system of checks and balances that allowed a few wealthy families to dominate the republic.

The machinery of the republic was designed to prevent any individual from acquiring enough power to reestablish monarchy. All elected magistrates served terms of only one year, and they were forbidden to seek reelection. The duties of the chief executive were shared by two consuls—the expectation being that each would keep the other in check. The consuls' authority over soldiers in the field (their *imperium*) was absolute, but their power in the city was limited. To prevent them from seizing control of Rome, their armies were strictly forbidden to cross the *pomerium,* the city's sacred boundary. If the Senate wished to honor a general, it showed its trust by suspending this rule and granting him a "triumph" (permission to parade his men through the city).

The struggle of the orders broke down many of the walls that divided plebeians from patricians. This did not do much for ordinary people, but it cleared the way for wealthy plebeian and patrician families to cooperate in running the republic. The diffusion of power in Rome made alliances necessary and encouraged influence peddling and a system of patronage. The poorer citizens needed the support and protection of those who were richer and more powerful. A patron advertised his importance by parading through the streets accompanied by a crowd of his clients. They gave him political clout, for they voted as he commanded or risked losing his support. (The secret ballot was not introduced until 139 B.C.E.) No poor man could marshal enough votes to be elected to an office, and if he had, he could not have afforded to serve. The republic's magistrates were not paid, and they were expected to fund the costs of their offices from their private fortunes. A man who wanted a major office also had to spend years pursuing it. A tradition known as the *cursus honorem* ("path of honors") decreed that a man had to win a series of lower offices before he qualified to run for higher ones.

The Roman Republic was so far from what we would regard as an equitable popular government that we might wonder why the Romans were so attached to it. They, of course, did not have the advantage of our perspective and did not feel deprived of rights they had never imagined. But they also had a good reason to be proud of their republic. It won them an empire.

The Republic Acquires an Empire   At the start of the fifth century, Rome was a tiny, landlocked city-state that had no obvious potential to become an imperialistic power. Its survival was threatened by enemies that attacked from every direction: Etruscan, Greek, Latin, and Celtic. Time and again, however, the Romans rose to the challenge and built on their victories by treating those whom they defeated generously. The republic annexed some territory and garrisoned a few places with military colonies, but it created more allies than subjects. One by one, Italy's city-states (some eagerly and others lacking alternatives) joined Rome in a federation. They retained control over their domestic affairs, but submitted to Rome's foreign policy and contributed to its armies. The rights some allies had to trade with Rome, to migrate to Rome, and to marry Romans helped spread Roman customs and language and create a common culture for Italy.

Rome's consolidation of Italy was viewed with suspicion by the western Mediterranean's other major power, the Carthaginian empire. While the Greeks were planting their colonies in Sicily and Italy in the mid-eighth century B.C.E., their seafaring competitors, the Phoenicians, were colonizing the Mediterranean's southern rim. Their chief outpost, the North African city of Carthage, emerged as the administrative center of a self-sufficient empire that closed the southwestern corner of the Mediterranean to outsiders. The primary threat to the Carthaginians came from the Greeks on the island of Sicily. Carthage believed that it had to hold the western end of Sicily to protect its sea lanes. (See Map 5–3.)

Sicily was perpetually at war. The Greeks fought among themselves and with the Carthaginians, and Syracuse, the largest Greek city on Sicily, sought to unite the island under its control. In 265 B.C.E., the Romans added to the confusion by acceding to a request from the Sicilian city of Messana for military assistance. (Messana commanded the narrow strait between Sicily and Italy through which Italy's shipping passed.) Carthage and Syracuse were both alarmed by Rome's intervention in their sphere of influence, and the situation quickly escalated into a major conflict called the First Punic (Phoenician) War (264–241 B.C.E.). The war dragged on because Carthage and Rome were incompatible military powers. Carthage fought at sea with its navy, and Rome campaigned on land with its army. Neither made much progress until Rome built a navy and set out to meet Carthage on its own terms. Carthage finally decided that the war was not worth its cost, and it ceded Sicily to Rome in exchange for peace.

The Romans had not set out to conquer Sicily, but the war convinced them that they had to hold the island to prevent anyone from using it as base for invading Italy. Because their

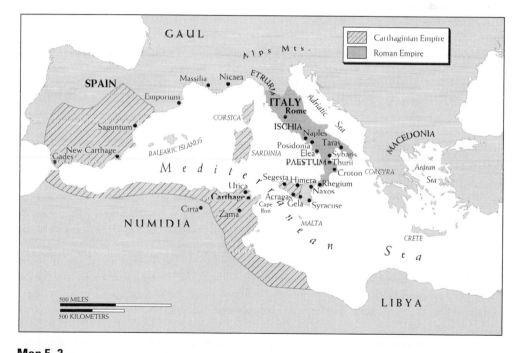

Map 5–3

Rome and Carthage Although the shaded areas on maps imply that the Romans and Carthaginians controlled large blocks of territory, in reality borders were vague, jurisdictions overlapped, and governmental authority was more effectively imposed in some places than on others. *Question:* Does the map support Rome's belief that Carthage was a threat to its security?

interests in Sicily were primarily defensive, they declared it a military province and turned it over to a Roman general. This first province in what was to become a Roman Empire altered the politics of the republic in unanticipated ways. Rome refused to shoulder the expense of maintaining its army in Sicily and ordered its commander to raise the funds he needed from the Sicilians themselves. This gave him an opportunity to loot the province and return to Rome much richer than when he left. He could then pour his new wealth into a campaign to win more offices and honors. As Rome's leaders discovered the advantage a provincial governorship gave a man in the game of Roman politics, the republic's foreign policy began to change.

By expanding into Spain, Carthage recovered from the First Punic War much more quickly than Rome expected. Its leading general, Hamilcar Barca (c. 270–228 B.C.E.), believed that things were not settled between his people and the Romans, and his suspicions increased in 238 B.C.E., when Rome ordered Carthage to cede it the island of Sardinia. Rome may only have wanted to make sure that Carthage could not use Sardinia to attack Italy, but by annexing Sardinia, it confirmed Carthage's fear that Rome was bent on its destruction. Hamilcar Barca's son, Hannibal (247–182 B.C.E.), inherited his father's belief that war with Rome was inevitable. The Romans, for their part, felt fairly secure. Control of the seas around Italy gave them confidence that if war came, it would be fought on Carthaginian territory.

When the Second Punic War (218–202 B.C.E.) broke out, the Romans dispatched their armies to Spain and Sicily. But Hannibal was not where they expected to find him. Publius Cornelius Scipio, the Roman commander of the Spanish expedition, was shocked to discover that Hannibal had already departed Spain with an army of thirty thousand men (and sixty famous elephants), crossed Gaul, and was heading over the Alps into northern Italy. Scipio hastily patched together another army, but the ease with which Hannibal routed it gave the Romans their first hint at the danger they faced. Hannibal won every major battle the Romans risked giving him (except the last). He devastated Italy and slaughtered its men, but the war dragged on for fourteen years. Hannibal had made a serious miscalculation. He had expected Rome's Italian allies to defect and join him, but most remained loyal to Rome. If Italy's cities were subjects of a Roman Empire, they were not eager to seize the chance Hannibal gave them to escape their subjugation.

Rome finally defeated Hannibal by refusing to fight him in Italy, while opening new fronts against the Carthaginians elsewhere. One Roman army dogged Hannibal's tracks in Italy and harassed his rearguard. Another overwhelmed his bases in Spain and his allies in Sicily, and a third finally took the war to North Africa. In 204 B.C.E. Hannibal was forced to pull his men out of Italy and take them home to defend Carthage. He fended off the Romans for two more years, but he was finally defeated by Scipio "Africanus," the son of the Scipio who had tried (and failed) to stop him when he first entered Italy. Carthage surrendered, and Hannibal fled to the Middle East, where he committed suicide to avoid capture by Rome's agents.

Carthage was allowed to survive—stripped of most of its territory and ships, and burdened with a huge war indemnity. Rome annexed Spain but ceded much of North Africa to Numidia, its ally in the war with Hannibal. The western Mediterranean was now indisputably Roman territory, but only portions of it were directly administered by Rome (which still had no plan for organizing an empire).

The Second Punic War had exhausted the Romans, but they leaped immediately into new campaigns in Greece. In 215 B.C.E. Philip V of Macedon (r. 221–179 B.C.E.) had allied with

Hannibal because he was afraid that Rome might use its naval bases at the mouth of the Adriatic to invade his realm. A war with his Greek neighbors prevented him from sending help to Hannibal, but that made no difference to Rome. Rome declared war on Philip in 200 B.C.E., and three years later he surrendered. Curiously, Rome annexed no territory but contented itself with liberating the Greek city-states from Macedonian control. So long as the Greeks were disunited and fighting among themselves, they posed no threat to Rome.

When a warring Greek faction invited the Seleucid emperor, Antiochus III (r. 223–187 B.C.E.), to come to its aid, Rome sent its armies back to Greece. Antiochus beat a hasty retreat. The Romans pursued him across the Aegean, and in 188 B.C.E. he yielded most of Asia Minor to Rome. Rome fought two more wars with Macedonia and the Greeks, and in 168 B.C.E. it tried to pacify Greece by taking a thousand prominent Greeks hostage (the historian Polybius among them). In 148 B.C.E. Rome finally turned Macedonia into a province, and in 146 B.C.E. Rome sacked the city of Corinth and put down the last of the Greek rebellions. In the same year, a Third Punic War (149–146 B.C.E.) ended with the obliteration of Carthage. Rome was now the dominant power in the Mediterranean world, but its imperial territory did not yet have an imperial government.

The Stress of Success   Rome's republican institutions were barely adequate for a city-state, and they were certainly not designed for the responsibilities of a vast empire. The new lands that Rome had acquired altered life for both the rich and the poor in ways that did neither class much good. Lax oversight of the provinces meant that most of the profits from the empire went into the pockets of military governors who used them to corrupt republican politics. The custom developed of giving a Roman magistrate a provincial command at the end of his year-long term in office. This prevented him from scheming to stay in power by getting him out of the city. But it also gave him a chance to recoup his finances and return to Rome with enough money to run for another office that would bring him another governorship. Because it was virtually impossible for an outsider to break into this cycle, about fifty families appropriated much of the empire's wealth and monopolized the republic's offices.

As the few rich grew richer, the empire's new provinces impoverished many of the soldiers who had conquered them. The Hannibalic war devastated Italy's farms, and long terms of military service prevented many men from caring for their land. When Rome's farmer soldiers finally returned home, many lacked the capital to rebuild their farms and those who had the money found that farming was no longer profitable. Grain was the small farmer's cash crop, but the Italian market was flooded with cheap grain from the provinces. Small domestic producers could not compete and had to sell out to wealthy investors who could afford to convert the land to more profitable uses. Rich families consolidated huge blocks of land and created *latifundia,* plantations that produced commercial crops (such as olives and wine) for the international market. These *latifundia* provided no employment for the Roman farmer whose land they absorbed, for Rome's wars created an excess of cheap slaves. As slaves took over much of the agricultural work, rural freemen had little choice but to flood into cities like Rome. The government distributed bread to keep them quiet, and they earned handouts by joining the armies of clients with which the great families fought their political battles.

The situation was so corrupt that by the middle of the second century B.C.E. even wealthy Romans feared that the republic might collapse. There were calls for reform, but two things made changing the system difficult. No one was sure what would work, and no one wanted anyone else to get credit for a program that did work. Matters came to a head in 133 B.C.E., when Tiberius Gracchus (168–133 B.C.E.), a tribune, proposed confiscating land from anyone who had more than 320 acres, dividing the surplus into small farms, and giving these to the poor. The office of tribune had been created to protect the plebeians, and each tribune had the power to block legislation that he thought was not in the people's interest by standing up in the assembly and saying *veto* ("I forbid!"). When Tiberius presented his land redistribution proposal, its opponents induced another tribune to cast a veto. Tiberius, however, was prepared for this. He persuaded the assembly to cast the man out of office—on the theory that he had not used his powers for the purpose for which they had been granted. Land reform passed, but at the cost of destroying one of the crucial checks and balances of the Roman constitution. If the mob could instantly depose any politician who displeased it, the republic would degenerate into mob rule. Tiberius's enemies, having no legal way to counter his maneuver, simply murdered him.

Tiberius's land redistribution plan was implemented, but it failed. Like many well-intended reforms, it addressed the symptom of a problem while ignoring its causes. It did nothing to change the situation that had forced small farmers off their land in the first place. Returning them to the land only set them up to fail again.

The strategy Tiberius invented to pass his reform program had a greater impact on the republic than did the reform itself, for it caused a new division in Roman politics. The *populares* ("people's party ") sought power, as Tiberius had, by championing ideas that appealed to the mob. The *optimates* ("aristocrats") defended the prerogatives of the Senate by affirming Rome's conservative traditions. Neither party had a platform of proposals designed to cure the ills of Roman society. Each was defined by the method it used for gaining political advantage.

In 123 B.C.E. Tiberius Gracchus's younger brother, Gaius (159–121 B.C.E.), took up the *populares* cause and made considerable headway until the *optimates* again took up arms. Rome's next leader, Gaius Marius (157–86 B.C.E.), learned a lesson from the fate of the two Gracchi that profoundly affected the course of Roman history. He concluded that to survive in the Roman political arena, a man had to have the backing of the army.

In 107 B.C.E. Marius won a consulship by promising to bring a war with Numidia to a speedy conclusion. He proposed beefing up the army by dropping the traditional property qualification for service. This was welcomed by the impoverished Roman masses who had no jobs and no prospects, for it gave them a chance to vote themselves military careers. The soldiers Marius created in this way were, however, more his than Rome's. By keeping him in office, they secured their own employment. Marius's reform turned Rome's army into a political machine that, contrary to tradition, elected its leader to one consulship after another.

Rome's Civil War

No one could compete with a man like Marius without building an army comparable to his, so every Roman politician who hoped to stay in the game now needed a military command. That meant that he also needed a war, for armies were only justified when there were wars. After years of being slow to acquire provinces, Rome's foreign policy changed. Its leaders began to look for lands to conquer as a means to the ultimate conquest: Rome itself.

Sulla   In 88 B.C.E. Sulla (138–78 B.C.E.), one of Marius's officers, revealed the danger at the heart of the new power politics. His army marched on Rome and forced the Senate to legitimate his command. After a profitable campaign in Asia Minor, Sulla retook Rome, assumed

✳ People in Context: Cornelia, Mother of the Gracchi

Roman women, like Greek women, were subject to male authority in theory, but they had much more freedom in practice. Roman girls could attend school, and Roman women were not confined to their homes. They followed politics and sometimes demonstrated in the streets to push for legislation they wanted. Women from prominent families were well-known public figures who exercised considerable influence. The most respected of these from the republican era was Tiberius and Gaius Gracchus's mother, Cornelia.

Roman women bore only one name, the feminine spelling of their father's *gens*. (All of a man's daughters had the same name.) Cornelia (c. 180–105 B.C.E.) was the daughter of Publius Cornelius Scipio Africanus, the victor in the Second Punic War. The husband to whom Scipio gave her (at age twelve) was a distinguished Roman considerably her senior, Tiberius Sempronius Gracchus. The marriage was fruitful. Cornelia bore him twelve children, alternating boys and girls. Only three survived to adulthood: Tiberius, Gaius, and their sister Sempronia (who married a Scipio to reaffirm the links between her parental families).

After her husband's death in 154 B.C.E., Cornelia elected to remain a widow and declined a proposal of marriage from the pharaoh of Egypt. She devoted herself to the education of her sons and was said to have fired their ambition by telling them that she was ashamed to be known as Scipio's daughter rather than the Gracchi's mother. Given Tiberius's bloody fate, she may have come to regret her words. Ancient historians cited letters (the authenticity of which modern scholars doubt) that she wrote to Gaius, urging him to moderate his radical politics. Her sons scored points with their audiences by mentioning her in their speeches, and her popularity was such that she became the first Roman woman, other than a priestess, to whom the Republic erected a statue. The bronze effigy has disappeared, but its inscribed base survives. We know what it looked like, for statues honoring other women took it as their model. It is hard to imagine such a monument being raised in Athens, where, according to Pericles, the best women were those who were totally invisible.

Question: What explains the fact that women were more liberated in the Roman republic than in the Athenian democracy?

---

dictatorial powers, and executed thousands of citizens. Although Sulla used the *populares* strategy to win control of Rome, he was an *optimates* reformer. He believed that Rome's difficulties had been caused by *populares* demagogues, and to prevent any more of them from appearing, he emasculated the popular assembly and restored the traditional dominance of the Senate.

Sulla's reform was as unrealistic as the Gracchan land redistribution scheme. The Senate could not defend the empire with magistrates who were hobbled by the traditional restraints of the republican constitution. A government in which every office changed hands every year lacked continuity and could not successfully wage lengthy foreign wars. Almost immediately, therefore, the Senate began to appoint "special commanders" to deal with its most difficult problems. What made a command "special" was its freedom from the limitations imposed on the regular magistrates. Ambitious men immediately recognized that the fastest route to power was not through the old *cursus honorem* but via a series of special commands.

The first of the great special commanders was Pompey (106–48 B.C.E.), a young *optimas* who was one of Sulla's supporters. His conservative credentials persuaded the Senate that he could be trusted, and his loyal service lulled the Senators into granting him one special command after another—culminating in a commission to sweep pirates from the Mediterranean. This warranted a massive army and navy, which Pompey used not only to suppress piracy but to extend the empire in the east to the borders of Egypt. The Senate ultimately awoke to the possibility that it had created another Sulla, and the only strategy it could think of to block him was to make more like him. They created special commands for Crassus (115–53 B.C.E.), reputedly Rome's richest man, and a brilliant blue blood named Julius Caesar (100–44 B.C.E.).

When Pompey returned from the east in 62 B.C.E., he surprised everyone by leaving his army behind. He was a conservative man who would have been content simply to be showered with lavish praise for his services to the republic. The Senators chose instead to undercut him by delaying the grants of land he requested for his veteran soldiers. The Senators also concluded that they could handle Pompey on their own and had no further need for Crassus and Caesar. This had the effect of uniting Pompey, Crassus, and Caesar against the Senate. In 59 B.C.E. they formed an alliance known as the First Triumvirate ("rule by three men").

The First Triumvirate   Together, Pompey, Crassus, and Caesar were invincible, but they had no common objective. Each man sought to use the triumvirate for his personal advantage. Pompey's army made him the dominant member, so Crassus and Caesar wanted assignments that would enable them to build up comparable forces. Crassus set out to conquer the Parthian Empire, a great Iranian state on the eastern edge of Rome's territory, and Caesar stirred up trouble with the Gauls in northern Europe. Caesar pushed Rome's frontier to the Rhine River and the English Channel and whipped up enthusiasm in Rome by publishing an account of his campaigns (*The Gallic Wars*). Pompey, who stayed in Rome, was distrustful of both his colleagues, and the Triumvirate unraveled after the Parthians killed Crassus in 53 B.C.E. The Senate concluded that Pompey, an *optimas,* was a lesser threat to its interests than Caesar, a *populiaris,* and it supported Pompey's efforts to bring Caesar down.

The situation came to a head in 50 B.C.E. Caesar's term as governor of his provinces expired, and the Senate refused to extend his command of his army. Caesar then marched on Rome and Pompey, and many of the Senators fled to Greece where large numbers of Pompey's troops were quartered. Although Caesar's army was much smaller and short of supplies, it went in pursuit, and in June, 48 B.C.E., Caesar routed the Senatorial forces at the battle of Pharsalus. Remnants of Pompey's army scattered to Africa and Spain, and Pompey sought refuge in Egypt, the only Mediterranean state still outside Rome's empire. Fearing Caesar's retribution, the Egyptians killed Pompey, embalmed his head, and sent it to Caesar as a token of their friendship. Caesar then invaded Egypt to avenge Pompey's murder. Egypt owed its survival as an independent country to the skill with which its young queen, Cleopatra (69–30 B.C.E.), a descendant of Alexander's general Ptolemy, handled Caesar.

It took some time for Caesar to clean out pockets of resistence, but by 45 B.C.E. he was master of Rome. Caesar was a good historian, and he probably concluded from his study of recent events that a republic could not govern an empire. Rome's urban mob had neither the wisdom nor the right to rule the world, and there was no way (given the primitive means of communications that were available) to enfranchise all the free men of the empire. Because monarchy was the only form of government efficient enough to run a large state in the ancient era, Caesar probably planned to establish kingship of some kind. That, at least, is what the

Figure 5–3 Coin Portrait of Cleopatra In the popular imagination Cleopatra is a beautiful seductress. Contemporary portraits on her coins, however, do not depict her as remarkably handsome. The legend about her beauty may owe much to misogyny—to the assumption that a woman's only power is her sexuality.

Senate suspected, and to prevent it, some sixty Senators mobbed him at a meeting on March 15, 44 B.C.E. (the ides of March), and stabbed him twenty-three times.

Brutus and Cassius, the plot's leaders, had no plan to replace Caesar. They saw themselves as reformers who were defending the republic, and like previous reformers, they mistook a symptom for a cause. They assumed that Caesar was the problem and that if he was removed, the republic would automatically thrive. It was the republic's inadequacy, however, that had brought Caesar to power. His death did not correct that. It simply created a vacuum to be filled by a new Caesar.

The man best poised to succeed Caesar was his popular second-in-command, Mark Antony (c. 83–30 B.C.E.). His plan was to stage a showy funeral for Caesar and distract Caesar's men until their desire to avenge themselves on the Senators abated. If they were under his control and the Senate was forced to rely on him for protection, he would be Rome's master. The problem with Antony's strategy was that Caesar had an heir. Caesar had no son, but he had adopted a nephew, Octavian (63 B.C.E.–14 C.E.), to carry on his name. Octavian was only eighteen when Caesar died, and he had little military or political experience. But when he charged into Rome demanding vengeance for the murder of his "father," Caesar's soldiers cheered. The Senate was perversely delighted. Even though Octavian was vowing to punish the senatorial assassins, the Senate granted him a military command. It assumed that he was too young to be a threat and that his existence would divide Caesar's men and set them to fighting among themselves. Octavian was too smart for that. As soon as he had something to offer, he joined forces with Antony and Lepidus (d. 13 B.C.E.), another of Caesar's officers. They formally established a joint dictatorship called the Second Triumvirate, and in 42 B.C.E. they defeated the armies of Brutus and Cassius at Philippi in Greece.

The Second Triumvirate The triumvirs had assumed dictatorial powers allegedly to restore the republic, but they were in no hurry. After Philippi, they divided up responsibilities for governing the empire. Antony's military reputation made him the dominant member of the triumvirate, and he awarded himself the best assignment. He headed east to prepare an invasion of Parthia—an excuse to raise a huge army with which to sweep the other triumvirs aside. Octavian remained in Italy and oversaw efforts to track down rebel armies led by Pompey's sons. Leppidus governed Africa until 36 B.C.E., when Octavian placed him under house arrest (which continued until his death twenty-four years later).

Octavian was a poor general but a superb politician, and when Antony committed a public relations blunder, Octavian moved in for the kill. Antony struck up a relationship with Egypt's Cleopatra. It was personal. (He fathered two of her children.) But it was also a sensible strategic alliance between two level-headed rulers. Antony needed Egypt's support for his invasion of Parthia, and Cleopatra extracted a promise of land in exchange for her aid. Octavian, however, convinced the Romans that the unpopular eastern queen had used her sexual wiles to captivate Antony—as she had previously captivated Caesar—and that Antony was the instrument through which she intended to rule Rome.

Octavian's charges would have had little effect if Antony's attack on Parthia had succeeded. But when it failed, Octavian made his move. In 32 B.C.E. he persuaded the peoples of Italy to swear a personal oath of loyalty to him and to support him in attacking Antony—allegedly to save the Roman Republic. The opposing armies again met in Greece, but they had little enthusiasm for the fight. The issue was decided by a sea battle off the western coast of Greece at Actium (31 B.C.E.). Antony and Cleopatra retreated to Egypt and committed suicide rather than submit to Octavian.

Octavian's victory confronted him with the challenge that had cost Caesar his life—the responsibility of creating a stable government for Rome's empire. Octavian had already publically eliminated the option of monarchy, for he had risen to power by promising to restore the republic. His ingenious strategy for reconciling what Rome wanted with what Rome needed

---

 ## Chronology: The Development of the Greek and Roman Worlds

GREECE	ROME
750 B.C.E., colonization movement	750 B.C.E., foundation of the city of Rome
510 B.C.E., Cleisthenes and Athens' democracy	509 B.C.E., Roman Republic founded
492–479 B.C.E., Persian Wars	"Struggle of the Orders"
432–404 B.C.E., Peloponnesian War	Rome fights in Italy
336–323 B.C.E., Alexander the Great	
323 B.C.E., Antigonids, Seleucids, Ptolemies (Zeno, Epicurus, Euclid)	
	287 B.C.E., Plebiscite established
(Archimedes)	264–241 B.C.E., First Punic War
	218–202 B.C.E., Second Punic War
200–196 B.C.E., Rome's war with Philip of Macedonia	
190 B.C.E., Rome defeats Antiochus and occupies Asia Minor	
(168 B.C.E., Polybius deported to Italy)	
	146 B.C.E., Corinth and Carthage sacked
	133 B.C.E., Tiberius Gracchus's tribunate
	123 B.C.E., Gaius Gracchus's tribunate
	107 B.C.E., Marius's first consulate
	88 B.C.E., Sulla's march on Rome
67–61 B.C.E., Pompey expands empire in the east	
	60 B.C.E., First Triumvirate
	45 B.C.E., Caesar defeats Pompey
	43 B.C.E., Second Triumvirate
	31 B.C.E., Octavian defeats Antony

was to create an "invisible monarchy," an imperial administration masked by a republican façade. By allowing the Romans to indulge the illusion of living in a republic, he was able to subject them to a monarchy. Sometimes governments grow powerful by claiming to be something other than they are. Citizens of modern democracies need to keep that in mind.

Larger Issue Revisited

Imperialism and monarchy have fallen out of fashion in the modern West. Western history is, however, studded with empires, and its ancient phase culminated in a Roman Empire that unified Europe, North Africa, and much of the Middle East and maintained something like world peace for over three centuries. This record compares very favorably with the chaos that followed Greece's experiments with democracy and Rome's struggle to create a viable republican government. It is often said that modern communications have shrunk our world and created a global village. If so, some kind of integrated government seems inevitable. What do the histories of popular governments and imperial monarchies suggest about the challenges that confront it?

Review Questions

1. What were Alexander's strategies for conquering an empire and for making that conquest permanent?
2. What do the arts, sciences, literatures, and philosophies of the Hellenistic empires imply about their sociopolitical environments?
3. Why did the breakthroughs made by Hellenistic scientists have so little impact on their world?
4. How did the Roman Republic differ from the Athenian democracy?
5. Did Rome set out to conquer an empire, or was the empire an unintended consequence of other developments?
6. Why was the Roman Republic unable to manage its empire?

Refer to the front of the book for a list of chapter-relevant primary sources available on the CD-ROM.

THE WEST INTERACTIVE

For web-based activities, map explorations, and quizzes related to this chapter, go to *www.prenhall.com/frankforter.*

CHAPTER 6

ROME'S EMPIRE AND THE UNIFICATION OF THE WESTERN WORLD

> [Octavian] seduced the military with gifts, the civilians with cheap food, and everyone with the benefits of peace. Then he gradually took over the functions of the Senate, the magistrates, and the law itself. . . . The prominent men who had survived [the civil war] found that the best way to prosper politically and financially was to offer him slavish support.
>
> —Tacitus

Larger Issue: *Do people prefer order to liberty?*

In 1937 a skillful feat of engineering recovered fragments of the Altar of Peace *(Ara Pacis)*, a first-century monument that lay buried beneath a sixteenth-century Roman *palazzo.* It had been erected about 9 B.C.E. to commemorate the *pax Romana* ("Roman peace") that descended on the Mediterranean world after Octavian's victory over Antony and Cleopatra. The altar stood on a platform open to the sky, and it was surrounded by a wall on which carvings depicted Octavian (63 B.C.E.–14 C.E.) and his family in a religious procession. Its style so brilliantly synthesized Greek idealism and Roman realism that Roman artists imitated it for centuries.

Near the end of his life, Octavian published a testament cataloguing his services to Rome. In addition to bringing peace, he noted that he had used his personal fortune to see the state through fiscal crises. He had rebuilt the city of Rome and entertained its residents with races and games. He had provided free food during famines. He had reduced the size of the army while expanding the empire, securing its frontiers, and maintaining its internal order. But the achievement of which he said he was most proud was the restoration of Rome's republican government.

Octavian had not restored the republic. He had used republican rhetoric to engineer Rome's transition to monarchy. At the time, few objected, for it seemed safe to trust him with overwhelming power. Few thought about what might happen when that power passed to other hands. Within a few years, the historian Tacitus (c. 55–120 C.E.) and other members of the senatorial class were so disillusioned that they even denigrated the peace the emperors created for Rome. It was purchased, they said, at the cost of the republican liberties that they had long enjoyed (and abused). Tacitus claimed that the victim sacrificed on Octavian's Altar of Peace was freedom.

Just societies aspire to reconcile the freedom of the individual with the needs of the group. This is difficult. Too much freedom leads to chaos, and too much control to tyranny— and fear of one may bring on the other. Octavian rescued Rome from a century-long civil war and established a peace that brought undeniable benefits. There was, however, a cost. As you examine the history of imperial Rome, reflect on what it teaches us about the problem of balancing liberty against the risk of anarchy.

TOPICS IN THIS CHAPTER

The Augustan Era • Order and Continuity: The Dynastic Option • Order and Continuity: The Elective Option • Life in an Imperial Environment • The Decline of Rome

The Augustan Era

The Roman Republic was able to conquer an empire, but not to rule one. The republic's strategy for heading off tyranny was to divide power among its magistrates. This risked disorder, for men often yielded to the temptation to use their offices to fight among themselves. A monarchy, which set one man far above all others, promised more stability, but the Romans equated monarchy with servitude. They were so attached to the image of themselves as citizens (not subjects of a king) that they clung to their faulty republic—even though it condemned them to a century of recurrent civil war.

An Invisible Monarchy   When Octavian returned to Rome from his eastern campaigns in 29 B.C.E., he was hailed as the savior of his country. He knew that its salvation would be short-lived unless fundamental changes were made in its political institutions, but he was acutely aware of the danger of making any changes that might be interpreted as threats to the republic. Suspicions of monarchical ambitions had cost Julius Caesar and Mark Antony their lives.

Rome's temporary need for a leader strong enough to restore order bought Octavian a period of grace. For eight years, he provided a legal basis for his authority by monopolizing one of the consulships, but this looked suspiciously like monarchy. In January, 27 B.C.E., he secured his position by threatening to give it up. He convened the Senate and offered to surrender all his powers and fully restore the republic. There was no risk that the Senate would accept his offer. Senators realized that things would fall apart if he gave up the reins of power. They acknowledged his services to the republic by granting him a title—Augustus ("majestic")—and prevailed on him to continue as consul and accept a ten-year term as governor of eighteen of the empire's twenty-eight provinces. The army had been split up and posted to trouble spots in the provinces, most of which, coincidentally, were the ones Octavian continued to control.

As the holder of *imperium maius* ("supreme military authority"), the new Augustus was Rome's *imperator* ("emperor"). This was an ancient republican term for a victorious general, not a monarch, but Augustus preferred to use a civilian title that the grateful Romans had lavished on him to recognize his record of public service: *princeps civitatis* ("first of citizens"). All of Augustus's titles were republican in origin, but they, like his adopted family name, Caesar (the origin of Kaiser and Czar), soon came to signify regal authority.

Augustus believed that the Romans would tolerate a *principate* (a government in which one man had the power to keep things on track) if it brought the blessings of peace and if its prince honored their republican traditions. He scrupulously avoided anything that looked monarchical. His home on the Palatine Hill was a typical upper-class residence. (Parts of it have survived.) He wore ordinary civilian dress, and he claimed that his togas (the garments that symbolized Roman citizenship) were homespun by his wife, Livia, and daughter, Julia. He did not surround himself with armed men or throw his weight around needlessly. He wandered the streets, entered into the fray of elections, solicited votes for candidates he backed, and treated his senatorial colleagues as equals.

Augustus's stated affection for republican tradition was not entirely insincere. He shared as much power as he thought he safely could with the Senate and the republican magistrates. He reduced the Senate from one thousand to about six hundred members and filled its ranks with experienced men of good reputation. Most were members of Rome's old families, but a few came from other Italian cities and the provinces. The reconstituted Senate had real responsibility. It managed the treasury, served as a kind of supreme court, and had the power to legislate. Augustus assembled a small company of trusted Senators and magistrates to serve as his personal advisors, and during his sometimes lengthy absences from Italy, the Senate was left to manage (or mismanage) on its own.

In 23 B.C.E. Augustus increased his republican cover by resigning the office of consul. His successive terms were unpopular, for they violated tradition and kept other men from enjoying the prestige of the office. Thereafter, he based his authority on his privileges as an honorary tribune and the periodic renewal of his provincial governorships. From time to time, he also held the office of censor, which allowed him to create Senators and "equestrians" (Rome's second highest social class), and he served as *Pontifex maximus,* the head of the state religion. Throughout his career he was careful to make sure that his powers derived from republican offices or precedents. By skillfully combining and prolonging these, he acquired mastery over Rome. His example suggests that the greatest danger to modern governments with constitutionally separated powers may not be an overt attack, but a covert strategy that quietly draws together key strands of legitimate authority.

Reorganization   The republican cloak that shrouded Augustus's monarchy rendered it officially "invisible" and allowed his fellow Romans to submit to it without sacrificing pride or patriotism. Even those who understood what was happening were inclined to go along with Augustus, for the benefits of his administration were obvious. On several occasions the Senate and the people of Rome begged him to take charge and see the state through an economic or political crisis.

The Augustan peace owed a great deal to Augustus's military reforms. Since the days of Marius, Rome's politicians had repeatedly involved its armies in their power struggles, and the empire's military had grown to immense size. At each stage in the civil war, the victor had added his defeated opponents' legions to his own. The army of which Augustus took command after Antony's fall was more than twice what he believed Rome could afford, and he knew that a smaller army would mean fewer threats from fewer generals. Augustus appropriated Egypt as his personal domain and used its wealth to retire about 300,000 men. This reduced the standing army from sixty to twenty-eight legions.

Augustus limited the legionnaires' opportunities to intervene in Rome's politics by posting them to camps along the frontiers. An elite troop of about forty-five hundred men, the Praetorian Guard, was created to maintain order in Italy. Its name associated it with the loyal soldiers who guarded the tents *(praetorii)* of republican generals. Augustus also eliminated motives that soldiers might have to meddle in politics by professionalizing military service. Legionnaires signed on for tours of duty lasting from sixteen to twenty years. They were paid according to a fixed scale and could earn promotion from the ranks to the officer corps (although the higher commands were reserved for men from the Senatorial and equestrian classes). In short, Rome's defenders became state employees and no longer had to look to maintain their generals in power to survive.

Figure 6–1 Portrait of Augustus Literary descriptions of Augustus suggest that he was a small, thin man who never enjoyed robust health (although he lived to be seventy-seven). It would not, however, have been appropriate for sculptors to show signs of weakness in their public portraits of Rome's leader.

Augustus's military reforms helped to consolidate, as well as pacify, the empire. His twenty-eight legions enrolled about 160,000 men—just barely enough to maintain Rome's four thousand-mile-long frontier. To back up the legions (which were composed of Roman citizens), Augustus created auxiliaries, companies of men recruited from the provinces. The legions and auxiliaries together provided about a quarter of a million men to protect and police a population of about 100 million. Auxiliaries were less well paid than legionnaires, but a term of honorable service earned citizenship for the veteran of an auxiliary unit and qualified his sons to join the legions. The army thus provided entree for provincials into Roman society.

Cities were central to the administration of the empire, for its primitive systems of communications meant that most government had to be local government. The army built Rome's famous network of roads to facilitate troop movements. Augustus began to extend the roads beyond Italy to the headquarters he established for the legions in the provinces. Many of these new military camps became permanent cities that assumed responsibility for administering the districts in which they were located, and they helped to spread Latin culture—particularly in the west. The eastern half of the empire had many ancient cities, but much of the west (particularly Spain, North Africa, and trans-Alpine Europe) had, until recently, been tribal territory. Augustus sponsored about one hundred colonies, many of which were settled by his veterans. Part of a soldier's pay was banked for him so that when he retired at about the age of forty, he had a nest egg with which to begin a new career. Many men invested in farms and businesses in the provinces in which they had served.

The Roman Empire was a kind of federation of city-states. Each of its urban centers operated within parameters set by the central administration, but each also accommodated local customs. The schools they supported and the opportunities for political participation they provided helped to romanize the provincial elites and foster their loyalty to the empire. As these elites learned Latin and Greek, the empire's upper classes developed a common culture. The cities in which they lived were similar, no matter where they were located. Each had temples, arenas, theaters, schools, monuments, baths, and public buildings, many of which the emperors funded. Each had its councils of local leaders. Romanization spread widely, but in many places classical civilization was a thin veneer over native cultures that outlasted the empire.

Augustus turned the republican hodgepodge of territories into a coherent empire. He redrew the boundaries of provinces and standardized their governments. He reduced corruption by establishing fixed rates of taxation and employing state officials, rather than private contractors, to collect and audit taxes. He waged campaigns to extend the empire to what he believed were defensible frontiers. In the east he set up a string of client kingdoms dependent on Rome. In the west he suppressed resistance in Spain and the Alps and extended Roman territory in the Balkans north to the Danube Valley. He planned to cross the Rhine and conquer more of Germany, but here he failed. In 9 C.E. the Germans ambushed and exterminated three legions. Augustus established peace, but Tacitus grumbled that in some provinces peace was only the quiet of a man-made desert. (See Map 6–1.)

Augustus's administrative reforms also helped to turn Rome's diverse holdings into a true empire. The republic had largely been run by amateurs and ad hoc arrangements, but Augustus created an imperial bureaucracy staffed by salaried professionals with specialized training. Wealthy Romans often relied on freedmen and educated slaves to run their plantations and staff their public offices, and Augustus continued this practice. Service in their government gave some men, who were legally inferior to citizens, considerable power over their social superiors. Senators and equestrians were also enlisted to help provide a growing list of government services. They oversaw grain and water supplies, police forces, courts, treasuries, public entertainments, and construction projects.

Moral Regeneration   Italy had built the empire, and in the minds of Augustus and most Romans a gulf existed between Italy and its provinces. Augustus's pledge to defend the republic was a promise to prevent dangerous foreign influences from corrupting its Italian essence. This could be done only by staffing and defending the empire with men who were thoroughly imbued with Roman values. Unfortunately, however, they were in short supply. The civil war had taken a toll, and birthrates were low. (Rome's upper classes preserved their fortunes by

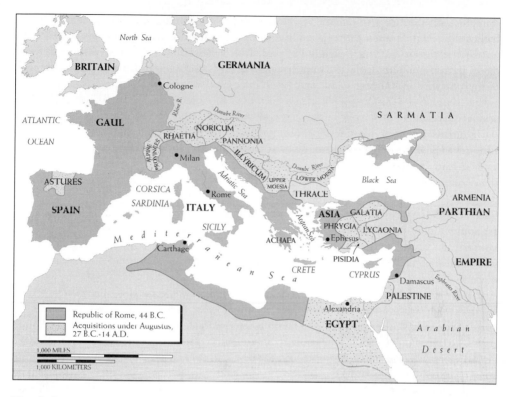

Map 6–1

Augustus's Empire   Under Augustus, Rome completed its encirclement of the Mediterranean, but the empire had not yet reached its full extent. His successors added territory in Britain, Germany, Central Europe, and the Middle East. *Question:* Was the Mediterranean Sea a help or a hindrance in the formation of Rome's empire?

limiting the number of their offspring.) Augustus tried to solve the manpower problem by passing laws that were designed to strengthen families, increase birthrates, and restore commitment to traditional values. He financially penalized women below the age of fifty and men younger than sixty who failed to marry early and remarry promptly when widowed or divorced. Sterile couples were heavily taxed, and families with three or more children were given preferential treatment by the government. Adultery for women and for men who had affairs with married women became a crime against the state, punishable by fine, exile, or death. Temples were restored and archaic patriotic ceremonies revived to promote patriotism and civic virtue.

Augustus's social legislation was a failure. His own family set a dismal example. He managed to produce only one child, a daughter named Julia, and her flagrant immorality ultimately drove him to exile her to a remote island.

Latin High Culture   The arts played a part in Augustus's program for the moral and patriotic regeneration of his fellow citizens, and Roman literature reached the pinnacle of its development during his reign. Romans did not produce much in the way of art, literature, or serious thought until they were stimulated by contact with the Greeks during the last century of the republican era. As Rome's armies moved east, Rome was flooded with looted objects and trade goods that Italian craftsmen eagerly imitated. Much classical Greek statuary survives today only in Roman copies. Influential upper-class Romans, such as the Scipios who led the city during the first and second Punic wars, were infatuated with all things Greek. They learned Greek, dressed as Greeks, bought Greek furniture and slaves, and sat at the feet of Greek philosophers.

Romans followed the Greeks more closely in some fields than in others. They also adapted what they copied and made some original contributions of their own. This is clearly evident in architecture. The Romans shared the classical taste for symmetrical designs, but their buildings were often larger and more complex than those of the Greeks. They added curves—arches and domes—to the linear elements (columns and lintels) characteristic of Greek buildings. They invented concrete and used it to construct new kinds of imposing but graceful structures. Sulla built Rome's first major building (a temple) in the Hellenistic style. Pompey and Caesar added a few more, but when Augustus came to power, his empire's capital still had few notable buildings. He boasted that he found Rome a city of brick and left it a city of marble.

Related to architecture was the Romans' unique gift for engineering. They drove arrow-straight roads across rough terrain, tunneled through mountains, and created immense systems of aqueducts to supply their cities with lavish amounts of water. Over 200,000 gallons a day eventually flowed into Rome to supply its fountains and baths. A leisurely daily bath was an indispensable ritual of civilized life for a Roman, and Roman cities were equipped with luxurious public bathing facilities.

Latin literature was pioneered by comic playwrights. Twenty-one plays by Plautus (c. 254–184 B.C.E.), an Italian, and six by his successor, a former Carthaginian slave named Terence (c. 195–159 B.C.E.), have survived. Both men imitated Greek models, but Terence's work was the more refined. Plautus served a Roman appetite for farce and slapstick that often served to diminish the literary significance of much Roman theater.

The authors of the early republican period were handicapped by the immaturity of the Latin language. The first Romans to try their hands at prose writing wrote in Greek. Cato the Elder (234–149 B.C.E.), a Senator remembered primarily for his political activities, attempted a history of Rome in Latin. It has been lost, but a book he wrote on agriculture survives to provide us with our earliest extended specimen of Latin prose.

Roman intellectuals were introduced to Greek philosophy in 155 B.C.E., when Athens dispatched a number of its prominent teachers to Rome as ambassadors. The traditional values of Roman culture disposed the Romans to reject philosophies that flirted with blasphemy and religions that undercut moral rigor. In 186 B.C.E. the Senate outlawed the worship of Dionysus (Bacchus), a cult associated with orgiastic excesses. In 173 B.C.E. it banished Epicurean philosophers for teaching what it regarded as self-indulgent quietism. The Greek philosophy that most appealed to the Romans was Stoicism, and Rome produced two of the most important Stoic authors: Epictetus (b. c. 50 C.E.), a Greek slave, and Marcus Aurelius (r.161–180 C.E.), an emperor (both of whom wrote in Greek).

Latin poetry began to flourish in the middle of the first century B.C.E. as Romans became acquainted with the work of Greeks associated with Alexandria's Museum. Among the best and earliest extant examples are the poems that Catullus (c. 85–54 B.C.E.) penned to describe his passionate, stormy, and disillusioning affair with the promiscuous wife of a prominent

Roman politician. Lucretius (c. 94–55 B.C.E.), the republican era's other major poet, chose a more serious theme for his work. He wrote to convince his countrymen that Epicurean materialism provided escape from the stress and anxiety of the wars that plagued his generation. He claimed that the universe was nothing more than bits of matter randomly colliding in empty space and that when people came to understand this, they would lose their fear of death and the gods and begin to behave rationally. Reason would persuade them of the wisdom of avoiding strong feelings—the pleasurable as well as the painful—by distancing themselves emotionally from the meaningless, uncontrollable world.

Because republican politicians had to solicit support from voters and sway the thinking of popular assemblies, they were drawn to study rhetoric, the art of persuasive speaking pioneered by Greek philosophers. The oratorical skills of Cicero (106–43 B.C.E.) helped him overcome the handicap of undistinguished ancestry, earn a consulship, and serve as one of the Senate's leaders during the era of the First and Second Triumvirates. Cicero was less an original thinker than a popularizer of Greek philosophy. He favored the Stoics and maintained that the infighting that plagued the republic would end if men allowed themselves to be guided by the rational laws that Stoics believed governed nature. A rational society would grant uniquely talented people (such as Cicero) special privileges and elevate them to positions of leadership no matter what their family backgrounds. Cicero claimed that, from time to time, the republic needed a *princeps,* an extraordinary citizen whose natural charisma, wisdom, and moral authority equipped him to guide the Senate and the popular assemblies in discharging their respective duties. To his dismay, Cicero discovered that a *princeps* might not be all that rational and benevolent. He attacked Antony in a series of fiery speeches, and when the Second Triumvirate came to power, Antony murdered him and nailed his tongue and right hand (the orator's instruments) to the speaker's platform in the Forum.

Art and Augustan Propaganda   The Golden Age of Latin literature dawned with Augustus's empire. The leading authors of his day helped promote his reforms, but their propagandistic works were inspired by sincere belief in his vision of Rome's strengths and his faith in its destiny. They were deeply grateful for the Augustan peace and brimming with patriotic enthusiasm. They shared Augustus's belief that the sturdy agrarian virtues that had enabled their ancestors to win an empire would equip them to lead the world into an era of peace and plenty.

Virgil (70–19 B.C.E.) was Rome's greatest poet. His father, a northern Italian landowner, wanted him to practice law. His work, however, came to the attention of one of Augustus's close associates, a wealthy equestrian named Maecenas (c. 63–8 B.C.E.), and his patronage freed Virgil to pursue his writing. Virgil's earlier poems, *Eclogues,* were mostly romanticized descriptions of the Italian countryside and the simple pleasures of rural life. He followed these with the *Georgics,* nationalistic poems giving thanks for the Augustan peace and celebrating the yeoman farmer, the type of hard-working citizen that Augustus claimed was the source of Rome's strength. Virgil's greatest project, which he did not live to finish, was the *Aeneid,* the story of the Trojan prince Aeneas, the legendary founder of the Roman people. Virgil intended the *Aeneid* to provide Rome with a national epic comparable to the *Iliad* and the *Odyssey,* and to tie the story of Rome's founding into Homer's mythic history. The poem justified the Roman Empire by claiming that the gods destined the Roman people to rule the world and establish universal peace. That was why the gods endowed the Romans with *Romanitas,* their characteristic virtues of self-sufficiency, strength, courage, devotion to duty, patriotism, and simple piety. Virgil's description of Rome's past was Augustus's vision for Rome's future.

The second major poet of Rome's Golden Age was Horace (65–8 B.C.E.), a freedman's son who saw military service in the civil war. Virgil recommended him to Maecenas, who gave Horace a rural estate on which to live and write. Horace worked on a smaller scale than Virgil (producing satires, odes, epistles, and hymns,) but joined Virgil in exhorting the Romans to practice the hardy, sober virtues that Augustus was eager to promote.

Augustus was less pleased with the third of the Golden Age's great poets, Ovid (43 B.C.E.– 17 C.E.). Ovid's prolific output dealt largely with sensuous subjects that appealed to the dissolute young aristocrats whom Augustus was trying to reform. Among his works was a textbook for seducers, *The Art of Love,* that was especially likely to offend the *princeps.* Scarcely less titillating were some of the 250 or so tales he retold in *Metamorphoses,* a kind of encyclopedia of classical mythology. In 8 C.E. Ovid's involvement (with Augustus's granddaughter) in a sexual scandal led to his banishment to a remote, barbarous town on the shores of the Black Sea. His pleas for forgiveness went unanswered, and he died in exile.

The greatest prose writer of Augustus's generation was the historian Livy (59 B.C.E.– 17 C.E.), who produced a monumental survey of Roman history from the city's founding to his own day. Thirty-five of its 142 books survive to provide us with most of what we know about Rome's early development. Like the poets, Livy was an advocate for the Augustan virtues. He believed that history's purpose was to teach moral lessons, and his history was filled with tales of Roman valor, self-control, piety, patriotism, and moral rectitude. For centuries, schoolmasters have used Livy's inspirational stories in their struggle to turn unruly boys into disciplined men.

Order and Continuity: The Dynastic Option

Augustus avoided assassination, gave Rome over forty years of stable government, and died in his bed at an advanced age. He knew that the empire needed someone like him to oversee it, but because Rome was still officially a republic, it had no provision for appointing someone to carry on his work. An invisible monarchy had to be passed on secretly. This was not hard to do, for Romans were not particular about the line that separates public from private authority.

In the testament that summed up Augustus's life's work, he gave an accounting of his private expenditures on behalf of Rome. On several occasions, he had distributed four hundred or more sesterces to at least a quarter of a million men. During famines, he had fed Rome at his own expense. He had spent 400 million sesterces to settle veterans from the army, and he had donated 150 million sesterces to the public treasury. Given that a laborer's daily wage was about four sesterces and that Augustus by no means impoverished his heirs, his fortune must have been staggering. By using it to fund public services, Augustus blurred the distinction between government agents and his personal servants. This created a confusion between his household and the state bureaucracy that allowed the latter to pass to his heirs when they inherited the former. The easiest way to perpetuate his invisible monarchy was to make it hereditary in his family.

Augustus's popularity and the length of his reign helped smooth the path for his heir. By the time he died, there were few Romans left who had experienced life under the old republic, and that republic was associated with painful memories of the civil war. The Romans did not want to return to the past, but they were not ready to repudiate their republican traditions and acknowledge the new political reality. This meant that they, in effect, surrendered to

Augustus's heirs, for they could not control the choice of their monarch until they admitted that they had a monarchy. Hereditary systems of succession are risky. An heir may not be qualified to handle his inheritance, or a ruler may fail to produce an heir. Augustus's family confronted Rome with both problems.

The Julio-Claudians   Augustus's only child was his daughter Julia, and his hopes for an heir were pinned on the two grandsons she gave him. When both these boys died, he had to make an arrangement that displeased all concerned. He compelled his estranged stepson Tiberius, the son of his wife Livia and her first husband (Claudius Nero), to divorce a wife he loved, marry Julia, and assume the duties of heir. Because Augustus was a Julian by adoption and Tiberius a Claudian by birth, historians refer to Rome's first imperial dynasty as the Julio-Claudians.

Augustus owed much of his success to his ability to cultivate the fantasy that he was only a first among equals in the game of republican politics. On his deathbed he reportedly asked a group of friends, "Have I acted my part well in life's farce?" Tiberius (r. 14–37 C.E.) tried to follow Augustus's example, but Tiberius was a moody man who lacked the ability to connect with people. He was soon loathed by both the masses and the Senators.

In 26 C.E. he left Rome and took up permanent residence on the island of Capri in the Bay of Naples. By now the imperial bureaucracy was sufficiently entrenched that Rome's *imperator* could ignore the Senate and popular assemblies and run the empire from any location he chose. This humiliated and infuriated the Senators, whom Tiberius disliked as much as they disliked him. He characterized them as "men eager to be slaves." To be fair, Augustus had put the Senators in the difficult position of having responsibility without power, and they reasonably feared being set up to take the blame for things that were beyond their control. Having few alternatives, they took up their pens and vented their frustrations by writing histories. Modern readers need to keep in mind that these Senators' assessments of many emperors were far from objective.

If Tiberius failed at public relations, he succeeded at government. He surrounded himself with good advisors and trained specialists, paid close attention to the administration of the provinces, reduced their taxes, built roads, economized by cutting back on Rome's gladiatorial games, and racked up a huge surplus in the imperial treasury for his successor.

Tiberius's only son died in 23 C.E., and his heir was a grandnephew, Gaius Caesar. He is better known by the childhood nickname his father's soldiers gave him when he strutted about their camp in a tiny military uniform: Caligula ("Little Boots").

Caligula (r. 37–41 C.E.), who is remembered as one of Rome's worst emperors, began well. He returned to Rome, was deferential to the Senate, courted the Roman populace with games, and recalled exiles. Then something went terribly wrong. Some historians believe that a serious illness disturbed his already precariously balanced mind. He was frenetic, high strung, given to insomnia, and plagued by insecurities. Many of the outlandish stories about him that are found in hostile senatorial histories defy belief. If Caligula was mad, there may have been a logic to his insanity. His extreme behavior makes some sense if it was an attempt to force the Romans to recognize that their republic was a farce and that they were subjects of a ruler like the god-kings of Egypt, Persia, and the Hellenistic East.

Caligula alienated those closest to him, and disaffected officers of the Praetorian Guard murdered him, his wife, and only child (an infant daughter). The Praetorians elevated his uncle, Claudius, to the throne.

Claudius (41–54 C.E.) was a bookish man who studied with the historian Livy and wrote on subjects ranging from Etruscan history to the alphabet. He was just what the faltering empire needed. The strength of the imperial bureaucracy and sheer momentum had carried Rome through Caligula's mismanagement, but inertia would not have preserved order indefinitely. Rome needed a conscientious leader, and Claudius had the right qualifications. He was a well-educated workaholic who enjoyed the details of administration. He had extensive knowledge of Roman law, which he put to work in the courts. He financed new colonies and public works—the most important of which was the rebuilding of Ostia, the port (at the mouth of the Tiber River) that served the city of Rome. He authorized the campaign that made Britain, an island that Julius Caesar had twice invaded, a Roman province.

Claudius's fourth and last wife was his niece, Agrippina the Younger. The unusual marriage was probably intended to safeguard the dynasty. Claudius was aging and ill and unlikely to live long enough to see his only son, Britannicus, reach maturity. The other possible heir to the throne was Nero, a son Agrippina had by an earlier marriage. Claudius's union with Agrippina and adoption of Nero joined the only surviving branches of the imperial family and created two potential heirs. Because both boys were young, Agrippina was groomed for the role of regent. Claudius gave her the title "Augusta" and minted coins in her honor. Ancient governments used coins to communicate with the masses. As they passed from hand to hand throughout the empire, people absorbed the messages the government stamped on them. By accustoming the Romans to an Augusta, Claudius prepared them, should it become necessary, for a situation they had never faced before: rule by a woman.

When Claudius died in 54 C.E., Nero (r. 54–68), the senior heir, was seventeen years old. He, like Caligula, has often been dismissed as a madman, but that may be too simplistic an interpretation of the ancient sources. On the one hand, he is accused of wanton murder of countless persons (including his half-brother, his mother, and his wife) and absurdly self-indulgent, self-deluding behavior. But on the other hand, Suetonius, an ancient Roman historian who never heard a scurrilous rumor he was not eager to repeat, claims that after Nero's death people raised statues to him in the Forum, annually decked his grave with flowers, circulated his edicts, and even claimed that he was not dead but would someday reappear to reclaim his throne.

The Roman concept of leadership was essentially military, but Nero was no soldier and was unwilling to pose as one. His strange behavior may have been an attempt to establish a new kind of authority over Rome. An *imperator,* a general, led by intimidating his subjects. Nero, a poet, may have embraced the romantic idea that an artist could lead by inspiring his followers. His education convinced him that Greek civilization set the standards to which Romans should aspire. He adopted Greek dress, promoted Greek customs, and tried to persuade the Roman mob to accept Greek athletic competitions in place of Roman gladiatorial combats. The more the Romans resisted his efforts to reform them, the more extreme his behavior became.

In 64 C.E. Nero proved that he was capable of governing effectively. When news reached him that a fire had destroyed ten of the city of Rome's fourteen districts, he hastened to Rome to supervise relief efforts. He then drew up plans for rebuilding Rome on a grander scale and issued new construction codes to make it a safer city. He also confiscated a large tract of land at the eastern end of the Forum on which to build a new palace-garden complex, the Golden House. His enthusiasm for these projects prompted rumors that he had started the fire to clear the way for them. Fires often swept through crowded ancient cities, and Rome's fire was

Culture in Context: The Roman Games

Public entertainments were integral to the operation of the Roman Empire. Every town of any size usually had both an arena and a theater. Rome's Colosseum seated fifty thousand, and 150,000 spectators or more could gather in its Circus Maximus to witness chariot races. Governments staged a constant round of spectacles to court public support and distract the masses. The Romans, like the Greeks, considered games to be religious festivals. Religion gave them many excuses for holding games. (About half the days in the year were dedicated to one god or another.) But it did not elevate the nature of their entertainments. Romans did not share the Greeks' passion for athletic competitions. They loved races, crude comedies, and bloodshed.

Republican politicians competed for office by bribing the voters with lavish games. When Augustus totted up his services to Rome, they included sponsorship of eighteen gladiatorial combats involving ten thousand men and thirty-five hundred animals. As each successive emperor sought to outdo his predecessors, tens of thousands of men and beasts were offered up at festivals that sometimes stretched on for months. Exotic animals were imported at great expense simply to be destroyed. To find the manpower for the games, jails were emptied of criminals, slaves purchased, and war captives driven into the arena. Contests between odd pairings of animals (a bear versus a bull, for example) or men with different weapons were invented to prevent the slaughter from becoming routine and boring.

Some of Rome's educated elite (including a few emperors) despised the games, but they knew that it was politically unwise to insult the masses by expressing contempt for the public's entertainments. The delight Romans took in witnessing bloodshed and death might prompt a modern American to look down on them, but no Roman was ever able to relish the kind of elaborate atrocities that Hollywood simulates. Modern audiences excuse their appetite for mayhem by pointing out that what they spend billions of dollars to watch is not real. If the Romans had special effects artists at their disposal, they too might have been content with make believe. The real moral issue is why such spectacles appeal to anyone in any age.

Question: Does a state's responsibility for maintaining order give it a legitimate right to supervise the entertainments of its people?

doubtless accidental. However, suspicion of arson fell on a band of Christians, followers of a new eastern religion that predicted the imminent destruction of the world. In the midst of Rome's holocaust, some of them had probably taken to the streets, announcing the fulfilment of their prophecies and urging last-minute conversions. Nero seized on this circumstantial evidence and made Rome's Christians scapegoats for the fire. It is important to note, however, that it was their alleged arson, not their faith, that led to their persecution and that only the small group of Christians in the city was affected. The Christian movement was not yet large enough to exert much influence on the course of Western history.

Nero's neglect of the army finally brought him down. In 68 C.E. the governor of one of the Gallic provinces organized a revolt that spread by fits and starts. Nero had no idea how to respond, and his confusion soon turned to panic. Assuming that all was lost, he ordered one of his servants to slit his throat.

The Flavian Dynasty   Nero was the last of the Julio-Claudians. Rome had become dependent on an emperor, but because it had created no constitutional machinery to govern succession to its throne, it had no legal way to fill the power vacuum left by the extinction of its first dynasty. The crisis reignited the civil war, but Rome was lucky. Three generals won and lost the city in rapid succession, and the fourth, Vespasian (r. 69–79 C.E.) restored order and established a new dynasty, the Flavian.

The Julio-Claudians were aristocrats of ancient lineage, but the Flavian family had a far less exalted equestrian background. The new emperor was a sixty-year-old career soldier with a lifetime of command experience acquired from postings to every corner of the empire. He was a tough, pragmatic man who spoke plainly and cracked crude jokes. The trappings of power did not seduce him into taking himself too seriously. On his deathbed he mocked the Roman custom of deifying dead emperors by quipping, "I think I'm becoming a god!"

Vespasian helped the empire recover from the colorful excesses of the Julio-Claudians. He had used his army to seize power, but he did not reignite the soldiers' political aspirations. He broke up dangerous concentrations of troops and transferred men frequently so that they did not put down roots and develop greater loyalties to specific regions and commanders than to the empire. Augustus had envisioned an empire run by Italians, but Vespasian (and later rulers) bridged the gap between Italy and the provinces. He encouraged romanization of the provinces, promoted provincials to the Senate, and added them to his administration. He established a budget for his government based on a census that estimated income from taxes. He funded the construction of roads, bridges, and public buildings throughout the empire and gave Rome a new temple to Jupiter on the Capitoline hill and its famous amphitheater, the Colosseum.

Vespasian's successor was his elder son Titus (r. 79–81 C.E.), whom he had groomed for the responsibilities of the imperial office. Titus was a seasoned general. At the start of his father's reign, he had put down a rebellion by Jewish nationalists. A triumphal arch at the eastern end of the Forum commemorates his victory and depicts the treasures the Romans sacked from Jerusalem's temple. Titus died before he could do much, but his reign was marked by a memorable event. In August, 79 C.E., Vesuvius, a volcano near Naples, erupted and (to the delight of generations of archaeologists and tourists) buried the towns of Pompeii and Herculaneum.

Titus's heir was his younger brother Domitian (r. 81–96 C.E.), an arrogant autocrat. The splendid residence he built on Rome's Palatine hill gave us our word "palace." He lived in constant fear that plots were being hatched against him, and his wanton executions of suspects ensured that they were. Thanks to his wife's cooperation, one of them finally succeeded.

Order and Continuity: The Elective Option

Domitian had no heir. His assassins therefore asked the Senate—Rome's most prestigious political assembly—to appoint a new emperor. By now there was no question of a republic, and the Senate knew that if it did not act to fill the throne, the army would.

Figure 6–2 The Streets of Pompeii The ruins of Pompeii and Herculaneum allow modern people to step back in time and walk the streets of Roman towns whose lives were abruptly frozen in place on August 24, 79 C.E.

The "Good Emperors"   Not surprisingly, the Senate chose one of its own, Nerva (r. 96– 98 C.E.), to be emperor. Nerva knew that there was little chance that the army's generals would allow a senatorial appointee to deprive them of the opportunity to make a bid for the throne, but he had a strategy for ensuring his survival. Nerva had no children and at age sixty-six was not likely to produce any, so he simply adopted Trajan, the commander of the legions along the Rhine and the general who was most likely to win a battle for Rome. The adoption set a valuable precedent. From 96 to 180 C.E. no emperor had a son, so each was free to choose his own successor. All chose wisely, and the result was the longest period of consistently excellent rule that the empire enjoyed.

People in Context: The Imperial Aristocracy: Pliny the Elder and Pliny the Younger

The Roman Republic had belonged to the aristocratic families that monopolized its political offices, commanded its armies, confiscated its wealth, and charted its destiny. The empire diminished their power. Emperors utilized a few men of senatorial rank as advisors, provincial governors, heads of departments of state, and military officers, but they kept a close eye on them. Association with the court or a too successful military career could be dangerous for a man from a prominent family. Most of the blood shed by Rome's "bad" emperors was the blue blood of upper class men who were suspected of plotting against the throne or who simply had fortunes their ruler wanted to confiscate. Given the risks of exposure, wealthy men often preferred the security of their country villas to life in Rome. Shut out from the world of politics, they devoted themselves to literature and to entertaining one another. Those who published took care not to write anything that might offend their emperor.

Prominent among the literary lights of the day were an uncle and a nephew, both named Pliny. The uncle, Pliny the Elder (c. 23–79 C.E.), was a close friend of Vespasian's, who found time in a busy military career to write poems, histories, and a huge encyclopedia of the ancient world's scientific and pseudoscientific lore. His scientific interests led to his death. He was living near Pompeii when Vesuvius erupted. The temptation to view the mountain up close was simply too great, and he was killed by a surge of volcanic gas. His nephew, Pliny the Younger (c. 61–113 C.E.), has left us a description of the eruption and the circumstances of his uncle's death.

Pliny the Younger studied rhetoric with Quintillian (35–95 C.E.), the author of Rome's leading text on the art of oratory, and by the age of eighteen he was representing clients in Rome's courts. He did not follow his uncle into the military, but he held prestigious offices. He was briefly a consul (a largely empty honor by his day), and the emperor Trajan (r. 98–117 C.E.) appointed him governor of Bithynia, a province on the southwestern coast of the Black Sea.

Pliny was an enthusiastic correspondent who edited his letters for publication. He wrote to and about many important people, among whom was his emperor. An emperor's servant was well advised to show deference and proceed with caution, and Pliny took no chances. He referred every decision about which he had the least doubt to the emperor, for, as he explained to Trajan, who "could better . . . guide my ignorance." If every Roman governor did likewise, Trajan's paperwork must have been overwhelming. Among the issues that puzzled Pliny was what to do with some practitioners of a new religion called Christianity. His letters reveal how little the Roman authorities knew (or cared) about the faith that would one day transform Western civilization.

Question: How might a society's interest in maintaining order affect the behavior of its artists and intellectuals?

Trajan (r. 98–117 C.E.) was eager to expand the empire. He created a new province called Dacia north of the Danube—a Latin enclave that became the modern nation of Romania. His other campaigns humbled Parthia, conquered Armenia, Assyria, and Mesopotamia, and brought the Roman Empire to its height. (See Map 6–2.)

Italy was the preferred recruiting ground for Trajan's legions, and his government implemented an ingenious program to boost its population. Italy's small farmers and artisans suffered as the empire's western provinces developed and began to compete with Italian products on the world market. To enable poorer Italians to raise more children, Trajan established the *alimenta,* an endowment that provided food and education for impoverished children of both sexes. The money came from interest that landowners paid on government loans that helped them improve their estates. Instead of handing out money, Rome funded its welfare program from investments that promoted economic growth.

Trajan was succeeded by a distant relative, Hadrian (r. 117–138 C.E.), who spent most of his reign away from Rome, touring the provinces and cultivating close ties with his troops. He was popular with his army even though he fought few wars and concentrated on strengthening

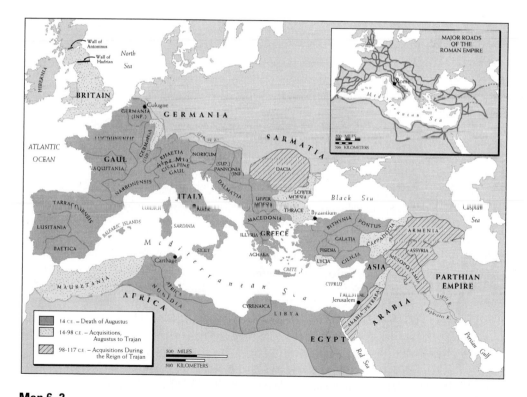

Map 6–2

The Pinnacle of the Roman Empire Augustus conquered territory that he thought would provide the empire with defensible frontiers. Claudius added Britain, but the major and final additions to the empire were the work of Trajan. Hadrian, his successor, concluded that some of the land Trajan had won was too difficult to defend, and he relinquished it. **Question:** Where, along Rome's long frontier, was the empire most likely to be attacked?

the empire's frontiers. He retreated to defensible positions, and where terrain offered no help, he built elaborate fortifications (the largest of which was a seventy-two-mile-long wall that spanned northern Britain).

Hadrian was a multifaceted person, a soldier and athletic outdoorsman as well as an aesthete and a scholar. He reformed Roman law to reflect Stoic principles of justice and protect slaves from abuse. He reorganized the empire's administrative system and held its bureaucrats accountable to high standards. He had such a passion for Greek literature and art that he was nicknamed "the Greek." He studied architecture, experimented with novel designs for buildings, and lavished buildings on provincial cities. The only major ancient temple still standing in Rome is one of his: the Pantheon, a drum-shaped hall roofed by a dome 141 feet in diameter.

Hadrian's last years were spent wrestling with a painful illness, but he outlived the first man he chose as his heir. When he finally died in 138 C.E., he commended the empire to the care of a senatorial aristocrat famous for his cultivation of the Roman virtues of dignity, sobriety, and simplicity: Antoninus Pius (r. 138–161 C.E.). Rome faced no wars or other crises throughout his long reign, but the quiet was deceptive. Beyond the empire's northern frontiers, hostile German tribes had been training in the use of Roman arms and tactics. Shortly after Antoninus passed the reigns of government to his successor, Marcus Aurelius (r. 161–180 C.E.), the world fell apart.

Marcus Aurelius was a remarkable leader—a determined soldier, a skillful executive, a faithful family man, and a Stoic philosopher who has left us an important collection of essays (*Meditations*). His Stoic detachment was severely tested, for his reign was a long series of crises: plagues, earthquakes, floods, famines, and wars.

Marcus Aurelius failed the empire in only one way. Alone among the "good emperors" he sired a son, a boy named Commodus (r. 180–192 C.E.). Although Commodus shared none of his father's virtues, Roman traditions of family and the inheritance rights of sons were too strong to deny him the throne. He spent his reign in dissipation and may have descended into madness. When he began to terrorize those close to him, they arranged his assassination and asked the Senate to appoint his successor. A similar maneuver had inaugurated the era of the "good emperors," but this time it did not work. The armies mutinied, and civil war broke out.

Military Rule   The winner was Septimius Severus (r. 193–211 C.E.), commander of the Danube legions. He restored order, but his methods augured poorly for Rome's future. He increased the army's size and nearly doubled its pay. His deathbed advice for his heirs was, "Enrich the troops, and despise everyone else."

The army may always have been the basis of an emperor's power, but it was dangerous for an emperor to acknowledge this too openly. Once the soldiers realized that they were in control, it was impossible to maintain their discipline. They killed the officers who tried to keep them in line and supported those who promised to do their bidding. Of the five emperors of the Severan dynasty, only the first escaped death at the hands of his own men.

Following the murder of the last Severan emperor in 235 C.E., the army spun out of control. Over the next fifty years approximately twenty-five men claimed the imperial title. They have been called the Barracks Emperors, for most began their careers as common soldiers. The administration of the empire languished while military factions fought among themselves, and large blocks of territory in both the east and west seceded and set up governments of their own. From 267 to 272 C.E. the eastern rim of the Mediterranean from Asia Minor to Egypt was ruled by a woman, Zenobia, queen of the desert city of Palmyra.

Figure 6–3 Marcus Aurelius Most bronze statues from the ancient world were melted down so that their valuable metal could be put to other uses.

Life in an Imperial Environment

Geography helped make Rome's empire, the ancient world's largest and most enduring, a viable entity. Although the empire's frontier was long, much of it needed minimal defense. The Atlantic Ocean protected the west, and the Sahara the south. There were wars with the Parthian Empire in the east, but most trouble on that front was stirred up by the Romans themselves. The frontier that needed the largest military investment was the northern line defined by the Rhine and Danube rivers. Communication, travel, and trade within these boundaries was facilitated by the empire's numerous rivers and its great central sea.

An Imperial Economy   Once the Romans secured the empire's frontiers, swept pirates from the Mediterranean, and began to spread urban institutions throughout their territory, the stage was set for the West's economy to thrive. The empire was abundantly supplied with natural resources. Most regions could provide themselves with fundamental necessities, but once secure trade routes were established, some districts began to specialize in what they could do best. Olive oil was exported from Spain, grain from North Africa and Egypt, and wine from Gaul and Greece. Metal ores were mined in Britain, Spain, Dacia, and Cyprus, and manufacturing centers sprang up in many places. Glass was shipped from Egypt and the Rhineland. A popular line of red-glazed pottery was mass produced in northern Italy. Textiles came from Asia Minor, and bronze work from Italy. Despite the success of some of these enterprises, shipment problems forced most industries to remain small and to produce for local markets. Water offered the only economical means for transporting goods. Wine brought from Gaul to Rome by sea (about 450 miles) was less expensive than wine carted to the city from vineyards only fifty miles away.

The economies of inland districts lagged far behind those of regions on coasts and waterways, and the empire's overall economy began to show signs of weakness as early as the Flavian period. Romans imported large quantities of luxury goods from India and the Far East and paid for them with gold and silver. This drained bullion from the West, and as the productivity of its mines decreased, emperors were hard pressed to find the precious metals they needed to mint an adequate supply of coins. The empire's success in suppressing war also had an economic downside. It diminished the supply of cheap slaves who were such an important element in the workforce of the late republican period.

Social Developments   Romans were generous in freeing slaves, and many of Rome's citizens were freedmen and their descendants. This may have given some of them sympathy for slaves. Philosophers urged respect for the humanity of slaves, and some emperors passed laws to protect them. But ideals and laws were difficult to enforce.

The gap that steadily widened between rich and poor in the Roman world blurred the line between freedom and slavery. Many of the free poor became *coloni,* tenant farmers who took over the work of slaves on the *latifundia* (large estates) of the rich. Lack of opportunity made them a virtually captive workforce. Large numbers of the indigent and unemployed also flooded into the empire's major cities and eked out livings on the public dole.

The distinction between Italy and the provinces that Augustus emphasized steadily eroded. By the end of the Julio-Claudian period, most of the old republican families had died out and a new aristocracy, drawn increasingly from the provinces, was taking its place. The settlement of Roman veterans on the frontiers, their intermarriage with local women, and the acquisition of citizenship by non-Italians who served in the auxiliaries all helped to create a larger, more inclusive class of people who identified with the empire. Stoic philosophers preached a doctrine of universal brotherhood, and Roman jurists posited the existence of a natural law that gave equal rights to all men. The principles of justice enshrined in Roman law have had tremendous influence on the development of Western thinking about courts, the rights of accused people, and the proper use of evidence in determining guilt and innocence.

Although citizenship and legal rights were usually viewed from a male perspective, women were not passive pawns in Roman society. They were required to have guardians to handle their legal affairs, but this had become a mere formality by the end of the republic. Diocletian finally did away with it. Aristocratic women had great power and influence, and despite Augustus's attempt to revive some version of the patriarchal family of the early republic, women added to their rights. Marriage was a private matter in the republican era, and the state had little to do with it. There were two kinds of marriage—one that transferred the bride entirely to her husband's *familia* and another that preserved her relationship with her father's household. The second form made divorce easier, for the bride and her family retained more power over her dowry. By the beginning of the empire, it had become the standard form of marriage, and divorce and remarriage, at least in aristocratic circles, were common. Augustus believed that this contributed to the decline of the Roman family, and he tried to reverse it by increasing the state's power over marriages. Legal procedures were instituted for divorces, and adultery became a crime prosecuted by the state. A sexual double standard was accepted. Husbands had nothing to fear from the law so long as they did not debauch another man's wife or conspire in the misconduct of their own mate. Because men could safely conduct affairs with women who were licensed as prostitutes, some aristocratic women safeguarded themselves and their lovers by registering as prostitutes. Augustus's laws had little effect, and there were few other attempts to legislate morality until the fourth century, when Christian emperors appeared.

Intellectual Life   Virgil, Horace, Ovid, and Livy provided Roman authors with models for the composition of Latin poetry and prose that ended their dependence on the Greeks. The intellectual environment created by the empire, however, prevented their successors from writing in the same spirit. The giants of the Golden Age were inspired by *Romanitas,* a vision of an idealized republican Rome that faded as the reality of life under autocratic emperors became clear. The risks they faced were revealed when Tiberius's government convicted the author of a history of the civil wars of treason and burned his books. Elections and popular assemblies also faded during Tiberius's reign as the imperial bureaucracy took over their functions. This struck at the heart of Roman literary education—the study of rhetoric. Without opportunities to debate real issues and influence important decisions and elections, rhetoric became a pointless end in itself. Students continued to be trained in the techniques of debate, but they wrangled over abstract hypothetical problems that had no connection with contemporary politics. Their elevation of style over substance caused formal writing to become increasingly elaborate, convoluted, and verbose.

Things improved when the scholarly Claudius took the throne and appointed the Stoic philosopher Seneca the Younger (c. 4 B.C.E.–65 C.E.) tutor to his heir, Nero. Literary activity revived and began what historians refer to as Rome's Silver Age. The empire produced many good writers, but none as influential as those who had been Augustus's contemporaries. Many of them, significantly, came from the provinces—a testimony to Rome's success in spreading Hellenistic civilization.

The first flush of the Silver Age was brief. During the course of his long literary career, Seneca produced plays, essays on Stoic philosophy, treatises dealing with ethical issues, and a book on natural science. Although he tried to tread carefully, his Stoic moralism raised Nero's suspicions, and the emperor finally ordered him to commit suicide. Seneca's nephew, Lucan (39–65 C.E.), joined him in suicide, leaving unfinished a passionately republican epic poem dealing with the war between Caesar and Pompey. Petronius (d. 66 C.E.), another of Nero's victims, wrote a novel, *The Satyricon,* from which only fragments survive. It wittily mocked the falsity, pretentiousness, and crass self-indulgence of wealthy Romans and their sycophants. Satire appealed to an age of cynical and disillusioned artists. The *Epigrams* of Martial (c. 40–104 C.E.) commented ironically on a wide spectrum of Roman society, and the *Satires* of Juvenal (c. 55–130 C.E.) are as amusing as they are filled with anger and scorn.

Nero's sensitivity to criticism and paranoia suppressed literary activity, and conditions did not improve much under his successors. The Flavians funded libraries and schools, but silenced philosophers of whose teachings they disapproved. A few historians, however, thrived in the era of the empire despite the politically sensitive nature of their material. Tacitus (c. 55–120 C.E.) reflected on the empire from the hostile perspective of the senatorial aristocracy. His elegant prose is replete with pithy, memorable phrases that sum up insights (often pessimistic) into human character. Josephus (c. 37–95 C.E.), a Jewish author, wrote to provide the Romans (and his Flavian patrons) with background on his people. Biblical scholars have found his work an invaluable source of information on the period between the testaments and the environment into which Jesus of Nazareth was born. Suetonius (c. 69–135 C.E.), the most colorful of the era's historians, wrote biographies of Rome's rulers from Julius Caesar to Domitian. He may have relied more heavily on amusing tales and titillating gossip than on objective research. Plutarch (c. 45–120 C.E.), a Greek author, produced a large set of biographies in which he compared Greek and Roman leaders whom he thought had similar careers. His work is as accurate, or inaccurate, as the literary sources on which he relied, and it reflects the belief of his age that the purpose of history is to provide lessons in morality.

The Decline of Rome

A famous historian has said that the question that should be asked about the Roman Empire is not why it fell, but how it managed to last as long as it did. His point is that the empire was inherently fragile, and to speak of its fall may be misleading. It did not come to a sudden end, and no single thing brought it down. The way of life that Rome represented was incrementally transformed until the world had changed so much that it no longer made sense to call it Roman. The western provinces of the empire were economically weaker, less populous, less urbanized, and more exposed to invasion than the eastern. They lost their Roman identity, but something that thought of itself as the Roman Empire survived in the eastern Mediterranean for a long time.

Rome's Weakness   Like most ancient societies, the Roman Empire's resources barely sufficed to meet its routine needs, and crises caused by invasions, civil wars, plagues, or crop failures could push it to the brink of collapse. Rome's longevity owed much to the absence of a major foreign enemy who might have taken advantage of the empire's internal problems. Parthia was the only civilized state with which Rome shared a border, and it seldom posed a threat. Rome's most vulnerable front was its fifteen-hundred-mile-long Rhine-Danube frontier. Occasional localized campaigns were enough to hold this line until the third century C.E., when the German tribes began to consolidate and adopt Roman military practices.

The Roman Empire was handicapped by the ancient world's failure to make much technological progress, and the empire remained an agrarian state supported by fairly primitive methods of cultivation. Some plantations and manufacturing industries produced products for the world market, but waterways provided the only cost-efficient transportation. The residents of coastal districts and regions near navigable rivers could trade profitably, but people who lived inland had to be self-sufficient. Wheat brought by sea from Egypt and southern Gaul, for instance, sold more cheaply in Rome than did Italian grain raised fifty miles from the city.

Some of the empire's trade depressed its economy. Romans had an appetite for luxury goods from the Far East, but the West produced little that India and China could not provide for themselves. The West, therefore, had to pay with gold and silver for the silks and spices it imported. The bullion this drained from the Roman Empire undermined its monetary system. By the second century C.E., the West's mines were being worked out, and gold and silver from which to mint coins were becoming scarce. Emperors stretched the shrinking money supply by debasing coins (that is, by mixing gold and silver with cheaper metals), but this backfired. Because these coins had less innate value, sellers demanded more of them for their goods. Prices rose, and the empire had to wrestle with the problems of inflation. The costs of administering and defending the Roman Empire steadily increased, while the economy that sustained the empire declined.

From our perspective, as beneficiaries of the Industrial Revolution, the ancient world's failure to grow its economy is perplexing. Hellenistic scholars made scientific breakthroughs that, if they had been exploited, could have transformed the ancient way of life. Physicists worked out the principles of levers, gears, and pulleys, and they built working models of steam turbines. Some slave-staffed businesses utilized assembly-line techniques. The ingredients for an industrial revolution existed, but somehow they never came together. Reliance on slavery and an aristocratic intelligentsia preoccupied with rhetoric and philosophy probably contributed to the lack of interest in making work easier and more productive.

Diocletian and the *Dominate*   The rapid turnover of leaders during the half century when the Barracks Emperors reigned created such confusion that Rome's imperial government lost control of large numbers of territory. But the last of the Barracks Emperors, Diocletian (r. 285–305 C.E.), restored the empire's unity and stability. His policies preserved the empire for another century, but at a cost of its traditional way of life. Augustus was a *princeps* ("first citizen") who led a principate, a civilian government. Diocletian was a *dominus* ("lord"), a divine king who wielded the power of a military autocrat.

Diocletian's first priority was to secure the person of the emperor, for the empire could not function if its leaders were frequently overthrown. To reduce the number of potential competitors for the imperial office, Diocletian divided and dispersed political authority. He doubled the number of the empire's provinces and gave each both a civilian and a military governor. This greatly diminished the strength of the provincial commanders, but at the cost of quadrupling the size of the imperial bureaucracy.

It was too dangerous to divide the army, so Diocletian consolidated an elite, mobile force under his direct command and settled a class of militarized peasants along the empire's frontiers. These farmer-soldiers were supposed to fend off attacks on their home districts long enough for the emperor to bring up the main army and restore order. Generous pay and preferential treatment (such as exemption from taxes) ensured the loyalty of the emperor's troops, his *comitatenses* ("companions"). Diocletian may have had half a million men under arms, and their maintenance imposed a tremendous burden on his treasury.

Similarly costly was Diocletian's court. A *dominus* ruled by intimidation—by radiating an aura of awe-inspiring majesty. He was a remote being insulated from contact with his subjects by court functionaries and elaborate protocols. When he appeared in public, he wore elaborate robes, jewels, and the golden diadem of the sun-god.

Diocletian believed that one emperor was not enough to defend Rome's frontier. The most secure arrangement, he decided, was to share the empire with a colleague named Maximian (r. 286–305 C.E.), a man whom he could intimidate. He stationed himself in Asia Minor to watch the Parthian and lower Danube borders, and Maximian established a base in northern Italy from which to guard the upper Danube and the Rhine.

Diocletian had no son to inherit his throne, and he tried to revive the practice of adopting successors that had worked so well throughout the second century. Each "augustus" (the emperor's title) was to choose a "caesar" (a vice-president) to assist him, and at the end of a twenty-year term, the augustus was to retire and the caesar ascend to his office. This tetrarchy ("four-man rule") gave four powerful men a vested interest in working together. (See Map 6–3.)

The Transformation of Roman Society   Government policies often have unintended consequences. Diocletian's innovations certainly did, for they all increased Rome's economic difficulties. Diocletian quadrupled the size of the empire's bureaucracy, built a larger and more expensive army, and established four imperial courts. Rome could not afford the burdens this imposed, for its simple agrarian economy may have required the labor of six farmers to support each soldier, bureaucrat, and court functionary who did not till the earth.

Diocletian tried to deal with this problem by carefully budgeting. He conducted censuses at five-year intervals to estimate the wealth of the empire and set tax rates. He debased the coinage to increase the money supply and encourage economic activity. He tried to halt the inflation that resulted by issuing an Edict of Prices. It decreed what could legally be charged for about a thousand items and services. All this did, however, was drive goods onto a black market that the government could not regulate.

Diocletian was driven to confiscate the property of his subjects to meet the expenses of his government, and this transformed the empire's social structure. Its wealthier citizens fled its cities, where they were too exposed to its tax collectors, and took up permanent residence on

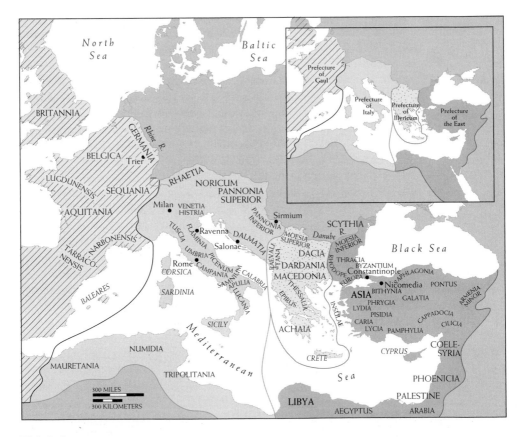

Map 6–3
The Divisions of the Late Roman Empire   Diocletian's creation of separate governments for the eastern and western halves of the Roman Empire forecast a division that became permanent. *Question:* Why were all the empire's administrative centers (Trier, Milan, Sirmium, and Nicomedia) on its northern rim rather than in a central location?

their rural estates. It was impossible for the government to track them all down, and to do so could be dangerous for tax collectors. This migration had a devastating impact on the empire's cultural institutions, for urban life was the dynamo that powered classical civilization.

Lesser individuals had fewer options for protecting their resources than the wealthy. When government confiscations bit into the working capital of farmers and artisans, they had to abandon their fields, close their shops, and go on the public dole. Each year the number of productive individuals declined. This increased the burden on those who remained and drove yet more people out of business. The state tried to maintain production of essential goods by nationalizing industries and conscripting laborers to work on state plantations. To maintain the workforce, men were required to teach their trades to their sons, and sons were forced to take up their father's professions. What had been, theoretically at least, a free society became a caste system. As masses of peasants *(coloni)* were bound to the lands they worked for the state and wealthy aristocrats, the empire began to break up into quasi-independent rural fiefdoms.

Larger Issue Revisited

The Romans often faced the unhappy choice between freedom and order. Theirs was never a democratic, egalitarian society in which everyone enjoyed the same liberties, but they honored ideals of citizenship and patriotism. These ideals have had a positive influence on the development of Western nations, but Roman history also illustrates what happens to such values when societies are under stress or subjected to unscrupulous or inept leaders. The insecurity of life in Rome's turbulent republic induced its citizens to submit to a powerful imperial government. For a long time, that government maintained stability and prosperity. Its decline into oppressive autocracy was neither inevitable nor accidental. It was the outcome of decisions that the Romans convinced themselves they were compelled to make.

Review Questions

1. Why was the Roman Republic unable to govern an empire?
2. Did Augustus save the Roman Republic or destroy it?
3. How did relationships between the military and the civilian elements in society change during the era of the empire?
4. Why might residents of the provinces and ordinary Romans have disagreed with the Roman Senate on which of Rome's emperors were good and which bad?
5. Could the Roman Empire have been saved?
6. Is popular government a luxury that only a people whose situation is relatively secure can afford?

Refer to the front of the book for a list of chapter-relevant primary sources available on the CD-ROM.

THE WEST INTERACTIVE

For web-based activities, map explorations, and quizzes related to this chapter, go to *www.prenhall.com/frankforter.*

PART THREE

THE DIVISION OF THE WEST
300 C.E. TO 1300 C.E.

During the ancient phase in the history of the West, the various civilizations that had sprung up around the Mediterranean blended into one, and for several centuries the whole of the Western civilized world was united under one government: the Roman Empire. There were significant cultural differences among the subjects of that empire. They spoke a variety of languages, practiced numerous religions, and preserved some ethnic distinctions, but at least for the governing classes, the things they shared were more important than the things that divided them. The Mediterranean Sea lay at the center of a world that was politically unified, economically interconnected, and intellectually in agreement.

The decline of Rome's empire was more than the end of a political system, for it signaled the start of an epoch in Western history in which the ancient trend toward unification reversed. The Mediterranean ceased to tie civilized peoples together, and the West divided against itself. During the ensuing Middle Ages, three distinct civilizations appeared: Latin Catholic Europe, Greek Orthodox Byzantium, and the Arab-Persian Muslim Empire. Although all three shared common legacies from the ancient world, they were more alert to their differences than to their commonalities. The defensiveness, misunderstanding, and hostility that came to characterize their relationships has yet to be overcome.

	CULTURE	ENVIRONMENT AND TECHNOLOGY	POLITICS
300	Christian persecution Edict of Toleration (311) Council of Nicaea (325) monastic movement begins	urban decay *coloni* two-field cultivation	Diocletian: the Dominate (305) Constantine (306–337)
		Visigoths at Adrianople (376)	
400	Christianity mandated (395) Augustine (354–430)	heavy, wheeled plows	Roman Empire divided Sack of Rome (410) Rhine frontier (406) Attila the Hun (d. 454) Romulus Augustulus (476)
500	*comitatus* Benedictine Rule, ca. 529 Byzantine civilization	*Hagia Sophia*	German kingdoms Clovis (d. 511) fds. the Merovingian dynasty Justinian (d. 565)
600	Islam and the *umma* (622) Shi'ite Islam (660)		Muhammad (570–632) caliphate (est. 632) Umayyad dynasty (660–750)
700		stirrup and heavy cavalry	Isaurian dynasty (fd. 717) Charles Martel (d. 741) Abbasid dynasty (fd. 750) Carolingians (fd. 751)
800	*capitularies* Carolingian Renaissance feudalism manorialism	mold board plow three-field cultivation system *minuscule* Byzantine *theme*	Charlemagne (768–814) Viking–Magyar invasions Macedonian dynasty (fd. 867)
900	Ottonian Renaissance Cluniac Reform (910)	horse shoe	Fatimid caliphate (fd. 909) Saxon dynasty (fd. 919)
1000		towns and trade revive capitalism	Capetian dynasty (fd. 987) Spanish crusade begins Salian dynasty (fd. 1024) Seljuk sultanate (fd. 1060) William the Conqueror
	Investiture Controversy (1075)		Battle of Manzikert (1075) Kingdom of Sicily (fd. 1092) I Crusade (1095–1099)
1100	Twelfth-Century Reniassance Peter Abelard (1079–1142) University of Bologna (1158)	scholastic method Romanesque architecture Gothic architecture	II Crusade (1144) Hohenstaufen dynasty Henry II (r. 1154–1189) III Crusade (1189–1192) Philip Augustus (1180–1223) Innocent III (r. 1198–1216)
1200	University of Paris (1200) troubadour lyric, romance		IV Crusade (1204) *Magna Carta* (1215)

# CHAPTER 7

THE WEST'S MEDIEVAL CIVILIZATIONS

> For all the differences that exist among the world's many great nations . . .
> there are only two kinds of societies, which . . . we have accurately characterized
> as two "cities." One is the "city of men," inhabited by people who are governed by
> the appetites of the flesh. The other is [the city of God], composed of people who
> live according to the spirit. Each of these communities decides what will make it
> happy, and when each gets what it wants, it lives with the consequences of its
> choice.
>
> **—Augustine of Hippo, *The City of God***

Larger Issue: *What role should religion play in society?*

Augustine (354–430 C.E.), bishop of the North African city of Hippo, was a highly educated
pagan who became a Christian in midlife. He wrestled with the decision for a long time, for to
be true to the Christian faith, he felt that he had to give up his flourishing secular career, break
off a socially advantageous engagement, separate from a mistress whom he loved, take a vow of
celibacy, and embrace a life of ascetic self-denial. Halfway measures would not do, for Augustine believed that people had to decide whether their allegiances lay with the "city of God" or
the "city of man." Those who trusted in Christian revelation were destined for eternal life in
communion with God. Unbelievers were damned beyond hope of redemption. On Earth,
these two groups were intertwined, but ultimately God would sort them out.

The Roman Empire unified the West and held it together for about three centuries. But
as the empire came apart, three new civilizations, whose identities were largely shaped by religion, staked claims to Rome's territorial and cultural legacies: Latin Christian Europe, Greek
Christian Byzantium, and an Arab-Islamic empire that extended from Spain across North
Africa and the Middle East to India. Each of these civilizations championed different (if related) faiths, and their respective religions profoundly influenced their internal politics and
their foreign relations.

The pagans of the ancient world were generally predisposed to religious tolerance, for
they believed that divinity was a multifaceted reality that manifested itself in many ways. As
polytheists, they were open to the discovery and veneration of new gods. Their governments
might go to war to win control of shrines and their treasures, or they might outlaw cults that
inspired immoral or treasonous behavior. But they did not usually regard religion as a source
of contention. This changed as the West entered the Middle Ages (the fifth through fifteenth
centuries), for the religions to which the three medieval civilizations were committed were
monotheistic faiths. The exclusive allegiance that each demanded to its own understanding of
God created the potential for misunderstanding and bloody conflict. Given that religion can
divide as well as unite people, how should society handle it?

TOPICS IN THIS CHAPTER

The Christian Element • The German Element •
The Byzantine Empire of Constantinople • Islam

The Christian Element

The steps that Diocletian took to save the Roman Empire changed it so much that it is reasonable to wonder if the empire he saved was still Roman. Its government was headed by a god-king and staffed by soldiers. Barter was replacing the use of money in its economic transactions. Many of its cities were declining. In some regions, powerful landlords were carving out quasi-independent domains, and people everywhere were being subjected to the restraints of a rigid caste system. Most of this was probably unintentional, for Diocletian did not set out to separate Rome from its past. His successor, Constantine (r. 312–337 C.E.), however, struck a purposeful blow at the roots of classical civilization. He shifted his allegiance from paganism to Christianity.

The Origin of the Christian Faith   Jesus of Nazareth, arguably the most influential individual in Western history, lived and died virtually unnoticed by his contemporaries. His brief career as the leader of a small band of Jewish disciples ended when he was crucified in Jerusalem during the reign of the emperor Tiberius. After his death, some of his acquaintances claimed that he had risen from the grave and that he was the *messiah* (or, in Greek, "the Christ," "the anointed"), a divine savior whose appearance the Jews had been anticipating. Their proclamation of this *gospel* ("good news") was not met with instant success. As late as the fourth century, when the emperor Constantine legalized Christianity, scholars estimate that only five percent (or perhaps as little as one percent) of Rome's subjects were Christians.

Jesus never strayed far from Galilee, a rural district north of Jerusalem that was populated by conservative Jewish peasants. Nothing is known about his activities until, at about the age of thirty, he began to wander about Galilee, preaching and healing. He continued this work for one to three years before going to Jerusalem to die on a Roman cross.

Jesus' history remains elusive. He wrote nothing, and no firsthand reports of his activities have come down to us. The oldest Christian writings are the letters of Paul (the former Saul of Tarsus) that form part of the New Testament, the Christian scriptures. Paul was a Jew from Asia Minor who came to Jerusalem sometime after Jesus' crucifixion. He never met the man Jesus but was converted to faith in Christ by a vision. He could have learned much about Jesus' earthly ministry from people who had been Jesus' companions, but this apparently did not interest Paul. His letters focus on the resurrected Christ, not the historical Jesus. The major sources of information about Jesus' life are the New Testament's four Gospels: Matthew, Mark, Luke, and John. They were written between thirty and sixty-five years after Jesus' death, and none of their authors claim to have been eyewitnesses of the events he narrates. The Gospels were testimonials of faith, not mere objective histories. They were written, as the Gospel of John (20:31) says, to induce those who read them to believe that Jesus is the Christ.

Jesus and his disciples were all Jews, and Jesus is never said to have sanctioned a break with Judaism. His brother James, the head of the Christian community in Jerusalem, was well known for his scrupulous observation of Jewish religious law. As Jews, the first Christians seem to have assumed that gentiles (non-Jews) who wished to join their community (the "church") would convert to Judaism. If gentile Christians did not become Jews, Jewish Christians could not associate with them without transgressing Jewish religious law. Paul, although he too was a Jew, saw things differently. He condemned any effort to impose Judaism on the church's gentile converts, and his position ultimately triumphed.

Although missionaries like Paul believed that the messiah's appearance meant that the era governed by Jewish religious law had come to an end, they clung to the Hebrew scriptures. The witness of this "Old Testament" was needed to understand the Christ, for the messiah was the fulfillment of the promise God had made to Abraham. God had said that Abraham's descendants would someday become a great nation. For generations the Jews had assumed that this meant that they would acquire land and political power, but by the second century B.C.E., their expectations had changed. They concluded that they were too few ever to triumph over the great gentile empires on their own. God, therefore, would fulfill His promise by intervening in history on their behalf. He would send them a messiah, an agent who was commissioned (anointed) to act with His authority. Some Jews expected the messiah to resemble the prophets, kings, or priests who had led them in the past. Others claimed that he would be an angel, a supernatural manifestation of God's power. No one anticipated a messiah like Jesus— a humble laborer who was crucified as a common criminal and whose passing left the world apparently unchanged.

Many Jews were shocked by the Christian claim that the transcendent and majestic deity of their faith had incarnated His power in a man like Jesus. Gentiles, on the other hand, were less likely to find this implausible. Pagan religious mythology was full of stories of gods who appeared as all too-human men and women—and of human beings who became gods. Jesus' crucifixion was, in Paul's words, a "stumbling block" to the faith of both Jew and gentile, but all things considered, conversion may have been easier for gentiles than for Jews.

The Church's Reception and Persecution

As the first century C.E. unfolded, Judaism and Christianity grew farther and farther apart. Jewish leaders condemned Christianity as a distorted version of their faith, and the political situation in Palestine made Christians eager to distinguish themselves from Jews. Palestine was restive under Roman control, and a radical Jewish faction, the Zealots, incited riots against the Roman authorities. (The Romans may have executed Jesus on the assumption that he was a Zealot.) Full-scale war finally broke out in 66 C.E. Rome destroyed Jerusalem and its temple, and fought for seven years to suppress the Jewish revolt. Given the circumstances, Christians were eager to assure the Roman authorities that they were on Rome's side in the conflict. The Gospels were written in this context, and that may explain their eagerness to shift responsibility for Jesus' crucifixion from the Romans to the Jews.

Rome's objectives in the Jewish War were political, not theological, for Romans preferred to adopt religions rather than suppress them. Romans worshiped simultaneously on multiple levels. The state honored numerous national gods: classical mythology's Greco-Roman Olympians, foreign deities such as Asia Minor's Magna Mater and Egypt's Serapis and Isis, and, of course, the emperors themselves. Countless localities had sacred caves, groves, and springs. Families maintained household shrines for their own private guardian spirits, and many individuals joined mystery cults. A mystery cult was a secret society that initiated its members. Its doctrines and rituals were inspired by the story of a divine being, a savior who defeated the forces of evil and opened the way for human beings to obtain personal immortality. These cults sometimes required converts to be baptized before admitting them to the key ritual: a meal that united worshipers with one another and their god.

Christianity's resemblance to the popular mystery cults doubtless helped it to grow, but it also had unique features that gave it advantages over these competitors. Its savior was not a fantastic being from a mythic past, but a real man from recent history. It accorded women and slaves the same spiritual standing as free men, and its conviction that the appearance of the Messiah heralded the imminent end of the world motivated it to proselytize with unusual zeal. The chief source of the young religion's friction with Roman society was its commitment to Hebrew monotheism—its insistence that its God was the only god.

Pagans feared that Christian blasphemy against the gods would anger the gods and prompt them to punish everyone. If a disaster occurred, the people affected might spontaneously rise up and attack their Christian neighbors. But there was no empire-wide effort to eradicate Christianity until the reign of Decius (r. 249–251 C.E.), one of the Barracks Emperors. Decius was fighting to save an empire that was on the verge of collapse, and he had no patience with disloyalty. Christians incited suspicion because they refused to perform a simple patriotic ritual—the sacrifice of a pinch of incense before the statue of the emperor. Their apocalyptic preaching, which maintained that the world (including Decius's empire) was soon to come to an end, also did little to assure the emperor that they supported his efforts to save civilization.

The Church's Organization   Persecution of the church was counterproductive. The willingness of Christian martyrs ("witnesses") to go to their deaths rather than compromise their allegiance to their deity made the strongest possible argument for the uniqueness and power of Christian faith. The threat of persecution also weeded out the weak, recruited the strong, and forced Christian communities to organize and work together.

Many religions fragment as they spread, but Christian congregations resisted this tendency. An increasing threat of persecution encouraged them to work together, but so did a sense of mission that was part of their faith from its beginning. Early Christians believed that the messiah's appearance meant that the end of the world was near. Christ would soon come again, and every human being would face God's final judgment. Christians believed that God, in His mercy, was granting them a brief period in which to take this message to the world. The urgency of the situation forced them to invest their limited time where it promised to do the most good. They ignored the people who were scattered thinly across the countryside and focused their attention on the urban masses. Consequently, Christianity became an urban religion, and paganism, the religion of *pagani* ("rural villagers"), lingered for a long time in the countryside.

As Christianity spread, the organization of the church began to mirror that of the empire. The empire was divided into territorial units centered on cities. The Christian missionaries who worked in these cities created ties among them. When a church in one town sponsored a mission to another, it forged an enduring link between them. Gradually, a network of such ties spread across the empire. It had no center, but it could diffuse information and financial aid widely. As the number of congregations grew in a town, its Christians would choose a bishop (*episcopus,* "overseer") to coordinate their work. Bishops of neighboring communities

Culture in Context: The Pursuit of Martyrdom

The earliest account of a Christian martyrdom is a description of the death by burning of Polycarp of Smyrna (c. 69–155 C.E.), a bishop who was said to have been a disciple of Jesus' apostle John. We are told that his followers rescued his charred bones and treated them like precious jewels. The medieval church vigorously promoted this sort of thing, and the veneration of relics—of anything that had been associated with a martyr or saint—became a staple of Christian worship. People made arduous pilgrimages to visit places where relics were enshrined, for these sacred objects were believed to work miracles.

Most of the church's martyrs were obscure men and women about whom little or nothing is known, but Vibia Perpetua, a twenty-two-year-old matron, who met her death in the arena at Carthage on March 7, 203, is an exception. During her imprisonment she wrote a kind of diary that gives us a rare glimpse into the mind of a Christian facing martyrdom. It is unclear why Vibia and the four people arrested with her were punished when other Christians seem to have been free to visit them in prison. She was a recent convert who was not yet baptized when she was arrested. She may have broken an imperial mandate that forbade further conversions to Christianity, or perhaps her neophyte zeal inspired her to commit some provocative act. Two of the Christians arrested with her were slaves, but she came from a prominent family. Her father, mother, and brother were allowed to visit her while she was in jail, and her father did his utmost to persuade her to save herself by sacrificing to the statue of the emperor.

Vibia was not dissuaded by the fact that her martyrdom was costly to others. She acknowledged that she was disgracing her family. Her aged father was nearly driven out of his wits by the behavior of a daughter whom he claimed to love more than his sons. His arguments and emotional distress failed to move her, as did the beating that the judge inflicted on him for disorderly conduct at her trial. Vibia had also recently given birth to a son who, she admitted, might die without her nursing, but even this did not shake her resolve.

In prison she had a foretaste of the influence she expected to exercise as a sainted martyr. She suddenly recalled a brother who had died years earlier at the age of seven, and she was overcome by the conviction that his soul was suffering in the afterlife. She prayed for him day and night until she was convinced that her intercession had liberated him from torment. Even the guards who imprisoned her, she says, respected her and her companions because "we had some great power in us."

Vibia had dream visions filled with symbols that she believed predicted her victory over the Devil and her personal welcome into heaven by Christ. In one of her dreams she imagined herself transformed into a male athlete and pitted against a vicious Egyptian in the arena. Her fate, however, was to be gored by a wild cow and finished off by a gladiator.

Question: Did martyrdom give ordinarily powerless members of Roman society a kind of power over others?

corresponded and occasionally convened meetings to discuss doctrinal and disciplinary issues. This helped create and maintain some consistency of faith and practice within large regions. Inevitably, the bishops of the larger and more important towns came to dominate their lesser brethren, and an administrative hierarchy began to evolve. No single bishop was ever recognized as the head of the whole church, but one had a unique claim to distinction. Peter, the chief of Jesus' disciples, was said to have been Rome's first bishop and to have been martyred in Rome. In the Gospel of Matthew (16:18–19) Jesus calls Peter "the rock" on which the church is founded and promises that whatever Peter does on Earth will be ratified in heaven. Rome's bishops insisted that, as Peter's successors, his status passed to them, but it was a long time before they could lay exclusive claim to the title *pope* (*papa,* a child's word for *father* common to many languages) or any other privilege.

Constantine and Imperial Christianity   Diocletian launched the empire's most concerted attack on the church, but his successor, Constantine (r. 312–337 C.E.), embraced Christianity and began the process of converting the empire. Constantine was not supposed to be Diocletian's successor. He became emperor by the tried and true method of persuading a portion of the army to help him eliminate other candidates for the office. Early Christian historians claim that he was converted by a vision on the eve of the battle that won him control of the western half of the Roman Empire. His faith was doubtless sincere, but it was also politically motivated. Persecution had been a conspicuous failure, and Constantine thought that the shaky empire might gain more by winning the church over than by continuing to oppose it. He did not go so far as to declare Christianity the empire's sole religion, but he made his preferences clear. He poured money into the construction of great basilicas, welcomed bishops into councils of state, and gave favorable treatment to Christians in the state bureaucracy. After he won control of the whole empire, he made his position even clearer. He moved the empire's capital east to a new city he called Constantinople. It was modeled after Rome, but where Rome had pagan temples, it had Christian churches.

The church benefited greatly from Constantine's patronage, but it was not as useful to him in shoring up the empire as he might have hoped. Once the threat of persecution was removed and church offices became stepping stones to wealth and power, Christians began to fight among themselves. The young faith had yet to resolve many theological questions, and now that it was safe for Christians to air their differences, fissures widened in the Christian community. Each faction accused the others of promulgating heresy (that is, false teaching), and each claimed that, as the sole arbiter of orthodoxy (correct belief), it ought to lead the church. Mobs took up the cause of one party against another, and violence erupted on the streets of Roman cities.

Constantine's first impulse was to use the power of the state to resolve theological disputes, but his experience with the Donatists, a group of North African Christians who had withstood Diocletian's persecution, taught him that this was unwise. The Donatists claimed that priests who had yielded to Diocletian's demands had forfeited the power to perform valid sacraments (the sacred rites that imparted God's grace to believers). The only valid priests who remained, therefore, were the Donatists' own. Their opponents disagreed, for, as they saw it, a priest's powers derived from his office, not from his personal merit as a Christian. A sinful priest could forgive other sinners their sins, for a priest did not act on his own authority. He was an agent of the church and therefore of God. Constantine's judges accepted this argument and ordered the Donatists to stop making trouble. The Donatists refused and rejoiced that the state was again giving them the opportunity to validate their faith through martyrdom.

Figure 7–1   The Arch of Constantine   By Constantine's day, Rome had not been the administrative capital of the empire for decades. The seats of imperial government had moved to places that had better communications with chronic trouble spots. Emperors still adorned Rome with monuments, but the arch erected to celebrate Constantine's triumphs suggests that the glory of the ancient world was fading. The structure's best components were looted from earlier buildings, and its new elements are of inferior quality.

Constantine's efforts to heal the split within the African Christian community had only made things worse.

When an Egyptian priest named Arius (c. 250–336 C.E.) initiated a furious debate over the relationship between Christ the Son and God the Father, Constantine was ready with a different strategy. At issue was whether the Son was the Father's equal or His first creation—the subordinate agent through whom He had created the world. Constantine decided to force the church to take responsibility for working this out for itself. In 325 C.E. he invited all the bishops of the empire to a council in the city of Nicaea (near Constantinople) and ordered them to resolve the dispute. The bishops hoped to unify the church by providing it with a creed (a statement of essential beliefs) that all Christians could profess. The council ratified a creed, but it failed to bring the warring factions together. Each group interpreted the creed as consistent with it own beliefs, and the squabbling continued. The exasperated emperor finally resorted to force and even tried switching from one side of the argument to the other, but the Arian debate raged on and spawned other doctrinal controversies.

The church did not unify Rome's crumbling empire, but it rescued much from the empire's decline. The eastern half of the empire survived longer than the western half, and Constantinople's powerful emperors treated the eastern church much like a department of state. The situation was different in Rome's western provinces, where fading imperial governments thrust freedom and responsibility onto the church. Each Roman city had a secular administration staffed by civil magistrates and an ecclesiastical administration headed by a Christian bishop. But as the empire declined in the west, the agents of secular government disappeared. Christian bishops, who were supported by the church's endowments, were the only public officials left in many cities. People inevitably looked to them for leadership. Cities came under the control of bishops, and they labored to preserve some of the administrative machinery of the former Roman state. When new kingdoms eventually began to rise from the ruins of the western empire, their rulers turned to the church's bishops for help in organizing them.

The church that bishops led served "the world"—the realm where men and women raised families and struggled to survive. As the empire declined, however, a kind of church within the church sprang up. It was populated by religious ascetics who wanted nothing to do with the worldly concerns of ordinary people. They believed that by disciplining their flesh, they could strengthen their spirits and draw closer to God. This was not exclusively a Christian impulse. The secular philosophies of the era also tended to be world-denying, and the speed with which the ascetic movement spread suggests that it matched the mood of the age.

The church's first ascetics were hermits—people who fled human company to live alone in remote, desolate places. This idea seems to have struck fire first in Egypt, and a biography of an Egyptian hermit named Anthony (c. 250–355 C.E.) helped to publicize it. It spread rapidly through the eastern empire and was somewhat slower to find a foothold in the west. So popular did it become that large numbers of hermits began to accumulate in some places. They were often drawn by the fame of a holy man (like Anthony) from whom they hoped to receive spiritual counseling. Practical concerns forced these spontaneous gatherings to organize themselves, and they evolved into institutions called monasteries—communities of *monks* (from a Greek word meaning "solitary"). The earliest monasteries were set up by one of Anthony's younger contemporaries, a former Egyptian soldier named Pachomius (292–346 C.E.).

The growth of monasticism accelerated after Constantine legalized Christianity and made the faith both safe and popular. Early Christians expected the world to resist their call for repentance and their warning of an imminent apocalypse. When the world suddenly capitulated and embraced their faith, some Christians were unsure how to respond. Many believed that faith required a witness against the world, and they were shaken when the world not only refused to martyr them, but offered them wealth and power. Fearing seduction, they literally fled into the wilderness and substituted voluntary ascetic disciplines for martyrdom. They became the spiritual heroes of the post-Constantinian church, and crowds of pilgrims sought their prayers and advice. Church officials saw this as a potential problem. Few hermits and monks were ordained priests, and their religious enthusiasm was not a reliable substitute for training in theology. To prevent them from drifting into heresy, church leaders devised rules to govern their communal lives. A rule penned by Basil of Caesarea (330–379 C.E.) won wide acceptance in the eastern empire, and a century later an Italian hermit named Benedict of Nursia (480–542 C.E.) wrote the rule adopted by most of western Europe's monks. Western monasticism emphasized ascetic disciplines less than eastern monasticism and focused more on a precisely regulated routine of work and prayer.

Although the hermit's flight from the human community ended with the formation of new communities, the monks who set up these communities still sought to isolate themselves from the world. They raised their own food and established schools to give their recruits the educations they needed to read the scriptures and chant the liturgies of worship. As the empire declined, its urban classes faded away—taking with them the schools and libraries that depended on their patronage. Monasteries survived, however, for they were largely self-sufficient, and the schools they maintained became, by default, the primary institutions keeping literacy alive in the West. Paradoxically, the men and women who fled the world saved its civilization.

The German Element

Constantine was survived by three sons who divided the empire he had spent much of his life uniting. One of these men, Constantius (r. 337–360 C.E.), outlived his brothers, reunited the empire, and passed it on to his cousin Julian (r. 360–363 C.E.). Christian historians dubbed Julian "the Apostate," for he withdrew state support for Christianity and tried to reform and revive paganism. Julian's reign was too brief, and his successor, a soldier named Jovian (r. 363 C.E.), restored the church's privileged status. Jovian reigned for only eight months, and at his death a coalition of military and civilian officials elevated another Christian soldier, Valentinian I (r. 364–375 C.E.), to the throne. Valentinian divided the empire, taking the western half for himself and assigning the government of the east to his brother Valens (r. 364–378 C.E.). Valens made a decision that precipitated a crisis from which the empire never recovered.

Invaders and Immigrants   The Germans who began to flood into the western Roman Empire in the fourth century have been called barbarians, but the term is misleading. They were not primitive people or strangers with an alien culture who suddenly appeared to threaten Rome. They had been the empire's neighbors for centuries and were thoroughly familiar with its civilization. They traded with Romans, worked inside the empire, and moved peacefully back and forth across the empire's vague boundaries. Roman diplomats even helped some German chiefs consolidate their tribes, for this stabilized turbulent regions and raised up kings with whom Rome could negotiate treaties. Roman merchants and Christian missionaries worked among the Germans, and some tribes converted to Christianity (albeit to the heretical Arian version) while still outside the empire. Germans envied Rome's wealth and power, and many were attracted to the empire in hopes of sharing the benefits of its civilization. Unfortunately, they came so quickly and in such numbers that the fragile, poorly governed empire could not absorb them.

The Germans were not only drawn to Rome; they were pushed against its frontiers by the migration of the Huns. The Huns had long preyed on China from their homeland in Mongolia. But when an aggressive dynasty arose in China and stiffened it defenses, the Huns were deflected to the west. They were formidable warriors whose equestrian skills were legendary, and they had invented a technique for making powerful bows that were small enough to be shot from horseback. In the mid-fourth century C.E. they reached the lands north of the Black Sea, where they encountered and subdued their first Germans, the Ostrogoths (East Goths). In 375 C.E. they routed the Ostrogoths' neighbors, the Visigoths (West Goths), who fled to the Roman border and begged permission to enter the empire.

This forced Valens, the eastern emperor, to make a difficult decision. As many as eighty thousand Visigoths were massed on his frontier. No ancient government could handle that many refugees, but if Valens refused the Visigoths entry, they were likely to attack and cost him soldiers he needed to fend off the Huns. Valens concluded that the lesser evil was to admit the Visigoths to the empire and use them to bolster its defenses. Things did not work out as Valens must have hoped they would. The Visigoths soon faced starvation in their refugee camps, and they were infuriated by the Roman profiteers who tried to exploit them. In desperation, they began to forage for supplies in the region north of Constantinople. Valens pursued them, and on August 9, 378 C.E., he blundered into an ambush near the city of Adrianople. He and Rome's eastern army were slaughtered. By then, the western half of the empire had passed to Valentinian I's son, Gratian (r. 375–383 C.E.). He gave Theodosius, a family friend, the job of restoring order in the eastern empire. Theodosius made peace with the Visigoths and enlisted them as *foederati*—independent allies resident within the empire and pledged to defend it.

By 394 C.E., various usurpers had overthrown Gratian and his brother Valentinian II (r. 378–392 C.E.), and Theodosius (r. 394–395 C.E.) had emerged as sole emperor. He was the last man to govern the whole empire and the first to proclaim Christianity its official religion (392 C.E.). At his death, the empire was divided between his sons. The west passed to Honorius (r. 395–423 C.E.), who was only ten years old, and the east to Arcadius (395–408 C.E.), who was eighteen. The shortsighted policies of their inept administrations were soon to extinguish the last vestiges of Roman power in the western half of the Mediterranean world.

The Decline of the Western Empire   About the time of Theodosius's death, the Visigoths acquired a new leader named Alaric (c. 370–410 C.E.). When he began to press Constantinople for new opportunities for his people, the eastern empire took the easy way out. It rid itself of the Visigoths by urging them to move west into Italy. Italy's defense was managed by Stilicho (c. 365–408 C.E.), a German general who commanded the emperor Honorius's army. He repulsed Alaric's initial assaults, but fear of the Visigoths caused Honorius's government to make some fateful decisions. Milan, the seat of the western empire, seemed too vulnerable to siege, so the court moved to Ravenna, a small port on the Adriatic. Ravenna owed the honor of becoming the last capital of the western Roman Empire to swamps that protected it from landward assault and to its proximity to the sea. The emperor wanted to be able, if threatened, to take ship and flee Italy. Honorius's advisors also chose to beef up Italy's defenses by recalling the troops that guarded the Rhine and Danube frontiers. With nothing standing in their way, large numbers of Germans from several tribes crossed the Rhine on the last day of year 406 C.E. and began to loot their way through Gaul.

In 408 C.E. the bad situation grew worse. Honorius became suspicious of Stilicho's ambitions and ordered the general's execution. This disrupted the defense of the western empire and gave the Visigoths a chance to break into Italy. Ravenna's swamps prevented Alaric from assaulting Honorius directly, but Alaric had a plan for putting pressure on the western emperor. He ordered the Visigoths to march on Rome. Honorius could not ignore this threat to the symbol of his authority. He opened negotiations with Alaric, but when he failed to implement their agreements, Alaric lost patience and made good his threat. On August 24, 410 C.E., he sacked Rome. This was of little practical consequence, for the city was no longer the seat of the western empire. But Rome's humiliation was a blow to the morale of the ancient world. It had been eight hundred years since the city last fell to an enemy, and its defeat was an ominous portent. Pagan intellectuals blamed the disaster on the rise of Christianity and the empire's neglect of the gods that had long protected it. The western empire's leading Christian thinker, Augustine (whose words are quoted at the head of this chapter), defended Christianity by putting the event in the broadest possible historical perspective. It was, he claimed, simply one in a long series of painful consequences of humanity's sinful rebellion against God. (See Chapter 8, "The Emergence of Europe.")

A SENSE OF PLACE:
THE WORLD THROUGH HUMAN EYES,
TO THE SEVENTEENTH CENTURY

Our eyes are not cameras that objectively record the external world. Our minds shape what we see. Ordinarily, this happens without us thinking about it, but when we consciously control the process, we become artists and make images that reflect us as well as the world. Each culture trains people to see the world from a particular perspective. The history of art, therefore, documents humanity's evolving relationship with the world.

The first artists found animals more interesting than themselves or the panoply of nature. As civilizations appeared, artists focused on the human. Classical artists often isolated and idealized human subjects. Hellenistic artists preferred realism. Apocalyptic, ascetic Christianity turned early medieval artists away from the transient world of nature and toward spiritual realities. Italy's Renaissance revived the classical point of view, and its artists described the world first as a context for human life and then as a subject in its own right. Faith's assumption that there is more to the world than meets the eye persists, and still leads Western artists, on occasion, to treat nature as a realm that hints at things unseen.

Cave Painting, Lascaux, France, 15,000–10,000 B.C.E. No one can be sure what prehistoric cave paintings mean. This one may describe a confrontation between two shamans, one of whom has taken the form of a bison that has been speared. A magical staff topped by a bird image lies next to the bison's rival, a magician wearing a bird mask. Lack of perspective makes it impossible to tell if this man is dead on the ground or standing triumphantly over the bison. The artist who painted the scene depicted a world where mysterious forces incarnate in animal species were humanity's companions. *The Art Archive/Musée des Antiquités St. Germain en Laye/Dagli Orti*

Hellenistic mosaic depicting sea creatures, Roman copy of a Greek original probably from Pergamon, 2nd century B.C.E., National Museum, Naples, Italy The Greeks of the Hellenistic era loved exotic subjects, and their artists delighted in demonstrating technical mastery. Hellenistic science also promoted an interest in exact, objective descriptions of natural phenomena. All these tastes came together in this mosaic, a kind of illustrated catalog of species of fish, eels, squid, and octopi. It was made for a patron who obviously believed that natural phenomena were worth studying for their own sake. *Scala, Art Resource, New York*

Wall painting from the Villa Livia at Primaporta, c. 20 B.C.E., Museo della Terme, Rome The great poets of the Augustan Golden Age celebrated Italy's fecund countryside and the pleasures of rural life. This painting from the walls of what may have been a dining room in a country home could serve to illustrate their works. The room was recessed in the earth to provide a cool retreat for summer suppers, and the painting creates the illusion that diners are viewing a luxuriant garden from the shelter of a rocky grotto. A wicker fence and stone balustrade serve as a border for an impenetrable thicket. Some 12 species of tree and shrub, ten of flowers, and 11 of birds can be identified. The fruits and flowers of different seasons all appear here together—representing the blessings nature bestowed on Italy. *Roman National Museum, Rome/Canali Photo-Bank, Milan/SuperStock*

Empress Theodora and Her Court, c. 547, Church of San Vitale, Ravenna, Italy This mosaic turns the lavish environment of the late Roman court into a symbol of transcendent reality. The empress Theodora sports an elaborately jeweled headdress and is accompanied by a retinue of richly robed attendants as she presents a sacred chalice to the church. The human figures and their costumes are described in minute detail and set against an architectural background, but they are not ordinary human beings occupying ordinary space. By depicting them in only two-dimensions, the artist has turned them into incorporeal beings detached from earthly time and space. *Scala, Art Resource, New York*

The 12th-Century Rock Monastery of Vardzia, Georgia Perched at 10,000 feet above a deep gorge, the monastery at Vardzia is a stunning example of the relationship between culture and the environment. It consists of over 3,000 caves that served as richly-frescoed churches, halls, refectories, bakeries, wine cellars, and animal pens. It housed up to 50,000 people and was a center for learning and the arts during the era when Georgian power and cultural influence reached its zenith. *Charles Cavaliere*

Decoration, The Alhambra Palace, Granada, Spain, 1377 Strict Islamic cultures eschewed naturalistic art, for attempts to create a world like nature's seemed to trespass on God's work. Instead, Muslim artists reminded people of divine truth by inventively replicating texts from the Qur'an. Elegant calligraphy and elaborate geometric abstractions celebrated the mathematic perfection God imparted to the universe. The 14th-century palace of the sultans of Granada contains superb examples of the kind of non-representational art that projected Islam's unique vision of a spiritual environment. *M. Freeman, Getty Images, Inc.—Photodisc*

The Month of September, from the Duke of Berry's *Book of Hours*, by Paul and Jean de Limbourg, 1410, Muséé Condé, Chantilly, France This elegant illustration from a calendar that was part of a prayer book commissioned by a member of the French royal family represents an activity, a grape harvest, associated with the month of September. Earlier medieval manuscript illustrations were often meant to be read as if they were pages of written text. That is, they consisted of clusters of images and symbols, each of which contributed something separate to the telling of a story or conveying of a message. Although the illustrations in the Limbourg brothers' *Book of Hours* are somewhat fanciful, they signify a renewed interest in the world of nature and in realistic representations of scenes from ordinary life. The artist who painted "September" had not yet mastered the rules of perspective that would have given depth to his composition, but he crowded his tiny picture with lavish details that help create the illusion that it is a window through which we can glimpse the real world. *"September: Harvesting Grapes by the Limbourg Brothers." Tres Riches Heures du Duc de Berry (early 15th century). Victoria & Albert Museum, London, UK. The Bridgeman Art Library*

St. Jerome in His Study, Antonello da Messina, c. 1460, National Gallery, London Italy's Renaissance humanists paid more attention to the environmental context of human life than most of their medieval predecessors. The world they described, however, was less the one they saw than the one humanist principles claimed ought to exist. Antonello da Messina, whom tradition credits with having introduced Venetian artists to the techniques of oil painting, placed the fourth-century church father, St. Jerome, in such a setting. There is no scholarly clutter in Jerome's study. His world is orderly, rational, and thoroughly under human control. The spiritual reality at which nature hints in Antonello's painting is not one of mystery and ecstasy, but reason and stability. *St. Jerome in His Study, Antonello Da Messina. (c) National Gallery, London*

The Miraculous Draft of Fishes, Konrad Witz, ca. 1444, Musée d'Art et d'Histoire, Geneva, Switzerland Most of the landscapes that appear in Renaissance art are imaginary, but eventually artists turned to the description of real places. The first to do so may have been Konrad Witz, who made Lake Geneva, not the Sea of Galilee, the setting for the Gospel's story of Christ walking on the water. It is hard for us to appreciate how shocked the Genevans must have been to be confronted, for the first time, by a picture of a place they recognized—and to see Jesus in it. *Museum of Art and History, Geneva, Switzerland/Bridgeman Art Library, London/SuperStock*

Danube Landscape, Albrech Altdorfer, c. 1520, Alte Pinakothek, Munich In the 16th century, landscape ceased to be a mere backdrop for human action and became a primary subject for painters. Albrech Altdorfer's view of the Danube Valley may be the first painting of a scene from the countryside into which human figures do not intrude. It suggests that Altdorfer and his contemporaries had begun to respect the world of nature as a reality that had worth apart from the uses people might make of it. Heaven was no longer the only realm that merited their serious attention. *Scala, Art Resource, New York*

Toledo, Domenico Theotocopuli— El Greco, c. 1600, Metropolitan Museum of Art, New York City The political confusion of the era of religious wars undercut the Renaissance humanists' faith in reason's ability to create an orderly, secure context for human life. Nature itself no longer seemed a beneficent, passive setting for human activities. It became a realm with dynamics of its own— some of which threatened life and civilization. The stormy context in which El Greco placed Toledo implies that even the existence of one of Spain's greatest cities is precarious. *View of Toledo, El Greco, Metropolitan Museum of Art, New York/Index/Bridgeman Art Library, London/New York*

The Visigoths did little serious damage to Rome. They were Arian Christians who respected the city's churches, and after three days of looting, they evacuated Rome and marched south along Italy's coast. Their plan was to collect ships and eventually to sail to North Africa. When a storm destroyed the flotilla they had gathered, they turned around and headed north to Gaul. Alaric died somewhere near Naples and was buried in a grave hidden beneath the bed of the Busento river.

Once the Visigoths were out of Italy, Honorius recognized them as *foederati,* and they settled in southern Gaul and Spain. They were far from the only Germans to stake claims to parts of the western empire. Many tribes had entered Roman territory in 406 C.E., when Honorius stripped troops from the Rhine frontier. The Vandals were part of the vanguard. As they looted their way across Gaul, others followed in their wake. Scattered bands of Franks occupied northern Gaul, and the Burgundians founded a kingdom in eastern Gaul. When the Visigoths pushed into southern Gaul, the Vandals wandered into Spain. In 429 C.E. they crossed the Straits of Gibraltar, conquered North Africa, established a capital for a kingdom at Carthage, and built a navy with which to raid Sicily and Italy. In 455 C.E. they sacked Rome. By then, Britain, whose defense Honorius had abandoned in 410 C.E., was being taken over by Angles and Saxons. Many other less significant tribes also grabbed bits and pieces of what was still, in theory at least, Rome's empire. (See Map 7–1.)

The western empire prolonged its existence as a legal entity by recognizing many of the Germans who settled within its boundaries as *foederati.* Rome had little power over these allies, but they responded to its calls for help when it was in their interest to do so. The last major occasion on which they served Rome was in 451 C.E., when Attila (c. 406–453 C.E.), king of the Huns, led his people into Gaul. Aëtius (c. 390–454 C.E.), a Roman general who served the emperor Valentinian III (r. 425–455 C.E.), met the Huns at Châlons, south of Reims. With the aid of his German allies, he fought the Huns to a draw, and Attila retreated to Germany. The following year, when the Huns struck south into Italy, Rome was abandoned by its allies. They fought only when their own lands were threatened. Diplomacy and a timely outbreak of malaria in Attila's army saved the city of Rome from another sack. The Huns withdrew to Germany's healthier environment, and Attila died the following winter. His empire did not survive him, but its sudden collapse did not guarantee Rome's security. It only freed Germans whom the Huns had enslaved to seek their fortunes in Roman territory.

By now, the western emperors controlled little more than Italy, and that was often only nominally theirs. The real power had passed to generals who were often of German descent. In 476 C.E. one of these, Odovacer (c. 493 C.E.), deposed the last of the west's figurehead emperors, a fifteen-year-old boy who bore the name of Rome's founder, Romulus, and who was mockingly called Augustulus ("Little Augustus"). The eastern emperor championed another claimant for the western throne, but he was powerless to seat his candidate.

After Attila's empire fell, the Ostrogoths advanced on Constantinople, and it dealt with them as it previously had the Visigoths—by diverting them to the west. In 489 C.E. the eastern emperor invited the Ostrogothic king Theodoric (r. 489–526 C.E.) to invade Italy and restore it to the empire. Theodoric theoretically served the eastern emperor, but in reality he was an independent monarch. He gave Italy a few decades of peace, during which attempts were made to rescue the West's faltering civilization. Two notable scholars, Boethius (c. 480–524 C.E.) and Cassiodorus (c. 490–580 C.E.), worked at his court, and the books they produced became the staples of education throughout Europe during the early Middle Ages. Theodoric gave Italy a valuable, if brief, respite from the confusion of a chaotic age. An

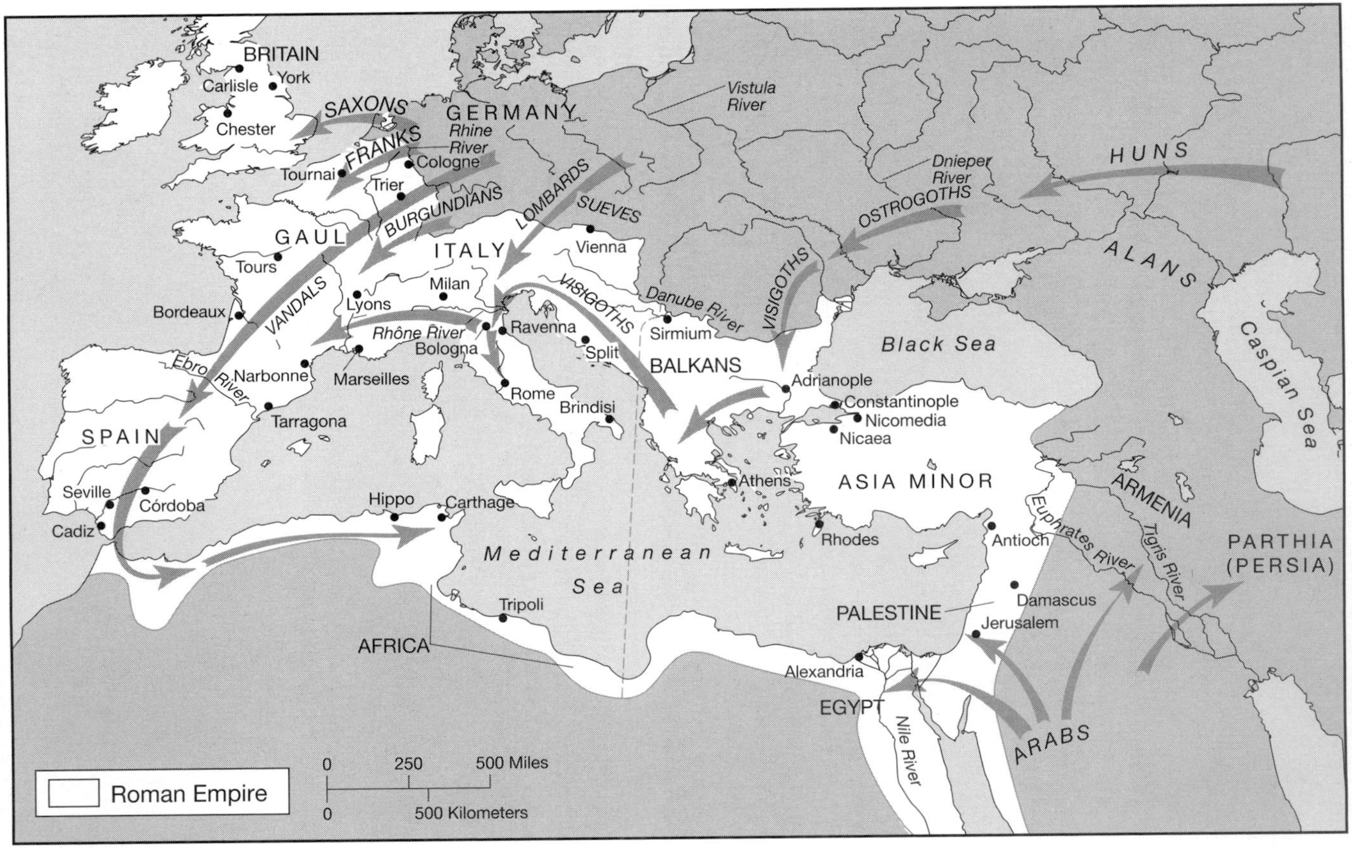

Map 7-1
The German Migrations into the Roman Empire Between 376 C.E. and 406 C.E., the western Roman Empire let down its defenses, and German tribes wandered freely throughout its territory. The eastern empire remained undisturbed because no one could get past Constantinople. *Question:* What different challenges did geography pose for the defenders of the eastern and western halves of Rome's empire?

attempt by an eastern emperor to regain control of Italy after Theodoric's death inflicted far more damage on the heartland of the ancient empire than anything the German "barbarians" had done.

The Byzantine Empire of Constantinople

When people speak of the fall of the Roman Empire, they are usually thinking only of its western half. The eastern Roman Empire, with its seat at Constantinople, was undisturbed by the German invasions, and its succession of emperors continued until 1453 C.E., when the city was conquered by the Ottoman Turks and renamed Istanbul. However, once the western Roman Empire was gone, Roman elements in the eastern empire diminished. It became an ardently Christian state with a largely Greek-speaking population and a partially Persian culture. Historians distinguish this emerging medieval civilization from its Roman predecessor by referring to it as the Byzantine Empire (from the Greek name for the site of its capital).

Justinian   In 518 C.E. a military coup elevated Justin (r. 518–527 C.E.), an illiterate soldier of peasant origins, to the eastern throne. He governed with the assistance of a gifted and well-educated nephew named Justinian. Justinian (r. 527–565 C.E.) followed his uncle to the throne and assembled a team of remarkable people to help him govern. Chief among them was his wife and virtual co-regent, Theodora (c. 500–548 C.E.).

As the only surviving Roman emperor, Justinian believed that it was his duty to recover the western territories that had been lost to the Germans. The empire had previously come apart on several occasions and been restored. Justinian had no reason to assume that history could not repeat itself. In 533 C.E. his loyal general, Belisarius (505–565 C.E.), made a promising start by quickly overwhelming the fragile Vandal kingdom and restoring North Africa and Sicily to Justinian's control. Diplomatic negotiations then persuaded some places along the coasts of Gaul and Spain to submit, but the Ostrogoths vigorously resisted Justinian's efforts to gain control of Italy. War there raged on until 552 C.E., when the Ostrogoths finally gave in and agreed to evacuate Italy. Justinian's victory was, however, Pyrrhic. Italy had been devastated. The city of Rome suffered such damage that over the course of the sixth century C.E., it lost nine-tenths of its population. Constantinople was left so exhausted by the struggle that it could not hold the prize it had won. In 568 C.E. another wave of Germans, the Lombards, swept into Italy from the north, and the Byzantines retreated to Ravenna and outposts in southern Italy. Rome's bishop defended his city and preserved its independence. But most of Italy was divided up among Lombard chieftains. The peninsula was to remain politically fragmented for the next 1,293 years.

Justinian could not concentrate all his attention on his western wars. Slavs, Germans, and various Asiatic peoples flooded into his Balkan provinces, and he faced a formidable opponent on his eastern frontier. Khusro I (r. 531–579 C.E.), the Persian shah, devoted much of his reign to preying on Byzantine territory. Justinian kept him at bay, but the fight drained both Byzantium and Persia, and made them easy targets for Arab Muslim armies in the seventh century C.E..

The eastern half of Rome's empire had always been more prosperous, populous, and urbanized than the western, and the east was not disrupted by the German migrations. The eastern emperors, therefore, still had formidable resources at their disposal—as Justinian's reign demonstrates. In addition to his costly wars, he funded building projects throughout his empire. The most famous of these was a massive church, called *Hagia Sophia* ("Holy Wisdom"),

Figure 7–2 The Church of *Hagia Sophia* Justinian's great church is one of the world's architectural masterpieces. Its architects used a cluster of domes to roof a huge, open room. The central dome is 107 feet in diameter and rises to a height of 180 feet. It collapsed shortly after it was built, but it was quickly reconstructed and has survived centuries of earthquakes. The four minarets were added when the Turks occupied the city and converted the church into a mosque.

next to his palace in Constantinople. Its innovative design and skillful engineering prove that the eastern Roman Empire was still capable of highly original and significant achievement during the era of Rome's "fall."

Byzantine Culture Constantine careful designed Constantinople to take Rome's place as the capital of a renewed Roman Empire. From the city's site on the waterway that connected the Aegean and Black seas, Rome's rulers could watch both of the empire's trouble spots: the German and Persian frontiers. The location was also economically advantageous. Constantinople became a focal point for major international trade routes, and its virtually invulnerable fortifications added to its attractions. As conditions in the western empire deteriorated, many of the empire's wealthy families moved themselves, their art collections, and their libraries to the new capital. Emperors stripped other cities to adorn Constantinople, and a steady stream of valuable records and objects flowed to "Second Rome."

Among the things that Justinian's government inherited was a mountain of legal documents—judicial records, imperial and Senatorial edicts, and lawyers' commentaries—that had been accumulating for centuries. It set up a commission to comb through this material, organize it, and distill from it the essence of Roman law. The result was a set of volumes, the *Corpus juris civilis (Body of Civil Law),* that had a major influence on the formation of Europe's medieval kingdoms and subsequently on some of modern Europe's nations.

Byzantine scholars produced encyclopedias and library inventories that make fascinating, if depressing, reading. They give us an indication of how much ancient literature once existed and how much has been lost. Byzantine intellectuals are not remembered for much original work, but they made contributions to history and theology. There was such an insatiable appetite for theological debate among Byzantines of all classes that it was said that a man could not get his hair cut without receiving a lecture on an obscure doctrinal point from his barber. Justinian had a reason for dedicating his empire's most important church to the wisdom of God. His people were devoted to pondering and rationalizing the mysteries of faith.

Islam

About five years after Justinian died, a man named Muhammad ("Highly Praised," c. 570–632 C.E.) was born in Arabia. At about the age of forty, he began to have religious experiences that transformed his life and the history of the world. He became "the Prophet," the man chosen to reveal the will of Allah, founded the religion known as Islam, and set in motion events that created an empire larger than Rome's.

The Arabian Context   At the start of the seventh century C.E. no one could have predicted that the next great world power would arise from Arabia. Most of the million-square-mile Arabian peninsula, with the exception of some oases and coastal districts, was desert inhabited by primitive nomads called Bedouins (*badu*, "desert"). Although Arabia was exposed to civilizing influences from Egypt and Mesopotamia, none of the ancient world's empires paid it much attention. The land was too barren to be worth the cost of conquest. Geography, however, gave Arabia some economic significance. Trade routes that connected the markets of the Mediterranean with those of India and east Africa passed around or through Arabia. As herdsmen wandered from place to place with their flocks, they could easily form caravans and move goods through their territory. Trade brought them into contact with Jews, Christians, Persians, Greeks, and Romans, and enhanced the importance of Mecca, Muhammad's birthplace.

Pre-Islamic Arabia was a politically chaotic country. It had no central government and no coordinated leadership. Arabs acknowledged few loyalties beyond those to blood kin. Scarcity of resources forced them to prey on one another and live by harsher codes than those that governed life in wealthier regions. Such order as existed in Arabia was maintained by fear of vendettas—by the knowledge that a man's kinsmen would avenge any harm done to him.

Trading was risky in a country where there was no governmental protection and in a culture where to display valuable items was to challenge others to try to take them from you. Fortunately, religion helped to compensate for the weakness of political institutions. Awe motivates people to restrain their behavior at sacred sites. Acts of violence or bloodshed are usually believed to pollute holy ground, and those who commit them risk divine punishment. Mecca was one of Arabia's sacred places, the site of a rectangular stone building of ancient, but uncertain, origin called the Ka'aba ("cube"). Various Arab tribes had deposited some three hundred holy images in the Ka'aba, and they venerated a black stone in its eastern corner. It was said to have been placed there by the Hebrew patriarch Abraham from whom the Arabs, like the Jews, claimed descent. They believed that their ancestor was Ishmael, Abraham's son by the maid Hagar, and that their cousins, the Jews, descended from Isaac, the son Abraham had with his wife Sara. Respect for the Ka'aba created a space around Mecca where a powerful tabu forbade the kind of fights that were routine elsewhere. Mecca was therefore a good place to trade.

Muhammad's tribe, the Kuraish, bore special responsibility for Mecca and the Ka'aba, but Muhammad was not born to a life of rank and privilege. He was orphaned at a young age, raised by a grandfather and then an uncle, and compelled as a youth to make his own way in the world. He worked on caravans, and about 595 C.E. he married a wealthy widow named Khadija, who was his elder by a decade or more. She may have born her husband seven children, but only one lived: a daughter named Fatima. After Khadija's death Muhammad acquired a harem of nine wives, but Fatima was his only descendant. The lack of a male heir may have confirmed his conviction that he was meant to be God's final prophet.

The Origin of Islam   In 610 C.E., when Muhammad was about forty, he began to receive visions that conveyed the precepts of a new faith. An angel (said to be Gabriel, who had earlier inaugurated Christianity by announcing the news of Christ's birth to Mary) ordered him to recite, and he spoke the first of the 114 *suras,* or divine messages, that compose Islam's sacred book, the Qur'an ("Recitation"). Muhammad's Arab audiences were stunned by the poetic beauty of his utterances, and they committed them to memory and circulated them as an oral tradition. About twenty years after Muhammad's death, the *suras* were collected, and an authorized text of the Qur'an was compiled. A collection of *hadiths,* "traditions" about the Prophet handed down by his acquaintances, provided additional religious guidance.

Muhammad's visions alarmed him, and he was reluctant to make them public. He had good reason. When he began to preach in 615 C.E., he set himself on course to collide with the Meccan authorities, the leaders of his tribe. Muhammad was disturbed by the growing materialism of the Meccan merchants, and he called for a return to traditional social values. He insisted that the rich had a duty to care for the poor. He personally had no taste for wealth or luxury and lived so frugally that he repaired his own clothing and helped his wives with household tasks. He advocated egalitarianism. All his followers were to be on the same footing, and no one was to claim superior social or spiritual status. None of this struck Mecca's leaders as new or alarming, but in 616 C.E. Muhammad crossed the line. He repudiated the polytheistic beliefs of his ancestors and embraced a radically consistent monotheism. This was an attack on the Ka'aba, and an attack on the Ka'aba was a blow at the foundation of Mecca's economy.

Muhammad claimed that his revelations came from *al-Ilah,* "the God," an ancient Arab term for a remote high god. Muhammad, however, declared Allah the sole deity—a unique, all-encompassing, transcendent divine power that defied human comprehension. Human beings could not hope to understand this ultimate reality; they could only surrender to it. Muhammad's core message was a call to submit (*salama,* "islam") to God's will. Muhammad repudiated every doctrine or image that might compromise Allah's unity or transcendence. He was acquainted with Judaism and Christianity, and he accepted their validity to a point. He said that the Hebrew prophets and Jesus were true spokesmen for God, but that their messages had been misinterpreted. He honored Jesus as a major prophet, but insisted that he was only a man and not an incarnation of God. He also forbade his own followers to pay him divine honors, and he claimed no miraculous powers. He was "the Prophet," God's final messenger, but that did not make him anything other than a mortal man.

By 620 C.E., the Prophet's situation in Mecca was deteriorating rapidly. As Muhammad pondered what to do, he had a vision in which he was carried to Jerusalem to the mountain where the Jewish temple had stood. From there he rose into heaven to meet the earlier

✴ People in Context: A'isha (614–678 C.E.), Wife of the Prophet

In 620 C.E. a girl named A'isha was informed that her father had arranged for her to marry his best friend and spiritual mentor, Muhammad. She was six years old, and her future husband was about fifty. The wedding took place three years later, and despite the gap in age between the bride and groom, the marriage was a great success. A'isha bore her husband no children, and he had other wives, but she became his favorite. He may have been intrigued by her independent spirit and her audacious sense of humor. (She once told him that she was amazed at how willing Allah was to do his will!) She narrowly avoided divorce when she blundered into a misadventure that raised doubts about her sexual fidelity, and on another occasion she led a harem revolt that brought Muhammad to the brink of repudiating all his wives. Despite occasional conflicts, the Prophet's affection for his feisty wife never waned, and when he was overtaken by his final illness, he asked to be taken to her room. He died with his head in her lap and was buried beneath her bed.

Muhammad's death committed A'isha, at the young age of eighteen, to perpetual widowhood, for the Prophet proclaimed his wives "Mothers of Believers" and forbade them to remarry. A'isha did not, however, sink into obscurity. As the only one of Muhammad's wives in whose presence he had received revelations from Allah, the leaders of the Muslim community turned to her when they were uncertain what to do. Her memories of what Muhammad had said and done served as precedents for deciding difficult questions. Tradition credits her with some 2,210 *hadiths,* the quasi-scriptural verses that supplement the Qur'an. A'isha knew how to make the most of her situation. She amassed wealth, dispensed influence, and intervened in the struggles that broke out for control of the Islamic community. At the start of Islam's first civil war, she raised an army and was captured on the battlefield when her men were defeated. Her reputation as the Prophet's beloved protected her, and she remained a force to be reckoned with until her death in 678 C.E. The early Islamic community was not exclusively a man's world.

Question: Given that priestesses were common in the ancient world, why did female religious leadership decline when the medieval West embraced Christianity and Islam?

---

prophets and to enter the presence of Allah. This experience confirmed his faith—as did a development that marked the turning point in his fortunes. He made six new converts from Yathrib, an oasis two hundred miles north of Mecca. Yathrib subsequently came to be called Medina ("city") of the Prophet, but it was not an urban community. It was a twenty-square mile patch of arable land inhabited by tribes of both Arabs and Jews. The people of Yathrib were having a hard time living together. They needed an outsider to mediate their disputes, and in 621 C.E. they offered Muhammad the job. Having found a safe haven, Muhammad instructed his followers to prepare for the *hijra* ("departure"). The *hijra* was a spiritual as well as a literal journey, for it meant a break with the tribe of one's birth and a commitment to a new *umma* ("community"), whose members were bound by faith, not blood.

***Umma* to Empire**   Because the *hijra* of 622 C.E. marked the start of Islam as an independent religious movement, it became the pivotal point of Muslim history—the event from which all other events are dated. However, it took more than a move to Yathrib to secure Islam's survival. At first, life in Yathrib was as challenging for Muhammad as it had been in Mecca. Some of the oasis's inhabitants were not happy about his arrival, and he had to find some way to support himself and his people. Yathrib's location near the caravan routes that served Mecca solved the latter problem. Muhammad ordered his men to prey on Mecca's trade, and he may have led as many as twenty-five raids in person. Christians find it hard to imagine Jesus doing such a thing, but Jesus lived in a different world. Muhammad's situation was more like the one that Moses faced as he forged the Jews he had led out of Egypt into a people and helped them wage war.

In 627 C.E. Mecca dispatched a large army to evict Muhammad from Yathrib, but its campaign backfired. The Prophet won a stunning victory over Mecca's superior forces, and as the news spread, converts to Islam multiplied. By 630 C.E. the Meccan authorities were ready to come to terms with the man whose spiritual vocation they had ridiculed. It was agreed that all pagan shrines throughout Arabia would be destroyed except Mecca's Ka'aba. The Ka'aba was purged of its idols, and Muhammad declared it the most sacred place on Earth.

Muhammad's insistence that loyalty to Allah superceded all other allegiances provided a way for the Arabs to transcend their tribal divisions and come together as a people. The new faith that the Prophet revealed founded a new nation, but Muhammad had little time to turn the *umma* into a state. He died in Medina on June 8, 632 C.E. His death did not shake the faith of his followers, for he had never denied his own mortality. It did, however, pose a problem. He had insisted that there would be no more prophets after him, and he had said nothing about choosing a new leader for the *umma*. Some tribes concluded that Allah's definitive Prophet could not have a successor, and they began to withdraw from the *umma*. Abu Bakr (r. 632–634 C.E.), the first of Muhammad's prestigious converts and a long-time friend, stepped in at this point and prevented Islam's dissolution. Muhammad had sometimes chosen Abu Bakr to stand in for him and lead the *umma*'s communal prayers. This and Abu Bakr's close association with the Prophet made him the logical choice to become Islam's first caliph ("successor"), the heir to Muhammad's duties as leader of the *umma*.

Abu Bakr was about the same age as Muhammad. He outlived him by only a few years, but this was long enough to secure the *umma*'s future. Faith helped preserve its unity, but so also did material success. Under Abu Bakr's leadership, Muslim raiding parties thrust into the lands of the Persians and Byzantines that bordered Arabia. Their timing was excellent, for both these empires had been locked in combat for decades. They were reeling with exhaustion. Raids quickly became conquests, and Islam began to acquire an empire. (See Map 7–2.)

Muhammad had forbidden his people to fight among themselves and decreed instead that they devote their energies to waging *jihad* ("holy struggle"). The word is difficult to translate and has often been misunderstood by non-Muslims and abused by Muslims. It asserts the *umma*'s right to defend itself, but it also extends to the religious duty to fight for a just society and do whatever is necessary to defeat evil. This may involve taking up arms against others, but it also entails the difficult spiritual struggle believers must wage against their darker impulses. There was no strain of pacifism in Muhammad's teaching, but he insisted that wars be fought only for just causes, that they be as brief as possible, and that they cease as soon as opponents offer honorable terms. He did not send his people forth to convert the world at the edge of a sword. Islam's rapid spread owed little to compulsion and much to its innate appeal.

Islam and Christianity   The church, in its various forms, had virtually captured the West by the seventh century C.E., and then Islam suddenly emerged to challenge Christianity's religious monopoly. The result was a division in Western and world civilization that has had—and

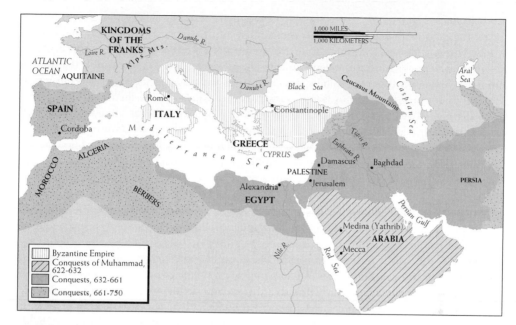

Map 7-2

The Growth of the Muslim Empire   This map shows the stages by which Islam spread in little more than a century from the interior of Arabia west to the Atlantic and the south of France and east to India and the frontiers of China. **Question:** Does the current tendency to use the term "west" to refer only to European civilization have anything to do with the rise of the medieval Muslim empire?

continues to have—troubling consequences. A history of conflict obscures the fact that Islam and Christianity have much in common. Both claim Hebraic ancestry. Both are monotheistic, and both have relied on Greek philosophy for help in developing their theologies. The so-called "Five Pillars of Islam" are usually mentioned when attempts are made to sum up the essence of Muslim practice:

1. Muslims affirm a monotheistic creed ("There is no god but Allah, and Muhammad is his prophet").
2. They pray at fixed times during the day.
3. They are required to contribute to charities that care for the poor.
4. They observe a season of fasting during the month of Ramadan.
5. They are expected to make at least one pilgrimage to Mecca.

What is seldom noticed is that medieval Christianity can be described in similar terms. Medieval Christians affirmed monotheistic creeds—although theirs tended to be much longer and more detailed. Christian monks prayed at fixed times during the day, and churches rang their bells at certain hours to encourage laypeople to pause in their labors and pray. The medieval church, like the Muslim state, had the power to levy taxes to support charitable works. Christians observed Lent, a longer period of fasting (forty days) than the Muslim month of Ramadan. Medieval Christians were also enthusiastic pilgrims, many of whom endured great hardship to fulfill the dream of visiting the Holy Land, the birthplace of their faith.

The most blatant contrasts seen today between the practices of Muslims and Christians reflect the gulfs that have widened between secular cultures in different parts of the modern world. There are also some significant differences between the faiths that reflect the particular environments in which their founders worked. The Christian church arose within the Roman Empire. This meant that responsibility for protecting and policing the society within which the church operated belonged to Rome's secular government and that the church had a narrowly defined religious mission. As the empire declined, the church was sometimes forced to fend for itself and lay claim to political authority. This created problems during the Middle Ages. Kings and popes sometimes disagreed as to which powers belonged to which leader, but the church and state were still assumed to be different entities. The *umma,* on the other hand, was a religious community that sprang up in a place where there was no state. It had to provide itself with the services of secular government. Consequently, the distinction between sacred and secular authority was far less clear in Muslim than in Christian societies. Islam did not create a priesthood at the head of an independent religious organization. It has no sacraments that require priestly intermediaries, and its mosques (*masjid,* "place of worship") have no altars. In this, Islam resembles Judaism. Mosques, like synagogues, are places for prayer, preaching, and study, and the duties of Islam's *imams* ("leaders" of prayers) are similar to those of Jewish rabbis. Islamic clergy interpret sacred texts and define *shari'a* ("required path") for the *umma.* The law of a Muslim society must reflect a belief that Muhammad shared with the Hebrew prophets—that God cares about how people treat one another and that He holds communities and individuals accountable to standards of social justice. Muhammad believed that God's justice would ultimately be revealed by a final judgment. Good people would be separated from bad, and individuals would receive the eternal reward or punishment their conduct merited. Many Muslims are convinced that because human actions have such transcendent significance, *shari'a* must govern every aspect of life and determine the policies of states.

The Muslim World   The Byzantine Empire was in bad shape when Muslim armies erupted from Arabia in the mid-seventh century C.E. Justinian's costly projects had driven taxes so high that some of Constantinople's subjects in Syria and Egypt welcomed the Arabs as liberators. Plagues had depopulated much of Asia Minor, and wars with Slavic invaders of Byzantium's Greek and Balkan provinces had drained the Byzantine Empire's resources. Fights over the throne and palace coups added to the confusion, and in 611 C.E. the Persians pushed through Byzantine territory to the Mediterranean coast, cut the empire in half, and sacked Jerusalem (614 C.E.).

The Byzantine Empire's decline was reversed when an army from its North African province staged a military coup and placed its commander, Heraclius (r. 610–641 C.E.), on the throne. By 627 C.E. Heraclius had driven the Persians back to their capital at Ctesiphon (near ancient Babylon), and regained the empire's lost provinces. He then, however, had to face the Muslims who were surging out of Arabia. In 636 C.E. they routed his army at the battle of Yarmuk and occupied Syria, Egypt, and Armenia. Constantinople then enjoyed a respite, for the Muslims shifted their attention to Persia. The Persian Empire collapsed in 651 C.E., and Constantinople's days also appeared to be numbered. Dynastic squabbles and brief reigns crippled the Byzantine Empire for the rest of the seventh century. The Muslim threat diminished, however, for divisions had begun to emerge within the *umma.*

As close associates of Muhammad's, the early caliphs were obvious choices for their office. But after Muhammad's generation died out, agreement had to be reached on a system for passing down the leadership of the *umma*. On November 4, 634 C.E., Umar (r. 632–634 C.E.), the man to whom Abu Bakr had bequeathed the caliphate, was stabbed by an assassin. He lived just long enough to charge a committee with responsibility for choosing his successor. Two candidates emerged, each representing different political philosophies. Ali, Fatima's husband and father of the Prophet's grandsons, was the favorite of those who believed that the caliphate should descend in Muhammad's family. Uthman, his opponent, was the head of the prestigious Umayyad family, the first of the great Meccan clans to convert to Islam. Wealth and connections won Uthman (r. 644–656 C.E.) the prize, but he had little aptitude for the office. In 656 C.E. a company of disgruntled soldiers from Egypt besieged his residence in Medina and killed him.

Uthman's assassins tired to save themselves from punishment by claiming that Uthman was unworthy of the caliphate and by offering it to Ali. Ali's acceptance infuriated Mu'awiya, governor of Syria and leader of the Umayyad family. Fighting broke out, and a schism developed within the *umma* that has never been resolved. In 660 C.E. a panel of judges declared

GRANADA. ∨ ALHAMBRA.   Sala de Justicia y Patio de los Leones.

Figure 7–3 Islamic Art, The Alhambra Palace, Granada, Spain Pre-Islamic Arabs were nomads who did not burden themselves with works of art, but as the empire of their Muslim descendants grew, Islam drew from a multitude of cultures to develop a unique artistic tradition. For some time, beginning in the eighth century C.E., artists were forbidden to represent living things, for this was considered a mockery of God's creative powers. The art and architecture of this period explored the aesthetic potentials of geometric abstraction and elaborate calligraphy.

that Mu'awiya was the legitimate caliph, and his Umayyad dynasty monopolized the caliphate for a century (660–750 C.E.). The *Shi'a* (the "party" of Ali), however, refused to acknowledge the Umayyad caliphate. When its leader, Ali, was killed in 661 C.E., the *Shi'a* split into factions that championed the rights of various individuals who claimed connections with Muhammad's family. Some Shi'ites insisted that the true caliph was a "hidden imam," an unknown messianic figure who would eventually emerge from obscurity to unite the *umma*. Today, the *Shi'a* is centered in Iran, but most modern Muslims are *Sunnis* ("orthodox" believers) who accept the legitimacy of Islam's historic dynasties.

The Umayyads settled in Damascus, a far more convenient location for running an empire than the remote religious centers of Mecca and Medina. Once in power, they resumed Islam's wars of conquest. The North African port of Carthage fell to them 698 C.E., and by 714 C.E. most of Spain was under their control. Muslim navies patrolled the western Mediterranean, and in 718 C.E. Muslim armies pushed into France. Islam's eastward expansion was equally rapid. In 711 C.E. the Muslims reached the Indus River Valley and began the conquest of what is now Pakistan, and in 714 C.E. a Muslim expeditionary force probed the frontiers of China.

The Umayyads' empire was too large, given the technologies of its day, to be administered by a central government. Local officials had considerable discretionary authority, and some of them established independent states. Arab rule was not unpopular. Muslims did not force conversions to Islam. Jews and Christians paid special taxes, but they were free to practice their faiths. The Umayyads, indeed, thought of Islam as a privilege Allah bestowed on Arabs. They allowed non-Arabs to convert, but treated them as second-class Muslims. Separate mosques were provided for them. They paid taxes from which Arabs were exempt, and Arabs were discouraged from intermarrying with them. This discrimination created tensions within the Muslim community that eventually unseated the Umayyads.

In 747 C.E. a family that claimed descent from Muhammad's uncle, Abbas (d. 653 C.E.), rallied non-Arab Muslims and launched a revolution that nearly exterminated the Umayyads. The Abbasid dynasty abandoned Damascus for a new capital called Baghdad ("Gift of God") near the ruins of Ctesiphon, the seat of the former Persian Empire. Baghdad's Abbasid court became legendary for its luxury and sophistication, and the civilization it represented was the most progressive of the early Middle Ages. The caliphs supported scholars who collected and built on the works of the Greeks and Persians, and the Islamic world began to make significant progress in philosophy and science.

The Abbasid dynasty survived for a long time, but its power steadily diminished. It failed in 750 C.E. to destroy all the Umayyads, and one Umayyad prince escaped to Spain, where his descendants established a rival caliphate. Another sprang up later in North Africa and Egypt. The Abbasid caliphs, like the last of the western Roman emperors, became figureheads for governments run by soldiers, and the dynasty was finally extinguished in 1258 C.E., when a Mongol army destroyed Baghdad.

Larger Issue Revisited

By bringing the peoples of the Mediterranean region and Europe together, the Roman Empire helped to create a unified Western civilization. As that empire declined, the political and cultural ties that held "the West" together weakened. Constantine and his successors probably hoped that religion would help to compensate for their loss. As the empire faded away, the Christian church had an unprecedented opportunity to influence the destiny of the West. It triumphed over all competitors and even over the paganism fundamental to classical civilization. It won recognition, insofar as such a thing was possible, as the West's sole legitimate faith. The effect this had on Western civilization was, however, ambiguous. Christians professed the same faith, but that faith often served more to divide than to unite them.

Islam's experience was similar. Muhammad's religion unified the Arab peoples and kept them working together long enough to build a huge empire. But like Christianity, Islam developed internal divisions that spawned intense hatred among persons who professed allegiance to the same religious tradition. Islam's spread into territory occupied by Christians created tensions that threatened further to fragment the world that Rome had united.

The fact that Islam, Christianity, and Judaism all spring from the same tradition and all honor many of the same sacred texts and shrines has often, paradoxically, made it difficult for them to tolerate one another. As monotheistic faiths, they share a tendency to assign people to opposing categories: the saved versus the damned, the sheep versus the goats, the citizens of the city of God versus the inhabitants of the city of man, us versus them. Given the nature and history of the West's three great religions, serious thought should be given to the role religion plays in society.

Review Questions

1. The famous eighteenth century British historian, Edward Gibbon, said that the fall of the Roman Empire was brought about by the triumph of barbarism and religion. Was he correct?
2. How did the eastern half of Rome's empire come to differ from the west? Why did the two have different fates?
3. How did Jesus' career compare with Muhammad's?
4. How does Christianity compare with Islam? How is the church different from the *umma*?
5. Why was religion the most powerful cultural influence on Western societies in the early Middle Ages?
6. Are Islam and Christianity both Western religions?

Refer to the front of the book for a list of chapter-relevant primary sources available on the CD-ROM.

THE WEST INTERACTIVE

For web-based activities, map explorations, and quizzes related to this chapter, go to *www.prenhall.com/frankforter.*

CHAPTER 8

THE EMERGENCE OF EUROPE

I am convinced that no one can describe these deeds [of Charlemagne's] more accurately than I can, for I was there when they transpired and, as the saying goes, witnessed them with my own eyes. Moreover, I cannot know for sure that anyone else will record these things. Therefore, I have concluded that it would be better to produce an account myself . . . rather than permit the amazing life of the most remarkable king, the leading man of his generation, to fade into the shadows of oblivion. . . .

—**Einhard**

Larger Issue: *How did Europe adapt the civilization it inherited from the ancient world?*

The explanation Einhard (c. 770–840 C.E.) gave for his decision to pen an account of the life of his king, Charlemagne, reveals how different his world was from ours. In our abundantly documented age, it is unthinkable that a man like Charlemagne, who ruled much of Europe, might be forgotten. Einhard, however, was right to be concerned. He was a member of Charlemagne's inner circle from 793 C.E. until the emperor's death in 814 C.E., but he knew nothing about his subject's birth and youth. There were no public records, and no one who knew Charlemagne as a boy was still alive. Only a few years had passed, but already part of the great man's history was lost. Under such circumstances, even the memory of extraordinary events could fade quickly. This worried Einhard, for he believed that his generation had witnessed one of history's turning points—the emergence of Europe as a world power.

Although Einhard's and his contemporaries' knowledge of history was limited, the past was a potent force in their lives. The line of emperors in the western half of the Roman Empire had ended in 476 C.E. with the deposition of Romulus Augustulus, but on Christmas Day 800 C.E., the people of Rome ended a 324-year-long interregnum by reviving the imperial title and bestowing it on Charlemagne. Charlemagne bore little resemblance to Rome's previous emperors, and his lands were not coterminous with those of their empire. His domain extended from the Pyrenees (the mountains between France from Spain) to the Oder River in eastern Germany and from the North Sea to Naples. Much of the territory that Rome had formerly governed, from Spain in the west across North Africa to Egypt and Syria in the east, had come under Muslim control. The Balkans, Greece, and Asia Minor were ruled from Constantinople, where Christian emperors stood in an unbroken line of succession that stretched back to the Roman Caesars.

The Greeks coined the word *Europe* (perhaps from an Assyrian term for west), but they were vague about the region it identified, and they knew little about it. It was on the periphery of their civilized world and remained peripheral even after the Romans added Gaul, Britain, and part of Germany to their empire. This changed following the western empire's collapse. Rome's former northwestern provinces began to expand, coalesce, and develop a sense of identity. Their emerging self-consciousness is reflected in what one of Einhard's colleagues, Alcuin (c. 737–804 C.E.), called Charlemagne: *Europae pater* ("father of Europe").

Charlemagne believed that the great continental state he had created entitled him to the prestige that the imperial title still conferred. His coronation was also meant to put the world on notice that the decline into which western Europe had slipped in the fifth century C.E. was ending and that Europe was asserting a claim to a share of the Western civilization that was Rome's legacy. Charlemagne's subjects were culturally inferior to the ancient empire's other heirs, the Byzantines and Muslims, but history more than vindicated Charlemagne's confidence in his people's future. Rightly or wrongly, Europeans came to regard themselves as the sole guardians of Western civilization.

When the Roman Empire broke up, what had been a politically unified territory with a veneer of common culture split into regions with ever more diverging identities. As distinctions between east and west—and north and south—increased, shared traditions diminished, and memories of common origins faded. Initially, the inhabitants of the lands along the eastern and southern shores of the Mediterranean, the Byzantines and Muslims, did the best job of preserving and building on the foundations laid by the ancient world, but by the end of the Middle Ages, the peoples who lived north and west of the Mediterranean (with help from their eastern and southern neighbors) had taken the lead and begun to spread the West's civilization around the globe. Much of the modern world, therefore, has experienced Western civilization in the form mediated by Europe. However, because Europe's physical and intellectual environments were different from those of the ancient Mediterranean region, Europe's version of Western civilization had to be adapted to fit Europe's unique context. As you work through this chapter, consider the changes that took place and the situations that inspired them.

TOPICS IN THIS CHAPTER

The Merovingian Kingdom: Europe's Nucleus • The Franks' Neighbors • The Carolingian Era • The Feudal Era • The Culture of Europe's Dark Age

---

The Merovingian Kingdom: Europe's Nucleus

When the Franks, for whom France is named, first appeared in history, they were a gaggle of German tribes inhabiting the eastern bank of the lower reaches of the Rhine River. The emperor Constantine's father, Constantius I (r. 306 C.E.), settled some of them (the Salian, or "Salt-water," Franks) in the Netherlands to create a buffer between the empire and wilder folk to the north. Some of the Franks who remained in the Rhineland (the Ripuarian, or "River," Franks) also entered Rome's service. In 406 C.E., after Honorius (r. 395–423 C.E.) recalled Rome's legions to Italy to fight the Visigoths, the Franks tried to hold the Rhine frontier for the empire. Franks were part of the army with which the Roman general Aëtius blocked the Huns' advance into Gaul in 451 C.E.. Thirty years later, a Frankish chief named Clovis united his people and founded a dynasty that turned Roman Gaul into medieval Francia.

Clovis and the Franks   Clovis (c. 466–511 C.E.) was about ten years old when the last western Roman emperor was deposed, and he was still in his teens when he succeeded his father as one of many Frankish tribal chiefs. His people lived near Tournai in Austrasia ("Eastern Lands"), a region between the Rhine and Somme rivers. Clovis's early campaigns extended his power south beyond Paris to the Loire Valley. The Franks called this territory Neustria ("New Lands"). Clovis pushed the Visigoths south to the Garonne River, eliminated rival Frankish chiefs, brought much of Germany under his control, and formed a marriage alliance with the Burgundians, whose kingdom lay on his southeastern border.

Two decades after Clovis's death in 511 C.E., the Byzantine Emperor Justinian still dreamed of regaining control of what had been the western Roman Empire. He succeeded in temporarily occupying Italy, but by then, much of western Europe was firmly established on the road to independence. This was thanks in large part to Clovis, who did more than conquer territory. He helped unify a world that had been culturally fragmented by the events that brought down the western empire. Germans like Clovis's Franks constituted a small minority of the population of the new lands their kings aspired to rule. Most of Gaul's residents were Romanized Celts, Catholic Christian descendants of the subjects of the old empire. Religion was important to them, for their native leaders were the bishops who had inherited responsibility for Rome's *civitates* (the city-states that composed the old empire) when the empire's secular government crumbled. Clovis's Gaul was a loose association of private, regional governments headed by Catholic bishops from powerful aristocratic families. If German kings, such as Clovis, were to be effective, they had to come to terms with these native magnates.

Clovis and the Franks were pagans who worshiped ancient Germanic gods, while the tribes of Visigoths and Burgundians, with whom the Franks competed for control of Gaul, were Arian Christians. This gave Clovis an advantage. Catholics despised the Arian faith as a heresy, a perversion of their religion. They regarded pagans, on the other hand, as candidates for conversion. Like Constantine a century and a half earlier, Clovis understood the political advantages of conversion, and like Constantine, he justified his conversion to his followers by claiming that the Christian God had given them victory in a crucial battle. The church welcomed him as its defender and patron, and it supported him in his wars with Arians and helped him maintain what was left of the imperial tax and administrative systems.

Many of the German tribes remained aloof from the peoples whose lands they occupied, but not the Franks. The conversion of the Franks made it possible for them to intermarry with the Romano-Celts and join them in developing a common culture. This required compromises on both sides. The Christian religion and Roman practice altered some German traditions—particularly those governing marriage, women, inheritance, and property rights. Frankish customary law influenced courts and the enforcement of justice—the prosecution and punishment of crime becoming a private matter rather than the duty of the state. Government's function was primarily to restrain the vendettas that threatened to break out among quarreling families. Accused persons could clear their names by undergoing physical ordeals or compurgations (that is, finding a number of individuals who would swear to their innocence). The guilty could avoid physical punishment by paying *wergeld* ("man money"), monetary compensation. Amounts were determined by the nature of the injury and the status of the person who had been harmed. As more formal governmental procedures evolved under Roman influence, the German laws, which had been preserved as an oral tradition, were translated into Latin and written down. Classical Latin survived as the language of scholarship and formal documents. The "street" Latin spoken by the majority of Gaul's residents edged out the

German spoken by the Frankish minority, and Francia evolved the Romance ("Roman") dialects that became modern French. As the Frankish and Romano-Celtic peoples fused, Gaul's cultivated, literate nobility disappeared, and the new aristocracy that emerged at the top of society adopted the lifestyle of the German warrior elite. In short, the contours of medieval civilization began to appear in western Europe.

The Merovingian Succession   Clovis's kingdom was a collection of virtually autonomous regions that he dominated by force. He did not think of it as a state, a political entity to be handed down intact from generation to generation. It was the private property of his family, the Merovingians (the descendants of Merovech, a quasi-mythical founding father). German tradition dictated that private property be divided among all a man's heirs, and this custom worked against the consolidation of Francia as a state. Its territory was repeatedly divided and recombined, and the battles that raged among the Merovingian princes weakened their dynasty. (See Map 8–1.)

Clovis divided his kingdom among four sons, who, fortunately, were more interested in wars of conquest than in fighting among themselves. One of the boys outlived the others and

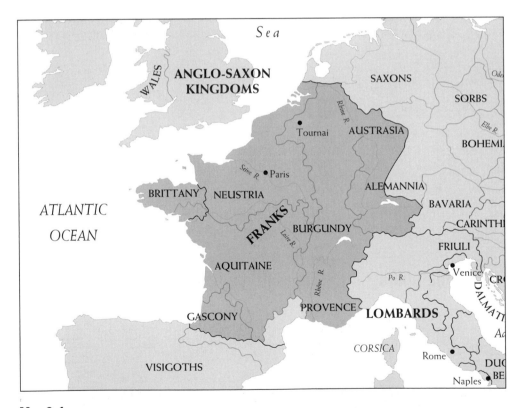

Map 8–1
The Merovingian Domain Clovis and his descendants conquered what might have become the core territory for a continental state. But they failed to overcome centers of regional power and develop an awareness of a common identity among their subjects. ***Question:*** Did geography work for or against the formation of a unified Francia?

briefly reunited the realm, but he divided it again for his heirs. From about 570 C.E. to 613 C.E. civil war raged between the Merovingian courts of Austrasia and Neustria. The survivor laid claim to all of Francia, but by then the Merovingians' power base was seriously eroded.

The Franks viewed kings less as administrators of territorial states than as tribal leaders. A king was a warlord whose duty it was to settle disputes among his followers and lead them on profitable raids. A Frank expected his loyalty to his king to be rewarded by a steady stream of gifts. Kings who acquired new lands through conquest were able to enrich themselves and their men. But when conquests ceased, kings sometimes had to give away their own lands to maintain the support of their followers. Over the long haul, some nobles greatly enriched themselves at the expense of the royal family, and the balance of power shifted as they became more wealthy than their Merovingian kings.

A proliferation of heirs also helped to weaken the Merovingians and encourage their tendency to fight among themselves. Royal marriages were fluid, and the distinction between a wife and a concubine vague. Kings often had children by many women, and because there was no tradition of primogeniture ("first born") mandating that the whole kingdom pass to a king's eldest son, every male with a bit of Merovingian blood could claim a share of the royal estate. This played into the hands of the Frankish nobility, for rival candidates had to offer them gifts in exchange for their support. The last significant Merovingian monarchs were Chlotar II (d. 629 C.E.) and his son Dagobert (d. 638 C.E.). After them, the throne passed to youths and weaklings whose fortunes steadily diminished until the last Merovingian kings were reduced to living modestly on a small farm outside of Paris.

The Franks' Neighbors

The Franks were not the only Germans to try to build new states amid the ruins of Rome's western empire. Other groups made promising starts, but like the Franks, they suffered reversals. The political contours of a new Europe were slow to emerge.

Italy and the Lombards   While Clovis was building a Frankish domain in Gaul, the Ostrogoths, under the leadership of their king Theodoric (r. 475–526 C.E.), were taking control of Italy. Theodoric restored political stability to Italy, protected its Roman inhabitants, and safeguarded its classical culture. After his death, the Byzantine emperor, Justinian (r. 527–565 C.E.), invaded Italy, and the peninsula was devastated by a war that dragged on to 552 C.E.. The Ostrogoths ultimately yielded and left Italy to join the Visigoths in Gaul and Spain. (See Chapter 7, "The West's Medieval Civilizations.")

In 568 C.E. the exhausted Byzantines fell back as another wave of German invaders, the Lombards, descended on Italy. Alboin, their king, established his seat at Pavia (south of Milan) in what came to be known as Lombardy. The Lombard kingdom was weak, and it failed to impose its authority throughout Italy. Lombard chiefs carved out independent duchies, and the Byzantines hung on to Ravenna and a few outposts in southern Italy. The peninsula was divided up by small states that preyed on one another and kept the region in turmoil.

Spain: The Visigoths and the Muslims   After sacking Rome in 410 C.E., the Visigoths settled in southern France and began to spread into Spain. Fighting among factions kept them weak, and in 507 C.E. Clovis and the Franks seized much of the land they had occupied in Gaul. Their hold on Spain was not much more secure. The Visigothic nobles elected their

> ### ✳ People in Context: Brunhild (d. 613 C.E.) and Fredegund (d. 597 C.E.): Powers Behind the Throne
>
> In 567 C.E. Sigibert, king of Austrasia, made a prestigious marriage that threatened the balance of power in Francia. He wed Brunhild, daughter of the Visigothic king of Spain. This gave him a powerful ally at the back of his brother, Chilperic, king of Neustria. Chilperic soon checked Sigibert's move by winning the hand of Brunhild's sister, Galswinth. For some reason, Chilperic quickly turned against his bride, murdered her, and returned to a former wife, Fredegund (d. 597 C.E.), a woman of humble origin with whom he was infatuated.
>
> Merovingian princes often wed commoners to avoid the troublesome entanglements associated with aristocratic marriages, but Fredegund did not make life easy for Chilperic. She persuaded him to repudiate his first wife and then cleared the way to the throne for her children by eliminating his sons by other women. An infant named Chlotar II was the only one of her boys to outlive Chilperic. Although his paternity was questioned, Fredegund defended his claim to the throne and served as regent during his minority.
>
> War erupted between Austrasia and Neustria after Galswinth's murder, but no contemporary source claims that it was caused by Brunhild's desire for vengeance. Dynastic ambitions may be enough to explain the bloody conflict that raged between her and Fredegund and Chilperic. In 575 C.E. Fredegund engineered the assassination of Brunhild's husband, Sigibert. Childebert II, Brunhild's young son by Sigibert, retained control of Austrasia with the help of an uncle, but Brunhild fell into Chilperic's hands. She tried to recoup her fortunes by marrying Merovech, one of Chilperic's sons who was trying to unseat his father. When their coup failed, Merovech committed suicide, and Brunhild escaped to her son's court. Two of Fredegund's agents, both clergymen, then tried but failed to assassinate Brunhild and Childebert.
>
> Although one of the Merovingian queens was a foreigner and the other a commoner, both wielded great power. The sources depict them as scheming behind the scenes, but both were well-known public figures. Fredegund's assassination of Sigibert reversed the course of a war, and the queen dominated her husband's successor until her death in 587 C.E.. Brunhild received flattering letters from Pope Gregory the Great (r. 590–604 C.E.), who assumed that

kings, and their preference was often for a candidate who posed no threat to their independence. The Visigoths' Arian religion was also a problem, for it drove a wedge between them and their Catholic subjects. The Visigoths finally converted to Catholicism in 589 C.E., but the continuing reluctance of the Visigoths to marry native Spaniards kept Spain's two peoples divided. The Visigoths spent much of their time fighting among themselves, and in 711 C.E. a group of rebellious nobles asked Tarik, the Muslim governor of North Africa, to help them overthrow their king. The army that Tarik landed at "Tarik's Mountain" (Jebel el-Tarik, or Gibraltar) chose instead to conquer Spain. Spain's Christians lost everything but the tiny state of Asturias in the northwest corner of the Iberian peninsula. Spain became, and for a long time remained, a Muslim country.

In 720 C.E. the Muslims crossed the Pyrenees bent on the conquest of Francia. By then the authority of the impoverished Merovingian kings had all but disappeared, and the Franks found a new leader in Charles Martel, the head of a powerful noble family. In 732 C.E. he halted the Muslim advance near the city of Tours. The Muslims retreated but retained control of a strip of France's Mediterranean coast until about 750 C.E.. In that year the Abbasids she had the power to reform the Merovingian church, and her husband and her son were both accused of being under her thumb.

Brunhild manipulated the feuds that divided Francia's aristocratic families, and by 585 C.E. she and her son Childebert were firmly in control of Austrasia and busily eliminating their opponents. In 584 C.E. Brunhild avenged Fredegund's assassination of Sigibert (Brunhild's husband) by murdering Fredegund's husband, Chilperic I. By 589 C.E. Brunhild and Childebert had become the dominant powers in Francia, and the death of an uncle in 592 C.E. allowed Childebert to add Burgundy to his possessions. Childebert died four years later, and Brunhild ruled as regent for his sons, Theudebert II and Theuderic II.

When Theudebert reached his majority (c. 600 C.E.), a coalition of Austrasian nobles forced Brunhild to flee to Burgundy, Theuderic's territory. She then announced that Theudebert was the bastard child of a palace gardener and that Theuderic was the legitimate heir to Austrasia. Her influence over her grandson increased as she encouraged his sexual affairs and dissuaded him from a marriage that would have raised up a rival queen. Reform-minded clergy were scandalized, but when they declared Theuderic's offspring illegitimate, Brunhild had the kingdom's bishops denounce them.

In 612 C.E. Brunhild finally persuaded Theuderic to attack Austrasia. Theuderic killed Theudebert and his son, and he was on the verge of invading Neustria to unseat Fredegund's son Chlotar II when he died of dysentery. Brunhild prevented the division of Theuderic's estate among his sons, and arranged for the eldest, her great-grandson Sigibert II, to inherit a unified kingdom. At that juncture, a block of aristocrats defected to Neustria and helped Chlotar II capture Brunhild and Sigibert. Chlotar claimed that Brunhild had been responsible for the deaths of ten kings, and he condemned the elderly woman to be torn apart by wild horses.

Question: What do the careers of Brunhild and Fredegund suggest about the roles that other less well-documented aristocratic women may have played in medieval politics?

overthrew the Umayyad caliph. He and most of the members of his family were slaughtered, but one Umayyad prince escaped and fled to Spain. He waged a bloody struggle that culminated in Spain's repudiation of the Abbasids and the establishment of a rival caliphate with its seat at Córdoba.

England The Franks and Goths who founded kingdoms in Gaul and Spain got their starts as *foederati* (allies) of Rome's empire. They were influenced by Roman culture, and they tried to save some of the empire's institutions. The situation in the Roman province of Britain was different. The cities the Romans founded in Britain failed to flourish, but the rural villas they scattered about the countryside prospered. During the fifth century C.E., when the migrations of the Germans disrupted production on the continent, demand for British goods soared and Britain's economy peaked. The island's Romano-Celts, the Britons, were understandably dismayed when, about 406 C.E., Rome withdrew its troops and told them to defend themselves. They faced raids from Ireland and Scotland, and without an army to back it up, the wall that the emperor Hadrian had built across northern England was useless.

Local strongmen emerged to fill the political vacuum left by Rome's departure, and some of them raised armies by recruiting German mercenaries from the tribes of Angles and Saxons who occupied the continent's North Sea coast. These soldiers-for-hire turned on their employers, and by 450 C.E., the homeland of the Britons was becoming Angleland (England).

The Anglo-Saxons, in contrast to other Germans, had been little exposed to Rome's civilizing influence, and the Britons gave them no help. The Germans who established the new kingdoms on the continent came from tribes that had a history of involvement with Rome, and when they settled into their new territories, they had the advantage of mixing with Rome's former subjects. But as the Anglo-Saxons moved into Britain, the native Britons either fled or were exterminated. So many emigrated to northwestern Gaul that it came to be called Brittany. Others moved to Ireland and Spain. Few attempted to convert the Anglo-Saxons to Christianity or instruct them in the arts of civilization. This period in England's history is largely undocumented, but the memory of at least one battle in which Britons triumphed over Anglo-Saxons survived into the twelfth century. It inspired a cycle of romantic tales about a King Arthur and a legendary land of Camelot. Scholars have proposed various Latin and Celtic roots for the name Arthur, but Camelot's king is a creature of mythology.

Ireland As civilization declined in Britain, it began to flourish in Ireland, a land that had never been part of the Roman Empire or had much contact with its civilization. Ireland was divided into clan territories headed by petty kings. It had no cities and no literate culture until a chance event set in motion a chain of events that fundamentally altered its culture.

In the fourth century C.E. Irish raiders sacked the coast of Britain and carried off a young man named Patrick, the son of a Roman official. Patrick spent six years in slavery in Ireland before escaping to the continent. For two decades, he studied in various monasteries, and about 432 C.E. he was consecrated a bishop and sent back to Ireland. He was phenomenally successful at converting the Irish to Christianity, and the new faith promoted the spread of monasticism and literacy

Because Ireland was, for some time, cut off from the rest of the Christian world, it evolved some unique religious customs. Each Irish clan established a monastery in its territory, and the abbots who led these houses were more important religious leaders than were Ireland's bishops. Irish monks were renowned for their asceticism and scholarship. Some embraced self-exile as an ascetic discipline and became missionaries to England and the continent. They helped to convert the Anglo-Saxons. They planted monastic outposts as far afield as Gaul and Italy, and one of them even tried to reform the morally lax court of the Merovingian queen Brunhild.

The Carolingian Era

In 751 C.E. the last of the Merovingians was deposed, and the Franks transferred their allegiance to the Carolingian dynasty. The new royal family is named not for its founder but for its most famous member, Charlemagne (a contraction of the French for "Charles the Great").

A Transition of Dynasties The Carolingian family was formed by the intermarriage of the heirs of the two most powerful men at the Austrasian court of the Merovingian king Dagobert. (d. 638 C.E.). The Carolingians controlled the office of "mayor of the palace," a kind of prime ministry, and were more powerful than the rulers they theoretically served. In 679 C.E.

Figure 8–1 The Book of Kells This page from an illuminated (decorated) text of the gospels was probably created about 750 C.E. at Iona, an Irish monastery on the western coast of Scotland. It is a supreme example of the original artistry that emerged from Christian Ireland.

Pepin of Heristal, the Carolingian mayor of Austrasia, extended his authority over Neustria and united both Frankish homelands under a Merovingian puppet king. When he died in 714 C.E., his illegitimate son, Charles Martel, dispossessed his half-brothers, who were minors, and assumed control of the family's enterprises. It was Martel (c. 688–741 C.E.) who repulsed the Muslim invasion of Francia in 732 C.E.. Further military successes won him the submission of Aquitaine and Burgundy, and new lands in Germany.

Some of Martel's contemporaries called him *rex* ("king"), but this was only a courtesy or flattery. It was Martel's son and heir, Pepin III, "the Short" (r. 741–768 C.E.), who formally elevated the Carolingian family to royal status. He might simply have appropriated the Merovingians' title, but that would have robbed it of its authority. Titles are only significant when people believe that they are legitimate, and it was hard for Pepin to challenge the Merovingians' legitimacy. Because the Franks had no memory of a time when they had not been ruled by Merovingians, the Merovingians seemed to have a divine right to the throne.

By Pepin's day, the Franks had embraced Christianity and no longer worshiped the gods who had made the Merovingians kings. The Christian God obviously had the authority to raise up new leaders for them, but the difficulty for Pepin lay in finding someone who could speak for God. The bishop of Rome claimed that right, and it was in Pepin's interest to take him seriously.

The Christian community had never acknowledged a supreme leader. The emperor dominated the church in Constantinople, and the groups of Christians that were scattered and isolated inside the Muslim empire attended to their own affairs. The church in western Europe was far from unified, but one of its bishops, the pope ("father"), could make a case for precedence over the others. The bishop of Rome headed the only diocese in the region that had been founded by one of Jesus' apostles, and its founder, Peter, was a very special apostle. Jesus (in the sixteenth chapter of Matthew's Gospel) had granted him the "power of the keys." Jesus had said that whatever Peter "loosed" or "bound" on earth would be "loosed" or "bound" in heaven. Catholic dogma holds that this authority passed to Peter's successors in Rome—giving them the right to speak for God. A wide gap existed, however, between the powers the early medieval popes claimed and the powers they actually exercised.

The church came of age as one of the institutions of the Roman Empire, and its leaders clung to the empire as long as they could. After the line of western emperors ceased in 476 C.E., the bishops of Rome looked to the eastern emperors for protection. But this was not a satisfactory arrangement. Byzantine emperors and popes quarreled over doctrine, and the military assistance that Constantinople could offer Rome steadily declined as the Lombards moved into Italy. Rome's Senate is last mentioned in 579 C.E., and as the city's secular government faded away, responsibility for defending and administering Rome fell to its bishop. During the seventh century C.E., some popes courted Frankish rulers in hopes of winning their help, but the Franks were reluctant to be drawn into a war with the Lombards.

In 751 C.E. the Lombards conquered Ravenna, Constantinople's major base in Italy, and the danger they posed to Rome increased. Pope Zacharias (r. 741–752 C.E.) made a desperate appeal to Pepin for help. Pepin was willing to respond, for the pope had something of value to offer him. Zacharias agreed with Pepin that the man who had the responsibility of king ought also to have the title, and he urged the Franks to declare Pepin their king according "to their custom." Pepin deposed the last Merovingian and confined him to a monastery. Pepin was then crowned in a ceremony that included a new ritual—an anointing, a spiritual consecration. This added dignity and awe to the new dynasty, but it raised troubling questions. Did it give kings clerical status and authority over the church? Or did it imply that the church, because it consecrated kings, also had the right to depose them? A serious struggle between church and state was to break out in the distant future, but in Pepin's day kings were so much stronger than popes that this would not have worried them.

Pepin's sons were both married to Lombard princesses, and his reluctance to offend his Italian allies delayed repayment of his debt to the papacy. In 754 C.E. a desperate Pope Stephen II (r. 752–757 C.E.) came to Paris to plead with Pepin in person—and to reconsecrate him as king. Pepin finally took his army to Italy, drove the Lombards back from Rome, and ceded the lands that he had liberated to the pope. This "Donation of Pepin" confirmed the existence of a papal kingdom (the future Papal States). The pope had conferred spiritual status on Pepin, and Pepin had reciprocated by acknowledging the pope's secular authority. The pope doubtless needed a base of his own so that he could resist domination by lay lords and kings, but the papacy's temporal interests inevitably conflicted with its spiritual role—to the detriment of the church.

Charlemagne Builds an Empire   When Pepin died in 768 C.E., his throne was well established. However, his decision to divide his kingdom between his two sons, Carloman (r. 768–771 C.E.) and Charles (Charlemagne, r. 768–814 C.E.), cast doubt on its future. Carloman's premature death in 771 C.E. prevented the outbreak of civil war, for Charlemagne quickly deprived Carloman's young sons of their inheritance and reunited the Frankish kingdom. He then set about building an empire.

Charlemagne's first acquisition was the Lombard kingdom in northern Italy. Its ruler, Desiderius, was Charlemagne's father-in-law, but that did not prevent Charlemagne from responding to another appeal from the papacy (in 774 C.E.) for help against the Lombards. He defeated Desiderius, imprisoned him, and appropriated the Lombard crown. This removed one threat from the papacy, but posed another. With much of France, Germany, and Italy under the control of the Frankish king, the pope had little latitude for independent action.

The papacy's concern for its independence may account for the appearance in the eighth century C.E. of a forged document called the Donation of Constantine. In fairness, the forging of documents was not quite the crime then that it is today. The decline of literacy meant that many people lacked documents confirming rights to which they were entitled. The forger's motive, therefore, was to create records that should have existed but did not. The popes believed that, as the only officials of the Roman Empire left in western Europe, they took precedence over the new German monarchs. The Donation of Constantine made their case by appealing to a popular, but groundless, legend that claimed that Pope Sylvester I (r. 314–335 C.E.) had cured the emperor Constantine of leprosy. The grateful emperor had supposedly repaid the pope by ceding the empire to the church, and the pope had graciously agreed to divide the empire and allow Constantine to rule the eastern half. The medieval popes did not claim, on the basis of this story, to be emperors. As early as the fifth century C.E., Pope Gelasius I (d. 496 C.E.) had declared the church and state to be separate and equal partners. Kings, like popes, were established by God, the former with a secular and the latter with a spiritual "sword." Each was to assist the other without transgressing on his colleague's turf. Popes, however, had a difficult time preventing royal encroachments on the church, and the Donation of Constantine was an attempt to intimidate kings by implying that popes were the final arbiters of the legitimacy of the West's monarchs.

The Donation of Constantine complicated disputes between popes and kings until it was proved to be a forgery in the fifteenth century C.E. Charlemagne was far too powerful to worry about its implications for church-state relations, and he may actually have found it useful in improving his position. His father, Pepin, wanted to become a king, and Charlemagne sought recognition as an emperor. The church helped both men reach their objectives.

If any German leader deserved recognition as an emperor, it was Charlemagne, for he came to control most of western Europe. Following his victory over the Lombards, he turned his attention to Muslim Spain. Spain seemed vulnerable, for the Muslims were fighting among themselves. But as soon as the Franks appeared, the Muslims closed ranks and forced Charlemagne to withdraw. As his army retreated through the Pyrenees, the native Basques attacked its rearguard. This inconsequential event captured the popular imagination, and stories began to be told about a Roland, a duke of Brittany, who allegedly died in the encounter. In the late eleventh century C.E. these inspired the first major piece of French literature, an epic poem entitled *The Song of Roland*.

Although Charlemagne's first Spanish campaign failed, he continued to probe Muslim territory, and by 801 C.E. he had taken Barcelona and created the Spanish *march* (a frontier military district). The march provided Christians with a base south of the Pyrenees from which they launched crusades in the eleventh century C.E. to reconquer Spain. (See Map 8–2.)

Most of Charlemagne's wars were aimed at winning German territory. From 772 C.E. to 804 C.E. he waged annual campaigns in Saxony (the region south of the Danish peninsula).

Map 8–2

Charlemagne's Empire   Western Europe had been civilized as part of a unified Roman Empire. After the empire fell, Europeans retained a sense of common identity, and the dream of restoring Europe's unity has never entirely faded. ***Question:*** Does geography encourage Europe's unification or its division?

Although mass executions and deportations were needed to pacify Saxony, it became one of Germany's stronger duchies. In 787 C.E. Charlemagne put down a rebellion in Bavaria, and a subsequent campaign culminated in the founding of the East March (*Ostmark,* or Austria). Next, he drove down the Danube Valley into the territory of the Avars, invaders from the Russian steppes who had grown wealthy extorting tribute from Constantinople and the Balkans. In 796 C.E. the Franks secured Germany's eastern border by defeating and dispersing the Avars, and Charlemagne returned home with massive amounts of treasure.

Charlemagne wanted the imperial title as a recognition of his achievement in uniting much of western Europe, but its quest confronted him with the same problem his father Pepin had faced. If the title was to be more than a presumptuous affectation, he could not simply assume it. His right to it had to be confirmed by an appropriate authority. The most obvious authority was the Roman emperor who still ruled in Constantinople, and in 780 C.E. Charlemagne began to negotiate with Constantinople for recognition as the eastern ruler's western colleague.

To bolster his claim to the imperial title, Charlemagne tried to look as imperial as possible. German kings had always led migratory existences. It was easier to feed the court by moving it from one royal estate to another than by shipping food from distant farms to a stationary court. Poor communications also meant that the king had to travel to stay in touch with his subjects. The lifestyle of a Roman or Byzantine emperor was, however, different. Monarchs of this kind resided in capital cities. Charlemagne, therefore, decreed the construction of a grand palace complex as a permanent seat for his court. The site he chose was an old Roman spa at Aachen (Aix-la-Chapelle) where there were hot springs in which he enjoyed swimming. The centerpiece of the new capital was a church in Byzantine style. It was as magnificent as the best European artists could make it, but it fell far short of the splendors of Constantinople's *Hagia Sophia.*

Charlemagne's negotiations with Constantinople dragged on for over twenty years without making much progress. The delay was due in part to political confusion in the eastern empire. In 797 C.E. the eastern emperor's wife, Irene, overthrew him and became the first woman to assert a claim of her own to either a Roman or a Byzantine throne. Because there was doubt about the legitimacy of a female emperor, it could be argued that the office was vacant and available for someone else to claim. In 800 C.E. Charlemagne went to Rome to extricate Pope Leo III (r. 795–816 C.E.) from some political difficulties. He stayed on to celebrate Christmas, and at the holiday mass the pope and the Roman populace hailed him as emperor. Einhard, Charlemagne's biographer, claims that the pope did this without Charlemagne's permission and that it infuriated Charlemagne. That seems unlikely. Leo was on shaky ground and could hardly have risked taking such a momentous step without Charlemagne's approval. It is also hard to imagine how he could have carried out a coronation ceremony without Charlemagne's cooperation. The story of Charlemagne's displeasure may have been circulated to smooth things over with Constantinople. It provided diplomatic cover for Charlemagne by shifting responsibility for the event to the papacy.

The patriarch of Jerusalem acknowledged Charlemagne's status as an international Christian leader of the first rank by sending him the keys to the Church of the Holy Sepulcher, the site of Christ's tomb. Harun al-Rashid (r. 786–809 C.E.), the Abbasid caliph of Baghdad, addressed him as an equal and sent him a gift befitting an emperor, a war elephant. Constantinople grumbled, but in 813 C.E. it accepted the *fait accompli* in exchange for resolving a dispute over some Balkan territories. A few months after Byzantine ambassadors hailed Charlemagne

Figure 8–2 Charlemagne's Chapel at Aachen The palace complex at Aachen was laid out as a rectangle with an area of about fifty acres. The palace occupied one side of the rectangle, and the church the other. A long covered gallery connected the two. The chapel rose in three tiers. Charlemagne's throne was situated on the second level opposite the altar.

as emperor in Aachen, he shared his title with his son and heir in a ceremony that pointedly excluded the clergy. Charlemagne did not want his coronation to set a precedent for the papacy to claim an exclusive right to crown emperors.

The Nature of the Carolingian Empire   Charlemagne's empire was held together by personal relationships that were maintained by the judicious use of carrots and sticks. The emperor was a daunting man who could physically intimidate his subordinates or seduce them with gifts, as the situation warranted. Their loyalty was essential to the functioning of his government, for primitive communications prevented Charlemagne from knowing much about what was occurring in his far-flung empire. Because he had to grant his officials a great deal of discretionary authority, he bound them to him with oaths and personal obligations. He filled most key offices with Austrasian nobles whose families had ties with his. He required all his male subjects over the age of twelve personally to swear loyalty to him, and he persuaded his leading men to take oaths of vassalage. His father was the first to impose vassalage on the nobility as a sign of their subservience to their king. *Vassus* (or *vassallus*) was a Celtic term for a slave, but by the end of the eighth century C.E., it had come to designate aristocratic status.

The empire had seven marches (militarized frontier districts) and about three hundred counties. The duke (*dux*, "general") or count (*comes*, "companion") who headed each of these was totally responsible for the government and defense of the lands assigned him. Because he was, in effect, a mini-king who was largely on his own, there were safeguards to prevent him from abusing his power. A man was usually assigned to a region where he did not have influential relatives to back him up, and he was moved from time to time to prevent him from building a power base that he might use against his emperor. Charlemagne frequently summoned his counts and dukes to court to remind them of their dependent status, and an annual mustering of the army at the beginning of the campaigning season (the Mayfield) gave him another chance to reinforce his ties with them. He circulated open letters called capitularies to establish guidelines for good government, but it was difficult for him to know if his orders were followed. About 779 C.E. he began to send out teams of auditors (*missi dominici*, "emissaries of the lord") to check up on his governors and hear complaints against them, but it is doubtful that this did much to stem corruption or halt abuse of power. Most of Charlemagne's subjects thought of their emperor as a remote figure who had little to do with their lives. Their fates were decided locally.

The Division of the Empire   Charlemagne's empire was held together by the vigilance and energy of its leader, and as age sapped his strength, it too declined. The emperor had a bevy of wives, concubines, and children. He avoided some dynastic complications by refusing to allow his daughters to marry, but he planned to divide his realm among his sons. The civil war that this invited was avoided when he outlived all but one of them. Unfortunately, the survivor, Louis the Pious (r. 814–840 C.E.), was probably the heir least suited to be an emperor.

Louis was a well-educated man who, had he not been destined for a throne, probably would have chosen a life in the church. Raised under the tutelage of a monk, he was a sober man who was appalled by the moral laxity of his father's court. One of his first acts was to purge the court of everyone (including his sisters) whose conduct was not up to his strict standards. He believed that the church too was in need of reform, but he was overly deferential to his clerical advisors. His father had crowned him to make it clear that the church had no control over the imperial title, but he submitted to a second coronation by his bishops. His vassals quickly discovered that their lord was as weak-willed as he was pious, and they began to take liberties. Louis's own sons ultimately turned on him and on one another. When Louis died in 840 C.E., his three surviving sons fought on for another three years before agreeing to a settlement of their father's estate. In 843 C.E. the Treaty of Verdun, which ended their war, foreshadowed the emergence of Europe's major nations. Charles the Bald became king of western Francia. Louis the German got the empire's eastern territories, and their senior brother, Lothair, claimed the imperial title and a long, narrow kingdom that ran between their realms from the North Sea down the Rhineland to Italy. The new kingdoms represented regions that were already evolving separate ethnic cultures. In 842 C.E. Louis and Charles had met at Strasbourg, and each swore an oath in a tongue that the other's followers could understand. The chronicle that records Louis's words preserves the earliest specimen of a Romance language.

Lothair's kingdom was divided among his heirs and eventually disappeared. The rulers of Francia and Germany appropriated parts of it, and France and Germany were still quarreling over Lorraine (Lotharingia) in the twentieth century C.E. The imperial title was allowed to lapse in 924 C.E., for by then, it meant little. It had become clear that Charlemagne's vision of a united Europe was only a dream.

Invasions and Fragmentation   Signs of the developments that were to dismember Charlemagne's empire appeared during the closing years of his reign. The western Roman Empire had fallen to the migrations of Charlemagne's German ancestors, and now a similar fate befell his empire.

In the second half of the eighth century C.E., Viking fleets began to sally forth from Scandinavia, driven by overpopulation or by opportunities for pillage. These Norsemen (Northmen, or Normans) had developed the best seafaring technology of their day. Viking ships could handle the high seas, but their shallow drafts also enabled them to navigate Europe's many rivers and strike deep inland.

While the Vikings attacked from the north, the Muslims renewed their assault from the south. In 800 C.E. the Abbasid caliphate ceded Algeria to the Aghlabids, a dynasty of local princes. The Aghlabids ended a long fight between Berber and Arab Muslims in North Africa by diverting their quarreling subjects to Christian targets. In 827 C.E. they began the conquest of Sicily, which was still Byzantine territory. From Sicily they raided Europe's Mediterranean coasts. They assaulted Rome in 846 C.E., and in 888 C.E. they established bases in the south of France from which they attacked traders who used the Alpine passes.

By then, a third threat to the Carolingian kingdoms had appeared on Germany's eastern frontier. The Magyars migrated westward from the Russian steppes and began to push up the Danube Valley into the heart of Europe.

The Carolingian states were poorly equipped to counter simultaneous attacks on multiple fronts, for they had little infrastructure to support centralized government. Some paved roads existed in those parts of Europe that had once belonged to Rome, but neither information nor troops could travel quickly. A king could not respond rapidly enough to fend off raids to his realm that might come from any direction or hit different places simultaneously. It made more sense to disperse resources and command authority, for every part of a kingdom needed a strong leader who was permanently in residence and able to defend it. Kings did not disappear, but power shifted decisively to their military vassals. Kings became firsts-among-equals who reigned rather than ruled. Their status was superior to that of their vassals, but their primary responsibility, like that of an ordinary lord, was to govern and defend their own estates.

The Feudal Era

The political fragmentation of Europe in the ninth century C.E. promoted the spread of a form of government called feudalism. *Feudalism* is a troublesome term. The word was invented by French scholars in the sixteenth century C.E. who believed that a coherent "feudal system" lay behind the myriad legal arrangements described in medieval documents. However, we now know that there were so many variations on, and exceptions to, what were once thought to be the rules of feudalism that some historians have suggested dropping the term. It remains useful so long as we remember that people are pragmatists when it comes to the struggle for survival. They do what works, not what a theoretical model or the pursuit of rational consistency may dictate.

Feudal Order Feudalism takes its name from *feudum* (fief), the estate that was given to a vassal to support him while he served his lord. Governments in early medieval Europe did not collect taxes in coin and pay their officials salaries from a public treasury, for money had nearly disappeared from circulation. Most financial transactions involved consumable items. Because it was too cumbersome to collect all the goods produced on the state's lands for redistribution to the state's servants, governments parceled out the land itself. A lord paid his vassals by giving them fiefs (usually farms equipped with laborers). They did not own the lands that supported them while they served their lord. They owned only the right to the income from those lands—and that only so long as they rendered the services that their fiefs were meant to fund. Once a vassal had a fief in his possession, however, it was hard for his lord to reclaim it. If a vassal had heirs who could perform the tasks for which his fief had been granted, it passed to them and soon came to be regarded as their hereditary property.

Because a vassal enjoyed all the income from his fief, he (and not his lord) bore all the costs of providing government services for the people who lived there. That meant that vassals had extensive power over everyone who lived on their fiefs, but there were some restraints on their authority. In simple, illiterate societies, custom acquires the authority of law, and feudal traditions could be quite explicit about the rights and duties of lords, vassals, and serfs.

Feudalism had deep roots in both the Roman and German pasts. Like the Roman institution of patronage and the German warrior *comitatus*, feudalism used personal oaths to organize societies. Citizenship ceased to have much meaning as the Roman state faded away, and the legal rights and protections it provided disappeared. People began to make private, individual arrangements to ensure their survival. That usually required them to commend themselves to the service of a protector. To commend oneself was to surrender freedom in exchange for help. Commendation could send an individual up the social scale to the rank of vassal or down to the level of serf (peasant farmer). These fates had different consequences, but legally they were the same. Neither vassals nor serfs were free people. Freedom was not a desirable condition in a feudal context, for free persons were outsiders who had failed to find a niche in society. They had no right to land or protection.

In the feudal world as in our own, birth often determined a person's options. Children of vassals had the chance to become vassals and those of serfs had few choices but to remain serfs. Individuals did, however, have to take the oaths their roles required for themselves, and there was some social mobility. Noble families could lose their standing, and talented people of humble origins might rise to great heights, particularly if they pursued careers in the church.

Feudalism of different kinds appeared in different places at different times. It flourished in northern France, but was slow to develop in Germany and very slow to spread to central Europe. In regions such as Switzerland, where small, scattered farms predominated, it never took root at all. Feudal obligations could also weaken or strengthen in response to fluctuating economic and political circumstances.

The standard model and technical vocabulary for feudalism reflect French customs that may have begun to evolve as early as the eighth century C.E. Medieval European feudalism was a form of decentralized government that associated land ownership with military service. It is linked with the rise of a military class that was supported by fiefs and that had legal jurisdiction over the people who lived on those fiefs.

The key feudal warrior was the knight (*cniht,* "boy" or "servant"), a heavily armed cavalry-man. The knight was the product of medieval inventions that exploited the military potential of the horse more effectively than the Romans had. Scholars debate when these inventions took hold in Europe and when the fully developed knight appeared. Early in the Middle Ages, Frank-ish soldiers used horses for transportation but preferred to dismount for combat. They had good reason. Saddles were in use in the West prior to the first century C.E., but they had no stirrups. This made it hard for a rider to thrust a spear or swing a sword without lofting himself out of his saddle and off his horse. The Koreans had stirrups by the fifth century C.E., and the Byzantines were using them by the sixth century C.E. They had certainly reached Francia by the eighth cen-tury C.E. It took time, however, for their potential to be recognized, and other inventions were needed before that potential could be realized. Larger, stronger horses that could withstand the rigors of battle had to be bred. They needed the protection provided by horseshoes, which were not invented until the late ninth century C.E. New weapons and armor had to be designed, and men had to master new kinds of combat. The fully equipped medieval knight was, therefore, probably not common much before the late ninth or the tenth century C.E.

A lance driven by the combined weight and momentum of a charging horse and rider de-livered a lethal blow, and a knight could slice through a company of foot soldiers. He marked an advance in military technology that every lord who wanted to remain competitive had to match. The process of making the transition to the new technology was, however, not easy, for knights were extraordinarily expensive. One knight might represent an investment equivalent to the cost of about twenty plow teams. As early as the generation of Charlemagne's grandfa-ther, Charles Martel, Frankish leaders were mobilizing the resources of their society for the support of their expensive armies. The church, as well as holders of secular property, had to provide lands for the maintenance of soldiers. Feudalism reached its peak in those parts of Eu-rope where the process of military mobilization was most thorough. Most land was assigned as fiefs, and landownership began to be thought of as entailing an obligation for military service.

Manorialism, the Feudal Economy   Given the economic burden that the new military technology imposed on medieval society, transition to the new kind of warfare would not have been possible if comparable advances in agriculture had not been made to support it.

The methods used to work the thin, dry soils of the Middle East and the Mediterranean's shores did not translate well to northern Europe. Farmers in Francia, Britain, and Germany had to contend with heavy, wet earth and short growing seasons. A simple "scratch plow" (a pointed stick) worked well in southern regions where the ground was easy to break up, and farmers wanted to conserve the moisture it contained by disturbing it as little as possible. A much heavier, animal-drawn plow was needed to work northern Europe's fields, and plow-shares had to be invented that did not merely break the earth but turned it over to promote drainage. It may have been the sixth century C.E. before such farming equipment was widely available.

Draft animals and metal plowshares were expensive, and farmers had to band together to afford them. This encouraged them to establish manors (*manere,* "to dwell"), medieval agricul-tural cooperatives. Manors differed from most modern communes in that they combined pri-vate ownership of land with common ownership of the tools that worked the land. Each serf (*servus,* "servant") who was commended to a manor held title to certain fields on the manor. He did not receive a percentage of the total production of the manor. He was entitled only to the crops that grew on his own fields. His holdings were not concentrated in one part of the manor, but divided up into small, scattered strips. This "open-field" system helped spread the risk entailed by farming with communal equipment. It prevented fights over who got to use the plow first and ensured that everyone had a bit of land in whatever part of the manor plowing began. This was important, for growing seasons were short in northern Europe. Serfs who had to sow their crops late ran a greater risk of starvation than those who could plant early.

Medieval farmers developed new methods as well as new tools to enhance their productivity. They understood the use of fertilizers (chiefly, lime and animal manure), but these were in short supply. The common method for maintaining the fertility of fields was fallow farming—plowing, but not planting, land, so that it "rested" for a season. Ancient farmers employed a two-field system. That is, they plowed all their land, but planted only half of it—alternating halves annually. Medieval farmers developed a three-field system that combined fallow farming with crop rotation. They divided their land into thirds and planted one-third in the fall with a grain crop, another in the spring with beans (that restored nitrogen to the soil), and left the third fallow. This reduced the amount of nonproductive plowing, provided some protection in case one of the crops failed, and increased harvests. Farmers made no major improvements on these early medieval techniques until the eighteenth century C.E.

Serfs were not slaves. They were unfree in that they were tied to the land (that is, obliged to live on the manor), but they had rights. They could not be separated from the land and sold like chattel. They were better off than many free people, for they were at least guaranteed a chance to earn a living. The vassal to whom the manor was given as a fief did not supervise his serfs' work. He was a soldier, not a farmer. His serfs managed their own affairs (guided by the customs of their manors). The vassal was supported in the same way as his serfs. He received whatever grew on his *demesne* (domain), the fields assigned to him. The serfs' chief obligation was to work these fields for him. His serfs also had to pay for the use of a mill and oven he provided, and he profited from fines levied by his manorial court. Unlike a modern landlord, he had legal jurisdiction over the people who lived on his property and could indict, try, and punish them for crimes.

The Culture of Europe's Dark Age

A Dark Age is an era that is dark to historians because it left behind few, if any, written records. By this standard Europe's early medieval period might best be described as shady rather than dark. Literacy declined in what had been the western Roman Empire, but it did not disappear. Scholarly work continued in scattered places, and there were even flashes of creative genius.

Scholarship in a Period of Transition   The fifth century C.E. produced a trio of great Latin intellectuals who laid the foundation for medieval Europe's Christian culture. Augustine (d. 430 C.E.), bishop of the North African city of Hippo, was one of the West's most important theologian-philosophers. Bishop Ambrose of Milan (c. 340–397 C.E.), who converted Augustine, shaped the preaching and liturgical practices of the Latin church. Jerome (c. 340–419 C.E.), an ascetic scholar, produced the Vulgate, the Latin translation of the Bible that was used throughout the Middle Ages.

During the years immediately following the deaths of these men, the confusion created by the migrations of the Germans into the western empire peaked, and intellectual activity in the Latin world declined. Whenever German kings restored a bit of stability, however, scholarly

Culture in Context: The Medieval Diet

Before they entered the Roman Empire, German tribes depended on herd animals for much of their food. Cattle rustling was one of the functions of the *comitatus*. The Roman historian Tacitus, writing in the first century C.E., claims that German males preferred to shed blood rather than sweat. They fought battles and duels, and left farming to women and slaves. As the Germans settled down, however, they came to rely more heavily on agriculture.

For the medieval as for the ancient world, grains formed the bulk of the human diet. Grain was baked as bread, stewed as porridge, and fermented as beer. Wheat was the most desirable grain, but it did not grow as well in northern Europe as barley, oats, and rye. All crop yields were low by our standards. A farmer was fortunate if one bushel of seed produced three bushels at harvest.

Meat was in short supply, and ordinary people derived much of their protein from beans, peas, and lentils. The banquets of the aristocracy were orgies of meat eating, for conspicuous consumption of scarce food reinforced their rank. Hunting for game was an exclusive privilege of the nobility, and peasant poachers were harshly punished. The meat ordinary people ate came primarily from excess draft animals that were slaughtered each fall because it was too costly to feed them through the winter. They also raised pigs, which could forage for themselves. Medieval animals did not produce much edible flesh, for they were generally less than half the size of modern breeds. Milk production was low, and fowl eggs were small.

Records provide little information about the consumption of fruits and vegetables. Except for varieties that could be dried or stored as roots, they were available only in season. Modern staples such as potatoes, tomatoes, and maize were unknown. (They were introduced into Europe from the western hemisphere in the sixteenth century C.E.) Only the rich could afford spices and sugar. Ordinary people made due with salt, local herbs, and honey.

Roman traders had shipped bulk foodstuffs (grain, wine, and olive oil) throughout the empire by sea. This meant that shortages in one region could be relieved by surpluses imported from another. This commerce declined in the early Middle Ages, and that meant that most places in western Europe had to depend on what they produced locally. This increased their vulnerability to famine, for there was no back-up system to provide aid when inevitable spells of bad weather or outbreaks of plant diseases caused crop failures.

Famines were common in medieval Europe, but even people who had adequate food supplies did not have healthy diets. They ate a lot of grain, and because salting was the most common method for preserving meat and fish, their sodium consumption was high. Diseases created by vitamin deficiencies and food contamination were common. The food that made life possible for medieval Europeans often also made life short. Fifty percent of Europeans in the early Middle Ages may have died before they reached the age of twenty. Few survived beyond their fortieth year, and people in their fifties were considered elderly.

Question: How does the impact that diet had on medieval lives compare with the way in which food affects life in the modern West?

Figure 8–3 Charlemagne No reliable portraits of Charlemagne exist, but this bronze statue from the second half of the ninth century C.E. may have been meant to represent him. It bears a resemblance to the equestrian statues of Roman emperors, and depicts the Carolingian king carrying a sword and an orb, a symbol of universal dominion.

work resumed. The thirty years of order that Theodoric the Ostrogoth (r. 493–526 C.E.) maintained in Italy gave Boethius (480–524 C.E.) and Cassiodorus (490–580 C.E.) the opportunity to create translations and textbooks that influenced education in Europe for centuries. (See Chapter 7.) Benedict of Nursia (480–543 C.E.), their contemporary, was no scholar, but he was largely responsible for the survival of schools and libraries in Europe. The rule that Benedict wrote for the monastery he founded in southern Italy at Monte Cassino so successfully adapted the ascetic vocation pioneered by the hermits and monks of the Middle East to the more pragmatic values of the Latin church that it accelerated the spread of monasticism throughout Europe. (The Carolingians mandated the Benedictine Rule for all the monasteries in their empire.) Benedict divided a monk's day into periods for worship, work, recreation, and rest. Part of their work was study and the production of books.

Turmoil returned to Italy following Theodoric's death in 526 C.E., but by then his contemporary, Clovis (c. 466–511 C.E.), had founded Francia's Merovingian dynasty. Over the years, several scholars surfaced at, or corresponded with, the Merovingian courts. The elegant Latin poetry of Fortunatus (535–605 C.E.), an Italian who was supported by Merovingian patrons, proves that excellent literary educations could still be obtained in Europe. Fortunatus's Frankish contemporary, Bishop Gregory of Tours (c. 538–594 C.E.), complained, however, that standards of literacy had declined dramatically in his part of the world. The Latin of his *History of the Franks* supports this, but scholars debate whether the obscurity that plagues the text is the fault of its author or of the copyists who transmitted it to us. Despite its literary weaknesses, Gregory's book is a major achievement. In his day, the writing of history was a nearly forgotten art, and had he not revived it, we would know very little about the Merovingians.

Gregory of Tours had a contemporary, also named Gregory, who was one of Rome's most important popes. Gregory I, the Great (r. 590–604 C.E.), defended Rome from the Lombards, laid a basis for the Papal States, and still found time for literary work that earned him the title, "Europe's schoolmaster." Gregory became pope at a time when the church in the Latin world was in near total disarray. His correspondence with bishops throughout Europe during an era of great confusion helped sustain them and retain a semblance of Christian unity. In addition to his many letters and sermons, he wrote several influential books. *Dialogues,* the most popular of his volumes, is a collection of stories about saints and miracles that had a tremendous impact on medieval preaching and spirituality. Gregory struggled to raise the standards of the church and further the spread of Christianity. He tried to interest the Merovingian queen Brunhild in church reform, and in 597 C.E. he sent missionaries to England to convert the pagan Anglo-Saxons. Augustine (d. 604 C.E.), the Benedictine monk who led the mission, set up headquarters in Canterbury, the capital of the Anglo-Saxon kingdom of Kent. The archbishops who head England's church today still have their cathedral there.

By the time the pope's emissaries arrived in England, Irish missionaries were already at work there. About 565 C.E., a monk named Columba (521–597 C.E.) had established a monastery on the island of Iona, off the coast of Scotland, and launched a mission that spread into northern England. The schools that the Irish and Roman missions established in England produced some of the era's greatest scholars. The most notable of these was a remarkably original thinker named Bede (672–735 C.E.). His interests ranged from natural science to theology and history. His major contribution to history, *The Ecclesiastical History of the English People,* is noteworthy for research methods that were far ahead of its time. Bede searched out evidence to document historical events and carefully critiqued his sources. He also helped establish the custom of dating historical events from the birth of Christ.

Visigothic Spain also produced a notable scholar in this period, Isidore of Seville (c. 570–636 C.E.), a contemporary of Pope Gregory. Isidore's major work, *Etymologiae* (or *Origines*), was a cross between an encyclopedia and a dictionary. It drew material from many ancient sources to construct explanations for the meanings of words and provided medieval readers with an immense amount of useful information and dubious speculation. Typical was Isidore's claim that the word "medicine" derived from "moderation" because excess causes disease.

Spain's intellectual life received a great boost about seventy-five years after Isidore's death. The Muslim conquest of the Iberian Peninsula exposed Spaniards to influences from the Islamic world, the seat of the most dynamic of the early medieval civilizations. Muslims, Christians, and Jews rubbed shoulders in Spain. They learned each other's languages, traded literatures, and engaged in learned conversations. The intellectual exchanges that took place in Spain helped northern Europe recover from the cultural slump into which it fell at the end of the Roman era.

The Carolingian Renaissance   About the time that Bede died (735 C.E.) another scholarly Englishman was born. His name was Alcuin, and the excellent training he received at the cathedral of York from a student of one of Bede's students equipped him to become Europe's most prominent educator. Charlemagne persuaded him to move to Francia and undertake the leadership of a project that historians call the Carolingian Renaissance.

Charlemagne knew that the level of civilization in Europe had declined dramatically since the days of the Roman Empire. His church was in a particularly lamentable condition. Many clergy were illiterate. Village priests, who were often peasants without formal educations, could not chant the mass accurately. Even some bishops could not read and found preaching a challenge. Charlemagne hoped to correct this by ordering monasteries and cathedrals to establish schools. To provide these institutions with teaching materials, curricula, and a model, he asked Alcuin to set up a school at court, and he combed Europe for scholars to staff its faculty. Italy yielded a historian, Paul the Deacon, and a grammarian, Peter of Pisa. Spain sent Theodulf, a poet. A couple of Irish scholars were in residence, and the most prominent Frank was Charlemagne's biographer, architect, and master of the palace works, Einhard (who was quoted at the beginning of this chapter).

The Carolingian Renaissance did not aspire to much original work. Its objective was to rescue literacy so that Europeans could access the intellectual legacy of the ancient world. Given the situation Charlemagne's scholars faced, their achievement was considerable. Following the example set by Roman textbooks, they designed an educational curriculum around the seven liberal arts, the knowledge needed by the *liber* ("freeborn man"). A liberal arts education emphasized literary skills. It began with the *trivium* (grammar, dialectic, rhetoric), instruction in reading and writing Latin. The *quadrivium* (arithmetic, geometry, astronomy, and music), which followed, taught clergy what they needed to know to manage estates, calculate dates for church feasts, and sing liturgies.

Alcuin and his colleagues wrote textbooks for their schools. They sought out manuscripts of neglected works to build library collections, and they published improved editions of ancient texts. They even reformed the mechanics of writing. So many different scripts had evolved in so many places in Europe that it was difficult for scholars from one region to read what those in another had written. Charlemagne's schools standardized shapes for the letters of the alphabet and taught students to leave spaces between words to make reading easier and more efficient. Our system of writing is based on this Carolingian "minuscule."

The Carolingian Renaissance had some notable successes. It reformed the liturgy of the church by building on Roman customs that it believed went back to the generation of Pope Gregory the Great. The tradition of Gregorian chant that it launched produced music that still moves worshipers. The Renaissance halted the loss of books and rescued what was left of the literary legacy of the ancient world. Few major works exist today in copies older than those made by Charlemagne's scholars. All told, the renaissance was a decisive moment in European intellectual history. It halted the cultural losses that had accompanied the passing of the Roman Empire in western Europe. The political confusion that broke out after Charlemagne's death set recovery back, but things were never again as bad as they had been before Charlemagne.

Charlemagne may have hoped for more than he got from his investment in Europe's re-education. The schools that he ordered monks and bishops to establish were not always able to fulfill their missions. His nobles ignored his call to educate themselves, and he may secretly have empathized with them. Einhard says that Charlemagne learned to read but that he started too late in life to master the motor skills that writing requires. He kept a slate under his pillow, however, and practiced the alphabet before falling asleep.

Larger Issue Revisited

Despite a healthy dose of barbarian ancestry, the inhabitants of early medieval Europe believed that they were legitimate heirs to the civilization of the ancient Mediterranean world, and they were determined to assert their claim to their legacy. They revered Rome's memory, the shreds of classical literature that had survived in their shrunken libraries, and the Christian religion. But they struggled with harsher and more primitive conditions than had faced the residents of Rome's Mediterranean empire. They survived by innovating new technologies. They integrated information from their tribal oral traditions with classicism's literary legacy. They adapted to a challenging physical environment, to an economy that offered little more than basic sustenance, and to a society that had nearly lost all order and structure. Their unique needs shaped what they did with their inheritance from the past, and the culture they pioneered was initially inferior to the civilizations of Islam and Byzantium. But it was preparing them for a great future.

Review Questions

1. When did the northwestern provinces of the Roman Empire cease to be Roman and become European? What changes mark the transition between the two eras?
2. How did the problems that led to the end of the Merovingian dynasty differ from the kinds of problems that caused the fall of Rome's dynasties?
3. How did Charlemagne's empire differ from the Roman Empire whose title he claimed?
4. Why was the ancient world able to sustain a single empire while medieval Europe was not?
5. In what ways were feudalism and manorialism adaptations to Europe's physical and political environment? What impact did they have on Europe's civilization?
6. How did the civilization of early medieval Europe differ from the classical civilization of the ancient Greeks and Romans? How was it similar?

Refer to the front of the book for a list of chapter-relevant primary sources available on the CD-ROM.

THE WEST INTERACTIVE

For web-based activities, map explorations, and quizzes related to this chapter, go to *www.prenhall.com/frankforter.*

CHAPTER 9

EUROPE TURNS OUTWARD

You race of Franks, the beloved whom God has chosen (as your many victories show) and set apart from other peoples by the location of your country, your Catholic faith, and your respect for the church—on you we call! There is grievous news from Jerusalem and Constantinople. A race from Persia—an accursed people who are totally opposed to God—has stormed Christian lands and depopulated them by looting and burning. . . . On whom does the task of avenging these crimes fall . . . if not on you, you on whom God has conferred—more than on any other nation—outstanding military valor, great courage, vigor, and strength to bring low all who oppose you?

—**Pope Urban II**

Larger Issue: *Was conflict among the medieval civilizations inevitable?*

On November 27, 1095 , Pope Urban II (r. 1088–1099) allegedly addressed the words quoted above to a crowd of knights assembled on a field at Clermont in central France. The knights who heard him may have been surprised to find themselves exhorted to fight, for they had come to Clermont to pledge themselves to the Truce of God. The Truce of God and an earlier movement called the Peace of God were efforts by the church to persuade feudal warriors to exercise self restraint. The Peace originated in 989 C.E. at a council at Charroux in Aquitaine. It decreed that knights should do no harm to noncombatants (clergy, women, and peasants). The Truce further curtailed bloodshed by declaring that no fighting should take place on sacred days: Sundays, religious festivals, and during the penitential seasons of Advent and Lent. Urban's call for a holy war was not, however, inconsistent with the objectives of the Peace and Truce. One way to pacify the home front was to divert Europe's military resources to foreign campaigns.

Urban's war is now known as the First Crusade, but the word *crusade* did not exist in his day. A Latin term meaning "war of the cross" ("crusade") was not coined until the thirteenth century C.E., and vernacular expressions appeared even later. Urban called his holy warriors pilgrims. Pilgrims were not supposed to bear arms, and the church had always said that it was a sin to shed blood, but Urban assured the knights who responded to his call that his was a new kind of war that merited new rules. The enemy Christians faced was so heinous, so anathema to God and civilization, that killing him was an act of self-sanctification. The crusader's sword purified a warrior's soul, for by wielding it against the enemies of the faith, he fulfilled the mission for which God created him.

Urban believed—correctly, as it turned out—that Europe had reached the turning point in its history. God, he claimed, had kept the Franks in reserve, tucked away from other peoples on the edge of the world. He had given them the true faith and the superior military virtues needed to defend it. The time had come, the pope said, for Europe's soldiers to be loosed on the enemies of God. For centuries Europeans had been in retreat and on the defensive. They had lost territory and suffered humiliating raids and invasions. Finally, however, they were ready to realize their destiny—to take the offensive and destroy all that they regarded as alien.

Urban's crusade was an early manifestation of the European impulse to thrust outward, both territorially and culturally. The descendants of his pilgrim-soldiers would one day build global-spanning colonial empires and attempt to make their civilization universal. In the process, they divided the world between "the West" and "the Other," and spawned resentments and misunderstandings with which modern nations still struggle. As you work through this chapter, ask yourself whether the warring cultures were as incompatible as they often seemed to assume.

 TOPICS IN THIS CHAPTER

Islam's Crest and Byzantium's Resurgence • The Reorganization of Feudal Europe • The Eleventh-Century Turning Point

Islam's Crest and Byzantium's Resurgence

The pan-European empire that Charlemagne hoped to build did not materialize. Europe lacked the infrastructure and cultural ties needed to support political unification, and the invasions of the Vikings, Magyars, and Muslims forced it to decentralize its defenses. The tendency toward political fragmentation was, however, not confined to Europe. The momentum of conquest preserved the Muslim empire until the mid-eighth century C.E., but once expansion ceased, the Muslim world, like Christian Europe, came apart.

Caliphs and Sultans   The Muslim empire was riven by ethnic tensions, new and old. The Umayyad caliphs did not impose Islam on all their subjects or even encourage them to come together to form a single people. They viewed Islam as a gift God intended primarily for Arabs, and they wanted Arabs to remain aloof from the natives of the lands they conquered. Umayyad "racism" had fiscal as well as cultural motives. The empire's non-Muslim subjects paid taxes from which Muslims were exempt. Many non-Arabs were, however, sincerely drawn to Islam. Although it was impossible to deny their wish to convert, Arabs often discriminated against them, and this created tensions within the *umma* (the Muslim community).

In 739 C.E. fighting erupted between Berber and Arab Muslims in North Africa, and in 750 C.E. Persian converts helped the Abbasids overthrow the Umayyad caliphate. In 756 C.E. Abd al-Rahman (731–788 C.E.), an Umayyad prince, wrested control of the Iberian Peninsula from the Abbasid caliphs and declared Spain an independent emirate. In 788 C.E. a Shi'ite leader won over the Berber Muslims and founded the Aghlabid dynasty in North Africa. In 800 C.E. the Abbasids acknowledged its virtual autonomy. The Aghlabids clashed with Spain's Umayyad emir, and they kept their Arab and Berber followers from feuding among themselves by sending them to raid southern Europe. In 902 C.E. they drove the Byzantines from Sicily.

In 909 C.E. the Aghlabids were overthrown by a Berber faction that supported a Shi'ite who claimed to be a descendant of Muhammad's daughter, Fatima. The Fatimid dynasty that he founded established a Shi'ite caliphate in opposition to the Sunni Abbasids. In 929 C.E. Spain's Umayyad emir rallied the Sunni Muslims in the western Mediterranean to his side by

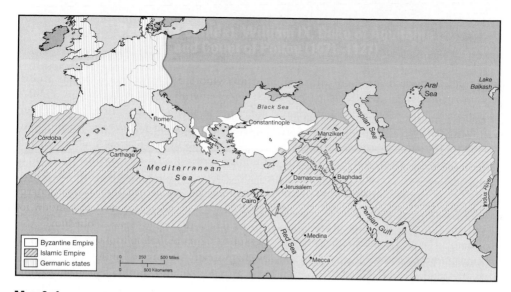

Map 9-1

The Medieval Muslim World   The Muslim Empire grew so quickly that it had little opportunity to consolidate before it began to come apart. The three caliphates that emerged (Umayyad Spain, Fatimid Egypt, and Abbasid Baghdad) reflected enduring religious, ethnic, and political divisions within the Islamic world. *Question:* Islam is sometimes contrasted with "the West." Does that description make geographical sense?

declaring himself their caliph. Baghdad's response was weak, for by then the political authority of the Abbasid caliphs was fading away. (See Map 9–1.)

The Abbasid dynasty had reached its peak during the reign of Charlemagne's contemporary, Harun al-Rashid (r. 786–809 C.E.). Harun al-Rashid's court in Baghdad was probably the most splendid and sophisticated of its day, but ominous developments shadowed the future of his empire. He had lost Spain to the Umayyads, and in 800 C.E. he relinquished North Africa to the Aghlabids. Wars between Harun al-Rashid's sons cost the Abbasid dynasty more territory, and in 820 C.E. a Persian prince wrested the eastern province of Khurasan from their control.

In the mid-ninth century C.E., the beleaguered Abbasid caliphs tried to secure their position by creating an army of Turkish slaves. The theory was that foreign slaves, who had no powerful families or local allies to support them, would be totally dependent on, and loyal to, the caliph. The Turks, however, developed their own leaders and wrested territory in Persia, Syria, and Egypt away from their caliph. Some Abbasids put up a good fight, but in 945 C.E. Baghdad's caliph submitted to the Persian Buyids. While the Buyids brought Persia and Iraq under control, the Fatimids moved across North Africa to Egypt. In 969 C.E. they evicted a Turkish ruler from Egypt and relocated the seat of their caliphate to a new city on the Nile, which they named Cairo (al-Kahira, "Victorious"). Sporadic warfare raged inconclusively between the Buyids and Fatimids for about a century, and in the end, both succumbed to a third Muslim power, the Seljuk Turks.

The Turks, like the early Germans, were an assortment of nomadic tribes that spoke related languages. They first made contact with Islam about 653 C.E., when the Arab armies that were sweeping across the Persian Empire reached the Oxus River. The Turks' relationship with Islam's new empire resembled the one the Germans had with Rome's old empire. They absorbed its religion and were attracted by its wealth, power, and culture. Some immigrated and integrated peacefully. Some were enslaved, and some set up their own states on its territory. During the tenth century C.E., Islam's eastern lands were overrun by Turks. Some of these planted Islam in northern and central India, and others, the Seljuks, took over Persia.

The Seljuks came from the region of the Jaxartes River and converted to Islam in the second half of the tenth century C.E. After occupying Khurasan, they set their sights on the Buyids, and in 1060 they took Baghdad. The Seljuks allowed the Abbasid caliph to serve as a religious figurehead, but their *sultan* (*shultana,* "governor") assumed responsibility for running Baghdad's empire and defending Sunni Islam against its primary enemies: the Shi'ite Fatimids and the Christian Byzantines.

The Fatimid dynasty was the lesser threat, for its power was fading. The Fatimids' early victories had raised unrealistic expectations among their Shi'ite followers. The Shi'ite faith was apocalyptic. It awaited a messiah—the revelation of a secret descendant of the Prophet, who would miraculously reunite the *umma* and complete Islam's triumph. As the tenth century C.E. dragged on, hope diminished that the Fatimid caliphate would produce such a savior.

The Fatimids turned Egypt into a strong state with a powerful navy, but they failed to make much progress against the Buyids, the Byzantines, or even rival Shi'ite groups. Wealth and power had their usual corrupting effect, and by the eleventh century, internal power struggles and inept caliphs were costing the Fatimids both followers and territory. The dynasty survived until an unexpected event altered political arrangements throughout the Muslim world. Constantinople triggered an invasion of the Middle East by western Europeans.

Constantinople   When the Arab armies first erupted from their homeland, they descended on a Byzantine Empire that had been weakened by a long war with Persia. In 636 C.E. the Byzantine emperor Heraclius (r. 610–641 C.E.) lost a major battle to the Muslims, and by the time of his death, his empire had been reduced to Asia Minor, parts of Greece and the Balkans, and nominal authority over Sicily, North Africa, and a few outposts in Italy. Then things got worse. Arabs annually raided throughout Asia Minor—sometimes threatening Constantinople itself. They challenged the Byzantine navy's power at sea, and in 670 C.E. they began a triumphal march through the Byzantine province of North Africa. Then things got much worse. In 679 C.E. the Slavs, who had long posed a threat to Constantinople's possessions in the Balkans, were joined by the Bulgars, a people similar to the Huns. Byzantium's efforts to deal with all these external threats were complicated by internal fights over its throne.

In 717 C.E. (just as Charles Martel was laying the foundations for Europe's Carolingian Empire) a great general, Leo III (r. 717–740 C.E.), seized power in Constantinople and drove the Muslims back from the city. Leo and his heirs, the Isaurian dynasty, restructured Byzantine government and society to mobilize support for a stronger military. They divided the empire into regions called themes. A regiment of soldiers was assigned to each, and each was governed by the commander of its regiment. Some soldiers were salaried, but many were supported, like Europe's vassals, by grants of land. Repeated Muslim raids had broken up many of the great estates and undercut the institution of serfdom. By redistributing lands among free peasants, the Isaurian dynasty created a class of independent farmers from which to recruit stalwart defenders for its empire.

Leo issued a new code of civil law (in Greek instead of the Latin that Constantinople's "Roman" emperors had previously used) and forced through a controversial religious reform. In 726 C.E. he promulgated the first in a series of edicts that forbade the use of icons (sacred images) in worship. Repugnance for religious art was widespread in the Middle East, for both Muslims and Jews regarded it as a temptation to idolatry. Leo apparently believed that the use of icons in worship promoted blasphemous worship of icons. By ordering their destruction, he also hoped to rein in some monasteries that had grown excessively rich from the offerings the superstitious masses made to the sacred images the monks possessed. Leo's iconoclasm ("destruction of sacred images") sparked revolts among his subjects and was roundly denounced by theologians who believed that a ban on religious images was tantamount to the denial of Christ's humanity. Church councils in western Europe objected to Leo's policy, and opposition to iconoclasm was probably a factor in the papacy's decision to ally with the Franks. The issue continued to make trouble for Constantinople until its rulers gave in and repudiated iconoclasm in 843 C.E..

In 867 C.E. Basil I (r. 867–886 C.E.), who had risen from slavery to become an imperial advisor, assassinated his emperor and seized the Byzantine throne. The Macedonian dynasty he founded restored the glory of Constantinople and reclaimed territory the Byzantines had lost to the Muslims and Bulgars. The ruthless Basil II (r. 963–1025 C.E.), "the Bulgar-slayer," brought Russia within the orbit of Constantinople and Christianity. Vikings who worked the river systems that linked the Baltic and the Black seas joined the Slavs of central Europe to form a people called the Rus ("Russians," after Ruric, the Viking ruler of Novgorod in 862 C.E.). Their ruler, Vladimir I (980–1015 C.E.) of Kiev, accepted baptism in exchange for the hand of Basil's sister, and the marriage forged strong commercial and cultural ties between Constantinople and Russia.

In 1057 a coalition of Byzantine aristocrats and clergy overthrew the last of the Macedonian emperors. Their coup was ill-timed, for it weakened Constantinople's defenses just as the Seljuk Turks were beginning to revive Islam's martial spirit. In 1071 the Byzantine emperor Romanus IV Diogenes (r. 1068–1071) lost a decisive battle with the Seljuks near an Armenian fortress called Manzikert, and most of Asia Minor—the region from which Constantinople recruited its armies—passed to the Seljuks. Constantinople survived. The city had strong fortifications, and it continued to prosper as a depot for international trade. The Seljuk threat also gradually receded, for the Turks began to fight among themselves for shares of the lands they had conquered.

The Reorganization of Feudal Europe

Europe bore the brunt of the devastation caused by the German invasions that brought down the Roman Empire, and for centuries it lagged behind the Byzantine and Muslim worlds. Charlemagne tried to close the gap, but the invasions of the Vikings, Magyars, and Muslims in the ninth and tenth centuries C.E. set Europe back once again. Charlemagne's successors were weak feudal kings who, like their vassals, were preoccupied with the struggle to protect their own estates. Once the invasions stopped, however, kings could give some attention to building centralized governments and consolidating the states that became the nations of modern Europe. This was a difficult project that did not always meet with success. By the end of the Middle Ages, England and France had emerged as stable, unified countries under different kinds of

Figure 9–1 A Viking Ship Primitive people may sometimes develop technologies that are superior to those of their more advanced neighbors. The Viking ship, which was adapted to both sea and river navigation, illustrates this. The civilized countries that the Vikings invaded had nothing to equal or counter it.

royal authority, but Germany and Italy remained politically fragmented until late in the nineteenth century C.E..

England and France   England was a small country (only a little larger than the state of New York) situated on an island, but that did not mean that it was easy to unify. After the Anglo-Saxons occupied it in the fifth century C.E., it may have been divided up into seven kingdoms. The Viking invasions of the eighth and ninth centuries C.E. obliterated all but one—the kingdom of Wessex that occupied England's southwest corner. Its ruler, Alfred the Great (r. 871–899 C.E.), confined the Vikings (Danes) to the Danelaw (the northeastern half of England) and founded a strong Anglo-Saxon state that endured for about a century. Alfred, like Charlemagne, was a patron of scholars and educators who set up a palace school. He was particularly eager to promote Anglo-Saxon literature, and unlike the Frankish emperor, he was able on his own to do some writing and translating.

In 954 C.E. one of Alfred's successors brought all of England under his control and converted the Vikings who had settled on the island to Christianity. Churches and monasteries began to be restored, but the opportunity to rebuild and consolidate was brief. At the end of the century King Ethelred the Unready (r. 978–1016 C.E.) confronted a second wave of Viking invaders. He tried to buy them off with the proceeds of a national tax called the Danegeld, but in 1013 a Danish army forced Ethelred to flee England.

England then became part of a North Sea empire headed by a king who also ruled Denmark, Norway, and parts of Sweden. The island's new ruler, Cnute (r. 1016–1035), was no barbarian. He visited Rome to consult with the pope and earned a reputation as an able monarch. Europe's history might have been quite different had his empire survived, but fights among his potential heirs destroyed it. Once England regained its independence, Edward the Confessor (r. 1042–1066), the Anglo-Saxon heir to its throne, returned from exile.

Edward, England's last Anglo-Saxon king, had Viking blood. His mother was the sister of a French duke, who was a descendant of a Viking chief named Rollo. In 911 C.E. the French king, Charles the Simple (r. 893–929 C.E.), had tried to limit his losses to the Vikings by coming to terms with Rollo. Rollo swore an oath of fealty to Charles in exchange for the title of duke and a fief consisting of the lower Seine Valley and much of the French side of the English Channel. The king hoped that Rollo's Vikings, the barons of the newly created duchy of Normandy (from Norsemen or Normans), would prevent other Vikings from raiding farther into French territory. The Normans acculturated quickly—adopting Christianity, the French language, and continental feudalism. Normandy produced a remarkable number of famous soldiers and adventurers who spread the duchy's influence from Ireland to the Holy Land.

Edward the Confessor had spent most of his life in Normandy and had no personal power base in England. He wed the daughter of the most influential man in his kingdom, an earl (an English title of nobility) named Godwin, but sired no children. He achieved little, and his death in 1066 set off a three-way race for England's vacant throne. The native Anglo-Saxon candidate was Edward's brother-in-law, Harold Godwinson. Harold Hardrada, king of Norway (r. 1045–1066), asserted the Viking claim, and Edward's distant relative, William, duke of Normandy, also entered the lists. In September 1066 Harold Godwinson defeated Harold Hardrada in northern England. But his involvement there gave William a chance to ferry the Norman army across the English Channel and land unopposed in southern England. Harold Godwinson dashed from one campaign to another, and England's fate was decided by a battle fought near the port town of Hastings. Godwinson and most of the Anglo-Saxon leaders were killed, and Duke William became King William I, "the Conqueror" (r. 1066–1087).

As England's conqueror, William was free to establish any kind of government he wanted. He imported the feudal institutions with which he was familiar in Normandy but wisely preserved English customs that gave the king advantages in power struggles with his vassals. Most feudal nobles preferred a weak king who could not interfere in their affairs, but England's new aristocracy needed the support of a powerful monarch. They were a tiny minority of French-speaking foreigners who were unpopular with the masses of their Anglo-Saxon subjects.

William succeeded in establishing a Norman ruling class in control of England, but his victory led to a struggle between the kings of England and France that dragged on for four hundred years. If William's estate had been divided as he ordered, however, the problem might have been avoided. At William's death, the duchy of Normandy passed by right of inheritance to his eldest son, Robert "Curthose." Robert showed little promise as a leader, and this may have entered into William's decision to separate the duchy he had inherited from the kingdom he had won. England needed a strong king, and the best candidate was William's second son, William II, "Rufus" (r. 1087–1100). In 1095 Robert pawned Normandy to his brother to

Figure 9–2   The Bayeux Tapestry   The Norman conquest of England inspired one of medieval history's unique documents, the Bayeux Tapestry. It depicts events in the life of William the Conqueror on a series of panels embroidered in colored wool on a 230-foot-long strip of linen. It is a source of invaluable visual information about William's world.

raise the money he needed to join the First Crusade. He survived that adventure, but he lost his duchy and his freedom to William's successor, their younger brother Henry. The duchy's reunification with the English crown might have seemed like good policy at the time, for many Norman lords owned lands on both sides of the English Channel. However, it created a diplomatic situation rife with confusion. Henry, as duke of Normandy, was the vassal of the king of France, but as king of England, he was the French monarch's equal.

William the Conqueror's third son became Henry I (r. 1100–1135), king of England, under suspicious circumstances. His unpopular brother, William Rufus, died in what was represented as a hunting accident but may well have been an assassination. Few lamented his death, but his demise by no means assured Henry's succession. Their older brother Robert had the stronger claim to England's throne. Henry, therefore, set about courting support. He dismissed William's unpopular officials, and at his coronation he issued a Charter of Liberties in which he pledged not to abuse his power. The document had little effect at the time, but it set an important precedent.

The church maintained that a king's power derived from God, not his subjects, and that subjects therefore had no right to sit in judgment on kings. Henry's charter, however, implied that a monarch was accountable to his people for how he governed them. A century later the famous Magna Carta reaffirmed this principle, but until the English Parliament was well established, there was no way to enforce it. The idea was kept alive in England by historical accident. It faded during the reigns of strong kings and revived when weak ones mismanaged their responsibilities. As fate would have it, strong kings alternated with weak ones throughout the

Middle Ages—leading to the development of a constitutional or limited monarchy in England.

The powerful monarchy that the Conqueror and his sons, William and Henry, established in England was nearly undone by a problem with the succession to their throne. The only one of Henry's legitimate children to survive him was a daughter, Matilda (1102–1167). Henry forced his reluctant vassals to promise to accept her as his heir. The idea of a reigning queen was so unconventional, however, that a case could be made for breaking such a promise. A medieval king was a warlord, and few people thought that a woman could do his job. Some of England's nobles repudiated Matilda (and her French husband, the count of Anjou) and declared her cousin Stephen the rightful heir to Henry's throne. Matilda had the advantage of descent from the Conqueror through the male line, but she was a woman. Ordinarily, Stephen's claim would be weaker, for his link with the Conqueror was through his mother, William's daughter. However, Stephen was a male, and his supporters argued that this tipped the balance in his favor.

Civil war erupted, and for twenty years the nobles had the advantage of being able to play one claimant to the throne off against the other. Stephen finally offered Matilda a compromise. In exchange for her recognition of his right to live out his life in peace as England's king, he acknowledged her son, Henry, as his heir. Stephen died a year later, and England's battered crown passed to a man who had the skill and resources to refurbish it.

Henry II (r. 1154–1189) was the right man in the right place at the right time—intelligent, well educated, crafty, physically vigorous, and charismatic. His family connections positioned him to make the most of his gifts. His uncle bequeathed him the kingdom of England. His mother and father left him the duchy of Normandy and the county of Anjou (much of northern France), and his wife, Eleanor (c. 1122–1204), brought him the duchy of Aquitaine (a large piece of southern France). Henry's sprawling Angevin (from Anjou) Empire made him a more powerful man in France than France's king. (See Map 9–2.)

The English monarchy began strong and was forced by circumstances to accept limits to its authority. The French monarchy headed in the opposite direction. France's early kings were weak, but by the end of the Middle Ages, they were well on their way to becoming absolute monarchs.

William, as England's conqueror, could impose any form of government on it that he desired. This got his dynasty off to a strong start. The French monarchy had a very different beginning. The invasions of the ninth and tenth centuries C.E. cost its kings considerable power and prestige. France was four times the size of England and exposed to attack on multiple fronts. A king could not offer as much protection as could a strong local lord. Consequently, France became the most thoroughly feudalised country in Europe.

In 987 C.E. the French nobles switched their allegiance from Charlemagne's ineffectual descendants to the family of Hugh Capet (r. 987–996 C.E.), count of Paris. Hugh's county was the front line in the war with the Viking invaders, and his fellow nobles concluded that it was in their interest to help him defend his small estate. The early kings of the Capetian dynasty, which he founded, had no power to compel obedience from France's nobles. Many of them controlled much more territory than their monarch. The Capetians also had to be careful not to offend their vassals by trying to assert their rights as kings. They were not born kings with a hereditary claim to the crown. They were elected kings by vassals who could, whenever they wanted, shift their allegiance to someone else. Little could be done to strengthen monarchy in France until the Capetians established exclusive rights to the French throne. For generations,

Map 9–2

Medieval France   For much of the Middle Ages, the country of France consisted of virtually independent feudal entities. Each of it regions had a distinct dialect and culture, and the kinds of nationalistic sentiments that seem natural to modern people had not yet appeared to bind them together. *Question:* Would geography have made the unification of France easy or difficult?

they threatened no one and always had a viable candidate (an adult son) ready for election before his father's death. Because the Capetians seemed a safe choice and none of the powerful lords wanted a competitor to have the royal title, the Capetians were repeatedly elected kings. Eventually, the succession of a Capetian became a foregone conclusion, and the nobles dispensed with pointless elections. Vassals, who based title to their fiefs on generations of family occupancy, could hardly challenge the Capetians' right to lay claim to the crown on the same grounds.

The first member of the Capetian dynasty who was secure enough to assert his authority was Louis VI, "the Fat" (r. 1108–1137), a contemporary of England's powerful Henry I. Louis did little more than exercise the rights that all feudal lords had over their vassals, but he also cultivated allies who wanted a stronger monarchy. The feudal nobles preferred a weak king who could not threaten their autonomy, but the clergy and many ordinary people wanted a king who could impose discipline on the marauding nobility. The residents of the new towns that sprang up in France in the eleventh and twelfth centuries C.E. were particularly eager to promote the development of centralized government. Townspeople depended on trade, and they wanted a king who could make the countryside safe for travelers and limit the tolls local lords imposed on merchants.

A feudal king was weak because he governed with the help of vassals who wanted him to be weak. If he hoped to become more effective, he had to find an alternative to working through the feudal hierarchy. Townspeople and clergy could help him by giving him money with which to hire salaried officials. It was hard to evict a vassal from his manors, but it was easy to cut off a salary. Salaried officials therefore tended to be more loyal than vassals, and they wanted a strong employer. The stronger the king, the more secure their wages.

Louis VI used his privileges as a feudal overlord to obtain for his heir a bride who promised to tip the balance of power in France decisively in the Capetians' favor. Louis VII (r. 1137–1180) wed Eleanor of Aquitaine, heiress to a huge duchy in southern France. Unfortunately for him, however, he was never able to compel his bride or her duchy to submit to his authority. In 1152 the flagrantly incompatible couple persuaded the pope to annul their union. Eleanor promptly chose as her second husband the man who posed the greatest threat to her first. She wed Henry of Anjou who, in 1154, became King Henry II of England, the architect of the Angevin Empire. Louis spent the rest of his life in an unequal struggle with Henry, but in the next generation the tide turned in the Capetians' favor. Henry's sons, Richard I, "the Lionhearted" (r. 1189–1199), and John (r. 1199–1216), were no match for Louis's heir, Philip II, "Augustus" (r. 1180–1223). Philip recovered many French fiefs from the English kings and kept much of what he won for the royal domain. He bequeathed his heirs a much stronger throne than the one he had inherited, but he did not resolve France's problems with England.

Germany, Italy, and the Papacy The medieval monarchy that made the most promising start and the most dismal finish was Germany's. In 911 C.E. the last of Germany's Carolingian rulers died, and the German dukes chose Conrad, duke of Franconia (r. 911–918 C.E.), to be their king. His primary achievement was to pass the crown to a more viable candidate, Henry I, "the Fowler" (r. 919–936 C.E.), duke of Saxony. Saxony was a much larger and more powerful duchy than Franconia, and thanks to its location in northwestern Germany, it had been spared the Magyar raids that had weakened the rest of the country. Germany's dukes submitted to Henry's authority because they needed the help he could give them in their fight with the Magyars. In 955 C.E. Henry's son and successor, Otto I, "the Great" (r. 936–973 C.E.), decisively defeated the invaders and reestablished Austria as a buffer state protecting Germany's eastern frontier. This contained the Magyars in a land of their own and encouraged them to settle down. Missionaries, whom Otto sponsored, quickly converted them, and in the year 1000 the pope recognized the existence of the new Christian kingdom of Hungary by sending its leader, Stephen (r. 997–1038 C.E.), a crown.

As Europe's most powerful monarch and the ruler of its largest kingdom, Otto saw himself as picking up where Charlemagne had left off. In 951 C.E. he began a war to bring Italy under his control, and in 962 C.E. the pope revived the imperial title and bestowed it on Otto. Romantic visions of Roman and Carolingian empires were not the only reasons for Otto's interest in Italy. His home duchy was in northern Germany, and he would have had difficulty holding his kingdom together if the leaders of either of its southern duchies, Swabia and Bavaria, had crossed the Alps and added Italy to their possessions. Otto and most of his successors believed that Germany and Italy (which had no native king) had to be united, but some Italians saw things differently. The papacy and the wealthy towns that flourished in northern Italy feared German domination and put up stiff resistance. (See Map 9–3.)

Constantinople was persuaded to accept Otto's coronation, and in 972 C.E. a marriage was arranged between his heir, Otto II (r. 973–983 C.E.), and a Byzantine princess named Theophano. She and her cosmopolitan entourage elevated life at the German court, and the close ties with Constantinople that the marriage established stimulated a burst of artistic and literary activity, which historians call the Ottonian Renaissance.

In the process of creating his empire, Otto acquired a lot of territory for the crown, but he knew that feudal kings had difficulty hanging on to land. A king's power depended on the number and loyalty of the servants who carried out his orders. He had to use his land to support those servants, but if he granted it to them as fiefs, their families established hereditary rights to those fiefs and became independent of him. Otto solved this problem by granting the bulk of his lands to the church. The church, like a secular landlord, owed the king military service for its lands. The advantage was that the leaders of the church could not marry and pass their offices down to their sons. Germany's bishops and abbots were appointed by its king. He could therefore make sure that the lands he gave the church remained in the hands of men loyal to him. His power was safe so long as his authority over the church was unquestioned, but in the late tenth century C.E. challenges began to be mounted to the power laity had over clergy.

In 910 C.E., shortly before Otto's Saxon dynasty was founded in Germany, the duke of Aquitaine funded an ecclesiastical experiment in France. He endowed a new Benedictine monastery called Cluny and gave its monks the privilege of choosing their own abbot and managing their own affairs. This was unusual, for the wealthy families that donated to ecclesiastical institutions usually assumed that they had the right to appoint the clergy who were supported by their gifts. The reformers who sponsored Cluny claimed that a lay patron who had a church office to give away tended to be more influenced by applicants' political connections than by their spiritual qualifications. The result was a lot of unworthy appointments and a general decline of religion. Things would improve, the Cluniacs insisted, if clergy were freed from secular interference and allowed to decide who was fit to be admitted to the clerical vocation. Cluny bore this out, for the monastery quickly earned the reputation of being the most reputable religious house in Europe. Other cloisters asked Cluny to reorganize them, and before long Cluniacs were spearheading a drive to reform the whole church.

Map 9–3

Medieval Germany and Italy Although the Roman Empire had never extended far into Germany, medieval Germany was haunted by the empire's memory. German monarchs claimed the Roman title and believed that it gave them the right to rule Italy. Italians disagreed and viewed the Germans as invaders. The failure of Germany's kings to overcome the combined resistance of the Italian towns, the papacy, and their own feudal nobles sapped their authority and led to the political fragmentation of both Germany and Italy. **_Question:_** Did geography encourage or hamper the attempts of the German kings to join their country with Italy?

✳ People in Context: Hroswitha of Gandersheim (fl. 935–1002 C.E.)

The most original of the Ottonian Renaissance's authors was a nun, Hroswitha of the Bene-dictine cloister at Gandersheim. Her personal history, beyond the little that can be inferred from her works, is a blank. She was probably an aristocrat, for Gandersheim was an elite house to which women from the royal family occasionally retreated.

Hroswitha was deeply grateful for the education she received at Gandersheim, and her teachers must have been women of considerable erudition. Hroswitha wrote excellent Latin and was a student of classical literature. Some of her works were what one might expect from a nun: saints' legends, apocryphal tales about the life of the Virgin Mary, and an ac-count of the foundation of her cloister. But Hroswitha also ventured into unusual literary territory. She tried her hand at a history of Otto I's reign (the first attempt, as far as we know, by a medieval woman to write secular history). But her crowning achievement was a set of six plays that she said she wrote to counter the negative image of women found in the comedies of Terence, a playwright from the era of the Roman Republic. Hroswitha's plays are surprising because we might not anticipate that anyone in remote medieval Saxony would know of Terence, that a nun would be drawn to his work, that she would write fine Latin, that she would decide to write plays, and that she would use theater to rehabilitate the image of women. Hroswitha's plays are the only ones known to have been written between the fall of Rome and the gradual emergence of religious drama from the liturgy of the church in the twelfth century C.E. It is unclear whether she intended them to be staged or simply read, but at least one of them seems to call for comic action to flesh out its words.

Hroswitha was that rarest of medieval authors, a woman who wrote about women. Her world offered women only three roles: wife and mother, consecrated virgin, and whore. Hroswitha's plays illustrated how women in each of these situations could become spiritual heroines. She believed that females were physically and mentally inferior to males, but this, she argued, gave them a spiritual advantage over men. In her opinion, the male's worldly strengths subject him to powerful temptations to which he is likely to succumb unless women, with God's help, courageously guard their virtue. Hroswitha placed women at the center of humanity's struggle for salvation.

Question: On what did women base their self-respect in the male-dominated medieval world?

The Saxon dynasty died out in 1024, before the Cluniac movement had become powerful enough to cause kings much trouble. The Salian dynasty (1024–1125), which succeeded the Saxons, was not so lucky. In 1049 its king, Henry III (r. 1039–1056), appointed his cousin, Leo IX (r. 1049–1054), to the papacy. Leo was a vigorous reformer. He traveled throughout Europe, convening councils to encourage spiritual renewal, and he improved the machinery of papal government by making more use of the cardinals (the Roman clergy who reported di-rectly to him). By the time Henry III's son, Henry IV (1056–1106), came to the throne, the

German king faced an ecclesiastical hierarchy that was determined to establish the papacy's independence of secular monarchs and to end the tradition of laymen appointing clergy.

Henry was crowned king at a young age, and the regents who governed for him were weak. This gave Pope Nicholas II (r. 1059–1061) an opportunity to establish a new procedure for papal elections that would exclude interference by kings. Before Nicholas created one, there was no formal method for choosing a pope. Popes were elevated by political factions in the city of Rome or chosen by whatever emperor or king had power in Italy. Nicholas decreed that henceforth only clergy could participate in a papal election, and because it was impossible to poll clergy throughout Europe, the cardinal clergy in Rome were given the job of choosing popes. In 1073 they elected an avid Cluniac reformer who took the name Gregory VII (r. 1073–1085). The new pope immediately made his position perfectly clear. He claimed that popes were the highest authorities on Earth, that no one had the right to judge how they used their office, and that they even had the right to depose secular rulers.

It was some time before Henry IV was able to respond to the papacy's challenges to his authority, for the Salian dynasty had difficulty bringing Germany's landed nobility under control. Once the king had Germany more or less in hand, however, he turned his attention to Italy and to Gregory. The result was the Investiture Controversy, an important episode in the ongoing struggle between church and state.

In 1075 Gregory ordered laymen to discontinue the practice of investing clergy (that is, appointing men to church offices). Henry promptly called the pope's bluff by investing an archbishop for Milan, a major Italian see. This set off a chain of escalating events. Gregory denounced Henry. Henry convened a council of German bishops that declared Gregory deposed, and Gregory reciprocated by excommunicating and deposing Henry. Gregory's deposition decree carried some weight, for it gave Germany's nobles an excuse to repudiate a king whose growing strength threatened their freedom. The nobles asked Gregory to come to Germany to cloak their rebellion with an aura of legitimacy, but Henry forestalled this by crossing the Alps in midwinter and ostentatiously begging the pope's forgiveness. Gregory had no choice but to reconcile with a king who made such a flamboyant public show of regret. But when he did so, the German nobles concluded that he had betrayed them, and they turned on him. Henry recovered his hold on Germany, and in 1084 he descended on Rome and forced the pope to flee.

Gregory was humiliated and died in exile, but this did not end the Investiture Controversy or solve the problem of church–state relations. The church was endowed with about one-third of the land in Europe, and kings would not relinquish the right to some say in the choice of the clergy who administered so much of the territory that lay within the boundaries of their kingdoms. The church therefore settled for a face-saving compromise. Kings agreed not to take part in the ceremonies that invested clergy, but candidates for investiture had first to take oaths of homage to kings for the secular services owed from the church's lands. This gave kings a chance to veto candidates whom they did not like without seeming to violate the church's independence. The church consistently claimed more freedom in theory than it exercised in practice. This was an excellent strategy, for practice tended to catch up with theory.

The Salian dynasty did not long survive Henry's victory over Gregory. The death of its last king in 1125 nearly extinguished monarchy in Germany, and a generation passed before a new dynasty was established. Despite the advantage of an early, strong start, Germany's kings were still a long way from providing their subjects with effective, centralized government.

The Eleventh-Century C.E. Turning Point

Feudalism, despite its weaknesses, was a successful adaptation to the chaotic conditions that prevailed in early medieval Europe. Feudal governments helped Europe weather the invasions of the ninth and tenth centuries C.E., and they provided enough security to prevent the loss of the cultural gains made during the Carolingian era. Feudalism also prepared Europeans for a new role in the medieval world. Europe had largely been on the defensive since the fall of the western Roman Empire, but in the eleventh century C.E. that changed. Europe took the offensive, expanded territorially and economically, and developed an environment in which artists and intellectuals flourished.

The Spanish and Sicilian Crusades   The most obvious sign that the eleventh century C.E. marked the start of a new phase in Europe's history was the threat Europeans began to pose to their neighbors. After centuries of being invaded, Europe became the invader. It waged crusades—holy wars motivated (at least in part) by a fervent desire to destroy persons whom it

Culture in Context: Pilgrimage

A desire for contact with the past inspires hordes of modern Americans to make pilgrimages to civil war battlefields, the homes of presidents, and the graves of dignitaries. Medieval people shared this human sensitivity to the aura of historically significant places, but they experienced it through the medium of religious faith. They believed that spiritual powers were stronger and more accessible in some locations than in others. The polytheists of the ancient world had assumed that different lands had different gods and that travelers should reverence the local deities of the countries through which they journeyed. Medieval Christians were, of course, monotheists who believed that one God had universal dominion. But they also felt that God was such a remote and awesome figure that He was best approached through the intercession of a saint. Although a saint might hear a prayer offered anywhere, the power of saints tended to be localized. Miracles were most likely to occur in the presence of a saint's relics. An arduous pilgrimage to a saint's shrine was also a form of penance that inclined a saint to look favorably on a pilgrim's petition.

When Christianity first began to spread through Europe, there was no procedure for canonizing (officially recognizing) saints. Saints spontaneously proliferated, and some were of dubious authenticity. A vigorous demand for their relics encouraged grave robbing and an unseemly trade in sacred objects—some of which were forgeries. This was, in part, a reaction to the paucity of sacred sites in Europe. The stage for biblical history was in the Middle East. Post-biblical legends claimed that saints Peter and Paul had preached and been martyred in Rome. More fanciful tales maintained that Mary Magdalene and Lazarus had retired to southern France and that Joseph of Arimathea, in whose tomb Christ had been buried, had settled in England. About 830 C.E. the story spread that the grave of the Apostle James, the son of Zebedee and one of Jesus' intimates, had been found at Compostela, a Christian outpost in northwestern Spain. However, no place in western Europe could equal the spiritual attractions of Palestine, the Holy Land. As early as the fourth century C.E., it was drawing pilgrims from the remote corners of Rome's empire. (The travel diary of a Spanish nun survives from the early fifth century C.E.)

regarded as enemies of its church. Crusades primarily targeted Muslims in foreign lands, but they also triggered pogroms (massacres of Jews) in Europe that continued to erupt sporadically well into the twentieth century C.E. The hatreds, misunderstandings, and suspicions the crusades nurtured are still a complicating factor in international relationships.

Europe opened its first front against the Muslim world at its point of closest contact: Spain. In the middle of the tenth century C.E. the Umayyad caliph of Córdoba united Spain's Muslims and attacked the tiny Christian states on the northern rim of the Iberian Peninsula. In 997 C.E. alarm spread throughout Europe when the caliph's vizier, al-Mansur ("Victorious"), sacked Compostela, a pilgrimage center that ranked in importance only behind Jerusalem and Rome. Al-Mansur died in 1002, and no comparable Muslim leader appeared to take his place. This created an opportunity for Sancho III, "the Great" (r. 1000–1035), ruler of Navarre, a kingdom on the slopes of the Pyrenees. He appealed to Europe's Christian knights for help in mounting a counter offensive. The church blessed his campaign as a holy war, and the monks of Cluny vigorously promoted it. The Christian forces advanced steadily, and in 1085 they captured the old Visigothic capital of Toledo in the heart of Spain. At this point, their Muslim opponents received

Merovingian and Carolingian authors loved to record reports of miracles witnessed by visitors to various saints' shrines, but the great age of pilgrimage awaited the dawn of the eleventh century C.E. The monastery at Cluny promoted pilgrimage as part of its program to reform the church and elevate the spiritual life of the laity. Monasteries established hostels along pilgrim routes, and the church formalized rules for pilgrimage. To be recognized as pilgrims and receive the church's protection, people had to reconcile with their enemies, pay their debts, make wills, confess to their priests, and be formally blessed before they set off. Pilgrims wore special garments that advertised their mission, for they were entitled to ask other Christians for help in completing their journeys. Most pilgrimages were undertaken voluntarily by individuals who sought healing, forgiveness for sins, and answers to prayers, but some pilgrimages were imposed as punishments. Criminals might be condemned to wander as perpetual pilgrims until they received a miraculous sign of forgiveness.

Although ordinary pilgrims were forbidden to bear arms, the supreme pilgrim of the High Middle Ages (eleventh through the thirteenth centuries C.E.) was the crusader, the soldier who "took the cross" and risked his life to restore the Holy Land to Christian control. Acts of violence for which a man would otherwise have to atone became the means of his salvation in a holy war. The soldiers who fought the First Crusade received the church's first plenary indulgence, a dispensation from punishment for the sins of a lifetime. Some crusaders even took the monastic vows of poverty, chastity, and obedience, and formed military orders. Instead of fleeing the world to engage in spiritual struggles, these monks waged literal combat with the forces of evil. The cloisters of crusading orders, such as the Templars and Hospitalers, were castles from which men devoted to the service of God sallied forth to slaughter His presumed enemies.

Question: Does the enthusiasm that medieval Europeans showed for pilgrimages imply that they had an interest in cultures other than their own?

reinforcements from North Africa, and the war bogged down. The Christian reconquest of Spain dragged on for four more centuries, for neither the Muslims nor the Christians were very successful at resisting the temptation to fight among themselves.

Europe's Christians launched their second offensive against Islam in the central Mediterranean. In 1017 a group of Norman knights stopped off in southern Italy on their way back from a pilgrimage to Jerusalem. The Normans discovered that Italy's petty wars provided plentiful employment for mercenaries, and as word spread, recruits poured in from France. Among these were Robert Guiscard ("Cunning") and his brother Roger, two of the numerous sons of Tancred de Hauteville, a minor Norman nobleman. They subdued or evicted the native lords of southern Italy and drove the Muslims from Sicily. In 1130 the pope conferred a royal title on Roger's son, Roger II (1103–1154), and recognized the existence of a Norman monarchy (the future kingdom of the Two Sicilies) ruling Sicily and southern Italy. Robert Guiscard also tried to conquer Byzantine possessions in the Balkans and Greece, but his dream of building a Mediterranean empire proved too ambitious.

The Crusades to the Holy Land   While the first crusades were altering the balance of power in the western Mediterranean, the situation in the Middle East was also changing. Constantinople had ceded most of Asia Minor to the Seljuk Turks after its defeat at Manzikert in

Chronology: The Three Medieval Civilizations: Leaders and Events

MUSLIM WORLD	BYZANTIUM	EUROPE
	Leo III (717–740 C.E.) Iconoclastic Controversy (726–843 C.E.)	Pepin III (741–768 C.E.)
Abbasid dynasty (750 C.E.) Umayyad Emirate of Spain (756 C.E.) Aghlabids (800 C.E.)		Charlemagne (768–814 C.E.) Vikings attack (860 C.E.)
	Macedonian dynasty (867 C.E.)	*England France Germany*
	Alfred the Great (871–899 C.E.)	
Fatimid dynasty (909 C.E.)		Cluny founded (910 C.E.) Saxon dynasty (919 C.E.)
Umayyad caliphate of Spain (929 C.E.) Buyids take Baghdad (945 C.E.)		
		Capetian dynasty (987 C.E.)
	Schism: Greek and Latin churches (1054)	
	Cnute (1016–1035)	
		Salian dynasty (1024)
Seljuks take Baghdad (1060)		
		William I (1066–1087)
	Manzikert battle (1071)	Investiture Controversy (1075) Toledo reconquered (1085) Sicily reconquered (1092)
	First Crusade (1095–1099)	

1071. A decade later, however, it saw a chance to recoup its losses. The Seljuks had broken up into mutually hostile states, and a competent military man, Alexius Comnenus (r. 1081–1118), had ascended the Byzantine throne. Alexius's diminished empire was short on manpower, but there were plenty of Christian knights in western Europe. Alexius therefore asked Pope Urban II (r. 1088–1099) to use the church's communication network to help him recruit soldiers.

Alexius's goal was the recovery of the Byzantine territory that had been lost in 1071, but Urban represented it as something much grander—nothing less than the eviction of Muslims from Jerusalem, a city they had held for almost 500 years. Urban had several motives for expanding the scope of the proposed war. First, he hoped that by cooperating with Constantinople, he could heal a schism that had erupted between the eastern and western churches in 1054. (They had quarreled over the relation of the Holy Spirit to the Father and the Son in the Trinity.) Second, Urban believed that by rallying an international army to wage a universal holy war, the pope would strengthen his claim to be Christendom's supreme leader. Finally, the diversion of Europe's soldiers to foreign lands might help to pacify European society, a cause for which the church had been working for over a century.

By Urban's day, an abundance of underemployed soldiers was posing a threat to the stability of European society. Knights trained their sons to be knights, for medieval men usually learned their fathers' professions. Population increased, but the number of fiefs available to support knights was limited. Changing customs also disinherited some men. German tribal tradition had decreed that a man's estate be divided among all his heirs. This worked well for primitive people whose wealth was largely moveable property, but it did not serve the interests of settled landowners. It subdivided viable farms into tiny plots that were too small to support anyone. Consequently, primogeniture (the right of the eldest male to inherit the whole estate) became the preferred method for preserving a family's fortune and status. It provided for the eldest brother but forced his younger male siblings to find heiresses to marry, to enter the church, to become knights-for-hire, or to take to the road as brigands.

The church tried to persuade knights that honor required them to discipline themselves. The Peace of God and Truce of God movements appealed to their idealism by declaring knighthood a sacred vocation—a divine commission to protect others. To drive this point home, the church was, by 1070, urging that quasi-religious dubbing ceremonies be used to admit men to knightly status. This was helpful, but Urban's plan to divert western Europe's excess soldiers to wars outside Europe was a more direct way of ensuring peace in their homelands.

On November 27, 1095, Urban preached a wildly successful sermon at a church council held at Clermont, France. It urged Europe's knights to go to the aid of the east's Christians and offered them all the spiritual and practical assistance the church could provide. The pope toured France for eight months, whipping up enthusiasm for the campaign, and numerous preachers fanned the fires he lit. The result was not just a crusade, but a crusading movement that inspired repeated European assaults on the Muslim world. Historians recognize seven or eight major crusades, but many more European armies departed for the Middle East before the Middle Ages came to a close.

No European king, at the end of the eleventh century C.E., could risk leaving home for an adventure in the Holy Land. The First Crusade did not acknowledge a supreme commander. It was managed (or mismanaged) by a committee of nobles who put themselves at the head of about four thousand knights, twenty-six thousand foot soldiers, and a horde of pilgrims and camp followers. Some who enlisted hoped to make new lives for themselves in the east, but most planned to return home once the campaign was over. The families of crusader knights endured financial hardship to equip them, and few seem to have made money from the venture.

Before the official crusade got underway, a charismatic preacher called Peter the Hermit led a horde of soldiers and pilgrims to Constantinople. His followers suffered a disastrous defeat as soon as they crossed into Asia Minor. They were not what Alexius had expected, nor were the French barons, when they arrived with their armies, what Alexius had envisioned. They did not want to work for him; they had plans of their own. (See Map 9–4.)

If the Muslims had not been so unwilling to cooperate in defending their territory, the First Crusade could never have succeeded. The Europeans knew little about the Middle East, and they were poorly equipped to deal with its geography and climate. They suffered from heat, thirst, hunger, and disease. Their leaders quarreled. Units defected from the main army to grab lands for themselves. But despite horrific blunders and misadventures, a remnant of the army reached Jerusalem on June 7, 1099. On July 15 they forced their way into the city and slaughtered everyone they found—including Jews and eastern Christians. An eyewitness reported that on the Temple Mount the knights' horses waded up to their bellies in blood and gore.

The crusaders declared Jerusalem the seat of a new Latin kingdom and established a string of crusader states along the Palestinian coast. These fragile European outposts owed their brief survival to the fact that the Muslims continued, for some time, to fight among themselves. In 1144, however, the Muslims recovered Edessa, the first state that the crusaders had won. The loss so alarmed Europe that two kings pledged to take the cross. Louis VII of France (accompanied by his wife Eleanor of Aquitaine) and Conrad III (r. 1138–1152) of Germany organized the Second Crusade—a costly and embarrassing debacle. This and the crusades that followed were distinguished primarily by the ways in which they failed.

The Cultural Environment   It is often assumed that if people from different cultures are given a chance to mingle, they will become more understanding and tolerant of one another. This, alas, is not always the case. Europeans learned a great deal from the Muslims who became their subjects in Spain and Sicily and their neighbors in the Holy Land. Muslims introduced Europeans to Arabic, Greek, and Hebrew texts that revolutionized intellectual life in the Latin west. Arab poets inspired the knightly troubadours ("inventors"), who appeared in the wake of the First Crusade, and reshaped European literature, music, and popular culture. The monastery of Cluny was curious enough about the Christian world's rival faith to sponsor a Latin translation of the Qur'an, but none of this made Europeans any more sympathetic toward Islam.

The eleventh-century C.E. *Song of Roland* assumed that Muslims worshiped an odd trinity of gods that included the Greek deity Apollo. The ludicrous picture of Islam it paints reveals just how ignorant many Europeans were of Islam on the eve of the crusades. A generation or two later, they were better informed but, if anything, less tolerant. They could not connect the Muslim scholars whose books they admired with the Muslim faith that they regarded as the antithesis of true belief. Some Europeans were exceptions to this rule, of course, but they could make things worse. The longer Latin Christians lived in the Holy Land, for example, the more like Muslims their lifestyles became. This horrified visitors from Europe and confirmed their assumption that Islam was a kind of Christian heresy that had to be exterminated to prevent the spread of its infection. Some Europeans took Muslim texts and practices out of context and unfairly interpreted them to create the impression that Islam was a religion of carnal self-indulgence and wanton blood lust. Many things worked to promote the belief that Christianity was engaged in a life-and-death struggle with Islam. Consequently, the pacific

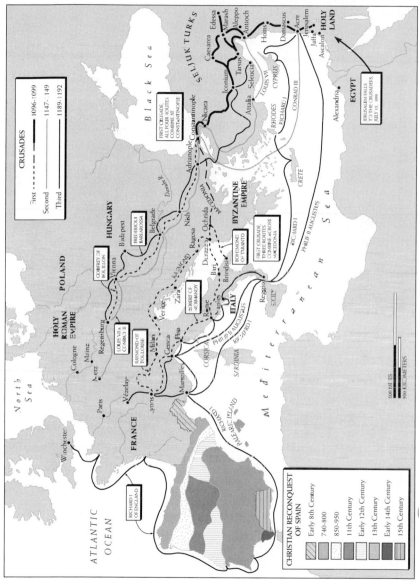

Map 9–4

Crusade Routes The earlier crusaders marched overland to Constantinople. The faster and easier sea route did not become popular until the twelfth century C.E.—after Sardinia and Sicily were in Christian hands and Italy's commercial cities had begun to wrest control of the Mediterranean from the Muslims. **Question:** Why did the Mediterranean unite the Roman empire but separate the medieval civilizations?

Figure 9–3 Fortress of Krak des Chavaliers, Syria To preserve their tenuous hold on their conquests, the crusaders invested heavily in the construction of massive stone fortresses. Their numerous ruins keep painful memories alive in the Middle East.

elements in Christ's teachings were submerged, and Christianity became a militant faith that mirrored the violence that it imagined to be a characteristic of its enemy.

Europe's Economic Revival The collapse of the western Roman Empire sent Europe into an economic decline that dragged on for centuries. Rome's western provinces had never been as wealthy or productive as its eastern ones, and although trade across the Mediterranean continued after Rome's fall, the west produced little that the east wanted. The repeated waves of attackers and migrants that swept across Europe disrupted commercial activity, and people adapted to the chronically chaotic environment by becoming as self-sufficient as possible. They never entirely abandoned trade, for vital supplies (salt and metals, for example) were not available in every locality. The church and the wealthy also wanted luxuries imported from the east.

As commercial activity picked up in the wake of the Viking, Magyar, and Muslim invasions, two foci for international trade appeared at opposite ends of Europe. Venice pioneered development of the southern pole of European commerce. At the start of the Middle Ages, Christians had lost most of the Mediterranean to Muslims but retained control of the Adriatic.

Venice, at the head of the Adriatic, conducted a thriving sea trade with Constantinople and shipped goods through nearby Alpine passes to markets in northern Europe. Pisa and Genoa began trading along the French and Italian coasts in the tenth century C.E., and in 1016 they drove the Muslims from Sardinia. A half century later, the Norman conquest of Sicily (1061–1092) made much more of the Mediterranean safe for Italian sailors, and the success of the First Crusade opened eastern ports to them.

Flanders, the northern center through which foreign goods flowed to European markets, appeared in response to the travels of the Vikings. While some Vikings sailed west to raid England and the coast of France, others headed east across the Baltic Sea and down Russia's rivers. Navigable river systems nearly converge in Russia, so that with a little portage overland from one to another, it is possible to sail from the Baltic to the Black Sea. The Vikings established bases at Novgorod and Kiev. From the latter, they sailed down the Dnieper River to the Black Sea and Constantinople. By the eleventh century C.E., Kiev was, after Constantinople, Christendom's largest city.

Constantinople's merchants were primarily interested in western Europe's raw materials and agricultural products, but Europe had one industry that served both foreign and domestic markets. Europe's climate produced a superior quality of wool, and the manufacturers who turned it into cloth played an economic role in the Middle Ages analogous to that of the makers of automobiles in twentieth-century America. Cloth was an ideal product for trade under medieval conditions. Everyone needed it, but not everyone could produce it. It was lightweight and could be transported over long distances without excessively increasing its cost to consumers. Europe's major cloth-producing centers were the cities of Flanders and northern Italy.

Commercial activity built slowly in the early Middle Ages, for merchants faced many obstacles. Their customers were widely scattered. There was little money in circulation to serve as a medium of exchange, and workers produced little surplus with which to trade. So long as opportunities to trade were limited, people had no motivation to produce surpluses. Surpluses that could not be sold represented useless expenditures of labor. Isolated communities aimed at self-sufficiency, but if commerce was to grow, merchants had to teach Europe's laborers to exert the extra effort needed to produce surpluses.

In the tenth century C.E. nature began to cooperate with human efforts to increase production. Europe's climate entered a warming phase that lengthened growing seasons and extended the ranges of some crops. The improving environment and the spreading use of new farming techniques (the three-field system) and tools (collars that allowed horses to be used as draft animals) increased the food supply. More food and the relative stability that feudal government provided encouraged population growth. Between 1000 and 1300 Europe more than doubled its population, and the expanding pool of producers and consumers stimulated economic activity.

Europe's economy did not just grow; it changed. Originally, Europeans had assumed that wealth was a finite resource and that the fundamental economic challenge was to figure out how to share it. That belief governed the thinking of the medieval craft guilds that monopolized production for local markets. Only members of a guild were allowed to manufacture and sell its product in its market area. The guild limited production to prevent saturation of its market. It regulated prices so that each guild member could make a reasonable living, and it policed manufacturing to ensure that shoddy goods did not alienate its customers.

Guilds could not establish monopolistic control over international markets, and the producers who traded on that level behaved more like capitalists. Capitalism maintains that wealth is not a finite resource, but something that can be increased by human effort. Capitalists try to maximize the production of surplus goods and then find markets in which to sell them at a profit. This profit becomes capital when, instead of being consumed, it is invested in the production of more goods to be sold to generate more profits. Scholars debate whether true capitalism appeared in Europe during the Middle Ages, but the medieval cloth industry was at least a forerunner of the system. Its investors employed a salaried workforce supervised by managers who ruthlessly served "the bottom line." When competition among them led to overproduction and market saturation, they simply fired their workers and ceased business until demand returned. One product of the commercial revolution of the eleventh century C.E. was a proletarian underclass of industrial workers who were vulnerable to such exploitation. During economic downturns, these hungry masses threatened social upheaval.

The Rise of Towns and the Middle Class   The early medieval merchant had to search far and wide for customers. The cities that had survived Rome's passing were ghosts of their former selves, and Europe's reduced population was thinly dispersed about the countryside. Few places had enough people to support a permanent market. Many medieval merchants were therefore simple pedlars who wandered about looking for people to buy their goods.

Commercial activity increased as pedlars learned to entice customers to come to them. Life on a medieval manor offered little excitement. Most Europeans lived in small, isolated communities where the arrival of an itinerant merchant was a major event. He offered a new face, desirable merchandise, and news from abroad. Merchants learned that if they let it be known that they would be in a certain place at a certain time, people would gather to meet them. They also discovered that by working together, they could create greater excitement and draw larger crowds. They preferred to display their merchandise near a castle or monastery that offered them protection, and the best time to appear at these places was when the people who lived nearby congregated to celebrate a religious holiday, a fair (*feria,* "feast day"). Fairs were exciting events. They provided entertainment as well as opportunities to stock up on goods that were otherwise unattainable. Medieval people shopped by the calendar, not by whim, and annual cycles of fairs constituted medieval Europe's primary distribution system. Some fairs served retail customers. Others—particularly those of the French county of Champagne, which was a convenient place for traders from Venice and Flanders to meet—primarily provided opportunities for merchants to restock their wares.

As population grew and the customer base increased, some fairs lasted longer and longer. By the eleventh century C.E., the merchant encampments next to some castles were becoming permanent. If merchants wanted to settle down, however, they had to come to an agreement with the lord on whose land they were squatting. They formed a commune and sought a charter from the lord that acknowledged its right to exist and manage its own affairs. The *bourgeoisie,* the founders of a *bourg* (a fortified settlement), sometimes took up arms to win their privileges, but often they simply purchased them.

Medieval merchant communes reinvented urban life. Some of Europe's new towns occupied the same sites as old Roman cities, but they bore little resemblance to their ancient predecessors. Most ancient cities served military or administrative purposes, but medieval towns owed their origin to commerce. They were created by traders and craftsmen who had no power over anyone but themselves. The feudal authorities that governed the countryside around them considered them to be exceptions to the divinely ordained social order. God, it was alleged, had (with consummate efficiency) created three kinds of people to perform the three tasks essential to human survival. Protection was the work of knights, provision was the duty of serfs, and prayer was the responsibility of clergy. Although there was no place in this system for artisans and merchants, they could not be ignored. Because their wealth and influence placed them somewhere between vassals and serfs, they were said to constitute a "middle class."

Townspeople may never have accounted for more than ten percent of the population of medieval Europe, but they drove the evolution of medieval society by injecting a new kind of freedom into the social order. Free persons were the outcasts of the feudal system, for because they had not commended themselves to the service of a lord, they had no rights to land or to protection. Townspeople, however, found ways to make freedom profitable, and their towns— oases of freedom in a sea of feudal obligation—gave people in the surrounding countryside options that had not previously existed. Lords who wanted to keep the serfs who cultivated their fields had to be careful how they treated them, for oppressed serfs might flee into a town. Because a town was an independent political entity, a feudal lord had no right to enter it to retrieve fugitives from his manors. If a serf stayed in a town for a year and a day, he became legally free. If a serf opted to remain on his lord's manor, a town in the neighborhood still gave him a chance to improve his lot. Townspeople did not raise their own food. Serfs who produced surpluses could sell them in a town's market and use the profits to buy privileges from their lords. Lords were inclined to negotiate with their serfs, for they wanted to keep their laborers—and they needed money. Conspicuous consumption was essential to maintaining a lord's aristocratic status, and the expanding economy created a rising standard of living that put him in a bind. He lived on a fixed income, for his serfs owed him only what grew on his *demesne*, the fields assigned him on his manors. To meet rising expenses, it made sense for him to give up his rights to labor services and simply rent his lands to his serfs. Tradition limited labor services, but rents were negotiable. As the new economy took hold, serfdom faded away, and feudalism became anachronistic.

Larger Issue Revisited

By the end of the eleventh century C.E., a newly assertive Europe was preparing to take on the world. As the weakest of the medieval civilizations, it had come to regard its cultural inferiority as a sign of moral superiority. It spurned the Greeks as devious quasi-heretics and the Muslims as enemies of God. It saw itself as the defender of true faith and authentic civilization—of the real West.

Today, the term *west* is usually reserved for European-American cultures, but limiting its use so severely distorts the memory of the West's historical development. The European institutions and attitudes that were transplanted to the Americas had deep roots in the ancient Middle East where the Christian religion was born from the much older Hebrew faith. The classical components of Western civilization also owed much to the ancient Middle East. Medieval Europe needed the help of Muslims from the Middle East to reclaim its Greco-Roman legacy, and Islamic and Christian cultures were nurtured by the same Hebraic and classical sources.

The subjects of the Roman Empire, despite their cultural diversity, felt that they shared a common civilization. But after the empire fell and Islam appeared, the peoples who lived at opposite ends of the Mediterranean began to stress their differences more than their similarities. The hostilities that erupted with the crusades encouraged this, and at the end of the Middle Ages, when Europe shifted its attention from the Mediterranean to the Atlantic, the cultures of Europe and the Middle East drew even further apart. Their alienation constitutes a serious threat to the peace of the modern world, but the study of history helps to overcome it by reminding us that the "Christian West" and the "Islamic East" have a shared legacy on which to build mutual respect.

Review Questions

1. How did the European environment differ from that of the Islamic world during the early Middle Ages?
2. Why were the Christians of medieval Europe suspicious of their fellow Christians in Byzantine and Muslim regions?
3. What things did the three medieval civilizations of the Mediterranean world have in common?
4. Were the political struggles faced by the English, French, and German monarchies unique to Europe or similar to developments elsewhere in the medieval world?
5. How did the crusades affect the three medieval civilizations? Did closer contact lead to better understanding?
6. What effect did the increasing volume of international trade in the tenth and eleventh centuries C.E. have on Europe and its neighbors?

Refer to the front of the book for a list of chapter-relevant primary sources available on the CD-ROM.

 THE WEST INTERACTIVE

For web-based activities, map explorations, and quizzes related to this chapter, go to *www.prenhall.com/frankforter.*

CHAPTER 10

EUROPE'S HIGH MIDDLE AGES

> Bernard of Chartres was in the habit of saying that we resemble dwarfs riding on the shoulders of giants. We see more and farther than they—not because we are physically or intellectually superior, but because we are elevated and supported by their great stature.
>
> **—John of Salisbury**

Larger Issue: *Why are some ages and cultures more optimistic and self-confident than others?*

Although John of Salisbury (c. 1115–1180) was an Englishman, he became bishop of Chartres, southeast of Paris. It would be unusual today for a man who was not French to occupy a major ecclesiastical office in France, but such appointments were common in the Middle Ages. Two of the medieval archbishops of Canterbury, the heads of England's church, were Italians recruited from a French monastery. When a job is important enough to a community, talent outweighs objections that might otherwise be made to an individual's candidacy. Because modern Western societies give science and technology the kind of priority that religion had in the medieval world, our scientific institutions are more likely to be staffed by persons with diverse backgrounds than our places of worship.

The clever remark quoted above, which John of Salisbury credited to his teacher Bernard of Chartres, captures the combination of humility and self-assertion that characterized scholars of John's generation. They were by no means prepared to claim equality with the great thinkers of the ancient world, but they were also no longer constrained by excessive respect for them. They assumed that by studying the works of their predecessors, they could pick up where "the giants" had left off, make more progress, and even correct the mistakes of the past.

As the intellectuals of the twelfth century C.E. shifted from merely assimilating the past to critiquing it, ideas and disagreements proliferated. They scrambled to develop techniques of analysis and inference that would reconcile conflicting opinions, for their goal was the production of a *summa*—a rationally consistent summation of all truths.

Medieval civilization hit its stride (the High Middle Ages) in the twelfth and thirteenth centuries C.E. States evolved more sophisticated instruments of law, justice, and government. Architects conceived radically new designs and spread awe-inspiring buildings throughout Europe. New kinds of schools promoted a new kind of learning, and new arts and vernacular literatures flourished. These advances required some painful adjustments, and the challenges they posed to traditional beliefs and institutions caused anxiety. But the era assumed that the positives outweighed the negatives and forged boldly ahead. As you study the High Middle Ages, ask yourself why some cultures cope with change more confidently than others.

TOPICS IN THIS CHAPTER

The Renaissance of the Twelfth Century C.E. • Universities and Scholasticism •
Religious Revival and Diversity of Opinion • The Artistic Vision of the High Middle Ages •
The Nation-State of the High Middle Ages

The Renaissance of the Twelfth Century C.E.

Europe's intellectual history is studded with renaissances—eras when a surge of interest in ancient Greek and Roman literature promoted cultural advances. Most Greek literature had disappeared from western Europe by the twelfth century C.E., but there were enough Latin classics available to sustain a humanistic renaissance. The intellectuals of the twelfth century C.E. took Virgil and Cicero as their mentors. They wrote elegant poems, letters, and treatises studded with allusions to Greco-Roman myth and history, and the artistic programs they designed to decorate churches spread their esoteric learning to the unlettered masses.

The twelfth-century C.E. renaissance was also stimulated by a flood of scientific and philosophical information from Arabic sources. Translations of the works of Muslim scholars introduced Europeans to important Greek, Muslim, and Hindu texts. Muslim scholars also provided commentaries that helped Europeans understand what they were reading and acquire the intellectual tools they needed to strike out on their own.

Christian Europe was preoccupied with theology, but it was the lure of science that drew its scholars to Muslim libraries (the nearest of which were in Spain). Constantine the African (d. 1087) specialized in translating Arabic medical texts. Adelard of Bath (d. 1126), an Englishman, translated an Arabic version of Euclid's *Elements of Geometry* into Latin. He also published an edition of the astronomical tables of the Arab mathematician al-Khwarizmi (d. 850 C.E.) that introduced Europeans to trigonometry. About 1145 another Englishman, Robert of Chester, translated al-Khwarizmi's *On the Restoration and Opposition of Numbers*—a text that was so fundamental to the study of mathematics that Arabs called it simply algebra (*al Gebra*, "the book"). A generation later, Leonardo Fibonacci (1170–1230), an Italian, introduced Europeans to "Arabic" numerals and the concept of zero, both of which Muslims had appropriated from Hindu sources.

The Popularity of Dialectic   The intellectuals of the High Middle Ages exalted dialectic (the craft of constructing logical arguments) over the other liberal arts that structured the medieval educational curriculum. This was due in part to the influence of Gerbert of Aurillac (c. 940–1003 C.E.), who was reputed to be the most learned man in Europe. Gerbert rose from humble origins in a French monastery to become the head of an influential school, tutor to an emperor, and (despite allegations of witchcraft) a pope (Sylvester II r. 99–1003 C.E.). He studied mathematics and astronomy in Barcelona, Córdoba, and Seville, constructed scientific instruments, and revived the use of the abacus (the ancient and medieval world's premier calculating device).

The great thinkers of the Middle Ages, Gerbert included, turned language into a tool for scientific research. Scientific breakthroughs in the modern era are often the result of new data provided by instruments that improve on the human senses. Medieval researchers had few such instruments. Because they could not improve on the information simple observation provided, their only hope for progress lay in improving on what their minds did with that information—on refining the language they used to describe it. They defined terms with technical precision and then explored the logical implications of their words. They focused on a task that scientists still acknowledge to be important: understanding how the mind represents the world to itself.

Gerbert taught his students dialectics with the help of what came to be called the Old Logic, the philosophical treatises that Boethius (see Chapter 8, "The Emergence of Europe") had assembled and translated in the sixth century C.E. This was familiar material, but it inspired a change of attitude for Gerbert's generation. Earlier scholars had been taught that truth rested on authority—that something was true because a respected source said that it was true. Truth was founded on revelation (on enlightenment by a superior power). The study of dialectic prompted men like Gerbert, however, to suspect that truth needed the support of nothing beyond itself. Its inherent rationality established its validity.

A famous debate between two eleventh-century C.E. theologians, Berengar of Tours (d. 1088) and Lanfranc of Bec (d. 1089), encouraged dialectic's advocates. At issue was what happened when a priest consecrated bread and wine in the sacrament of the mass. The church had not yet taken a stand, but it was widely believed that consecration turned the bread and wine into Christ's body and blood (the doctrine of transubstantiation). Berengar claimed that this could not be so, for human senses could spot no differences between consecrated and unconsecrated bread and wine. The traditional method for dealing with skeptics like Berengar was to remind them that human understanding was limited and that some truths could only be grasped by faith. Lanfranc, however, opted to use dialectic to argue for the rationality of faith. Philosophy, Lanfranc noted, distinguishes between a substance and an attribute. A substance is the essential nature of a thing, while an attribute is a feature of that thing that can change without affecting its identity. (A cloak, for example, remains a cloak no matter what color it is dyed.) In ordinary experience, Lanfranc argued, attributes change but substances do not. Logic dictates, however, that an omnipotent God could make an exception in the case of the mass—changing the substances of consecrated bread and wine but not their attributes. Lanfranc did not claim to have proved that this was the case, but only to have shown that what faith believed was not a logical absurdity.

Lanfranc's reconciliation of faith with reason had a significant implication. If the truths that come from revelation are, as he suggested, compatible with those acquired by ordinary human experience, the universe must be fundamentally intelligible and its mysteries should yield to dialectical analysis. Theologians quickly discovered, however, that reason was a two-edged sword that required skillful handling.

Reason and Authority   Europe's dialecticians were fascinated by a problem that the Old Logic raised but left unresolved: the status of words that refer to classes of things versus those that refer to individuals. *Nominalists* maintained that a word that referred to a category of objects was a mere *nomen* ("name") that the mind invented for its own convenience. Their opponents, the realists, insisted that the fact that the mind wants to assign individual objects to classes means that it perceives something that transcends their separate existences that is really in them. Individual chairs come and go, but the essential reality that makes all chairs into chairs is eternal. Both these positions had unfortunate theological implications. Nominalism suggested that the Trinity was only a name for a group of three deities: the Father, Son, and Holy Spirit. Realism, on the other hand, led to the heresy of pantheism (the belief that God is simply the sum total of everything that exists). Neither of these alternatives was acceptable to

Christians, and the search for a rational alternative to them inspired exploration of the subtleties of logic.

The dialectical method's most famous advocate was Peter Abelard (1070–1142), the eldest son of a minor Breton nobleman. Abelard relinquished his patrimony to a younger brother and, freed of family obligations, left home to seek an education. He drifted from school to school, immersing himself in the debate between the nominalists and the realists, and soon began to challenge prominent spokesmen for both sides. As his brilliantly constructed critiques revealed the flaws in the arguments of one famous scholar after another, he earned enemies, followers, and (in 1115) a position as a teacher at Ste. Geneviève in Paris. Abelard was a brilliant, charismatic educator who enthralled his students with poetry as well as dialectic. The crowds of scholars who flocked to Paris to hear him established the city's reputation as Europe's premier center of intellectual activity. At the height of his popularity, however, Abelard made a serious blunder.

One of Paris's prominent clerics had a niece named Heloise (d. 1163). He sent her to a convent school where she mastered Latin, Greek, and (possibly) Hebrew, and earned a reputation as an intellectual prodigy. Because it was impossible for a girl to mix with the rowdy adolescent males who populated Paris's schools, Heloise's uncle was at a loss as to how to continue her education—until it occurred to him to ask Abelard to tutor her privately. Abelard was intrigued by her intellect (more than her looks, he said), and she fell passionately in love with him. They became sexually involved. After she became pregnant, he persuaded her, although she argued against it, to marry him. His plan was to keep the marriage secret. Medieval scholars were considered clergy, and the reward they aspired to was appointment to a well-funded office in the church. Because clergy had to be celibate, an acknowledged wife would have ended Abelard's career. Heloise's uncle concluded that Abelard, in order to gratify himself, was sacrificing Heloise's reputation, and he took drastic steps to avenge her and his family's honor. He hired some thugs who broke into Abelard's rooms and castrated him.

Abelard sought refuge in a monastery, and Heloise (for love of him and not God, as she explained to him in her letters) entered a convent. The cloister, however, brought Abelard no peace. New controversies arose, and his enemies seized the opportunity to accuse him of attacking the church. Abelard had written a book called *Sic et Non (Yes and No)*. It listed conflicting opinions (those who had said "yes" and those who had said "no") on points of doctrine lifted from the works of famous theologians. By showing that authorities sometimes disagreed, it was intended to demonstrate that scholars had to do more than quote respected thinkers. Abelard claimed that if his contemporaries hoped to discover truth, they had to use dialectical methods to critique all opinions, even those of the most revered fathers of the church. The church hierarchy was not convinced, and in 1141 a council condemned him. Abelard set out for Rome to appeal to the pope, but he died on the way. His career might have been less stormy if he had been less brash, for the spirit of the age was with him. Dialectic was in the ascendancy, and his younger contemporary, Peter Lombard (d. 1160), produced a book *(Sentences)* similar to *Sic et Non* that became one of the medieval world's standard student texts.

Universities and Scholasticism

Monasteries dominated education in the early Middle Ages, but during the twelfth century C.E., leadership passed to cathedral towns. The move reflected a fundamental change in the nature of education. Monks were taught to respect authority and tradition and to sacrifice individuality to a communal ideal. Twelfth-century C.E. Europe, however, with its flourishing economy, rising towns, more complex institutions, and increasing contacts with the wider world, needed men who were trained to innovate, solve problems, and take initiative. Urban schools, which had access to the wealth and the new information flowing into Europe, were best situated to meet this need.

The Academic Guild   Universities developed from local schools that became famous enough to attract an international clientele. The needs of this clientele prompted organization of a university. The medieval world had no embassies or consulates and no international agreements to assist travelers and protect resident aliens. Foreign students and faculty had no legal rights in the towns where they worked. They were therefore vulnerable to exploitation by landlords and abuse by government authorities. To strengthen their position, they banded together and formed a guild or union—a *universitas* ("university"). They had leverage in negotiations with local political leaders, for students were a source of income for a town. They rented rooms and bought food and other supplies. Because schools had no campuses or buildings, students and faculty could easily pack up and take their business to another community. Many of Europe's famous universities were created by migrations of disgruntled academics.

The earliest known charter to accord legal recognition to an academic university was issued in 1158. It was granted to a school in Bologna, Italy, that was governed by students. The student council employed the university's professors, oversaw its curriculum, and even regulated methods of instruction. Bologna emphasized the study of law and attracted older, career-driven students. Most medieval universities, such as the famous one chartered in Paris in 1200, were faculty guilds.

Teachers and students in the first medieval universities made do with whatever facilities they could find. A man who was licensed by a university guild to teach would set up a lectern (reading desk) in the side aisle of a church or some other public building. His students would stand or sit on the floor around him. Latin was used for instruction and much casual conversation, for it was the only language that all members of the academic community had in common. Many students had no books or writing materials, for these things were expensive. They might use wax-covered boards for taking notes, but medieval scholars trained themselves to memorize what they heard and read. They carried prodigious amounts of information in their heads. Professors (*profiteor,* "to educate") taught by glossing texts. That is, they read a passage from a book and then commented on it, explaining its meaning and spelling out its implications. There were no course finals and no grading system. Students (sometimes as young as ten) were completely on their own. They drifted from teacher to teacher and school to school until they felt that they were ready to apply for membership in the teachers' guild. As with any guild, those who aspired to join (that is, become "masters") were required to produce a masterpiece that demonstrated their command of their craft. A would-be shoemaker, for instance, submitted a pair of shoes for examination by the officials of the shoemakers' guild. Candidates for academic guilds submitted theses—propositions that they were prepared to defend in public debate before the whole university community. Graduate programs in modern universities perpetuate this custom. Candidates for degrees conduct original research, develop theses, and then defend them before committees composed of experts in their fields.

Entry-level students in medieval universities were "bachelors of arts," young males who were learning the basics of medieval education, the seven liberal arts of the *trivium* and the *quadrivium* (see Chapter 8). The masters of the guild that taught these subjects were masters of arts. A lengthy course of advanced study in a specialized field earned a scholar the highest academic title, *doctor* ("teacher"). Medieval society was organized hierarchically, and people dressed to reflect their social rank. Academics wore gowns appropriate to their place within the university, and on ceremonial occasions the members of American university communities still don the hoods and robes that served their medieval predecessors as hats and overcoats.

Scholasticism and the Influence of Aristotle   Medieval scholars never completely threw off their respect for the authority of ancient texts. They took it for granted that the Bible, the Church Fathers, and the great ancient philosophers all spoke the truth, and they trusted what these sources said more than they trusted the evidence of their own eyes. Universities, however, promoted a more liberal way of thinking that diminished faith in authority and valued independent investigation. As their scholars struggled to understand and reconcile the diversity of opinions found in the books that were flooding into Europe from Muslim and Byzantine sources, they embraced the rational, critical approach to the search for truth. The medieval university nurtured the open-minded spirit of inquiry that characterizes modern Western civilization at its best.

The men who worked at the new schools were called Scholastics. Modern students may find their dialectical methods and arguments tedious, but the great Scholastics were exciting, original thinkers. Some of them took breaks from dialectic—from the refinement of definitions and logical arguments—to compose poetry, but their primary interest was in language as science, not art. They used language with the precision of mathematics.

The Scholastics owed much to the arrival in Europe, during the second half of the twelfth century C.E., of the New Logic, the surviving treatises on logic by the ancient Greek philosopher Aristotle. Europeans' appetite for Aristotle had been whetted by their study of the works of his great Muslim interpreters Avicenna (Abu ali ibn Sina, 980–1037 C.E.) and Averroës (Ibn-Rushd, 1126–1198 C.E.). During the thirteenth century C.E., all of Aristotle's works (in Latin versions taken directly from the Greek) that had survived from antiquity gradually became available to European scholars, and their impact was revolutionary. Aristotle was the fulfillment of a medieval scholar's dream. He was the primary authority on the rules for constructing logical arguments, and he wrote on a huge range of subjects.

The church was initially alarmed by the enthusiasm scholars manifested for Aristotle, for some of his ideas contradicted Christian theology. Aristotle, for instance, maintained that the universe had to be eternal, for the concept of creation out of nothing was a logical absurdity. In 1210 C.E. a church council tried to protect faith by censoring Aristotle's works and limiting their use, but it was impossible to force the Aristotelian genie back into his bottle. Aristotle quickly became required reading for every serious scholar. Some medieval thinkers simply accepted the apparent incompatibility of his philosophy with Christian theology and declared that there were two kinds of truth—one of faith and one of reason. But the era's greatest thinkers—notably, Albertus Magnus (1193–1280 C.E.) and his student Thomas Aquinas (1225–1274 C.E.)—devoted their lives to reconciling Aristotle's insights with Christian doctrine. Aquinas did such a masterful job that the Roman Catholic Church has endorsed his theological *summae* (comprehensive surveys) as definitive explications of its faith. Aquinas believed that reason and faith were complementary methods for understanding reality. Reason began a journey that only faith could complete. Some medieval scholars attacked Aquinas's work. But the logic of his *summae* was compelling, and they were so comprehensive that there was little that his followers could add to them.

Not all medieval intellectuals were equally enthusiastic about dialectic and Aristotle. John of Salisbury, among others, complained that dialectic substituted narrow vocational training for true education. He championed a broader humanist curriculum based on the study of classical literature. Even at the peak of Scholasticism's popularity, there were critics who used the tools of dialectic to counter what they regarded as the Scholastics' excessive rationalism.

Religious Revival and Diversity of Opinion

A surge of religious enthusiasm energized the cultural creativity of the High Middle Ages. It was a source of constructive intellectual tension, for it challenged the era's drift toward excessive rationality by championing the importance of intuition and feeling. By exalting the practice of faith and the experience of God over mere speculation about divine mysteries, it inspired defense of—and attacks on—traditional beliefs and institutions.

Monastic Innovations   The religious fervor of the High Middle Ages sparked a renewal of interest in monasticism. But recruits did not flock to the older Benedictine houses that Cluny had reformed in the tenth century C.E. They were drawn to new, stricter orders that restored the asceticism and simplicity of the original Benedictine Rule.

The emergence of new monastic ideals was forecast by a hermetical movement at the end of the eleventh century C.E. that was officially recognized (about 1130) as the Carthusian order. Carthusians worshiped as a community but lived alone in isolated cells where they worked with their hands and practiced rigorous self-denial. Their order was too strict to attract large numbers, but it was so disciplined that it never needed reform. Far more popular was the Cistercian order that sprang up in the first half of the twelfth century C.E. Cistercians eschewed the richly ornamented sanctuaries and elaborate rituals characteristic of the old Benedictine houses. They refused gifts of rich estates worked by serfs and established their houses on wasteland, where they labored to support themselves. They were such successful developers that the barren lands to which they fled in pursuit of simplicity and spirituality made them rich and powerful.

So many monastic orders appeared during the twelfth century C.E. that the papacy finally decided to authorize no more. But in the early thirteenth century C.E., it made an exception for some orders that redefined the monastic vocation. Monks traditionally withdrew from the world to devote themselves to prayer. In part, this was a judgment on the world as a worthless realm of sin that was doomed to pass away. The confident atmosphere of the High Middle Ages, however, nurtured a greater sense of responsibility for the world, and this led some of the people who felt the call to devote their lives totally to God to embrace asceticism while remaining engaged with the world. The practitioners of this new religious vocation called themselves friars (*frater,* "brother"). The pattern for their lives was set by the son of a prosperous Italian cloth merchant, Francis of Assisi (1181–1226).

Francis was initially attracted to all the pleasures life holds for handsome, wealthy young men. But a gradual religious conversion convinced him to pattern his life after the life of Christ. Francis believed that Christ and his Apostles had no possessions and relied on God to support them in their ministry of preaching and healing. He therefore gave away everything he had and became a mendicant, a wandering beggar. Francis drifted about, preaching and doing what he could for the poor. He ordered his followers never to keep anything in reserve for the future, but immediately to share with the needy everything they were given or earned. His radical vision of a religious fellowship that trusted entirely to God for its survival was soon moderated by church authorities (who insisted on more secure financial arrangements). But the friars' highly visible work among the laity made them the most popular and respected of medieval clergy.

In 1216 a second order of friars was founded by a Spanish priest named Dominic de Guzmán (1170–1221). Dominic was attracted to evangelism, and he initially hoped to become a missionary. The pope, however, sent him to southern France to deal with another product of the religious revival of the twelfth century C.E., heresy. The Dominicans—officially, the Order of Preachers (or Black Friars, from the color of their robes)—were educators. They were trained to preach and to supplement the limited religious instruction and pastoral care the laity received from parish priests. They hoped that by engaging people's intellects and by setting them an example of Christlike living they could combat religious error. The Franciscans' founder was a poet who imbued their order with a deep appreciation for the emotional, mystical aspect of faith. The Dominicans, on the other hand, appealed to people who preferred a cooler, more rationalistic religion. They produced some of the era's most important scholars and made a major contribution to medieval university life. Their skills as scholars and debaters, however, proved less effective than Dominic had hoped in fulfilling their original mission: combating heresy.

Return of Heresy   The general decline of European culture during the early Middle Ages had reduced the threat of heresy by diminishing intellectual speculation of all kinds. But as levels of education and literacy rose in the twelfth century C.E., heresy returned. People who gained access to the Scriptures and other documents for themselves acquired a perspective from which to judge the conduct of the church, and some concluded that the church's clergy fell far short of the standard Christ set for them. The lives of the pope, who claimed to be Christ's vicar on Earth, and his servants bore little resemblance to those of Christ and his disciples. The Franciscans and Dominicans were able implicitly to criticize the church without breaking with it, but others were less successful at steering such a delicate course.

A few years before Francis of Assisi's birth, a merchant from the French city of Lyons named Peter Waldo anticipated the call to live a Christlike life that motivated Francis and the friars. He gave away his property and devoted himself to serving the poor. When local clergy objected to what they regard as Peter's transgression on their turf, he and his followers became more radical. Like the Protestants produced by the Reformation of the sixteenth century C.E., they insisted that the Bible was the only authority binding on Christians. They repudiated the pope and the priesthood and claimed that faithful laypeople could administer the sacraments for themselves. The pope condemned them in 1184, but the movement spread and survives today in Italy.

A more extreme heresy rooted itself in the south of France. Some historians believe that the religion of the Cathars ("the Pure"), or Albigensians (from Albi, a town that a contemporary may have unfairly branded as a center of the heresy), spread into western Europe from the Balkans with the trade that began to surge in the eleventh century C.E. The Cathars preached a dualistic faith similar to one that had competed with Christianity during the last centuries of the Roman Empire. They claimed an evil demon, not God, created matter and flesh. They believed that extreme asceticism was needed to free the soul from a cycle of reincarnation and return it to the realm of pure spirit where the true God reigned. The Cathars attracted a large

People in Context: William IX, Duke of Aquitaine and Count of Poitou (1071–1127)

Saints and scholars were not the only contributors to the robust civilization of the High Middle Ages. The era had a thriving popular culture that produced breakthroughs in art, music, and literature. Early medieval entertainers had chanted epic poems featuring stolid, one-dimensional warrior-heroes, such as Beowulf and Roland. But the audiences of the High Middle Ages had a taste for something more individual, passionate, and intimate. They were attracted to lyric poetry and music. Students at universities composed Latin lyrics, but the pioneers of secular poetry were the troubadours (*trovar,* "inventer") who appeared first in southern France. The names of about 460 troubadours have survived (some of whom were women).

Troubadours were (or served) feudal aristocrats, and the first of their line, William IX of Aquitaine, was a lord of exalted rank. As duke of Aquitaine and count of Poitou, he presided over about one-third of France. His domain was not only large, it boasted a uniquely rich and sophisticated culture—thanks, in part, to contact with Muslim Spain (whence the inspiration for the new poetry may have come). William was a worldly man who was more inclined to enjoy this life than prepare for the next. The great adventure for noblemen of his generation was the crusade, and the success of the First Crusade prompted him to raise an army and set off for Jerusalem. Unfortunately, he blundered into an ambush while crossing Asia Minor and lost almost all his men. His defeat and those suffered by similarly ill-fated campaigners were blamed for restoring the confidence of the crusaders' Muslim opponents.

William was not a man to dwell on setbacks. His poetry is enlivened by a sense of humor, self-mockery, and sheer physical joy at being alive. The songs he composed celebrate the pleasures of rides through the sunny Provençal countryside and his delight in the company (apparently intimate) of beautiful women. The troubadour's primary theme was love—a passionate emotion but one governed by an elaborate etiquette. Modern literary critics call it "courtly love," an elegant game of courtship played by medieval aristocrats. The troubadour placed the woman he adored "on a pedestal." He praised her as a paragon of beauty and virtue and pledged to endure any hardship in exchange for the slightest sign of her favor. His love for her drove him to realize the best in himself. William's granddaughter, the Eleanor of Aquitaine who became England's queen, continued the duke's tradition of providing patronage for poets, and the troubadour culture that she and her daughters spread through Europe did much to turn its rude feudal warriors into civilized, cultivated courtiers.

Question: Would the kind of praise that troubadours heaped on women have contributed to the empowerment of women in medieval society?

following, for their ascetic leaders were more admirable spiritual exemplars than were many of the church's clergy. When preaching and threats failed to counter the heresy, the church opted for force. In 1208 the pope called for a crusade to root out the Cathars, and the lords of northern France seized on it as an excuse to grab lands for themselves in the south. The war raged for twenty years and devastated what had been one of Europe's most culturally advanced regions.

Mysticism and the Limits of Reason   Mystical currents have always flowed within Christianity, but they ran more strongly at the start of the twelfth century C.E. Mystics have experiences of God that transcend reason and understanding, and that give them, in the opinion of other Christians, a kind of prophetic authority. The twelfth-century C.E. renaissance produced one of the greatest of the medieval mystics, Bernard of Clairvaux (1090–1153). Although he was a Cistercian abbot, he was no recluse. He advised kings and popes, and was the driving force behind the Second Crusade (see Chapter 11, "Challenges to the Medieval Order.") He devoted some of his considerable energy to destroying Abelard and opposing the kind of dialectical theology Abelard advocated. Bernard believed that knowledge of God came from an encounter with God—that it was mediated by love, not reason.

Many of Bernard's contemporaries shared his passionate approach to faith, and mysticism was not confined to monks and clergy. It influenced the pious practices of the laity. It inspired artists. It motivated reform movements, and it helped some women escape the constraints medieval society imposed on their gender. Female mystics and visionaries were particularly plentiful during the second half of the Middle Ages. Some were counselors to kings, popes, and prominent male intellectuals. Bernard had little respect for womankind—although he made exceptions for the Virgin Mary and Hildegard of Bingen (1098–1179). The latter was a visionary nun, a poet, a composer, a physician, and an astute dialectician who carried on a large correspondence with the leading men of her day. In recent years, modern audiences have rediscovered the pleasures of her music.

Mysticism was not willful ignorance. Some of the great thinkers of the High Middle Ages were mystics who used dialectic to explain their point of view. Bonaventure (1221–1274), a Franciscan scholar and faculty colleague of Thomas Aquinas's, was one of the most influential of mystics. He, like the early Latin theologian Augustine of Hippo (354–430 C.E.), believed that human reason is untrustworthy because it, like the rest of human nature, is corrupted by original sin. Reason, he argued, describes the surface of things and provides superficial knowledge, but only a mind that has been enlightened by love and divine grace can intuit truth—the ultimate reality that the created world merely symbolizes. Aquinas himself may finally have come around to Bonaventure's point of view. Toward the end of his life Aquinas is said to have had a mystical experience that so overwhelmed him that he ceased to write.

The Artistic Vision of the High Middle Ages

For medieval mystics such as Bonaventure, the world was filled with visible things that symbolized the invisible truths of faith. That was the purpose of much ecclesiastical architecture, and nothing better captured the spirit of Europe's medieval civilization than the great churches that were erected during the High Middle Ages.

New churches sprang up everywhere during the twelfth and thirteenth centuries C.E. In France, where much of the era's architectural innovation took place, more than eighty cathedrals and thousands of lesser churches were built. A town of five thousand people might have as many as fifty parish churches, and some cities built cathedrals large enough to house their entire populations. The sheer volume of construction was remarkable, but so were its products. The new churches of the High Middle Ages so perfectly expressed Christianity's transcendent faith that they still influence the design of Christian houses of worship.

Origin of Christian Architecture   Early Christianity had no architecture of its own. The first Christian congregations were small and poor. They met in the homes of their members or in the open air. So long as persecution threatened, Christians were not free to design buildings that advertised their activities. Only after the emperor Constantine legalized the faith in the fourth century C.E. were conditions right for Christianity to evolve an architectural vocabulary of its own.

The Constantinian church grew so rapidly that there was no time to invent a new kind of space to house its proliferating congregations. Its bishops simply appropriated and consecrated existing public buildings. The Roman Empire's standard multipurpose building was the basilica, a simple rectangular hall (nave) with a rounded bay (apse) at one end to house the office of the building's administrator. Additional floor space was sometimes created by running parallel corridors (aisles) down the sidewalls of the building. Basilicas had flat roofs and were lit by windows cut in the wall above the level of the aisles (the clerestory).

The basilican design was gradually altered to serve the needs of Christian worship. When the growing numbers of clergy who chanted the liturgy needed more room, the apse was pushed out to create a space called the choir. Altars multiplied along the walls of the nave, and some grew into side chapels. Large chapels on opposing sides of a nave created a transept or "crossing" that gave the floor plan of a church the shape of a cross. But the most overtly religious aspects of the early basilican churches were their decorations. Most had large expanses of wall covered with frescoes or mosaics with sacred themes.

In addition to rectangular basilicas, a circular church design also appeared in the late Roman period. It probably evolved from shrines built over the graves of saints. It was particularly popular in the Middle East, and its association with the lavish sanctuaries of the Byzan-

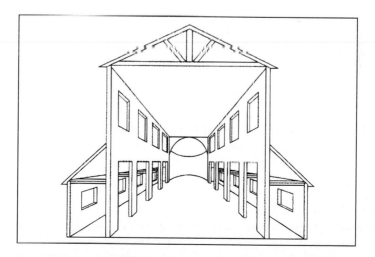

Figure 10–1 The Basilica This drawing shows the standard features of the Roman basilica. By combining aisles and nave, a builder could cover a large space by using several simply constructed roofs rather than a single wide-span roof that would have been difficult to engineer.

tine Empire may explain why Charlemagne chose it for his great church at Aachen. It appealed to the crusaders as well. The Templars, one of the orders of warrior monks, often built round churches.

Romanesque Style   Basilican churches spread to northern Europe in the early Middle Ages, but they were not well adapted to its environment. Their low-pitched wooden roofs were prone to rot in climates damper than those of the sunny Mediterranean. The weight of northern snows stressed them, and they were vulnerable to fires. A pious desire to honor Christianity's eternal God with eternal buildings may also have motivated the search for ways to replace wooden roofs with vaults of stone, the most durable material then available.

Medieval architects began by copying the vaulting techniques used by the Romans. Roman buildings employed round arches. The simplest way to vault a nave is to span it with lots of these arches, one next to another like slices of bread. This creates a barrel vault, a tunnel-like room that is difficult to light. Because each part of the vault is supported by the wall immediately beneath it, it is risky to cut holes in the walls for windows. Walls have to be very thick to counterbalance the lateral thrust from the arches that rest on their tops. The use of round arches also imposes design limitations. The ratio between the span and the height of a round arch is fixed. The only way to make a barrel-vaulted nave wider is to make it higher, but size does not have to increase much before the weight of the vault becomes too great to manage.

The medieval architect's Romanesque style featured round arches, thick walls, and small windows. It was popular in Italy, Spain, and southern France, for hot, sunny regions welcomed the shelter of dark, cavelike buildings. Romanesque churches continued to be erected in southern Europe long after the north had switched to the later Gothic style.

Romanesque architects tried to make their heavy buildings look less ponderous by covering them with elaborate decoration. False arcades were cut into walls to lighten their appearance, and blank spaces were filled with paintings, mosaics, and sheets of colored stone arranged in geometric patterns. But the Romanesque's fortresslike appearance fit the defensive mood of the early Middle Ages, and it served well for monastic retreats from the world. The optimistic, expansionistic spirit that pervaded the towns of the High Middle Ages, however, called for something more open, confident, and audacious.

Gothic Style   The first church in the Gothic style (the supreme achievement of the medieval architect) was erected about 1140 at France's royal monastery, St. Denis, near Paris. It was the work of the cloister's abbot, Suger (1081–1151), chief counselor to kings Louis VI (r. 1108–1137) and Louis VII (r. 1137–1180). By integrating a series of structural innovations, some of which dated back to the eleventh century C.E., Suger invented a new kind of sacred space—one where light symbolized God's presence. The inscription Suger placed on the door to his new church explained the purpose of the artistry that went into its design: "Meditation on material things lifts the intellect from lethargy and enables it to grasp the truth."

The most distinctive feature of Gothic architecture is the pointed arch. Gothic architects escaped the limitations imposed by the geometry of the Romanesque's round arch by "breaking" it at its apex. A pointed arch has no fixed ratio between its height and span. Its apex can be pitched at any height to serve as a kind of hinge for halves of an arc that can be as wide or as narrow as a builder wants.

By combining pointed arches with rib-vaulting (a technique that Romanesque architects developed), Gothic architects could erect vaults over rectangular or irregular spaces. Rib-vaulting was a significant improvement over the simple barrel vault. If the nave of a church was divided into squares, each square could be vaulted by running round arches not from side to side, but between diagonal corners. These arches (the ribs) intersected over the center of the square and light masonry was used to fill in the spaces between them. They functioned as a built-in scaffolding that bore much of the vault's weight, and they gave an architect more control over the thrust from a vault. Ribs focused the weight they carried on the points where they intersected with the wall. Walls had to be buttressed (thickened) at these places to compensate for that weight. But the reduction of pressure on the wall space between them meant that more wall could be cut away to create larger windows.

Gothic architects got even more light into their churches by preventing buttresses from shading the windows near them. They planted buttresses some distance from their buildings and used arches to link them to the pressure points where ribs intersected with walls. These "flying buttresses" turned a Gothic building into a kind of stone tent. The sheet of stone (the vaulting) that roofed it was held in place by stone "ropes" (arches) tied to stone "pegs" (buttresses) around its perimeter. Because the ribs and buttresses carried most of the weight of the building, its walls could be replaced by huge windows. Well-designed Gothic churches were so filled with light that medieval people called them glass houses.

During the second half of the twelfth century C.E., the Gothic style spread rapidly from its birthplace in northern France throughout Europe. Towns spent phenomenal sums to construct ever larger, brighter, and more awe-inspiring sanctuaries. The record was set by the builders of the cathedral at Beauvais who, after several failed attempts, pitched a vault at the height of 157 feet—high enough to shelter a fourteen-story building.

The Gothic style captivated medieval people because it was so congruent with their faith and spiritual experience. This becomes evident when Gothic churches are compared with the temples of the ancient Greeks. Classical architecture reflected a humanistic faith. A Greek temple, like the Parthenon, was meant to assure people that the world was a humane, rational place. It did this by making the principles of its construction immediately obvious: vertical pillars supporting horizontal lintels and stone doing what stone is expected to do. A Gothic church creates the opposite impression. To convey Christianity's faith in a transcendent reality (a reality quite different from our own), it offers an experience of a supernatural world. A Gothic church encloses a divine space where nature's laws are transcended. The Gothic architect conceals the principles of his building's construction so that the logic of its design is hidden from those who enter it. Vertical lines dominate the interior and pull the eye upward. The ribs of the vault seem to converge at infinity, and far overhead tons of rock appear to float on walls of light. There are windows on every side, but their tinted glass prevents the worshiper from connecting the world inside with the world outside and fills the sanctuary with unnatural light. From the engineering point of view, a Gothic church is a supremely rational structure, but one that uses reason to create the experience of irrational space. It is a place where nature, by seeming to behave supernaturally, fulfills Suger's mandate and turns the intellect from the seen to the unseen. A Gothic church is not just a place to hear about God's transcendence; it is a place to experience it.

The Nation-States of the High Middle Ages

The High Middle Ages were a decisive moment for the formation of modern Europe. Carolingian dreams of empire receded, but feudal fragmentation was also overcome. The contours of powerful nation-states, with their rich mix of ethnic cultures, emerged—creating an ever more

Figure 10–2 The Cathedral of Notre Dame Gothic churches, such as Paris's Cathedral of Notre Dame (begun in 1163), are the strongest association that many modern people have with the medieval world. This is fitting, for they are products of the dynamism and ingenuity of the medieval mind. Nothing like them existed before the Middle Ages.

complex environment for European civilization. The unity that religious faith promoted was challenged by Europeans' growing sense of themselves as peoples of distinctly different countries.

England A pattern of alternating strong and weak reigns helped define the institutions of the English monarchy. William the Conqueror (r. 1066–1087) and his sons, William Rufus (1087–1100) and Henry I (1100–1135), exploited the opportunity that conquest gave them to lay the foundations for a powerful monarchy in England, but their work was undermined by the twenty-year-long civil war (1135–1154) that raged between Matilda (1102–1167), Henry's daughter and only surviving legitimate child, and her cousin Stephen (r. 1135–1154). However, the truce that ended that war and brought Matilda's son, Henry II (r. 1154–1189), to the throne began the restoration of the authority of England's kings.

The French lands that Henry II inherited from his parents and acquired by marrying Eleanor of Aquitaine (c. 1122–1204) gave him immense resources, but he was no autocrat. His grandfather, Henry I, had implicitly conceded that England's king was accountable for the use of his powers, and Henry II affirmed the "liberties" that Henry I had promised the English people. Henry's attention was not focused exclusively on England. He had not been raised there and, like many of medieval England's kings, he did not speak English. He ruled a vast Angevin Empire (see Chapter 9, "Europe Turns Outward") that included about half of France, and he was eager to expand his holdings on the continent.

Although Henry was often abroad, he did not neglect England. He stabilized its frontier with Scotland, brought parts of Wales under control, and invaded Ireland to win recognition of his lordship over the outposts that Norman warrior-entrepreneurs had established there. In 1172 the pope recognized the English king's claim to Ireland, but the Irish and English are still disputing their relationship.

Henry I greatly improved England's governmental institutions, and Henry II continued his grandfather's work. The fact that William I had claimed all the land in England by right of conquest helped centralize its monarchy, for all property owners owed feudal obligations to the crown. William had also preserved the old Anglo-Saxon system of shires. This helped keep feudalism in check by reducing the English king's dependence on his vassals. He could govern with the help of the shire-reeves, the sheriffs who were not part of the feudal hierarchy. Henry II shifted some political tasks from feudal lords to professional bureaucrats (trained in Europe's new schools), and he raised enough money to salary most of the men who worked for him. Instead of fighting in the king's army, vassals were encouraged to pay scutage ("shield money"). This gave the king funds with which to hire professional soldiers, and it had the added benefit of pacifying the feudal nobility by turning them into a class of tax-paying civilian landowners.

Henry strengthened support for monarchy by increasing the services his subjects received directly from the crown. Chief among these was the provision of justice. The right to hold a court and administer justice was a coveted feudal privilege, for the fees and fines a court levied produced income for a feudal lord. Henry took business away from the courts of his vassals by reserving some categories of crimes to the royal justice system. His judges rode circuits about England so that people could have access to the king's justice. Henry also expanded the use of writs, documents, which people purchased, that ordered royal officials to take some action.

The royal courts brought England under a "common law," a single standard of justice, and developed procedures that are still in use today. Henry's courts empaneled two kinds of juries. Grand (large) juries put local men under oath and ordered them to report any crimes that might have occurred in their communities. This created business for petit (small) juries, which heard cases and rendered verdicts. Juries could usually settle disputes about property, for local people could provide evidence about who owned what and for how long. It was often impossible, however, to gather evidence in criminal cases, so other methods were used to resolve them. Compurgation allowed the accused to clear their names by finding a certain number of people who would swear to their integrity. By identifying the most trustworthy party in a dispute, it increased the probability of rendering a just verdict. Sometimes suspects were forced to undergo ordeals—physical tests that risked injury or death. The theory was that God would protect the innocent, but by Henry's day, enlightened governments were reducing their reliance on ordeals. In 1215 the pope contributed to their demise by prohibiting priests from hearing the oaths of innocence that ordeals supposedly tested.

As royal governments became more effective and assumed broader responsibilities, the potential for conflict between the church and the state increased. In England the fight was triggered by Henry's efforts to improve the enforcement of justice. In 1164 Henry's Constitutions of Clarendon clarified the relationship between his courts and those of the church. Two years earlier he had thrust priesthood and the office of archbishop of Canterbury on his friend, Thomas Becket (1118–1170), a commoner who was serving as England's chancellor (chief minister). Ordination had changed Becket's loyalties and led him, in the opinion of some of his fellow bishops, to make extreme claims for the church. At issue was the treatment of clergy who were accused of crimes. Henry did not dispute that the church had the right to judge their cases, but he insisted that the guilty should be stripped of their clerical status and turned over to the state for punishment. This would ensure that lay and clerical criminals received the same penalties for the same crimes. Becket refused to accept this, fled England, and spent six years trying to turn international opinion against Henry. In 1170 he and Henry declared a truce. But when Becket returned to England, he infuriated Henry by excommunicating some royal officials. Henry made some intemperate remarks that his men interpreted as orders to kill Becket, and on December 29, 1170, they forced their way into the cathedral of Canterbury and profaned its sanctity by slaughtering its archbishop. The scandalized medieval world instantly hailed Becket as a martyr. Miracles were credited to him, and three years after his death he was officially declared a saint. His tomb at Canterbury became a major pilgrim shrine, and Henry submitted to a whipping by Canterbury's monks as a penance for his part in Becket's murder.

The Becket defeat was humiliating, but the greatest threat to Henry came from his family. Queen Eleanor bore him five sons, and she and they plotted against him. Henry placed Eleanor under house arrest in 1174, and he managed to outlive three of their boys. But the remaining two (with the help of the French king) disrupted the last years of his reign.

Henry's heir was Richard I, "the Lionhearted" (r. 1189–1199), a king whose popularity with the English is hard to understand. Richard spent only eight months of his reign in England, and his interest in his kingdom was primarily as a source of revenue for foreign wars. Chief among these was the Third Crusade. In 1187 Saladin (1137–1193), a warrior of Kurdish descent, united the Muslims of the Middle East and retook Jerusalem. Europe clamored for a new crusade, which Richard eagerly promoted. He compelled France's young king, Philip II, "Augustus" (1180–1223), to take the cross with him, and Frederick I "Barbarossa" (r. 1152–1190), Germany's aging emperor, agreed to go as well. The venture yielded little for all that was invested in it. Barbarossa drowned on his way to the Holy Land, and Philip Augustus withdrew as soon as possible. Richard lingered in the east, while Philip and Richard's brother, John, worked against him at home. In 1193 Richard tried to hurry back to his kingdom through the territory of a German enemy and was captured. Eleanor raised a huge ransom to win his release, and he spent his remaining years fighting to regain the possessions in France he had allowed to slip away. He died from a wound received in a skirmish with one of his vassals.

Richard's successor was his disloyal brother, John (r. 1199–1216). John was neither stupid nor cowardly, but he was headstrong and had a talent for alienating people. He was no match for Philip Augustus, who took Normandy from him, and he picked a needless quarrel with Pope Innocent III over the appointment of an archbishop for Canterbury. The pope closed all the churches in England and excommunicated John. John held out for six years, but in 1213, when the pope threatened him with deposition, he suddenly reversed course and took an oath of vassalage to the pope. John was developing an elaborate plan for winning back his French lands, and he did not want his vassals to have an excuse to rebel against him.

In 1214 John, his cousin Otto of Brunswick, and the count of Flanders joined forces to invade France. Philip Augustus decisively defeated them at the battle of Bouvines, and John fled back to England, where his disgusted vassals were on the brink of revolt. He met them at Runymeade, west of London, and agreed to terms spelled out in the famous Magna Carta ("Great Charter"). Within two months, the document was a dead letter. The pope absolved John from his oath to honor it, for subjects, the pope believed, had no right to limit the authority of the kings God sent them. John's barons, however, sought to influence God's choice by inviting Philip Augustus's son, Louis, to invade England and claim its throne.

The Plantagenet dynasty was saved by John's timely death. His heir was his nine-year-old son, Henry III (r. 1216–1272), and England's rebellious barons, who preferred a weak child king to a powerful French prince, promptly switched their allegiance back to the English royal family. Henry's reign was one of the least successful in England's history, but its weakness had the effect of inching England further toward constitutional or limited monarchy. Henry mismanaged England so badly that civil war broke out under the leadership of Henry's brother-in-law, Simon de Montfort. In 1264, when the rebels captured their king, Simon decided to convene a council to rally national support for this act of treason. He invited the barons and church leaders who usually attended such meetings, but he also included representatives of England's shires and boroughs (towns). The result was the first session of what the French-speaking English court called Parliament (*parler*, "to speak").

Henry's son Edward, who was far more competent than his father, rallied the royalist forces, killed Simon (d. 1265), restored his father to the throne, and reversed the monarchy's decline. Edward learned from his enemies. Although the first Parliament had been a rebel organization, Edward continued to convene parliaments for purposes of his own. England's kings were expected to meet the costs of government from their own incomes. If they needed more money, they had to ask their subjects for it. Parliament was an expedient way to do this and to conduct other kinds of business. Medieval Parliaments were weak. Only the property-owning classes were represented in them, and they met only at the king's pleasure. But they survived, grew in importance, and set an example that has influenced popular governments throughout the modern world.

Edward I (r. 1272–1307) accomplished a great deal. He brought Wales under control. He strengthened England's hold on parts of Ireland, and he was on the brink of subduing Scotland when he died. On the civilian front, he promulgated so much legislation that he has been called "the English Justinian." His interest in justice, however, did not prevent him from raising money by expelling the Jews from England and confiscating their property. He also destroyed Italian banks by failing to repay the money he borrowed from them.

France   France's Capetian dynasty made slow progress during the twelfth century. Its kings struggled with the powerful English rulers and their own vassals. The monarchy reached a turning point in 1214, when Philip Augustus defeated England's king John at the battle of Bouvines. Philip's victory secured his hold on northern France and tripled the king's estates and income. When the pope called for a crusade against the Cathar heretics of southern France in 1208, Philip's soldiers answered and extended his influence into that region.

Philip reorganized royal government to enhance its ability to administer the lands he won. Earlier kings had relied on tax farmers to collect their dues. These men paid the treasury a fixed sum in exchange for the right to collect what was owed to the crown. Whatever additional money they extracted, they could keep for themselves. Philip ended the corruption, abuse, and cheating this system invited by replacing tax farmers with salaried officials.

When Philip died and passed the crown to his mature, experienced son, Louis VIII (r. 1223–1226), the future of the Capetian dynasty seemed secure. Philip had charged Louis with protecting royal interests in the crusade against the Cathars, and Louis acquired lands that extended the king's domain to the shores of the Mediterranean. Louis, however, endangered the future of France's monarchy in two ways. He died young—leaving the throne

Culture in Context: Castles and Military Strategy

The Romans erected walls along some frontiers and built fortified towns and permanent military camps, but they preferred to protect their empire with mobile armies rather than fixed defenses. The German barbarians, for their part, created fortified enclosures to which they could retreat with their herds when attacked. The castle was primarily a medieval invention, and over 100,000 castles may have been erected in western Europe during the Middle Ages. Most were not residences for rulers or refuges for civilians. They were headquarters for military garrisons.

The earliest castles were simple mounds of earth (mottes) surrounded by defensive ditches and walls (baileys). A tower (donjon), usually constructed of wood, was erected on the motte to provide storage space for supplies and shelter for soldiers. One of the common duties of a feudal vassal was to spend time each year on guard duty in his lord's castle. Given the crowding, noise, and smells of such places, garrison duty was probably not a popular assignment. It was, however, important, for castles were key elements in the calculations of military strategists.

Castles enabled a region that was threatened with attack to use its manpower with maximum efficiency. It took a much larger army to lay siege to a castle than to defend one, and because an invader could not afford to leave a castle's garrison at his rear, he had either to halt until he took it or leave soldiers behind to besiege it. The former plan destroyed his momentum, and the latter fragmented and scattered his forces.

Discounting treachery, a castle could only be taken by assault, starvation, or sapping (tunneling to undermine walls). None of the options was easy. Sapping only worked on certain kinds of ground and was dangerous. Assaults were costly in men and equipment, and architects were constantly improving castles to make them easier to defend. Machines, such as battering rams, catapults, and moveable siege towers might be constructed, but they were not always available or effective. Starving a garrison into submission could be a lengthy process, and it was not easy to feed an army while it besieged a castle. Armies lived by foraging for food around their camps, and if they stayed in one place for long, they depleted local stocks.

As the Middle Ages progressed, governments invested heavily in castles that grew ever larger and more complex. England's Edward I constructed eight extraordinarily expensive castles in Wales alone. New designs featured concentric rings of walls, castles within castles that provided fall-back positions, traps for invaders, and huge towers or keeps. The military worth of these costly buildings diminished in the late Middle Ages as cannon became more effective. Soaring castles continued to be built as imposing royal residences, but these edifices owed more to romantic nostalgia than military science. They housed courtiers, not soldiers. Military purposes were served by new kinds of buildings that were harder targets for artillery: low-lying forts with walls cunningly angled to deflect projectiles.

Question: Because states must match the military advances of their enemies if they hope to survive, might military technology help to break down cultural boundaries?

Figure 10–3 Pembroke Castle, Wales England's Norman conquerors quickly recognized the military importance of Pembroke's site at the mouth of a river in southwestern Wales. They erected the first castle there in 1093—an earth and timber structure protected by cliffs and water. The construction of the current stone castle began in 1180. Its two walled courtyards are anchored by a massive keep, a four-story round tower with walls fifteen-feet thick.

to a minor (a first for the Capetians), and his will carved out appanages (quasi-independent territories) from the royal estates for the new king's three younger brothers.

Louis IX (r. 1226–1270) was only twelve years old when he inherited the throne. He faced a horde of powerful nobles who relished the opportunity a weak regency government gave them to cripple a monarchy that was becoming too strong for their tastes. Fortunately, the young king had an able defender, his mother, Blanche of Castile (1188–1252), granddaughter of Eleanor of Aquitaine and England's Henry II. Her job was made easier by the tendency of France's nobles to squabble among themselves. England was small enough that its barons knew one another and sometimes agreed to form a common front against their king. This was less likely in France, which was four times England's size. Regionalism was strong in France, and awareness of common interests developed slowly among nobles from different districts.

Louis IX grew up to become the most popular and respected of France's kings, and his reputation obliterated whatever doubts remained about the Capetians' divine right to the throne. Twenty-seven years after his death, the church declared him a saint. Louis was pious and inclined to personal asceticism, but these traits did not diminish his effectiveness as a king. He was a strong, courageous leader who sincerely believed that it was a Christian monarch's duty to protect the poor and weak, and to deliver justice. Louis restrained France's nobles and halted the private warfare that ravaged the countryside. He made himself accessible to the humblest of his subjects and acted to right their grievances. He sent out *enquêteurs* ("investigators") to audit the accounts of his officials and hear complaints against them. He relied on the *Parlement* of Paris (a group of legal advisors) to help him improve the professionalism of his administration. He settled territorial squabbles with neighboring kingdoms by making generous concessions, and his reputation for fairness was so great that other countries asked him to adjudicate their internal disputes.

France flourished under Louis's leadership, but the Christian principles that inspired his virtues as a leader could also cloud his judgment. He persecuted Jews and persons accused of heresy, and he squandered his country's resources on crusades that had little hope of success. In 1249 he led an elaborately equipped expedition into Egypt. The Muslims cut off his supply lines. Disease broke out in his army, and it was forced to surrender. A huge ransom was paid to win Louis's release, but even then he was reluctant to give up and return to France. He never relinquished the dream of winning back Jerusalem, and in July 1270 he set out on a second crusade. This time he attacked Tunis, intending to work his way across North Africa and Egypt to the Holy Land. Seven weeks into the campaign, he died of a disease that ravaged his army.

Louis had prepared his son, Philip III (r. 1270–1285), for the duties of kingship, but Philip lacked his father's talent and charisma. Philip was overawed by his forceful uncle, Charles of Anjou (1227–1285), who was determined to carve out a kingdom for himself in Italy and Sicily. Philip died shortly after leading a futile expedition into Spain in support of his uncle. The throne then passed to Philip's much more competent son, Philip IV, "the Fair" (1285–1314).

Germany and Italy   France, like Germany, was tempted to try to expand into Italy, but the German experience should have warned the French of the risks of such a policy. Two strong German dynasties, the Saxon and the Salian, tried to join Italy to Germany, and both were defeated by the combined efforts of popes, Italian cities, and truculent German nobles.

The premature death of Henry V (r. 1105–1125) ended the Salian dynasty and began a quarter-century-long tug of war for the German throne. Two factions contended: the Welfs (Guelfs) who backed the duke of Saxony-Bavaria, and the Waiblingens (Ghibellines) who supported the duke of Swabia. Kings were chosen, but none was more than a figurehead.

In 1152 the Waibling candidate, Frederick "Barbarossa" ("Red Beard"), won out over the young Welf duke, Henry the Lion (1129–1195). Frederick I (r. 1152–1190), whose mother was Henry the Lion's aunt, was a compromise candidate, and it was hoped that his ties to both ducal factions would persuade them to work together. Frederick established his authority and broke up some of the German duchies. But whereas France's Capetian kings added the lands they conquered to the royal domain, the German nobles forced Frederick to grant his acquisitions as fiefs. Germany therefore remained a fragmented collection of feudal principalities.

The Hohenstaufen dynasty that Frederick founded pinned its hopes on Italy. Its base, the duchy of Swabia, in the southwestern corner of Germany, was poorly situated to be the capital of a German kingdom, but it was ideally located to become the center of a Roman Empire. Frederick acquired the kingdom of Burgundy (west of his duchy) by marrying its heiress. The rich towns of northern Italy (Lombardy) resisted him. In 1161 he forced them to come to terms, but as soon as he turned his attention to Germany, they and the pope colluded against him. In 1176 he lost a battle to the Lombards and was forced to recognize the wisdom of compromise. The cities recognized his overlordship, but retained the right of self-government. A decade later a bit of luck tipped the balance of power in Italy in the Hohenstaufens' favor. Frederick's daughter-in-law, Constance, inherited the kingdoms of Sicily and Naples from her nephew, William II (r. 1166–1189). This surrounded the Papal States with Hohenstaufen territory and opened the way for Frederick to consolidate his hold on Italy. But the Third Crusade distracted the aging king, and in 1189 he headed for Constantinople at the head of the greatest crusading army ever assembled. He drowned before reaching the Holy Land.

Frederick's son, Henry VI (r. 1190–1197), was a competent king, but his reign was brief. His son (another Frederick) was only two when Henry died. The Hohenstaufens' enemies seized the opportunity this gave them to try to topple the dynasty. The young heir was shunted aside in Sicily, and his uncle, Philip of Swabia, contested possession of the throne with Otto of Brunswick (c. 1174–1218), head of the Guelf party. Pope Innocent III (r. 1198–1216), whose reign began just as this war was breaking out, tried to prolong their fight in order to keep them out of Italy. But in 1209 Philip was assassinated, and Otto emerged victorious. When Otto then staked a claim to Italy, the pope remembered Frederick, the forgotten Hohenstaufen heir.

Frederick II (r. 1215–1250) was such a remarkable man that his contemporaries called him *Stupor Mundi,* "Wonder of the World." The young king was an athlete, a warrior, and an intellectual. He was fluent in six languages. He sponsored scientific research, wrote a book on the art of falconry (which survives), founded a university, and gave Sicily a constitution that was a model of centralized monarchy. Frederick believed that a king's duties extended beyond policing and protecting his state. Frederick managed Sicily's economy, and he even issued environmental regulations to protect air and water quality.

In exchange for the church's support, Pope Innocent elicited a promise from Frederick that he would not rule both halves of Italy, but Frederick had no intention of keeping his word. He was an Italian who had little interest in Germany. He allowed the German barons to do as they wished in order to be free to concentrate on Italy. In hopes of distracting Frederick from Italy, the pope persuaded him to go on crusade. But he was so slow in acting on his vow that when he finally sailed for the Holy Lands in 1228, the pope had excommunicated him. He opened negotiations with the Muslims, and they handed Jerusalem over to him without a fight. The pope was appalled that an excommunicate had succeeded where so many faithful crusaders had failed, and he declared war on Frederick. Frederick spent the rest of life battling with the papacy and the Lombard cities. The pope fled into exile, and the cities would probably have yielded to Frederick had he been a bit more compromising. In the end, his opponents were saved by an attack of dysentery that carried off the king.

Frederick had so alarmed his enemies that they joined forces, tracked down his heirs, and exterminated his dynasty. Germany's emptied throne once again became a prize for which many were eager to compete, but the German barons, who fattened on bribes from candidates, were in no hurry to choose a new king. From 1254 to 1272 the throne remained in dispute, and without a strong king, there was no hope of countering the forces that were fragmenting Germany.

As Germany retreated, a new threat to Italy's cities and the papacy appeared. Louis IX's brother, Charles of Anjou, invaded and seized control of southern Italy and Sicily. In 1282 the Sicilians drove out the French and offered their throne to the king of Aragon. The French held

Chronology: Political Leaders of the High Middle Ages

ENGLAND	FRANCE	GERMANY	THE PAPACY
Henry I (1100–1135)	Louis VI (1108–1137)	Henry V (1106–1125)	
Stephen (1135–1154)	Louis VII (1137–1180)	[Civil War, 1125–1152]	
Henry II (1154–1189)		Frederick I (1152–1190)	
	Philip II (1180–1223)		
Richard I (1189–1199)		Henry VI (1190–1197)	
John (1199–1216)		Philip and Otto (1198–1214)	Innocent III (1198–1216)
Henry III (1216–1272)	Louis VIII (1223–1226)	Frederick II (1215–1250)	
Edward I (1272–1307)	Louis IX (1226–1270)	[Interregnum 1254–1273]	
	Philip III (1270–1285)		
	Philip IV (1285–1314)		
Edward II (1307–1327)			

on to Naples, but instead of focusing on Italy, they opened new fronts in Hungary and the Balkans. The High Middle Ages witnessed progress toward the consolidation of England and France as nations, but the story was very different in Italy and Germany.

Larger Issue Revisited

The dominant intellectual faith of the High Middle Ages was a belief in reality as a coherent unity—a confidence that everything that human beings learned from experience or received by revelation could be integrated into an intelligible, universal system. Progress toward this goal was made on some fronts. An international intellectual community appeared. Feudal particularism was overcome in parts of Europe. Clearer rationales for institutions and policies were developed, and new arts created visual summaries of the medieval worldview.

Bernard of Chartres's "dwarfs" had much of which they could be proud, but their *summae* remained frustratingly incomplete. Dialecticians fought among themselves and with mystics. Reformers and heretics rebelled against traditional institutions and authorities.

Consolidation of states led to larger wars, not peace, and promising crusades ended in defeat. None of this, however, challenged their belief that Europe had found its footing and was finally in the ascendancy. This faith was soon to be severely tested.

Review Questions

1. How did intellectual life change in Europe with the invention of the universities of the High Middle Ages?
2. Why were the scholars of the High Middle Ages preoccupied with dialectic? Did it promote agreement or disagreement among them?
3. How did religious enthusiasm affect the cultural environment of the High Middle Ages? Were its effects positive or negative?
4. How did Romanesque architecture differ from Gothic? Do the impressions each style makes suggest that each was inspired by a different theology?
5. How did the development of the French and English monarchies differ?
6. Were there environmental factors that promoted the development of monarchy in France and England but handicapped it in Germany and Italy?

Refer to the front of the book for a list of chapter-relevant primary sources available on the CD-ROM.

THE WEST INTERACTIVE

For web-based activities, map explorations, and quizzes related to this chapter, go to *www.prenhall.com/frankforter.*

PART FOUR

REORIENTATION
1300 C.E. to 1700 C.E.

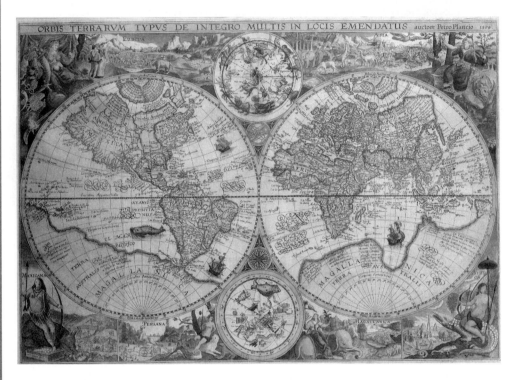

Throughout the Middle Ages, Europeans believed that they were tucked away in the northwestern corner of the world. They knew that the world was round but assumed that their avenues for exploring it were severely limited. They could not head north through the impenetrable Arctic wastes or west across the unfathomable Atlantic, and they did not think that they could travel south indefinitely. They assumed that because temperatures grew warmer as one moved south, a zone of intolerable heat formed a barrier between the northern and southern hemispheres. Europe's only access to the lands of the Far East that produced exotic silks and spices was therefore through Russia and the Middle East, journeys of thousands of miles across hostile territory. A few European merchants and missionaries made the trip, but direct contact with these fabled places seemed almost impossible.

All of this changed at the end of the fifteenth century when Europeans discovered that the Atlantic was not a barrier to their exploration of the wider world, but a highway providing them with access to lands both known and unknown. Europeans were amazed to find that the world was much larger than they had ever imagined, and the initiative they took in exploring it gave them a new sense of their place in it. The Mediterranean and the Middle East became less important to them, and they began to regard Europe as the center of a new world order.

	CULTURE	ENVIRONMENT AND TECHNOLOGY	POLITICS
ca 1200		Western Europe: population growth and land clearance	Ayyubid Empire Mamluk sultanate Mongol invasions
	Marco Polo (1254–1324)		German *Interregnum* (1254–1273)
	Dante (1265–1321)		Habsburg dynasty
ca 1300		"Little Ice Age" commences	Estates General (1302) Avignese papacy (1305–1377)
		The Great Pestilence (1347–1350)	Timur the Lame (1336–1404)
	Italian Renaissance		Hundred Years' War (1337–1453)
	Petrarch (1304–1374) Chaucer (1340–1400)	Cannon appears	Golden Bull (1356) Great Schism (1378–1415)
ca 1400	Conciliarism		Ottoman dynasty Council of Constance
	Joan of Arc (1412–1431)	Portugese explorations, 1430 printing press, 1446	
	da Vinci (1452–1519)		Constantinople falls (1453)
	Erasmus (1466–1536)		Ottoman Empire Tudor dynasty
ca 1500	Michelangelo (1475–1564)	Columbus's first voyage, 1492	Safavid dynasty
	Martin Luther (1483–1546)	global circumnavigation, 1522	
	Protestant Reformation	disease ravages the Americas	Aztecs fall, 1519
	Diet of Worms 1521		Charles V (r. 1519–1556) Süleyman (r. 1520–1566) Incas fall, 1529
		American imports change Europe	Habsburg-Valois Wars (1525–1544)
	English Reformation (1534) Council of Trent (1545–1563)		
			St. Bartholemew's Day Massacre, 1572
	Edict of Nantes (1598)		Spanish Armada 1588
ca 1600	Shakespeare (1564–1616)		Thirty Years' War (1618–1648) English Civil War (1642–1646) Puritan Republic (1649–1660)

CHAPTER 11

CHALLENGES TO THE MEDIEVAL ORDER

Age of sorrow and temptation, of tears, jealousy and torment,
Time of exhaustion and damnation, declining to extinction,
Era filled with horror and deception, lying, pride and envy,
Time without honor and meaning, full of life-shortening sadness.

—Eustache Deschamps

Larger Issue: *What did the crises of the late medieval era reveal about the strengths and weaknesses of Europe's civilization?*

The verses quoted above are from a poem by Eustache Deschamps (c. 1346–1406) in which he laments the dismal prospects of his generation. His disillusionment is understandable. He trained for the law at a university, won royal patronage, traveled in the service of his king, and held a series of important political offices. But his career unfolded against a background of disasters that would have undercut the confidence of the most determined optimist. Deschamps was born about the time that a great plague carried off a third of the population of Europe, and those who survived were never free of the threat of its return. A devastating war between England and France also disrupted his life. He endured sieges. His home was burned, and he lost his job. From his perspective, the world was drifting toward anarchy, and he had no confidence in the leaders whose duty it was to maintain order and provide justice.

During the twelfth and thirteenth centuries C.E. Europe had expanded on all fronts. Population grew. Commerce, cities, and artistic and intellectual life flourished. Then, early in the fourteenth century C.E., things began to go wrong—some suddenly and dramatically, others slowly and insidiously. Food shortages became common. Epidemics spread. Europe was threatened with invasion. The leadership of the church broke down, and the efforts of government leaders to cope with these crises often made them worse.

People of Deschamps's generation had reason to believe that their world was in decline, but it would be inaccurate and unfair to accuse their civilization of having failed them as a survival strategy. The stresses of the fourteenth and fifteenth centuries C.E. certainly forced Europeans to make painful adaptations, but many of their problems were signs of evolving circumstances more than cultural failure. Some were the dark side of the achievements of the twelfth and thirteenth centuries C.E., and others were the result of natural and historical processes that were beyond human control.

Historians have rightly described the late medieval period as the Age of Anxiety, a time characterized by pessimism, skepticism, and self-doubt. But the fourteenth century C.E. also witnessed the flowering of Italy's Renaissance, a movement associated with a surge of optimistic humanism (see Chapter 12, "Renaissance and Exploration.") Some of Deschamps's contemporaries shared his opinion that they were sorely afflicted, but they also anticipated the dawn of a glorious new era. It was their destiny to be born at a time of testing for the institutions that the dynamic High Middle Ages had created. The crises they weathered revealed weaknesses in Western civilization but also signs of future strengths.

TOPICS IN THIS CHAPTER

Challenges from Nature • Turmoil in the Middle East • Spiritual Crises •
Political Responses: The Burdens of War

Challenges from Nature

Because most modern people live in artificial environments, they forget how dependent even an advanced civilization is on the processes of nature. Such forgetfulness is dangerous, for scientists have discovered that the natural environment that sustains all life is not fixed and stable. Earth has experienced such drastic shifts in climate that tropical plants have flourished in what is today the arctic, and glaciers once reached the Mediterranean. The whole history of civilization has unfolded during an unusually warm and stable period in Earth's cycle of climates. This is a sobering fact, for even minor shifts in climate can threaten the stability of human institutions.

Climate Change   From 1000 to 1300 Europe enjoyed a benign climate warmer than our own, but then the Little Ice Age, an era of slowly diminishing average temperatures, set in and continued into the nineteenth century C.E. Climate change posed a great threat to medieval Europe's largely agrarian economy. Weather patterns changed. Precipitation increased. Growing seasons shortened, and in some places, crops that had thrived would no longer grow. Much of Europe lies at the latitude of Canada. (Paris is farther north than Nova Scotia.) Europe's climate is moderated by the Gulf Stream and warm seasonal winds from Africa. A change in the behavior of these phenomena can have serious repercussions.

Sporadic famines had always been a part of medieval life, but in the fourteenth century C.E. they came more frequently and affected larger areas. In 1309 there was a continent-wide famine, the first in 250 years. Crops failed throughout northern Europe in 1315, 1316, and 1317, and there was another widespread famine in the 1330s. Death by starvation was not unusual. People ate dogs, cats, and rats, and there were even rumors of cannibalism. Governments could do little to respond to such crises. Even if they found supplies of food, they lacked the distribution systems to get emergency relief to afflicted regions.

Food supplies were critical, for increasing political stability and economic growth had allowed Europe's population to triple between the eleventh and the fourteenth centuries C.E. Although population density was not great by modern standards, it reached previously unprecedented heights. There were perhaps 80 million Europeans in 1300 compared with 732 million today. But given the available agricultural technologies, Europe began, by the fourteenth century C.E., to exceed the carrying capacity of its land. Farmers responded by bringing more (and often marginal) land into production. They drained swamps, reclaimed fields from the sea, and cleared so much forest that Europe may have more trees today than it did then. As the climate began to cool, however, the poorer land stopped producing, and society's agricultural base began to shrink. The demand for food soon outstripped supply, and people started to go hungry.

Wealth was unevenly distributed in medieval societies, and there was no social safety net. In any age, economic depressions can trigger migrations from the starving countryside into cities by people who are desperate for food and work. But as large numbers of destitute, chronically malnourished people crowded into Europe's medieval towns, they increased their vulnerability to the second blow that nature struck the West in the fourteenth century C.E.: plague.

Plague   Between 1347 and 1350 a great epidemic spread across the world and carried off between thirty and fifty percent of Europe's population. Medieval people called it simply "the pestilence." The name Black Death appeared in the sixteenth century C.E., and the term Bubonic Plague only describes one form of the disease. A bubo is an infected lymph node, usually in the groin or armpit. Plague can also rupture blood vessels and cause bleeding from bodily orifices or infect the lungs and be spread by coughs and sneezes.

The diseases that afflicted the ancient and medieval world are hard to identify, for the records describing symptoms are often inadequate. Diseases also mutate over time, and modern diseases may differ from their earlier versions. For a long time, historians have assumed that the pestilence that afflicted Europe in the fourteenth century C.E. was caused by a bacterium called *Yersinia pestis*. It is indigenous to parts of China and Africa and lives in the digestive tracts of fleas that infest certain species of rats. When the bacteria multiply excessively, they block their host flea's digestive track. The starving insect then begins to bite other warm-blooded creatures, and its bite injects them with infected material from its blocked gut. Recent research has raised doubts about the cause of the great medieval pandemic, for it did not conform in many ways to modern plague. Rather, it bore a closer resemblance to the virulent influenza epidemic that swept the globe in 1918.

The fourteenth century C.E. was not the first to confront an epidemic. Smallpox spread through the Roman Empire about 180 C.E. Measles erupted in 251 C.E. *Yersinia pestis* may have spread from Africa north through the Byzantine Empire and into western Europe around 540 C.E. and burned itself out by the eighth century C.E. From then until the fourteenth century C.E., Europeans suffered few epidemics, for once the pool of diseases to which they were exposed stabilized, their immune systems were able to adapt.

If the fourteenth-century C.E. plague was *Yersinia pestis,* the global climate shifts that were taking place at that time may help to explain its arrival in Europe. Humidity and temperature affect the activity of the fleas that are the plague's hosts. As Europe's climate grew wetter, central Asia suffered drought, and flea-infected rodent populations migrated into regions inhabited by nomadic tribes of Turks and Mongols. The medieval epidemic began in China in approximately 1330 C.E. and reached Samarkand in 1339, the Crimea in 1345, and Sicily in October 1347. Within months the disease had spread throughout Europe as well as the Islamic world. Muslim countries may also have lost thirty to fifty percent of their population. The rapidity with which the epidemic spread, however, is one of the reasons for doubting that it was caused by *Yersinia pestis.*

Modern people are all too familiar with acts of genocide and natural disasters that devastate limited regions, but it is hard to imagine what it was like to experience the universal spread of a mysterious, lethal illness. Medieval people were baffled. They knew that it was infectious, but they did not know how it spread. There were no effective treatments for it, and it was almost always fatal. There seemed to be no logic to its behavior. It struck unevenly, obliterating some places and skipping others. Thousands of villages disappeared. Tightly packed communities such as monasteries and nunneries were obliterated. The general upheaval reduced the number of universities from about thirty in 1349 to ten in 1400. Disease and deteriorating climate led to abandonment of the country of Greenland, and Europe did not recoup its population losses until the mid-sixteenth century C.E.

Social Consequences   Frightened people often turn on one another, and the plague prompted persecution of Europe's resident outsiders, the Jews. They were dying along with everyone else, but rumors that Jews were poisoning wells still spread. The physicians who taught at the universities of Paris and Montpellier dismissed this, and Pope Clement VI (r. 1342–1352) ordered the clergy to protect the Jews. But over two hundred Jewish communities were destroyed.

University scholars resorted to astrology and attributed the disease to an unfortunate alignment of planets, but humbler Christians assumed that God had sent the plague to chastize a sinful Europe. In desperation, they did penance. They fasted and made pilgrimages. They increased their acts of charity, and some tried to appease God by tormenting their flesh. Processions of flagellants whipped one another into bloody, ecstatic frenzies. The church condemned the flagellants, but it had no effective alternatives to propose for dealing with the crisis. It may have lost forty percent of its clergy in the first onslaught of the epidemic, and there was no evidence that sacraments, intercessions, and traditional acts of piety did much good. Some Christians responded to the crisis by turning inward and cultivating an individual, mystical piety that helped them come to terms with mortality. This and other developments in late medieval societies accustomed people to assuming greater responsibility for themselves.

Death became the preoccupation of the age. Artists covered the walls of churches with pictures of the Last Judgment that emphasized the punishments of the damned. Grave monuments focused on the gruesome aspects of death. The tomb effigies of earlier generations represented the deceased in the full bloom of their youth and vigor, but now the dead were depicted as corpses in states of decay. The intent was to abase earthly pride and affirm that life's fulfillment lay beyond the grave.

Every cloud is said to have a silver lining, and this held true even for the fourteenth-century C.E. epidemic. Many of those who survived it found their prospects improved. The disease reduced pressure on Europe's food supply by reducing the population. Land became available. Small holdings were concentrated into larger, more viable farms. Wages rose, for a labor shortage put workers in a good position to bargain. Prior to the epidemic, overpopulation had glutted the labor market and driven wages down. Now the process was reversed. Landlords had to give their workers better terms to keep them. In western Europe the wage-laborer replaced the serf, but in central Europe, where towns and strong kings were few, serfdom spread. The powerful landowners of that region could exploit their peasants, for poor laborers had nowhere to flee to and no source of alternative employment.

The rising wages that workers in western Europe demanded threatened employers' incomes, and their employers' reaction prompted social upheaval. The propertied classes controlled medieval governments, and they used their political power to keep wage earners in their place. Sumptuary laws preserved class distinctions by regulating how people dressed and by limiting indulgence in certain luxuries to the aristocracy. More galling, no doubt, were ordinances that kept wages low by imposing caps.

Figure 11–1 The Image of Death The brevity and fragility of life were favorite themes of late medieval artists, who graphically depicted the horrors of death and death's power to sweep away all human protensions to pomp and glory.

People tolerate bad situations if they assume that misery is inevitable. The dangerous time for a society is when improving conditions raise hopes that are subsequently dashed. Europe was little troubled by popular uprisings until its depressed economy began to improve in the second half of the fourteenth century C.E.. In 1358 the first of the Jacquerie rebellions (named for the poor man's cheap leather jacket) erupted in France. In 1381 the English throne was shaken by a Peasants' Revolt. Similar uprisings took place later in Spain and Germany. The commoners, especially in England, won concessions, but the upper classes remained in control. The aristocracy was, however, not a closed order. Wars, feuds, dangerous sports, and political executions put medieval male nobles at great risk. The average life expectancy of a male born into an English ducal family in the fourteenth and fifteenth centuries C.E., for instance, was only twenty-four years. His sister could anticipate living into her thirties. Aristocratic families had difficulty preserving their male lines for more than a few generations, and this created opportunities for new families to climb the social ladder. Commoners broke into the upper class by intermarriage and by acquiring fortunes with which to purchase titles and estates.

Turmoil in the Middle East

By the fourteenth century C.E., the world that Europeans viewed beyond their borders was undergoing significant changes, and few European leaders may have grasped the dire significance of what these developments portended. During the thirteenth century C.E. a series of events disrupted life for both the Byzantines and Muslims. Europeans tried to take advantage of the situation to regain footholds in the Middle East, but their interventions backfired disastrously. They weakened Constantinople to the point where it could no longer protect Europe's eastern frontiers from Muslim incursions. The Muslim world was temporarily disrupted by invasions from the East. But the newcomers converted, and a reenergized Islam embarked on a new age of empire building. The Middle Ages were to end as they had begun—with Muslim and Christian powers contending for control of the Mediterranean Sea. The crusaders' repeated thrusts into Muslim territory were repulsed, but Islam's late medieval counteroffensive succeeded. Muslim armies seized Greece, the Balkans, and parts of central Europe, and held them for centuries.

Constantinople   The crusades cast a lengthy shadow over Europe's relations with its eastern neighbors. Byzantine emperor Alexius Comnenus (r. 1081–1118) had unintentionally launched the Holy Land crusades by asking Pope Urban II (r. 1088–1099) to help him recruit soldiers for Constantinople's wars (see Chapter 9, "Europe Turns Outward.") What seemed a good idea at the time proved in the long run to be a disaster for Alexius's empire. Constantinople lost trade as the crusaders took control of ports on the eastern coast of the Mediterranean, and Constantinople itself became a target for Europe's crusaders.

In 1202 the armies of the Fourth Crusade gathered in Venice. They planned to sail to the Holy Land. But when they proved not to have enough money for their passage, they agreed to earn their way by selling their services to Venice. Venice diverted them to Constantinople to support an exiled Byzantine prince's bid for the imperial throne. Once the Venetian candidate was in power, Venice expected to dominate trade with Constantinople. The intimidated Byzantines crowned the prince, but he soon fell victim to a plot. The angry crusaders assaulted the city, and the Byzantines bungled its defense. The Christian city that for centuries had withstood multiple attacks by barbarian and Muslim armies fell, for the first time, to soldiers who fought in the name of Christ. The crusaders sacked Constantinople, claimed it for themselves, and enthroned a Latin emperor. Many of the treasures the city had preserved from antiquity were lost in the fires and looting that ensued.

The triumphant crusaders forgot about Jerusalem and rushed to stake claims to Byzantine territory. However, a rival Greek emperor established a base in Asia Minor and rallied resistance to the Catholic Latins, who were loathed by their Orthodox subjects. The Latin Byzantine empire, like the earlier crusader states, was a feudal kingdom whose ruler had little power and few resources. The last of Constantinople's Latin emperors was so desperate for money that he hawked relics from the city's churches and sold the lead that roofed his palace. In 1261 C.E. Venice's competitor, the Italian city of Genoa, helped the Greek emperor, Michael Palaeologue (r. 1261–1282), regain control of a depopulated and impoverished Constantinople. Michael's Byzantine Empire was a shadow of its former self, and it faced a world in turmoil. Europe's crusaders had set in motion events that were to lose Christians their last outpost in the East. For centuries, Constantinople had blocked Muslim advances into Europe, but its ability to do so was now seriously compromised. The city survived in Christian hands for almost two more centuries, however, for its Muslim enemies had more important matters to attend to.

The Islamic Middle East The First Crusade succeeded because the Muslims of the Middle East were fighting among themselves. This continued until a Kurdish warrior named Saladin (1138–1193) brought them under his control. In 1174 he terminated the Fatimid caliphate and occupied Egypt. Syria and Mesopotamia were his by 1186, and in 1187 he took Jerusalem. After he repulsed Richard the Lionhearted's Third Crusade (see Chapter 10, "Europe's High Middle Ages"), he built an empire that stretched from Tunisia in North Africa to Armenia and the Caspian Sea. His Ayyubid dynasty reigned over a loose feudal federation that posed no threat to the Christian West. It wanted good trade relations with Italy's cities and was primarily interested in preserving the status quo.

The Muslim lands east of the Ayyubid Empire (roughly modern Iran) passed from the Seljuk sultans to the shahs of Khwarazm, the region south of the Aral Sea. It was there, in 1218, that the Muslims first encountered a threat that renewed hope in Europe for their ultimate defeat. The shah's lands were invaded by the Mongols, nomadic tribes who roamed the vast stretch of grasslands bordering northern China. The Mongols were not Muslims. European leaders thrilled at the prospect of converting them to Christianity and enlisting them in a joint effort to exterminate Islam.

Mongols The Mongols owed their entrance onto history's stage to the leadership of a man named Temujin (c. 1167–1227), who is better known by his well-deserved title, Genghis Khan ("Universal Lord"). The Mongols had evolved a unique and very effective military technology. They bonded different materials together to make powerful bows that were small enough for efficient use by mounted soldiers. Temujin made the most of these weapons by forging the Mongols into an army with a unified command and training them to execute strategic maneuvers. The Mongols routed much larger opponents who had little grasp of tactics and lacked the Mongols' mobility on the battlefield. Temujin concentrated on conquering northern China while his generals made progress on other fronts. In 1221 a Mongol army overthrew the shah of Khwarazm and then split into two branches. One headed north of the Aral and Caspian seas into Russian territory, and the other moved across Persia. (See Map 11–1.)

In 1258 the Mongols took Baghdad (in a siege of only four days) and slaughtered all its inhabitants—including the last Abbasid caliph. They reached the Mediterranean, where they met strong resistance from the Mamluks, Turkish slave soldiers who had overthrown Egypt's Ayyubid ruler in 1250. The Mongols withdrew to Baghdad. The Mamluks emerged as the dominant Muslim power in the Middle East, and in 1291 they took the last crusader outposts on the Palestinian coast.

The pope and France's crusader king, Louis IX, tried to establish contact with the Mongols. In 1245 they dispatched a Franciscan friar, John of Piancarpino, to Mongolia. He returned two years later, bringing Europeans their first eyewitness account of the exotic Far East. In 1255 a second Franciscan, William of Ruybroek, repeated his feat, and late in the century another Franciscan, John of Montecorvino, established a Christian bishopric in Peking. The most famous account of the Mongol Empire derived, however, from the autobiography of a Venetian merchant named Marco Polo (1254–1324). He claimed to have visited the Mongol court with his father and uncle in 1275. He said that he spent seventeen years in China, and even became an official in the Mongol government. Some historians question whether Marco Polo ever visited the East and suggest that he may only have cobbled together stories about China that sifted back to Venice along its trade routes. Their doubts arise not so much from what he said about China but from prominent Chinese customs (tea drinking and foot binding, for example) that he failed to mention.

Culture in Context: Medieval Medicine

Medicine was ill-served by the principles that governed intellectual activity in the Middle Ages. Respect for ancient authorities and reliance on dialectical arguments to ferret out truth diverted people from the kinds of observation and experimentation that are needed to make progress in the natural sciences. The ancient Greeks and Romans had accurately described symptoms, categorized diseases, and devised some useful treatments through trial and error. Arabic medical treatises and the medical books of Galen (c. 130–c. 201 C.E.), antiquity's most respected physician, acquainted Europeans with some of this, but medieval medical practitioners were inclined to base their treatments on philosophical speculations.

Greek philosophers claimed that natural phenomena could be explained as the products of interactions among a few elemental principles. Aristotle identified four types of these: hot, cold, wet, and dry. Physicians inferred from this that the human body was influenced by four fluids called humors: blood, phlegm, black bile, and yellow bile. The relative proportions of these humors in each individual were said to govern his or her character, and illness was alleged to be the result of an imbalance among them. The appropriate treatment for most ailments, therefore, was to open a vein and drain blood to allow the body to purge itself of excesses. Astrology was also believed to explain the onset of an illness and provide an essential guide to its treatment.

Late in the eleventh century C.E. a medical school was founded in Salerno, Italy, and the study of anatomy was revived. The church forbade dissection of human cadavers, so researchers worked on the carcasses of pigs. A surgical text was published early in the twelfth century C.E., but surgery was considered an inferior branch of medicine. Physicians were scholars who did not deign to dirty their hands. They delegated the work of bloodletting and opening human bodies to inferior healers—often to barbers who were practiced in the use of razors. The modern red-and-white-striped barber pole recalls the bloody rags that medieval barbers hung out to dry.

The plague sent Europe's philosopher-physicians down a disastrously wrong path. They concluded from the contagious nature of the disease that it spread through the air. It was, they assumed, caused by miasmas (harmful humors) penetrating the body. They recommend, therefore, that people make their bodies as impenetrable as possible. This involved wearing tight clothing and avoiding bathing, for water opened the pores and made the body easier to penetrate. Prior to the plague, medieval towns were well-supplied with public bathhouses, but fear of infection led to the demise of these institutions and a widespread distrust of bathing. Physicians had reasoned logically from what they thought they knew about the plague, but dialectic led them to erroneous conclusions that supported potentially harmful therapies.

Question: What does medieval medical theory indicate about the strengths and weaknesses of medieval civilization?

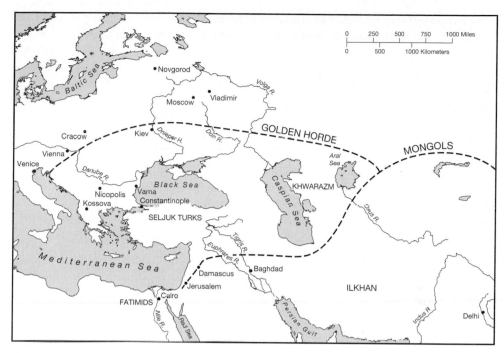

Map 11–1
The Mongol Invasion   The Mongols resembled the Huns and Magyars who had earlier
emerged from the Russian steppe to threaten Europe, but their military organization
was much more sophisticated than that of their predecessors. *Question:* Does geography suggest any clear line of division between the East and the West?

European hopes for a Mongol alliance were dashed late in the thirteenth century C.E. when
the Mongols converted to Islam. By then, Europeans had come to view the Mongols more as
potential enemies than friends. The Mongols had charged almost unopposed across the lands
north of the Black and Caspian seas. In 1238 they sacked the Russian cities of Vladimir and
Moscow, and in 1240 they took Kiev. By 1241 they were nearing Cracow in Poland and pushing up the Danube to the gates of Vienna in Austria. Here their momentum was broken less by
Vienna's Christian defenders than by the confusion that followed the death of their khan.

The Mongols organized the territory north of the Black and Caspian seas as the khanate
of the Golden Horde (named for the color of its ruler's tent). The prince of Moscow was assigned to collect the tribute their Russian subjects owed them. This gave him a chance to
establish his authority over the Russians, and in 1480 Moscow's Ivan III, "the Great"
(r. 1462–1505), threw off the Mongol yoke and began to pull together a large Russian state.

In the late fourteenth century C.E. another Mongol army under the command of a Timur
"the Lame" (Tamerlane; 1336–1404), who claimed to be a descendant of Temujin, erupted
from the east. He raided across Russia as far as Lithuania, struck south into India, leveled the
city of Delhi, and then occupied Baghdad, Damascus, and much of Asia Minor. Europe, with
a population diminished by plagues and famines, had reason to anticipate the worst. But
Tamerlane suddenly died, and his numerous descendants divided up his empire.

Far from assisting Europe's Christians in the destruction of Islam, the Mongols added vigorous new blood to the ranks of Muhammad's followers. Their advance thrust Europe back on the defensive and raised the specter of yet another thrust of alien eastern peoples into the heart of the continent. A weakened Constantinople, disillusionment with crusades, and the loss of the initiative in foreign affairs added to the anxieties created by plague, famine, and social unrest.

Spiritual Crises

Even in the modern world, where religion is far more marginalized than it was in medieval society, people often turn to religious institutions for help in stressful times. Unfortunately, when the Europeans of the late Middle Ages turned to their church, they found an institution that was in disarray. Instead of offering aid and comfort, it added to the problems of an anxious age.

Innocent III and Papal Monarchy   The pope who most successfully exercised the exalted rights that medieval pontiffs claimed for their office was Innocent III (r. 1198–1216). Innocent was a Roman aristocrat with relatives in the papal court. He studied law at the University of Bologna and theology at Paris. He wrote several books, one of which was a piece of devotional literature that enjoyed great popularity. He was only thirty-seven when he became pope, and in addition to youth, he had the advantage of good timing. For most of his reign, the Germans were too busy with a civil war to intervene in Italy and threaten the papacy's independence.

The text on which Innocent preached at his coronation set forth his understanding of the powers of his office: "I have set you today over nations and kingdoms" (Jeremiah 1:10). Innocent maintained that all Christians, including kings, were subject to the spiritual authority of the pope. He agreed that kings derived their power directly from God, but as Christ's representative on Earth, it was the pope's duty to hold kings accountable for how they used the office God entrusted to them. He urged Europe's kings to become his vassals. This would not have made him Europe's ruler, but as feudal overlord of Europe's kings, he would have had the right to adjudicate their disputes. Innocent wanted the church to become a kind of high court in which nations could resolve their difficulties without resorting to war.

Few kings accepted the pope's invitation to become his vassals, but Innocent, on several occasions, challenged great monarchs and forced them to back down. He owed his success to the care with which he chose his fights. He confronted kings when they blundered and made themselves vulnerable.

Like his predecessors, Innocent hoped that by sponsoring crusades, he could strengthen the pope's role as Christendom's supreme leader. This was the least successful of his undertakings. The first army he intended for the Holy Land (the Fourth Crusade) sacked Christian Constantinople in 1204. The crusade he called against the Cathar heretics in 1208 devastated southern France. The Fifth Crusade (1218–1221), an attack on Egypt that he was planning at the time of his death, was a debacle.

Innocent's greatest achievement was the strengthening of papal authority over the church and its clergy. In 1215 his Fourth Lateran Council affirmed that the church was a papal monarchy, endorsed the doctrine of transubstantiation as the explanation of the Eucharist, enforced clerical celibacy, and imposed new pious duties on the laity. Innocent bluntly asserted that the state had no power over the church and denied kings the right to tax or exercise judicial authority over the clergy. Given the growing strength of some of Europe's monarchies, Innocent committed his successors to a position that they were ill-equipped to defend, and their failure produced a century-long crisis for the church.

Humiliation of the Papacy   In 1295 France's powerful king, Philip IV (r. 1285–1314), informed the French clergy that he was imposing taxes on the church. The clergy appealed to Pope Boniface VIII (r. 1296–1303), and the pope informed Philip that the church (as the Fourth Lateran Council had made clear) was totally independent of the state and not subject to taxation by kings. When Philip responded by blocking funds flowing from France to the papal treasury, the financially strapped Boniface tried to make a face-saving retreat. He explained that although kings had no right to tax the church, the church would, of course, help out a king who faced a national emergency—and that a king had the right to decide when such an emergency existed.

Having won de facto taxing authority, Philip next challenged the pope's claim that clergy did not fall under the jurisdiction of the state's courts. In 1301 he charged a French bishop with treason and threw him into prison. Boniface fired off a letter to Philip, warning him of the spiritual penalties awaiting him if he continued to attack the church. Philip circulated a distorted version of the letter to inflame his subjects against the pope, and then, in 1302, he convened a national assembly to see where they stood. This first meeting of France's Estates General, like England's Parliament, represented only the politically significant classes—the higher clergy, nobility, and townspeople. With its assurance that France was solidly behind him, Philip dispatched troops to Italy to arrest Boniface. The French held the pope prisoner for three days, and he died a few weeks later.

The cardinals who met to elect a new pope had learned a hard lesson. If people were forced to choose between their king and their pope, they were likely to side with the king. It was also clear that Europe's leaders would not unite and take action to punish a king who assaulted the head of their church. The cardinals therefore concluded that they had to make peace with France. Boniface's successor, Benedict XI (r. 1303–1304), lifted the spiritual penalties Boniface had imposed on Philip, and at the end of his brief reign, a French archbishop (whose diocese was in English territory) was elected pope. Clement V (r. 1305–1314) was in France at the time of his election, and he stayed there to negotiate with Philip. He established temporary residence at Avignon, a city in southern France on the border of Philip's territory. One problem followed another, and Clement never had an opportunity to go to Rome. At his death, the college of cardinals, which was now largely French, elected another French pope who opted to remain in Avignon. The pattern repeated itself, and for more than seventy years (1305–1377) the bishop of Rome never visited the city of Rome. Lavish facilities were built for the papal court at Avignon, and it began to appear that the papacy had no intention of ever returning to Rome.

Critics branded the papacy's sojourn in Avignon a "Babylonian captivity," a reference to the Bible's account of the exile of the Jews in ancient Babylon. They accused France of having abducted the papacy. French influences were strong at Avignon, but the Avignese popes were no one's puppets. Many were excellent executives who improved the power and efficiency of the church's central government. Having lost control of the Papal States, they were ingenious at finding other sources of income. They claimed the right to appoint candidates to all major clerical offices, to collect the revenues of those offices during vacancies, and to hear appeals from all ecclesiastical courts. They created an elaborate bureaucracy dedicated to attracting as much business as possible to the papal court, and they collected fees (and bribes) for all services. The papal administration at Avignon became a model of efficiency for Europe's secular governments, but the popes' fiscal skills hardly enhanced their reputations for sanctity.

The church to which Europeans turned for spiritual help with the crises of the fourteenth century C.E. seemed to be becoming ever more worldly and materialistic. Saints—notably Bridget of Sweden (1302–1372) and Catherine of Siena (1347–1380)—begged, and reformers demanded, that the popes return to Rome before they irreparably damaged the church. In 1378 Pope Gregory XI (r. 1370–1378) yielded to the pressure and took the cardinals back to Rome.

Papal Schism   The Papal States were out of control, and the Roman buildings that housed the papacy had been neglected for seventy years. Gregory and the cardinals, who were accustomed to the comforts of their elaborate palace in Avignon, soon concluded that Rome was unliveable. Gregory decreed a return to Avignon, where the papal bureaucracy was still headquartered. Death, however, intervened, and Gregory's demise forced the cardinals to stay in Rome until they had chosen his successor. This proved difficult, for the college of cardinals split in support of rival French candidates. To break the stalemate, the cardinals decided to placate the Roman people by elevating an obscure Italian, Urban VI (r. 1378–1389), to the papacy. The cardinals expected to be able to dominate Urban, and prior to his election they required him to promise to take them back to Avignon. Once seated on the papal throne, however, Urban changed his mind. He knew that in Avignon, as one Italian in a sea of Frenchmen, he would have little power.

When Urban informed the cardinals that they would stay in Rome, they refused and returned to Avignon without him. In Avignon they declared his election invalid and chose a new pope, Clement VII (r. 1378–1394). Urban responded by appointing a new college of cardinals in Rome. Europe suddenly had two popes, and because there was no way to decide which one was valid, kings simply supported the pope who best suited their political agendas. France and its allies endorsed Avignon. England, France's enemy, favored Rome, and other nations lined up accordingly.

This division of the papacy—the Great Schism (1378–1415)—plunged a generation of Europeans into spiritual confusion. Catholic doctrine maintained that allegiance to the true pope was essential for salvation, but there was no way to determine which of Europe's rival popes was Christ's authentic representative. A Christian's salvation depended upon receiving valid sacraments, but a sacrament—the power to act in God's name—was something delegated by Christ to the clergy through their superior, the pope. If the pope was really an antipope, the clergy who served him had no authority to act in God's name. A divided papacy therefore posed a major threat to medieval Christian faith and practice.

Prominent Europeans pressed the popes to settle the issue between themselves. But neither man was willing to sacrifice himself for the good of the church. Attention then shifted to the cardinals. They were urged to repudiate both their popes and unite behind a new one. The cardinals welcomed this plan, for it confirmed their belief that they were the arbiters of papal legitimacy. In 1409, when they met in the Italian city of Pisa and chose a new pope, the popes they had forsaken in Rome and Avignon appointed new colleges of cardinals. Ironically, the strategy for resolving the schism multiplied the number of popes.

Conciliarism and Popular Government   The Avignese papacy and the Great Schism forced Europeans to think seriously about the nature of authority—secular as well as sacred. To end the schism, they needed a justification for forcing popes, who claimed to be accountable only to

Figure 11–2 The Papal Palace at Avignon The facilities constructed to house the pope and papal court at Avignon were more lavish than the palaces of contemporary kings. Religious reformers were scandalized by their luxury and the impression they created that St. Peter's successors had abandoned their Roman see

God, to do what they did not want to do. Whatever rationale they developed for sitting in judgment on a pope could easily be adapted to argue for limiting the authority of their kings.

William of Ockham (1285–1349), an English Franciscan philosopher, insisted that because popes were human, they were as prone to error as anyone else. The most reliable way for fallible human individuals to determine the truth about an issue, he insisted, was to seek a consensus of opinion from all persons qualified to comment. Ockham warned, however, that even experts make mistakes and that it was important, therefore, that minorities be listened to and coercion minimized.

Marsiglio of Padua (c. 1278–c.1342), an Italian philosopher, claimed that the church was not some supernatural entity, but only a community composed of individual Christians. The people who were the church had an obvious right to control it, but because they were also part of the larger institution of the state, they had to operate their church within limits set by the state.

The Englishman John Wyclif (d. 1384) offered a different justification for empowering the masses. He admitted that dominion (the right to rule) was traditionally understood to be a sacred power delegated to men by God. But he argued that this logically implied that dominion had to be used for the purpose God intended—for the welfare of God's creatures. If popes (and kings) failed to use the authority God gave them for the good of their subjects, they forfeited legitimacy. The subjects of any ungodly ruler had a duty to replace him, for he had no right to dominion over God's people. Wyclif also denied that the pope had ultimate authority to interpret the Scriptures. He urged that the Bible be translated from Latin into the vernacular languages so that laypeople could study it and decide for themselves what it said. At the time, the church forbade vernacular translations, for it claimed that simple folk, who were not trained in theology, would misread the text and fall into error.

Critiques of papal authority and arguments justifying action by the masses led to the proposal that finally ended the Great Schism. A group of scholars known as the Conciliarists argued that a universal church council would have the authority to end the schism. Church lawyers warned that only a pope could summon a council and that a council had no power over a pope, but the Conciliarists found ways around these obstacles. They pressured the weakest of the popes, the one in Pisa, to convene their council, and they argued that if an essential institution (such as the church) breaks down, logic gives its members the right to act to restore it.

In 1415 the Swiss city of Constance hosted a council at which most of the powers in Europe—kings, cardinals, bishops, abbots, lawyers, and prominent scholars—were represented. The Great Schism ended when they all agreed to withdraw their support from the rival popes and unite behind a new one chosen by the cardinals at the council. The new pope, Martin V (r. 1417–1431), then did his best to get the council to disband, for the schism was not the only business on the Conciliarists' agenda. They wanted the council to reform the church. Martin feared that if this happened, the council would replace the pope as the ultimate authority over the church.

Once the schism was healed, much of the excitement went out of the meeting, and its member were eager to go home. However, before they left, they passed two revolutionary decrees. The first, *Sacrosancta,* declared that the church was to be governed by councils—implying that popes were simply the church's chief executive officers, agents who were accountable to councils and subject to their supervision. The second decree, *Frequens,* ordered popes to summon councils at regular intervals. If these decrees had succeeded, the church would have become an institution governed by a representative assembly. This did not happen, because kings knew that what councils did to popes they might try to do to kings. In 1431 a council that met in Basel, another Swiss city, made a fatal mistake. It quarreled with the pope, deposed him, and elected a rival. To prevent a new schism from developing, Europe's kings withdrew their support for councils and allowed popes to stop convening them. In 1460 Pope Pius II (r. 1458–1464) declared it a heresy to claim that anyone or any council has authority over a pope. In 1870 Pope Pius IX (r. 1846–1878) and the First Vatican Council confirmed this by promulgating the doctrine of papal infallibility. The church emerged from the crises of the fourteenth century C.E. with the claims it made for the authority of its leader intact, but its reputation as a spiritual institution tarnished.

Private Faith, Mysticism, and Skepticism   The medieval church claimed to be the sole intermediary between God and His people. Pope Boniface VIII had clearly stated to King Philip of France and the world that there was no salvation outside the communion of the church. Yet for much of the fourteenth century C.E., the church did not inspire trust as a mediator. Rival popes excommunicated one another and insisted that their opponents' sacraments were invalid. Faithful Christians had no way to determine the truth. They were therefore thrust back on their own spiritual resources: private prayer, study, and meditation. Laypeople took the initiative and invented new kinds of religious communities and disciplines that had little to do with the church and clergy. The mystical element in medieval religion thrived, for mysticism was an avenue to a direct, personal communion with God. The breakdown of the church forced people to assume responsibility for themselves, and the autonomy to which they became accustomed in the religious sphere spilled over into other areas of their lives.

Even the authority of reason, the thing in which medieval dialecticians placed their greatest trust, was questioned by late medieval philosophers such as William of Ockham. Ockham denied that reason could be used to support faith. He argued that the only reality of which the mind can be certain is the one conveyed through the body's senses. The mind infers classes and abstractions from the specific bits of data that the senses provide, but it has no way of knowing if such words refer to anything that actually exists. The truths of faith are grasped by intuition, and because an omnipotent God is not bound by the rules of logic (else logic would be greater than God), faith need not be rational or comprehensible. Ockham's skepticism severely limited what human beings could hope to learn. But by separating faith from reason, he liberated science from constraints imposed by theology.

Political Responses: The Burdens of War

The governments of the young nation-states that were taking shape in the late Middle Ages faced the challenge of managing populations unsettled by plague and famine. The tools available to them were as limited as their experience. Kings were still primarily warlords, but war was an unlikely cure for the problems of their unstable world.

France and England   England and France were late medieval Europe's most fully formed nation-states. Both had well-established dynasties and relatively centralized bureaucratic governments. Unfortunately, however, they also had an unresolved territorial dispute. Ever since 1066, when the Norman dukes became kings of England, the jurisdictions of the French and English monarchies had overlapped. Henry II of England had controlled about half of France. His son, John, lost most of it, and by the fourteenth century C.E., England's holdings on the continent had been reduced to Gascony, the region around Bordeaux in southwestern France. England's kings were, however, eager to recoup their losses.

Edward I (r. 1272–1307), the warrior-king who conquered Wales and nearly subdued Scotland, reopened war with France to support allies in Flanders. Flanders and England had close economic ties, for English wool merchants supplied the Flemish cloth industry. France evened the odds by helping the Scots fend off the English king. In 1308 the French and English dynasties agreed to a truce, and a royal marriage was arranged to seal peace between the two kingdoms. Edward's son and heir, Edward II, married Isabella, daughter of Philip IV of France. The union was supposed to ensure future good relations between France and England, but instead it prompted a conflict called the Hundred Years' War.

Edward II (1307–1327) was as weak a king as his father had been strong. He led his army to disastrous defeat in Scotland, and his excessive devotion to a few unworthy friends alienated his barons and his wife, Isabella. In 1325 she traveled to Paris on a diplomatic mission to her brother's court, and there she began an affair with an exiled English nobleman, Roger Mortimer, the Earl of March. Isabella and Mortimer raised an army, returned to England, and forced Edward to abdicate in the name of his son, Edward III (r. 1327–1377). The ex-king died, or probably was murdered, a few months later, and Isabella and Mortimer governed England as regents for his son. In 1330 Edward III overthrew them and at age eighteen began his independent rule.

Edward II had seriously damaged the prestige of the monarchy, but Edward III was just the man to restore it. He was a handsome, athletic youth who looked like a king, and he had a gift for what the modern world would call public relations. Enthusiasm for the Arthurian romances was at its height when Edward came to the throne, and he encouraged his subjects to think of him as a new Arthur. He hosted feasts and tournaments at which he and his friends played at being knights of the round table, and in 1348 he founded the Order of the Garter, a fraternity of knights like the one that the legendary King Arthur had assembled at Camelot.

Ceremonies help build a royal image, but a medieval king who aspired to glory had to win repute as a warrior. Edward led several forays into Scotland, but his commanders were not excited by the prospect of plundering such a poverty-stricken land. Much more tempting were the rich provinces of their traditional enemy, France. Moreover, Edward believed that he had a justification for a war with France. He claimed to be the rightful heir to the French throne.

Ever since its founding in the tenth century C.E., France's Capetian dynasty had enjoyed remarkable biological success. Whenever a king died, there was always a son to take his place. Philip IV had seemingly ensured the future of the dynasty by siring three sons: Louis X (r. 1314–1316), Philip V (r. 1316–1322), and Charles IV (1322–1328). Each succeeded to the throne, but surprisingly, none produced a male heir who survived infancy. When Charles died in 1328, the senior line of the Capetian house died with him. The dynasty, however, had a collateral branch founded by Philip IV's brother, Charles of Valois (1270–1325), who had a son named Philip. When Charles IV died, the throne passed to his cousin Philip of Valois, France's king Philip VI (r. 1328–1350).

Edward did not protest when Philip was crowned in 1328, but in 1337 the English king's eagerness for an excuse to invade France prompted him to claim that the French crown should have come to him. Philip VI was only Philip IV's nephew. Edward was Philip IV's grandson, a more direct heir. France's legal authorities disagreed. Edward's link with the Capetian line was through his mother, Isabella, and the lawyers claimed that ancient Frankish tradition—the so-called Salian Law—barred women from occupying France's throne or transmitting title to it. The legal wrangling was beside the point. The French did not want an English king, and Edward hardly expected France to surrender voluntarily. Nor was he likely to conquer it with the resources of a kingdom that was one-quarter France's size. His claim, however, provided a noble justification for looting and pillaging.

The Hundred Years' War   Edward could do little more than harass the French by staging quick raids on their territory, but in 1346 one of his forays turned into a major battle. A large French army surprised Edward while he was charging across Normandy and forced him to take a stand near the village of Crécy. The English were outnumbered, but an unconventional strategy saved them. Edward took up a defensive position and waited for the French to charge him. Archers armed with a uniquely English weapon, the longbow, were stationed on both wings of his army. Their arrows reduced the heavily armored French cavalry to a flailing heap

People in Context: Christine de Pizan (c. 1364–1430): Professional Female Writer

In 1368 France's King Charles V (r. 1364–1380) offered Tommaso de Bologna, a professor of medicine and astrology at the University of Bologna, the post of royal astrologer, and Tommaso moved his family to Paris. His daughter Christine surely absorbed much from the conversations of the learned men who were her father's colleagues and friends, but her only formal education was the elementary training that medieval society gave most girls.

Christine was destined for a completely conventional life. At about the age of sixteen she married Etienne de Castel, one of the king's secretaries. The couple produced two sons and a daughter, and then the family's fortunes began to fail. Charles V died, leaving the throne to a more frivolous monarch, Charles VI (r. 1380–1422), who provided little patronage for the scholars who had adorned his father's court. Christine's father died in poverty about 1387, and three years later her husband followed his father-in-law to the grave. Christine, at the age of twenty-five, was left alone to support herself, three young children, a mother, and a niece.

Christine had no training for a trade or profession, but she was literate. She appears, at first, to have maintained her household by working as a copyist. In the days before the printing press, book sellers got their wares from scribes who wrote them out by hand. One benefit of being a copyist was the opportunity the job provided for self-education. A copyist was lent books to work with that otherwise might have been hard to come by, and copying a book meant reading it. This provided Christine with sufficient education to become an author herself.

In 1402 Christine published her first collection of poems, and she soon established herself as one of France's more popular and prolific writers. Some of her works dealt with the theme of love and drew on the romances that were staples of medieval popular literature. But she also treated more serious topics. She discussed politics and education and advised kings, dukes, and princes. She was particularly interested in the condition of women. She wrote extensively about the roles they had played in history and offered them advice on how to make the best of their current opportunities. Fittingly, Christine's last poem was a celebration of the deeds of a contemporary who vindicated her faith in the potential of women: Joan of Arc.

Question: What does the career of a woman like Christine de Pizan indicate about the strengths and weaknesses of late medieval society?

of wounded horses and men before its charge reached the English lines. Edward's knights then dashed in, completed the rout, and won a victory that was as complete as it was unexpected.

The lesson of Crécy was that the era of cavalry's dominance on medieval battlefields was coming to an end, and the reluctance of the French feudal aristocracy to accept this explains why the Hundred Years' War dragged on for so long. Small English armies using new methods repeatedly defeated larger French forces that insisted on fighting with outmoded techniques. England, however, never had the strength to exploit its victories and occupy France. All the

English could do was go home and celebrate their victories while the French prepared for the next round.

The medieval aristocracy owed its social and political supremacy to its military technology, but by the fourteenth century C.E. new weapons were making expensive aristocratic training and equipment anachronistic. Little instruction was needed to teach a man how to shoot a crossbow, a small bow that was bent by a crank and released by a trigger. But the crossbow was so lethal that the church tried to outlaw its use. It cost little to arm large numbers of men with longbows. Their six-foot length gave them great range and power, but a lot of practice was needed to master them. They were therefore used primarily by men from Wales and England who grew up with them. The Swiss developed a weapon called a pike—a combination long-handled spear, axe, and grappling hook. With it, a company of infantrymen could easily repulse a cavalry charge. By the fourteenth century C.E., gunpowder was also bringing primitive cannon and small arms onto battlefields—although these weapons were not yet very effective.

Knights defended themselves against the new weapons by increasing their armor, but heavier armor meant less mobility and vulnerability of a different kind. Infantry had dominated the battlefields of the ancient world. At the start of the Middle Ages, inventions such as the stirrup had permitted cavalry to gain the upper hand, and by the fourteenth century C.E., new inventions were again reversing the balance of power. This was clear to objective observers, but people are reluctant to abandon behaviors that are fundamental to their sense of identity and way of life. France's knights resisted acknowledging that the traditional military skills of their class were no longer effective, and their obduracy nearly cost France its independence.

As Edward aged, his son and designated heir, Edward "the Black Prince" (1330–1376) took over the reins of government. In 1356 at Poitiers the prince won a second major victory over the French that was nearly a repeat of his father's triumph at Crécy. He captured the French king, John II, "the Good" (r.1350–1364), and carted him off to captivity in England. John was a dubious prize. The rules of chivalry required that his English hosts foot the bill for maintaining him in a style appropriate to his rank, and during his absence, France was governed by his far more competent son, Charles V, "the Wise" (r. 1364–1380).

Charles earned his reputation for wisdom by giving up pitched battles with the English and turning conduct of the war over to a guerilla fighter, Bertrand du Guesclin (1320–1380). Du Guesclin's army was composed of mercenaries who valued victory and survival more highly than chivalry. The long war multiplied the numbers of men who fought for pay, and this added to the problems of the Age of Anxiety. Governments hired mercenaries for specific campaigns and then discharged them. Between bouts of employment, these professional soldiers, who had no fiefs to fall back on, supported themselves by freelance looting and raping.

There was a long lull in the Hundred Years' War in the second half of fourteenth century C.E. while England struggled with internal problems. The Black Prince, who had been raiding France from his base in Gascony, diverted his attention to civil wars in Spain. By 1367 his overtaxed Gascon subjects were in revolt, and he was suffering from an illness that slowly killed him. Edward turned his duties over to his brother, John of Gaunt, the Duke of Lancaster (1340–1399), and retired to England, where he died in 1376. By then, the aging Edward III was mentally incompetent. Because his heir, the Black Prince's son Richard, was still a minor, John of Gaunt governed England as a regent. But given the anomalous situation, he was barely able to restrain the quarrelsome English nobility.

When Richard II (r. 1377–1399) reached maturity, he was determined to exercise what he believed was his God-given right to autocratic power. This necessitated the destruction of some of England's powerful noblemen. When Richard attempted to strip his cousin, Henry of Lancaster, of his estates, England's barons realized that if Richard succeeded with Henry, none of them would be safe. They forced Richard to abdicate, and because he had no son, Henry, his nearest relative, took the throne.

Henry IV (r. 1399–1413) spent his reign defending his hold on the crown. His son, Henry V (r. 1413–1422), decided that the best way to promote his popularity with his subjects was to revive the war with France. In 1415, in what was virtually a repeat of Crécy and Poitiers, a large French army cornered the English invaders at Agincourt and was decimated by the English longbow. This time, however, the aftermath of the battle was different, for the situation in France had changed.

In 1392 France's king, Charles VI (r. 1380–1422), began to suffer bouts of insanity that required his confinement. His uncle, Philip of Burgundy, and his brother, Louis of Orléans, contested control of the regency for the disabled king. In 1407 Philip's heir, John "the Fearless," assassinated Louis, and war broke out between the Burgundian and Orléanist (or Armagnac) factions. The army that Henry V defeated at Agincourt was Orléanist. After their loss, the Orléanists tried to heal the breach with the Burgundians, but at the peace conference a disgruntled Orléanist avenged Louis's death by assassinating the Burgundian duke. The Burgundians promptly allied with Henry and helped the English capture Paris and Charles VI. Henry married Charles's daughter, Catherine, and in due course the union produced a male infant, the future Henry VI, who was declared heir to both England and France.

Charles VI's son, Charles "the Dauphin" (the title given to the heir to the French throne), fled to a region that was still under the control of the Orléanists, but his supporters were too dispirited and disorganized to put up much of a fight. Their prospects improved in 1422 C.E., when both Charles VI and Henry V died. The regents who governed for the infant King Henry VI (r. 1422–1461) were his two uncles. Although it was apparent that they could not work together, another seven years passed before the Dauphin's party took advantage of England's weakness. The Orléanists were finally prodded to action by a seventeen-year-old peasant girl named Joan of Arc (c. 1412–1431). She suddenly appeared at Charles's court and informed him that God had sent her to save France. Faith in Joan inspired the Dauphin's soldiers, and they began to role back the poorly led English. In 1429 they regained Reims, the city in whose cathedral France's kings were crowned, and the Dauphin was enthroned as King Charles VII (r. 1429–1461). The new king concluded that Joan had served her purpose and began to shunt her aside. When the Burgundians captured her in 1430, he declined to ransom her, and her captors sold her to the English. England hoped to demoralize the French by convicting Joan of heresy. After a lengthy trial, they burned her at the stake, but her death did not improve their situation. (The pope declared Joan's innocence in 1455, but the church did not canonize her until 1920.)

Duke Philip "the Good" of Burgundy sealed England's fate by making peace with Charles VII in 1435. England had no hope of resisting a united France, and by 1453, it had lost everything on the continent but the port city of Calais (which it retained until 1558). The French monarchy emerged from its humiliation stronger than ever. The long war, which was fought entirely on French territory, convinced the French that they needed a strong royal defender. The king's subjects knew that he had to have the power to act quickly and decisively. Therefore, they did not resist his efforts to tax them or force him to consult with them on major decisions. Wartime conditions prevented the Estates General from aspiring to the kinds of powers sought by the English Parliament and promoted the development of absolute monarchy in France.

Figure 11–3 Joan of Arc The art of portraiture began to be revived in the late Middle Ages. This picture of Joan of Arc dates to her era, but no one can be sure how accurately it describes her.

The situation in England was different. After a century of famous victories, the English king had to admit to his subjects that he had won the battles but lost the war. This damaged the prestige of the crown, and Henry VI lacked the talent to rebuild it. He was a weak, distracted ruler, and in 1453 he suffered a mental breakdown. A powerful faction formed in support of his more competent cousin, the duke of York, and in 1455 civil war erupted. The heraldic symbol of the king's Lancastrian family was a red rose, and that of his Yorkist cousins was a white rose. The conflict between them has therefore been dubbed the War of the Roses.

The Yorkists triumphed over the Lancastrians, but their tenure of the throne was brief. Edward IV (r. 1466–1483), who deposed Henry, left a thirteen-year-old heir who disappeared shortly after his father's death. The boy and his brother had been entrusted to an uncle who claimed their inheritance and declared himself King Richard III (r. 1483–1485 C.E.). Richard's title was quickly challenged by the exiled leader of the Lancastrian faction, Henry Tudor. Henry invaded England, and Richard died in battle, deserted by his followers. With Richard, the Plantagenet dynasty and England's medieval era came to an end. The new king, Henry VII (r. 1485–1509), founded the Tudor dynasty and began to rebuild the battered monarchy. Much was yet to happen, however, before England settled on what kind of royal government it would have.

Larger Issue Revisited

Periods of stress pose challenges that reveal the weaknesses and prove the strengths of individuals and institutions. The civilization that blossomed in Europe in the twelfth and thirteenth centuries was tested by the crises of the fourteenth and fifteenth. The church did not fare well. But the lapses in its performance gave the faithful the freedom to assume more responsibility for themselves and scholars a motive to think deeply about the nature of legitimate authority.

Plagues and economic difficulties confronted states with problems that were beyond their understanding and control, and the use to which they put the tools of government—legislation and war—probably made bad situations worse. The result, however, may have been a stronger, more open society. Feudalism declined in Western Europe. Economic opportunities improved for the masses. Wars decimated the ranks of the aristocracy, and popular uprisings hinted at new assertiveness on the part of ordinary people. Few persons outside of university circles were probably familiar with the philosophical treatises that developed rationales for individual autonomy, free inquiry, and representative government, but these characteristic features of modern Western civilization were beginning to affect people's lives.

Review Questions

1. What environmental factors helped render Europe vulnerable to pestilence?
2. Was religion the only source of medieval Europe's hostility to Islam?
3. How did traditional institutions, such as the church and state, respond to the challenges posed by the tense environment of the late Middle Ages?
4. How did reformers justify sitting in judgment on the popes (and kings) who were believed to be established by God?
5. Why was tiny England able to win so many victories and sustain such a long war with the much larger nation of France?
6. What strengths and weakness did the Age of Anxiety reveal in the fabric of European civilization?

Refer to the front of the book for a list of chapter-relevant primary sources available on the CD-ROM.

THE WEST INTERACTIVE

For web-based activities, map explorations, and quizzes related to this chapter, go to *www.prenhall.com/frankforter.*

CHAPTER 12

RENAISSANCE AND EXPLORATION

God gives man the power to have whatever he wants and be whatever he chooses. Animals possess at birth—from their mothers' wombs—all that they will ever have. At the Creation (or shortly thereafter) the angels became what they will be forever. But when man appeared, God the Father endowed him with the potentials of all living things. Whatever each person cultivates will mature and bear its fruit through him.

—**Giovanni Pico della Mirandola**

Larger Issue: *How should a society use its history?*

Giovanni Pico della Mirandola had high ambitions for himself and for all humanity. The youngest son of the ruler of a tiny state in Italy's Po Valley, he studied at the universities of Bologna, Padua, and Paris, where he was particularly attracted to Hebrew literature. Pico believed that the insights of major thinkers from all the ancient Western civilizations—Greek, Latin, Hebrew, and Arabic—could be reconciled, and at the young age of 23 he set out to prove this by defending some nine hundred theses. When the church condemned thirteen of his propositions as heretical, Pico fled to France. A powerful patron interceded for him, and he was allowed to return to Italy to live out the remainder of his short life in Florence, the capital of the Renaissance.

Pico's celebration of human potential—his faith in the power of people to shape their own destinies—signaled a shift in European intellectual history. Early medieval thinkers, such as Augustine of Hippo (354–430 C.E.), claimed that sin rendered human nature impotent and turned the world into a worthless realm doomed to extinction. They denigrated earthly life as something from which people waited to be rescued by God's grace. There was much in both pagan philosophy and sacred literature to support their view, but Renaissance optimists like Pico believed that these thinkers had missed a more fundamental truth. The Bible's Creator-God had imparted His image to human beings, pronounced their world good, and ordered them to go forth to populate and subdue it. God's prime directive was a command that human beings share the divine work of bringing Creation—themselves included—to completion.

Pico was not alone in proclaiming the "dignity" and "excellence" of humanity. The architect Leon Battista Alberti (1404–1472) spoke for many when he asserted that "man can do everything that he sets his mind to." This, the Renaissance's proponents argued, was not a groundless faith but a truth taught by scripture and the Greek and Roman sages. What set men like Pico and Alberti apart from their medieval predecessors and made them "modern" men was their rediscovery of ancient wisdom.

The church and conservative scholars of the Renaissance era believed that it was wrong to put too much trust in human virtue, rationality, and self-sufficiency. Much in history undercut Pico's kind of confidence in human nature, and this, they claimed, was the true ancient wisdom. This pessimistic view of human history cautioned against bold departures from tradition and attacks on the *status quo*.

Western civilization has repeatedly reengaged its own history. Sometimes the past has served as a "dead hand," a legacy that caps what people permit themselves to think and do. It inspires a kind of religious fundamentalism, a belief that certain ideas or institutions transcend history and may not be challenged. Excessive veneration for the past may retard development, but it can also provide security during turbulent times. Conversely, a revival of interest in a historical era may prompt people to think about their own era in new ways. It can inspire critiques of received truths and launch reform movements. Either way, the past shapes the present and, therefore, the future. Much depends on how a society handles its history.

 TOPICS IN THIS CHAPTER

The Context for the Renaissance • The Culture of the Renaissance • The Northern Renaissance • Europe: Centers of Conflict • The Middle East: The Ottoman Empire • Europe and Atlantic Exploration

The Context for the Renaissance

The Renaissance is controversial. Historians debate when it began, how it should be defined, and even its importance. Some scholars stress the Renaissance's role in ending the medieval era and launching the modern world. Others emphasize its continuity with the Middle Ages and note that its effects were limited. All, however, agree that Italy holds the key to understanding it.

Formation of City-States in Italy   The Renaissance was the product of late medieval Italy's unique urban institutions. The commercial revolution of the High Middle Ages scattered towns across the map of Europe, but city life flourished more vigorously in Italy than elsewhere. By 1400, four of Europe's five largest cities (Genoa, Florence, Milan, and Venice) were in Italy. Only Paris (at about eighty thousand) was their equal. Italy had about twenty cities in the second rank with populations of about twenty-five thousand. In the rest of Europe, there were only four.

Size and number were not all that made Italy's cities noteworthy. In most of Europe a city's jurisdiction ended at its walls, but Italy's cities controlled the countryside around them. Cities in northern Europe were tiny islands in a sea of feudalism, but Italian cities became self-governing city-states that bore some resemblance to the towns of the ancient Greeks and Romans. The territories they controlled were, however, usually small. Often, their farthest frontiers were only a day's ride from their urban centers.

Geography encouraged the growth of city-states in Italy, for the peninsula was divided into separate agricultural districts. In some of these, traces of the old Roman *civitates* survived. Politics also prodded towns to become city-states. When the Carolingian Empire disintegrated in the ninth century C.E., local kings survived in France and Germany, but not in Italy. Because there was no native dynasty fighting to centralize government, Italy's regional governments were unopposed. Italians supported them, for they offered the only defense against the German kings who repeatedly invaded the peninsula. Italians also had to deal with the complications created by the Papal States. Rome was the seat for a papal government that claimed international jurisdiction. Popes regarded any attempt by a secular ruler to unite Italy as a threat to their independence, and their diplomatic and military maneuvers caused endless problems for Italy's other leaders.

Italy's feudal nobles had no native king behind whom to rally as they struggled to fend off Germany's invasions. However, the nobles were inclined to cooperate with the governments of the urban communities that sprang up in the eleventh and twelfth centuries C.E., for townspeople shared their opposition to German domination. Town and country had economic as well as political interests in common. Towns bought the products raised on the nobles' rural estates. Over time, nobles moved into town, intermarried with bourgeois families, integrated into urban life, and, as the distinction between town and country faded, a city-state appeared.

Different kinds of states developed in different parts of Italy (see Map 12–1). The southern half of the peninsula was a feudal kingdom centered on Naples. Its rulers were preoccupied with Sicily and expansion across the Adriatic into Greek territory. The Papal States, which spanned the center of Italy and extended up the Adriatic coast into the former Byzantine exarchate of Ravenna, were unstable. Entrenched aristocratic families competed for control of the papacy, and the popes, who were often elderly men with short reigns, had difficulty maintaining order. Northern Italy was divided among major and minor city-states that experimented with different kinds of governments. Some (primarily Venice, Florence, Genoa, Lucca, Pisa, and Siena) called themselves republics. Others (Milan, Ferrara, Mantua, and Modena) were duchies. Functionally, all were oligarchies. That is, they were dominated by wealthy minorities.

Italy's cities were politically turbulent, for their governments were constantly evolving. Many began as republics of one kind or another, for they were founded as communes—as associations of people who voluntarily banded together for mutual benefit. Most communes were administered by a town council (of a hundred or more members) assisted by a pair of executive officers. Checks and balances and short terms in office prevented individuals from becoming too powerful. Town life was chaotic, however, for family and clan groups competed for control of communes. They built fortified towers inside towns and sallied forth to battle one another in the streets. Trade and merchant guilds and various kinds of fraternities also had their agendas, and their shifting alliances kept factions volatile and politics in turmoil. A commune's leaders had a constant struggle to persuade the numerous self-interested groups that composed it to work together. If a hopeless stalemate developed, it became common by the second half of the twelfth century C.E. for a town to suspend its constitution and temporarily turn itself over to a *podestà*. A *podestà* was an outsider who was empowered to govern a town for a limited period of time. Because he was a neutral stranger, factions trusted him to arbitrate their disputes and get their community back on track. The danger, of course, was that a *podestà* might make his lordship permanent. This happened frequently, for republics were far less efficient and less able to defend themselves than states ruled by autocrats.

Italy's Economy and the Renaissance   The Renaissance was, partially, a response to Italy's challenging political situation, but the country's economy made an even greater contribution to its development. Renaissance society was preoccupied with possessions and conspicuous consumption. Its materialism reflected conditions that caused unusual amounts of wealth to accumulate in Italy. Geography allowed Italy to dominate trade between Europe and the Middle East. Profits from this commerce provided capital to fund banks, and Italy's bankers became Europe's leading financiers. Italians sent little of their money abroad to pay for

▤	Duchy of Milan	▨	Republic of Venice
▥	Republic of Genoa	⬚	Papal States
▦	Republic of Florence	▨	Kingdom of Naples

Map 12–1  **Renaissance Italy** This map simplifies Renaissance Italy's complicated political geography. Boundaries shifted frequently. States appeared and disappeared, and leagues and alliances repeatedly rearranged the political landscape. **Question:** What sorts of features of geography and environment might explain why Italy's cities clustered in the northern half of the peninsula?

imported goods, for Italy had sufficient raw materials to supply its industries, enough agricultural production to feed its population, and monopolies on the manufacture of many of the luxury goods its people consumed. Additional wealth entered the country with the German, French, and Spanish armies that repeatedly invaded, and the papal treasury in Rome siphoned funds from every corner of Europe. Political fragmentation prevented a single ruler from monopolizing these resources, and chronic instability kept society open and wealth circulating. Italy, in short, provided an ideal environment for the growth of a capitalist middle class. The Renaissance was, in many ways, an affirmation of the lifestyle of a prosperous, powerful, and self-aware bourgeoisie.

The Culture of the Renaissance

Most modern people associate Italy's Renaissance with the arts—sculpture, painting, and architecture. But the Renaissance was above all a literary movement focused on the study of ancient Greek and Roman texts. Its scholars searched for forgotten manuscripts, and they found a few long-disregarded works by ancient authors. But the Renaissance owed less to the discovery of new documents than to the development of a new way of reading old ones. Medieval scholars had mined classical literature for useful ideas. But when Renaissance scholars began to read this literature for itself, they discovered an ancient way of life that seemed to affirm their own.

The Renaissance's Humanist Agenda

The intellectual leaders of the Renaissance are classified as humanists, for they advocated what they called *studia humanitatis,* the study of humanity. They were not, however, what modern America thinks of as secular humanists. They were far from hostile to religion, as the art collection of any major museum (with its Renaissance Madonnas and religious paintings) will demonstrate. They did, however, value the material world and secular life more highly than their medieval predecessors had.

Renaissance humanists were professional scholars. Their academic specialty was rhetoric, the study of the works of ancient orators such as Cicero and Seneca. Their more traditional faculty colleagues, the scholastic dialecticians who worshiped Aristotle, believed that the function of language was to construct logical arguments. The humanists, on the other hand, thought of language as an instrument for persuasion. Rationality was all that mattered for the scholastics. But humanists maintained that will and passion also were important, for people were more than reasoning machines. Logic and detached contemplation were not enough; to be convinced of truths and fulfilled as individuals, people needed action, empathy, and engagement with the world.

The humanists's philosophy of life affirmed the values of Italy's urban classes. Humanists believed that people should marry, have families, shoulder political responsibilities, develop their individual talents, and enjoy the beauties and pleasures of the material world. They maintained that a fully human life was packed with action and achievement, and that a fully developed human being was a multifaceted individual who was interested in everything and able to do all things well. This was more than a theory; it was a reasonably accurate description of some of the giants of the Renaissance.

Poets and Prose Writers

Early signs of the Renaissance appear in the work of the poet Dante Alighieri (1265–1321) and emerge more clearly in the writings of two of his fellow Florentines of the next generation: Petrarch (1304–1374) and Boccaccio (1313–1375). All three, as was the medieval custom, wrote in Latin when addressing the scholarly community, but their fame derives in large part from what they wrote in Italian. Humanists dedicated themselves to the study of the classical languages, but they understood that Latin and Greek had been the speech of ordinary people in the ancient world. They concluded, therefore, that poets and serious thinkers ought to use the tongues common to the era in which they lived.

Dante's thought was deeply rooted in the Middle Ages, but he lived like a Renaissance intellectual. Most medieval scholars took clerical orders, but not Dante. He married, had a family, and pursued a political career. He became a professional man of letters after his party's fall from power forced him to leave Florence and spend the rest of his life in exile.

Among Dante's Latin works was a treatise *(De vulgari eloquentia)* that urged scholars to break with tradition and write in the vernacular so that a wider audience might profit from their discussions. Dante practiced what he preached—with phenomenal success. About 1293 C.E., while he was still living in Florence, he finished *Vita Nuova (New Life),* a cycle of lyric poems and prose narratives celebrating his passion for a woman he called Beatrice. She was not his wife or mistress, but a feminine ideal whom he adored, like a medieval courtly lover, from afar. His masterwork was a huge poem written during his years in exile. He called it *Comedia,* not because it was funny, but because, unlike a tragedy, it was a story with a happy ending. *The Divine Comedy,* the title Dante's readers gave his poem, purports to describe a dream in which the poet journeys through Hell and Purgatory to Heaven, where he is granted a vision of God. Dante's guide during the first stages of his trip is the pagan Roman poet Virgil (70–19 B.C.E.). Because medieval scholars thought that one of Virgil's poems had predicted the birth of Christ, Virgil served Dante as a symbol for the truths that reason can intuit without the help of faith. Because reason does not require scripture or revelation to understand society's need for laws and their enforcement, Virgil is equipped to lead Dante through the realms of punishment—Hell and Purgatory. But because reason cannot grasp the mysteries of divine grace, Virgil halts at the gates of Heaven, and Beatrice, Dante's love, appears to lead him into Paradise. *The Divine Comedy's* cosmology and theology are medieval, but its respect for the dignity of human nature and human love hints at the emerging Renaissance. Dante has a higher opinion of some of the sinners whose punishments he describes in Hell than of spiritless people who go to their graves having done nothing either good or bad.

Petrarch studied at a university, was ordained a priest, and sought ecclesiastical stipends to support his work. At first glance, therefore, his scholarly career looks more conventional than Dante's, but the two men had much in common. Petrarch formed an attachment with a woman and was a family man with a son and daughter. He shared Dante's interest in the poetry of courtly love, and his equivalent of Dante's Beatrice was an unidentified woman whom he called Laura. The sonnets she inspired him to write in Italian are his most popular compositions.

The Renaissance shines more clearly in Petrarch's work than Dante's primarily because of the emphasis Petrarch placed on the study of the classics. Petrarch has been called "the father of humanism" because of the role he played in sparking the Renaissance's passion for classical literature. Petrarch claimed that intellectual darkness had descended on Europe after Rome's fall, but that the light of civilization was being rekindled for his generation. Progress, he argued, required an educational reform based on a curriculum that emphasized literary skills (Latin grammar, rhetoric, and poetry) and moral edification (Roman history and Greek philosophy). He urged scholars to comb through Europe's libraries for forgotten works by ancient authors, and he himself found a collection of Cicero's letters. Petrarch believed that he and his contemporaries could pick up where the ancients had left off. He encouraged the use of classical Latin rather than the simpler ecclesiastical Latin that had evolved during the Middle Ages. His most ambitious attempt to honor the classical tradition was a poem entitled *Africa,* a Latin epic on the life of the Roman republican general, Scipio Africanus (237–183 B.C.E.). It dealt with the struggles leading to the triumph of the Roman Republic. In 1341 the people of Rome gathered on the Capitoline Hill to award Petrarch the ancient symbol of artistic achievement, a crown of laurel. Petrarch's love for the classics persuaded him that fame was a noble pursuit, but it did not override his Christian concern for the sin of pride. He took his pagan trophy to the Vatican and dedicated it to God.

Boccaccio, the illegitimate son of a Florentine banker, was Petrarch's devoted disciple. Petrarch's influence persuaded Boccaccio to abandon the poetry and storytelling of his youth and take up classical studies. He wrote a number of books in Latin that served his contemporaries as useful compendia of information from the ancient world. The most popular of these were a genealogical encyclopedia of the pagan gods and collections of biographies of famous men and women. His more well-known compositions, however, are his earlier vernacular works, the most famous of which is a vast collection of bawdy and serious tales entitled *Decameron.* It purports to be an account of the stories that ten young men and women told to entertain themselves while they hid from the plague in the comfort of a luxurious country house. Like Dante and Petrarch, Boccaccio was inspired to write poetry by love for a woman. But unlike Dante and probably Petrarch, he had a physical relationship with Fiammetta, the lady whom he idolized. When she deserted him, he poured out his anguish in his poetry. The intimacy and personal nature of these poems reflect the Renaissance's belief that the emotions and interior life of the individual are worthy of study and documentation.

Boccaccio's contemporary, the English author Geoffrey Chaucer (c. 1340–1400), shared this faith. Chaucer, like many of the pioneers of the Renaissance, was a son of the middle classes with a background in business and experience in politics. He is not usually thought of as a Renaissance figure, but he read Italian and modeled some of his poems on Boccaccio's. Italy's Renaissance would not have spread so readily to the rest of Europe if cultures north of the Alps had not, on their own, been evolving similar values and interests. Chaucer's most popular work, the *Canterbury Tales,* describes a company of pilgrims en route to the shrine of St. Thomas Becket at Canterbury. Chaucer introduces each pilgrim and then repeats the stories each of them tells to amuse the others. The characters in the *Canterbury Tales* are unique, memorable persons, and Chaucer bestows individuality on his pilgrims by matching his descriptions of them with the stories they tell.

Sculptors   Vernacular literature helped to spread the Renaissance beyond the narrow circle of humanist scholars, but literature was not the only thing that helped the Renaissance extend its influence. Artists and architects created urban environments that exposed ordinary men and women to the spirit of the new age.

Artifacts of Roman civilization were more abundant in late medieval Italy than they are today, and their influence on Italy's sculptors is apparent as early as the thirteenth century C.E. Real bodies seem to exist beneath the classical robes with which Nicola Pisano (c. 1220–1284) and his son Giovanni (c. 1250–1320) draped their figures. Renaissance artists did not, however, simply copy ancient models. They combined the idealism of classical art with a new realism that reflected the humanists' emphasis on the individual. Many ancient Greek statues have a detached, timeless quality that renders them static. Renaissance sculptors, for their part, tried to convey a greater sense of existing not in eternity, but in a particular moment. They portrayed ideal types, but with a novel vibrancy. Their medieval predecessors had conceived of statuary as architectural ornament and subordinated it to the lines of the buildings it decorated. But the Florentine sculptor Donatello (1386–1466) revived the art of carving statues that, like those in the ancient world, were meant to stand alone and be viewed in the round. They were so natural and imbued with life that some people found them shocking. The early work of Michelangelo (1475–1564), particularly the gigantic *David* he created to stand in front of Florence's town hall, represents the humanist ideals of the Renaissance at their best. *David's* heroic nudity proclaims the glory of an idealized human body, but *David* is not an abstract study of mathematical proportions. The statue's outsized head and hands impart tension to its design, and the look on David's face hints at the youth's thoughts as he heads into his unequal contest with the giant, Goliath (I Samuel 17).

Architects   Because Italians had never cared much for the Gothic style that originated in France in the twelfth century C.E., they had continued the older Romanesque tradition and thus maintained more continuity with the classical world. The Renaissance's architects drew

People in Context: Elisabetta Gonzaga (1472–1526)

Feminist historians have pointed out that the Renaissance did not affect men and women in the same way. The respect the period accorded individual talent and achievement in the secular realm—in politics, business, and family life—opened doors for some men. But the ancient Greek and Roman societies that the Renaissance admired were thoroughly patriarchal, and their attitude influenced the humanist perspective on the family. It gave new currency to the ancient belief that women (despite the independence some of them enjoyed in the Roman era) should be confined to the domestic sphere and subordinated to the male heads of their households. Economic reality had more to do with the status of women in most poor and middle-class families than did humanist ideology, for these women had to work to help support their families. But the upper class could afford to curtail the activities of its women. This deprived aristocratic women of some of the rights and opportunities they had enjoyed under the feudal system, and their fate ultimately affected their lesser sisters. The upper class set the standards that the middle class adopted whenever it could afford to—an aspiration for status that gave Elisabetta Gonzaga's life an importance she could never had anticipated.

At the age of sixteen, Elisabetta, whose family, the Gonzaga, ruled the tiny Italian state of Mantua, wed Guidobaldo da Montefeltro, the duke of Urbino. Her husband was a friend of humanists, an art collector, and the owner of one of the larger libraries in Italy. As the duchess of Urbino, Elisabetta presided over a court famous for its refinement and elegance.

Baldassare Castiglione (1478–1529), the count of Novellata and a distinguished papal diplomat, spent his early career in the service of Urbino's duke. Near the end of his life, Castiglione drew on his extensive experience with court life to write *The Book of the Courtier,* a kind of guidebook to the upper reaches of Renaissance society. The volume was translated into numerous languages and remained a best seller for over a century. It made Elisabetta famous.

The Book of the Courtier purports to be an account of conversations at Elisabetta's court. It describes a kind of salon where Elisabetta and her guests debate the nature of gentility and, not surprisingly, come to the conclusion that their hostess is the ideal Renaissance lady. Elisabetta is praised for her humanist education—for a knowledge of literature, art, and music that ensures that cultured men find her conversation worthy of their time. But her special vocation as a woman is to keep her court running smoothly and, by her charm and elegant behavior, elevate its tone. The physical activities in which men indulge—riding, hunting, and warfare—are beneath her. She attends to the domestic sphere and serves the world by civilizing the men who run it.

Some of Elisabetta's aristocratic female acquaintances were cut from different cloth. They governed states and did not shrink from violence and bloodshed. She, however, appears really to have been the kind of gracious, but submissive, woman that Castiglione described. Thanks to the success of his book, generations of Europeans thought of her as the embodiment of the feminine ideal to which all women should aspire.

Question Do a society's theories about ideal gender roles accurately describe how its people actually behave ?

Figure 12–1 Michelangelo's *David* Several of the Renaissance's most famous artists sculpted statues of David, the young shepherd who became king of Israel. Most depict him after his victory over the Philistine giant, Goliath. However, the fourteen-foot-tall *David* that Michelangelo completed for Florence in 1504 shows the youth before the battle—before anything is resolved. The nude males sculpted by the ancient Greeks inspired Michelangelo, but unlike their timeless images, his *David* is focused on a particular moment and seems to have an interior life.

both inspiration and, unfortunately, building materials from Italy's abundant Roman ruins (from which marble, columns, and bronze ornaments were plundered for use in new structures). A book on architecture by Vitruvius, a first-century C.E. Roman engineer, that came to light in the fifteenth century C.E., also helped spread knowledge of the principles underlying classical designs.

The first of the great Renaissance architects was Filippo Brunelleschi (1377–1446). The dome he designed for Florence's cathedral is an engineering marvel, and it still dominates the city's skyline. Brunelleschi intensively studied Roman buildings, but, like the sculptors of the Renaissance, he did not merely copy his models. He admired their symmetry, simplicity, and proportions, and he used their standard design elements (pillars and round arches, for example). But by the way in which he manipulated these things, he mated Renaissance energy with classical stability.

The most ambitious of the Renaissance's building projects was the reconstruction of Europe's largest church, St. Peter's at the Vatican. The basilica that the Emperor Constantine had built there for the popes in the fourth century C.E. had deteriorated so badly by the end of the Middle Ages that Pope Nicholas V (r. 1447–1455) proposed to tear it down and replace it. The work dragged on for two centuries and involved over a dozen architects, the most important of whom were Donato Bramante (1444–1514), Michelangelo (1475–1564), and Gianlorenzo Bernini (1598–1680). Michelangelo was not only a superb sculptor, but also a brilliant architect, an extraordinary painter, and a competent poet. The frescoes he created for the vault and altar wall of the Vatican's Sistine Chapel (named for its builder, Pope Sixtus IV, r. 1471–1484) are a miracle of design and execution.

Painters   Unlike sculptors and architects, Renaissance painters had few ancient examples of their art to study. They were influenced by classical sculpture but had to invent the techniques that translated its lessons to the two-dimensional surfaces of their paintings.

Medieval artists thought of paintings as pages of text. Influenced by Byzantine design, they drew two-dimensional figures against blank backgrounds and often combined different scenes from a story in the same composition. A single painting of the Virgin Mary might, for instance, depict the annunciation, the birth of Jesus, and the Virgin's ascent to heaven. Its overall design could be aesthetically pleasing, but its meaning only became clear when its elements were separated and read like words on a page. Renaissance paintings were not pages, but windows. They framed a scene—a view of a realistic, three-dimensional world into which a spectator could imagine stepping.

The Florentine painter Cimabue (c. 1240–1302) worked in the medieval Byzantine style but anticipated the Renaissance by experimenting with techniques of perspective drawing and by giving the faces of his subjects individuality and emotional intensity. Giotto di Bondone (1267–1337), his student, went much farther in these directions. His human subjects manifest strong feelings and move in real space—like actors in theatrical scenes. The epidemic that began to spread through Europe in 1348 may explain why Giotto had no immediate successor. Eventually, however, a Florentine called Masaccio (1401–1428) picked up where Giotto left off, and an extraordinary number of great artists appeared over the course of a few generations.

Renaissance painters added a new medium to their art. Medieval and early Renaissance painters usually worked in tempera, that is, with pigments mixed with a binder such as egg

Figure 12–2 Brunelleschi's Church of San Lorenzo In 1418 Brunelleschi remodeled the church in Florence where the Medici family, the wealthy and powerful patrons of the Renaissance, worshiped. He revived the ancient basilican plan favored by Rome's early Christians, but the room he designed had a greater rhythmic intensity than usually found in a classical building.

yolk. They painted on wooden boards or walls covered with wet plaster. Tempera was a restrictive medium, for it dried quickly and its colors did not blend well. Northern European painters were the first to discover that these difficulties could be overcome by mixing their pigments with oils. Oils dried slowly, and translucent oil-based paints could be applied in multiple layers to produce an infinite variety of intense, glowing colors. There is literary evidence for oil painting as early as the twelfth century C.E., but the first great practitioners of the art were the Netherlanders, Hubert (c. 1366–1426) and Jan van Eyck (c. 1390–1441) and

✦ Chronology: Leading Artists and Authors of Italy's Renaissance

```
ca. 1220 Nicola Pisano 1284
        1240 Cimabue 1302
           1250 Giovanni Pisano 1320
              1265 Dante      1321
              1267 Giotto       1237
```

```
1295 Andrea Pisano 1348
     1304 Petrarch      1374
     1313 Boccaccio 1375
```

```
1377 Brunelleschi        1446
  1378 Ghiberti            1455
    1386 Donatello          1466
      1395 Fra Angelico  1455
        1399 Della Robbia          1482
          1400 Jacopo Bellini   1470
          1401 Masaccio 1428
            1406 Filippo Lippi 1469
             1407 Lorenzo Valla 1457
               1415 Piero della Francesca  1492
                  1429 Gentile Bellini       1507
                  1430 Giovanni Bellini        1516
                  1431 Mantegna        1506
                  1435 Verrocchio 1488
                    1444 Bramante   1514
                    1445 Botticelli  1510
                      1452 da Vinci      1519
                       1457 Filippino Lippi 1504
                          1469 Machiavelli        1527
                            1475 Michelangelo        1564
                            1475 Giorgione 1510
                              1483 Raphael    1520
                                1485 Titian                1576
                                   1500 Cellini 1571
                                    1518 Palladio 1580
```

Dirk Bouts (1415–1475). They filled their pictures with a wealth of detail—precisely describing the physical world and representing the gleam or texture of all kinds of materials. Northerners also pioneered landscape painting.

Venetian artists introduced oil painting to Italy in the late fifteenth century C.E., along with a second northern invention: the use of a canvas on stretchers as a surface for a painting. By reducing the cost of pictures and improving their portability, this expanded the market for art and broke the church's monopoly on patronage. The prospering urban classes began to commission paintings, and artists found plenty of work producing decorative objects to satisfy the Renaissance's taste for luxury and conspicuous consumption. The era's renewed respect for the individual also created a demand for a kind of art that had virtually disappeared during the Middle Ages: portraiture.

The Northern Renaissance

The Arts   Toward the end of the fifteenth century C.E., the Renaissance began to make its influence felt north of the Alps, where it competed with a still vibrant medieval tradition. Gothic architecture was far from dead, particularly in England where a refined and delicate "perpendicular Gothic" style flourished. The work of northern painters, such as Hubert and Jan van Eck, owed more to the tradition of medieval manuscript illumination than to Renaissance classicism.

Albrecht Dürer (1471–1528) was the first northern artist to take an interest in Italy's Renaissance. He was a citizen of Nuremberg, an independent German city that had extensive commercial ties with Italy. Many of Italy's Renaissance artists were trained in the shops of goldsmiths. Dürer's father was a goldsmith, and Dürer practiced the related art of engraving. His interest in prints probably alerted him to what Italian artists were doing and motivated him to make several trips to Italy. Dürer immersed himself in the rapidly growing literature dealing with the laws of perspective and the relationship between draftsmanship and mathematics. He read classical authors, studied ancient statuary, and became convinced that art had to be informed by a close, scientific study of nature. His filled his files with detailed sketches of plants, animals, and people with interesting faces. He was excited about the artistic potential of the newly invented printing press. He produced a large number of woodcuts and engravings that, because they were issued in multiple copies, were cheap enough to be purchased by art lovers of modest means. The printing press acquainted an ever widening spectrum of European society with the arts of the Renaissance, and politicians quickly realized what print makers could contribute to their propaganda campaigns.

Northerners came to Italy to study the Renaissance, but Italian artists also found work in northern capitals. Leonardo da Vinci (1452–1519), whose *Mona Lisa* may be the most famous portrait from the Renaissance era, was employed by King Francis I (r. 1515–1547) of France. Francis's political aspirations may explain why he was the first of northern Europe's kings to take an interest in the Renaissance. After the Germans retreated from Italy, the French tried to move in. Francis mounted an expedition in 1525. It failed spectacularly, but even futile military ventures spread the Renaissance. The hordes of foreign soldiers they brought into Italy absorbed its Renaissance culture and took it home.

Northern Humanism   There were environmental differences between northern Europe and Italy that help to explain differences in the interests of their scholars. Northern Europe had few if any Roman ruins to remind people of the grandeurs of classical civilization, and its towns bore little resemblance to the classical world's city-states. It was not the pagan past that attracted northern scholars, but the early Christian era.

Northern humanism was energized by a religious revival—the Modern Devotion—that originated in the Netherlands in the fourteenth century C.E.. It inspired the foundation of quasi-monastic organizations devoted to charitable work and education. The schools maintained by the most famous of these, the Brethren of the Common Life, were noteworthy for the training they provided in the ancient languages—an education needed for the intensive study of the Bible in which the Brethren engaged.

The most prominent of the northern humanists, Desiderius Erasmus (1466–1536), was schooled by the Brethren of the Common Life. He was the illegitimate son of a learned priest who developed an interest in humanism while visiting Italy. Erasmus, as was customary in the Middle Ages, sought support for a life of scholarship by entering the church. He became a monk and was ordained a priest, but soon realized that this was a mistake. He found monastic life stultifying, and he was no happier when his superiors sent him to study theology at the University of Paris. The scholasticism that held sway in Paris repulsed Erasmus and drove him into the humanists's camp.

Erasmus, like other Renaissance intellectuals, believed that scholars should not keep their work to themselves, but use it to benefit the masses. His major scholarly achievement was a superior edition of the Greek New Testament based on a critical study of ancient manuscripts. The text improved the accuracy of Latin and vernacular translations. Erasmus wanted the church to jettison much of the baggage it had accumulated during the Middle Ages and revert to the simplicity of the New Testament era. Authentic Christianity, he argued, was a way of life guided by a personal faith, and the best way to build that faith was to give ordinary people a Bible they could read for themselves. He had little sympathy for clergy who wanted to keep their congregations ignorant and subservient. One of his most popular books, *Praise of Folly,* was a social satire that targeted the clergy. Erasmus was such an outspoken critic of medieval Catholicism that his contemporaries joked that he laid the "egg" that the Protestant reformers hatched. When the Reformation broke out, however, Erasmus, like his friend the English humanist, Thomas More (1478–1535), was unwilling to leave the Catholic Church. He agreed with the Protestants that the church should be reformed to bring it more in line with the New Testament, but as a humanist, he preferred a more tempered and rational faith than the Reformers were preaching (see Chapter 13, "Reformation, Religious Wars, and National Conflicts").

Europe: Centers of Conflict

England had separated from France by the end of the fifteenth century C.E., but many political borders on the continent continued to be disputed long after the Middle Ages drew to a close. The contours of the modern European nations were slow to emerge—due in large part to the persisting fragmentation of Italy and Germany. Their weakness invited foreign invasions, internal struggles, and various schemes for carving up their territory.

Italy and France   The Hohenstaufen emperor Frederick II had alarmed the papacy and the cities of northern Italy by nearly winning control of Italy. They eagerly seized on the opportunity his sudden death (1250) gave them to attack his heirs and exterminate the dynasty. In 1266 the pope invited France to intervene in Italy to help him eliminate Frederick's descendants. King Louis IX's brother, Charles of Anjou (1226–1285), invaded and took possession of the kingdoms of Naples and Sicily. In 1282 Sicily repudiated Charles and turned itself over to Aragon, a kingdom on the northeastern coast of Spain that was becoming a maritime power. However, the French retained Naples, and Naples gave them an excuse to continue to dabble in Italy's politics.

Italy's city-states used the intervals between foreign invasions to fight among themselves. One of the largest and most powerful of these was Milan, a northern duchy that lacked access to the sea but controlled approaches to vital passes through the Alps. The Visconti family ruled Milan until 1447. Then it passed to a Visconti son-in-law, the founder of the Sforza dynasty. Genoa, Milan's western neighbor, was a small coastal republic dominated by a powerful merchant oligarchy. It had a large navy and was one of Italy's richest ports. Venice, the island city at the top of the Adriatic that ruled the northeast corner of Italy, was Genoa's chief competitor for Mediterranean trade. Its wealth derived from its commercial ties with Constantinople and the Byzantine Empire. Venice, like Genoa, was formally a republic and functionally an oligarchy. Thanks to a complicated constitution that minimized the formation of political power blocks, it enjoyed unusually stable government for its era. Factionalism plagued most Italian city-states and none more than Florence, the cultural capital of the Renaissance.

Florence, an inland city on the Arno River, was a textile manufacturing center that expanded into banking and international finance. By 1350 Florence's first bankers, the Riccardi, Frescobaldi, Peruzzi, and Bardi families, had all failed—due in large part to the refusal of kings to repay their loans. However, the bank that Giovanni de' Medici (1360–1429) subsequently founded restored Florence's financial leadership. His fabulously wealthy Medici family won control over the city's republican government and then turned Florence into a duchy. Giovanni's son, Cosimo (1389–1464), was the family's first great patron of Renaissance humanists and artists, and his grandson, Lorenzo "the Magnificent" (1449–1492), attached some of the Renaissance's greatest artists, including the young Michelangelo, to his household.

Disputes among political parties threatened Florence's internal stability, and the city was deeply enmeshed in the convoluted power struggles of the papacy and rival city-states. Its troubles prompted some deep thinking about politics and the lessons of history. *The Prince,* a book by Nicolò Machiavelli (1469–1527), the most famous of Florence's historians and political theorists, is a fundamental text for the study of political science. It purports to be a primer written to instruct a young Medici heir in the arts of government. Its overriding message is that a ruler should allow nothing—religion, morality, law, or conscience—to stand in the way of the pursuit of power. The book so bluntly advocates the use of "Machiavellian" methods to achieve success at any price that some readers believe that Machiavelli, who expressed republican sympathies in his other works, intended it as a joke. Ultimately, however, Italy's turbulent history may have convinced Machiavelli that nothing mattered more than the establishment of a government strong enough to maintain order.

In 1516 (three years after *The Prince* appeared), Machiavelli's English contemporary and Erasmus's friend, Thomas More, published a witty satire that was similarly pessimistic in its assessment of politics. More called his book and the mythical society it described *Utopia* (Greek for "No-place"). More's Utopians behave completely rationally, which, as More's descriptions of their customs illustrate, Europeans clearly did not. Like Machiavelli, More was acutely aware of the gap between what human beings are and what they might aspire to be.

Germany and the Holy Roman Empire   Frederick II had largely ignored Germany as he struggled vainly to win control of Italy, and after his death, the German nobles were slow to seat a new dynasty. The German imperial throne remained vacant from 1254 to 1274. In the interim, no one challenged the independence of the country's hundreds of political entities. Some regions were governed as hereditary duchies. Some were ruled by the church. Many were tiny feudal baronies or urban republics and oligarchies. The most interesting political organization was a powerful league of cities.

The German merchants who operated in the Baltic region compensated for the absence of a royal protector by forming a corporation *(Hanse)* and working together to defend themselves. The cities of the Hanseatic League, which was formally established in 1359, did not occupy contiguous territories, but the army and navy they maintained controlled the land and sea routes that connected them. At the league's peak, it had about 170 members and exercised a virtual monopoly over Baltic and North Sea commerce. It dominated the Scandinavian kingdoms, and England and France treated it as if it were a sovereign state. The development of Atlantic trade routes finally eroded its economic clout, but it survived into the seventeenth century C.E.

The most significant political developments in Germany involved its eastern borderlands. In 1248 the family that ruled the duchy of Austria died out. Austria should then have returned to its overlord, Frederick II, but he was too preoccupied with wars in Italy to assert his claim to it. A year after his death in 1250, Ottokar II (r. 1253–1278), king of Bohemia (the region around Prague), annexed Austria. So long as Germany had no king, there was no one to challenge him.

The situation changed in 1273 when Pope Gregory X (r. 1271–1276) persuaded the German barons to end the squabbling over their vacant throne by electing a king. They chose a minor nobleman, Rudolf of Habsburg (r. 1273–1291), who, they assumed, would pose no threat to their independence. Because Rudolf's barons feared the powerful king of Bohemia more than their new Habsburg leader, they agreed to help Rudolf reclaim the duchy of Austria for the crown. When the Bohemians withdrew, Rudolf left his tiny ancestral barony on the Aar River east of the Swiss city of Bern and moved his family to Vienna. The Habsburgs remained in power there until 1918, the end of World War I.

The German barons elected their kings, and their preference for weak rulers cost the rapidly rising Habsburgs their support. After Rudolf's death, they transferred the royal title to less consequential men, but in 1310 history repeated itself. Ottokar of Bohemia's dynasty died out, and the Bohemians offered their throne to the son of Germany's king, Henry VII (r. 1308–1313). Henry's family, the Luxemburgs, followed the example set by the Habsburgs and relocated to central Europe. In 1347 Bohemia's Luxemburg king, Charles IV (r. 1347–1378), became Germany's Holy Roman Emperor, and in 1356 he issued a decree that virtually guaranteed that his descendants would keep the imperial title. Charles's Golden Bull *(bullum,* the seal that ratifies a document) helped to stabilize Germany by limiting participation in imperial elections to the heads of seven great principalities (four secular lords and three archbishops). This established a rough balance of power among the German magnates and ended the pope's meddling in Germany's affairs. Because Charles recognized the independence of the electors, they felt safe in allowing the crown to remain with the Luxemburg family.

In 1440 the Luxemburgs died out and the throne passed to the Habsburgs with whom they had intermarried. By then, the imperial title was a largely empty honor, and the Habsburgs were far less interested in Germany and Italy than in an empire they were building in Central Europe. They faced an enemy on that front who posed a threat not only to them but to all of Europe.

The Middle East: The Ottoman Empire

The states that the Seljuk Turks had established in the Middle East in the eleventh century C.E. were undermined by the Mongol invasion in the thirteenth century C.E. The Mongols' grip on the western edge of their empire was, however, tenuous, and by the early fourteenth century C.E., petty warlords were carving out new centers of power. One of them, a Turkish chief named Osman (r. 1299–1326), had a unique opportunity to pull ahead of the others. His domain in western Asia Minor on the frontier of the fading Byzantine Empire provided a base for a holy war with Islam's Christian enemies. By 1340 Osman's descendants, the Ottomans, had brought most of Asia Minor under their control. In 1354 a Byzantine emperor, in exchange for their help against a rival, foolishly allowed them to establish a base at Gallipoli on the northern (European) shore of the channel that links the Black and Aegean seas. From there they moved into the Balkans and began to encircle Constantinople. In 1389 they defeated the Serbs at the first battle of Kosovo, and a year later the remaining parts of Asia Minor as far east as the Euphrates submitted to them.

Expansion of Ottoman Power   In 1402 Timur the Lame (Tamerlane), the greatest Mongol emperor since Genghis Khan (see Chapter 11 "Challenges to the Medieval Order"), inflicted a major defeat on the Ottomans. The Mongols soon retreated, however, leaving rival Ottoman chiefs to fight among themselves. One of them, Mehemmed I (c. 1389–1421), finally won the upper hand and reunited the Ottoman territories. His son, Murad II (1421–1451), conquered Greece and the Balkans, and pushed into Hungary. The defeats he gave the Hungarians at the battle of Varna in 1444 and at the second battle of Kosovo in 1448 crippled the Christian state that Europeans hoped would halt the Ottoman juggernaut.

Murad's son, Mehemmed II, "the Conqueror" (r. 1451–1481), secured the Ottomans' position by winning a prize that had eluded Muslim armies for nearly eight hundred years. On May 29, 1453, the twenty-year-old Turkish sultan took the city of Constantinople—with the help of some European technology. In 1452 a Hungarian gunsmith offered to construct a huge cannon for the last Byzantine emperor, Constantine XI (r. 1448–1453). When Constantine failed to raise the money for the project, the Hungarian approached the Ottoman sultan, who commissioned several pieces of artillery. The largest was a cannon twenty-six feet long that fired missiles weighing eight hundred pounds. With weapons like this, it took only a few weeks to pound the impoverished and depopulated capital of eastern Christendom into submission. Venice and Genoa might have helped Constantinople, but they did not want to do anything that risked harming good commercial relations with the Ottomans.

The Turks renamed Constantinople Istanbul and turned its great church, the Hagia Sophia, into a mosque. The loss of the last great Christian outpost in the Middle East was a shock to Europe, but it had little practical significance. Constantinople had ceased to protect the eastern frontiers of Christendom, and its Muslim rulers had no intention of severing its mutually profitable commercial ties with Europe. Italy actually profited from the disaster that befell Constantinople. Greek scholars fleeing the Ottomans sought refuge in Italy, and their linguistic expertise and libraries helped fuel the Renaissance. Cultural influences also flowed in the opposite direction. Mehemmed employed Italian artists and architects, and despite Islam's occasional hostility to representational art, he sat for a portrait by one of Italy's great Renaissance painters, Gentile Bellini (1429–1507).

Figure 12–3 Mehemmed II This portrait of Mehemmed II portrays the conqueror of Constantinople as a hard but introspective man. The classical style of the frame seems somewhat at odds with the artistic traditions of Mehemmed's own culture (although the jeweled cloth draped over it hints at eastern opulence). *Library of Congress.*

Mehemmed and his successors could not concentrate all their attention on Christian targets, for they had much to do in the divided Muslim world. In 1502 Shah Ismail I (r. 1502–1524) founded a rival empire in Persia (Iran). Religion complicated the situation, for the Ottomans were Sunni Muslims and Ismail's Safavid dynasty was Shi'ite (see Chapter 7 "The West's Medieval Civilizations" for a discussion of these two branches of Islam.) Each empire regarded the other as heretical and tried to purge its territory of inhabitants who professed its opponent's faith. In 1517 the Ottoman sultan took the title of caliph and laid claim to religious as well as political authority.

Persian culture powerfully influenced the Ottomans, but the Ottomans failed to break the Safavids's hold on Persia. The Ottomans added Iraq, Syria, Arabia, Egypt, and North Africa to their empire, and in 1522 they won control of the eastern Mediterranean by capturing the island of Rhodes. A year earlier they had taken Belgrade and occupied most of Hungary, and by 1529 they were besieging the Habsburgs in Vienna and attacking European shipping in the western Mediterranean from their ports in North Africa. Although the Habsburg defenses held, the threat to Europe posed by the Ottoman advance further estranged Islam and Christianity.

Ottoman Civilization   The civilization of the Ottoman Empire was shaped by the Turks' devotion to Islamic religious law. Classic Islam maintained that all laws issue from God and that God's eternal and unchanging laws were all revealed in the life and teachings of the Prophet Muhammad. Further legislation is therefore impossible, but when questions arise about what to do in new situations, religious scholars can answer them by interpreting the law. The Ottoman ruler's function was not to make law but to enforce *shari'a* (divine law) with the help of *muftis* (religious jurists). Islam had no priests, for it had no sacraments. Its religious leaders, like Orthodox Jewish rabbis, were specialists in the interpretation of sacred law.

The Ottomans' devotion to *shari'a* did not make them intolerant of other faiths. The empire had many Jewish, Christian, and even Shi'ite Muslim subjects, and there were divisions within its official Sunni faith. Muslims who found the legalism and formal liturgies of their state religion emotionally unfulfilling turned to sufism. Sufis were mystics who used music, song, poetry, and dance to cultivate ecstatic trances and visions.

The Ottoman concern for orthodoxy and the enforcement of *shari'a* may have stifled intellectual activity in the Muslim empire. Medieval Europeans had learned much from Muslim philosophers, mathematicians, physicians, and scientists, but Islam fell behind Europe in all these areas as the West entered the modern era. Its religiously inspired confidence that all truth was enshrined in a set of revealed texts promoted an educational system that stifled curiosity about the outside world and was hostile to innovation and critical thinking. Whatever the cause, an intellectual, technological, and eventually military gulf began to widen between European and Islamic civilizations, the full implications of which are only now becoming clear.

Ottoman power reached its peak during the reign of Süleyman "the Magnificent" (r. 1520–1566), and the Ottoman Empire lasted into the twentieth century C.E. As early as the seventeenth century C.E., however, Turkish historians were lamenting the empire's decline. The fault, they claimed, lay with sultans who allowed unworthy favorites and corrupt servants to usurp their authority. The Ottoman method for passing on the throne may have weakened its leadership. The Ottomans established hereditary succession, but the heir to the throne was seldom the previous sultan's eldest male child. All his sons were contenders, and the one who was chosen executed his brothers to prevent them from fomenting rebellion. This custom was apparently well established by the fourteenth century C.E., when Mehemmed the Conqueror formalized it as a law derived from the Qur'an. In 1603 concern for the preservation of the dynasty ended the executions, and it became customary for the throne to pass to the eldest male Ottoman prince—often the brother of the previous sultan. To prevent the others from causing trouble, they were confined to luxurious prisons. This meant that sultans were chosen from a pool of men who had no experience with government or the world. Rulers of ability and fortitude were therefore rare, and few of them were able to exert much control over the empire's bureaucratic and military elites.

Ottoman sultans tried to counter the power of the entrenched factions that developed within their empire by relying on the services of a special class of totally dependent individuals. Early in the fifteenth century C.E., the sultans began to impose a tax on the empire's Christian communities that was paid in boys. These youths were separated from their families and homelands, forced to convert to Islam, and trained to serve the sultan. Europeans called them Janissaries (*yeni cheri*, "new soldiers"). They were formidable military men, and some occupied the highest government offices. In time, however, they became just another one of the self-interested groups competing for advantage within the empire.

Europe and Atlantic Exploration

The rise of the Ottoman Empire meant that once again Western Europe was under siege from the east. By the sixteenth century C.E., however, the anxiety this initially created was receding (except perhaps in central Europe, which was directly threatened by Ottoman armies). Europeans had discovered that the Atlantic was not, as their ancestors assumed, an impassable wall at their backs, and for the first time in history, they shifted their attention from the

Mediterranean and the Middle East to the Atlantic and to a much larger world than they had ever imagined existed.

Portuguese Explorations   The tiny state of Portugal led the way in Atlantic exploration. It had little choice, for its only access to the Mediterranean (the center of the medieval world's trade network) was through the straits of Gibraltar, which were controlled by Spanish and Muslim enemies. In 1415 Prince Henry "the Navigator" (1394–1460), third son of Portugal's king, John I (r. 1385–1433), earned his knight's spurs in a battle that won Portugal the Muslim port of Ceuta on the African coast opposite Gibraltar. Henry's subsequent military campaigns were inconsequential, but his sponsorship of voyages of Atlantic exploration paid huge dividends.

The Portuguese initially worked their way down the Atlantic coast of Africa, searching for the source of the gold that Muslim caravans brought across the Sahara Desert from Africa's interior. By 1432, they had discovered the Atlantic islands, the Canaries, Azores, and Madeiras, where they developed sugar plantations worked by African slaves. Successive expeditions inched farther and farther down the African coast until Bartolomeu Dias (c. 1481–1500) rounded the southern tip of the African continent in 1488. In 1498 Vasco da Gama (c. 1460–1524) charted the east coast of Africa and a sea route that linked Portugal to the port of Calicut in southwestern India. News of his return with a cargo of spices (particularly pepper) sent shock waves through the markets of Europe. By importing directly from India, the Portuguese could now undersell merchants who used the older and more expensive routes overland through the Middle East. The Portuguese wasted no time in exploiting their advantage. They dispatched a fleet of ships armed with cannons to bring the Indian Ocean and its ports under their control. Then they pushed farther east and established bases in Indonesia, China, and Japan.

One of the puzzles of world history is why Europeans rather than Chinese established the sea route between the West and the Far East. The third emperor of the Ming dynasty (1386–1644) built ships that were many times larger than any that Europeans were then capable of constructing, and between 1405 and 1433, he dispatched fleets of sixty or more vessels to Africa's eastern coast. His successors, however, terminated the project, and China withdrew into itself. What the Chinese had learned of the outside world evidently did not intrigue them.

Spanish Explorations   Italy, with centuries of seafaring experience to draw on, produced excellent navigators and cartographers, some of whom were eager to share the Atlantic adventure. About 1478 Christopher Columbus (1451–1506), a Genoese sailor and map maker, emigrated to Portugal, where he married the daughter of a ship's captain who had sailed for Prince Henry.

Columbus's study of the geographical information available in his day led him grossly to underestimate the size of the globe. Otherwise, he never would have proposed trying to reach the Far East by sailing west across the Atlantic. Had the Americas and certain Pacific islands not been where they are, no ship of Columbus's day could have survived a journey directly from Europe to the other side of the world. Columbus tried to persuade the Portuguese government to fund an expedition to prove his theory that the shortest route to the East lay west, but Portugal decided that its African explorations, which were just beginning to pay off, were a better investment.

Culture in Context: Invention and Social Change

Some societies value their traditions so highly that they regard change as a threat. The European West, however, came to equate change with progress. The positive effects that inventions and discoveries had on European lives (particularly at the start of the modern era) helped to establish this attitude.

Europe made considerable technological progress during the Middle Ages—thanks primarily not to scholars but to artisans and workers who wanted to improve their products and lighten their labors. New farming tools and techniques appeared early in the medieval era. By the eleventh century C.E., the horse's potential on the farm (as a draft animal) and on the battlefield was being fully realized for the first time. The Romans had watermills, but medieval people also harnessed the winds and tides and invented many machines driven by these powers of nature. They built sawmills to make lumber and water-powered hammers to pulverize ore and full cloth. By the fourteenth century C.E., water-powered bellows were easing the work of ore smelting and forging.

Some societies resist learning from others, but medieval Europeans readily appropriated (and improved on) ideas from many sources. They learned paper-making from the Muslims, and then created a superior product that dominated the market. The Chinese invented gunpowder, but Europeans made the cannons that used it—weapons that gave them a decisive advantage in building colonial empires. A Chinese astronomer of the eleventh century C.E. constructed a mechanical clock, but his invention, like the steam turbine of the Hellenistic Greeks, led to nothing. When the clock appeared in Europe in the early fourteenth century C.E., however, it revolutionized human behavior. Once time could be accurately measured, the activities of whole communities could be coordinated and work planned with unprecedented efficiency. Towns all across Europe, therefore, began to erect clock towers as a public service. The Chinese also discovered the properties of the magnetized needles that Europeans were using as compasses by the twelfth century C.E.. Europeans combined compasses with

Columbus considered going to France next, but he finally decided to try his luck at the Spanish court. Spain was a new nation, which had been formed in 1469 by the marriage of Queen Isabella I of Castile and King Ferdinand V of Aragon (joint reign, 1474–1504). The royal couple were intrigued by Columbus's proposal, but the time was not propitious for a new project. In 1484 Ferdinand and Isabella had set out to conquer Granada, Spain's sole remaining Muslim state, and until that costly campaign was resolved, they were not prepared to take on anything else. Granada finally surrendered on January 2, 1492, and, thereafter, things moved quickly. Columbus received his commission on April 17. He set sail with a fleet of three small ships on August 3, and seventy days later he planted Spain's standard on what was probably one of the Bahamian islands—although he was certain that it was not far from Japan. Columbus had been lucky. By striking south to avoid the Portuguese, he had discovered the prevailing winds that offered the easiest passage across the Atlantic.

Columbus's largest ship ran aground and he was forced to leave half his crew (44 men) behind as he hastened back to Spain to announce that he had reached outlying portions of other inventions to revolutionize shipping. By the thirteenth century C.E., they had ships that relied entirely on sails, and by the fourteenth, they had large vessels with multiple masts and lateen rigging—an idea they may have picked up from the Muslims. A host of inventions that improved sailcloth, rope, carpentry, metals, and navigational instruments contributed to the creation of the ships that enabled Europeans to take the lead in global exploration late in the fifteenth century C.E..

Simple inventions, such as the spectacles that an Italian glassmaker produced about 1285, made incalculable contributions to society by extending the productivity (and improving the quality) of the lives of innumerable people. But nothing accelerated the development of European society more rapidly than the printing press with movable type that Johannes Gutenberg (1400–1468) constructed about 1446. The Chinese or Koreans pioneered printing by stamping images on paper and cloth with carved, inked blocks of wood. By the fourteenth century C.E., Europeans were using this method to print pictures, short texts, and the newly popular decks of playing cards. Before anything as elaborate as Gutenberg's press became possible, a host of contributing inventions that improved ink, paper, metal casting, and die cutting was required. In 1455 Gutenberg combined all these things with a press adapted from those used to crush grapes and olives and produced the first printed book, a glorious Bible. In short order his invention spread across Europe, and for the first time in history, the world was flooded with books. There may have been only about 100,000 volumes in all of Europe in 1450, but by 1500, there were probably nine million. No previous society had ever had to cope with the effects of such a rapid and broad dissemination of information. The effect was comparable to the impact the Internet has had on modern society.

Question: What sorts of things open a society to change, and what kinds of experiences might make it hostile to change?

India and contacted "Indians." He received a hero's welcome, a title of nobility, and a much larger fleet for a return to what he claimed, until the end of his days, was the perimeter of Asia. The four expeditions Columbus led explored the Caribbean and the coast of Central America, but they never found the passage to Japan that their admiral was certain had to be in the vicinity.

England occupied the extreme western end of the lengthy medieval trade routes that linked Europe with the Far East. The shorter Atlantic passage that Columbus claimed to have found promised to be an economic godsend for England. News of his discoveries therefore persuaded King Henry VII (r. 1485–1509) to fund an expedition by another Genoese explorer, whose anglicized name was John Cabot (1450–1498). In 1497 Cabot reached the islands off the coast of Canada and returned to England to inform the king that he had reached Asia north of Japan. A second voyage in 1498 took Cabot as far south as Labrador. England's financiers contemplated more expeditions, but because Cabot had found nothing of value aside from some furs, plans were slow to materialize.

In 1500 a Portuguese fleet bound for India via the African route went off course and sighted a land it named Brazil (for a species of tree that grew there). A year later, the

Portuguese dispatched a follow-up expedition piloted by Amerigo Vespucci (1454–1512), one of Columbus's associates. Vespucci was among the first to suggest that what the Europeans were exploring was not the outer reaches of Asia, but a "New World." The geographers who used his reports labeled the continent whose outline was emerging on their maps "the discoveries of Amerigo" ("America"). Any lingering doubts about the place America occupied on the globe were resolved in 1522 when the remnants of a Spanish fleet that had set out under the command of Ferdinand Magellan (1480–1521) completed the first circumnavigation of the Earth. (See Map 12–2.)

Columbus never found the gold he promised his Spanish sponsors, but in 1519 the longed-for instant wealth finally began to flow. Hernán Cortés (1485–1547) invaded Mexico and looted the Aztec Empire. Ten years later Francisco Pizarro (c. 1475–1541) overthrew the New World's other major civilization, the empire of Peru's Inca. Small companies of Spanish soldiers subdued large native populations with surprising ease, for the invaders had advantages that more than compensated for their numbers. First of all, they had superior weapons, and they had horses—animals that were new to the Americas. Native armies had never confronted mounted warriors with guns. But second, and most effectively (if unintentionally), Europeans practiced germ warfare. Migration and trade among the peoples of Asia, Africa, and Europe had exposed the inhabitants of these regions to many diseases to which they had gradually evolved immunities. However, peoples of the western hemisphere had different immune systems, and they were devastated by diseases that were minor childhood afflictions for

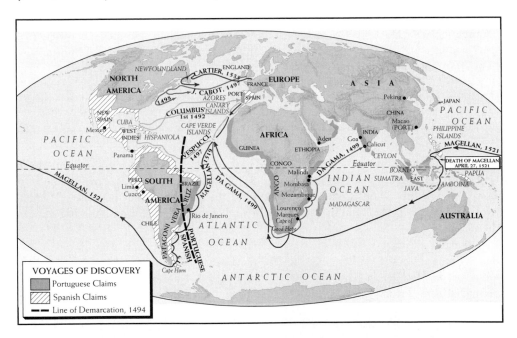

Map 12–2
Europe's Initial Global Explorations   This map shows the routes taken by the Portuguese, Spanish, English, and French explorers as they ventured into the Atlantic and beyond. ***Question:*** What effect would the increasing attention that Europe gave to global exploration have had on relations between the Christian and Muslim worlds?

Europeans. Smallpox, chicken pox, measles, and other illnesses swept ahead of the European invaders and cleared the way for their conquests. Native populations declined so precipitously that the European entrepreneurs who established plantations and mines in the New World had to reconstitute its workforce by importing slaves from Africa—people who shared the Old World immunities.

In 1494 the pope presumed, as Christ's vicar on Earth, to draw a longitudinal line that divided the globe into Portuguese and Spanish spheres of influence. Territories east of his "Line of Demarcation" (which ran through Brazil) were declared Portuguese, and anything to the west was supposed to belong to Spain. Other European nations with access to the Atlantic refused to be restrained by the papal decree. Three years after the pope's proclamation, John Cabot staked England's claim to the New World, and in 1534 France sent out the first of its explorers, Jacques Cartier (1491–1557). He made four trips to a land he thought the natives called Canada (their word actually meant "village"). Cartier searched for a waterway through the Americas to the Far East and a North American kingdom that was rumored to be as rich in gold as Mexico's Aztec Empire. Although he found neither, France sent out more explorers and added the Mississippi watershed and some Caribbean islands to the American territories it claimed. In 1595 tiny Holland established bases in the East Indies to compete with the Portuguese. England and France eventually followed. As Europeans moved out into the world, they spread their civilization and the power of their colonial empires around the globe.

Larger Issue Revisited

A handful of European explorers needed only a few decades to effect the greatest alteration that has yet to take place in the course of world history. In their wake, Europe's civilization and the political and economic power of the colonial empires Europeans built transformed life for peoples around the globe. Dramatic changes took place in Europe as well. The gold and silver and raw materials that poured into Europe greatly enriched its economy. Luxury consumables, such as sugar, rice, and spices, became much more affordable. The new plants that explorers brought back for cultivation in Europe revolutionized society at every level. Europeans tasted maize, squash, and tomatoes for the first time and discovered the pleasures of tobacco, coffee, tea, and chocolate. The potato, which was indigenous to Peru and Chile, flourished in Europe's cool, wet climate. As it replaced wheat as the staple food of the poor, famines diminished and populations grew. The national cuisines of European countries today feature foods, drinks, and flavors that were unknown to Europeans until relatively recently.

The New World's creation of a new Europe caused Europeans some anxiety. The flood of information that suddenly became available to them about peoples, places, and things whose existence they had not previously suspected posed immense challenges. For the first time, they became aware of viable alternatives to their way of life, and this forced them to rethink the fundamental assumptions of their civilization and religion. They were, however, accustomed to dealing with change. Their Renaissance, despite its name, was less a rebirth of the past than a creative response to it. It revived beliefs and institutions of an earlier age, but treated these things as the beginning, not the end, of its search for truth. The situation in the Ottoman Empire, the other major heir to the Western tradition, was different. There, the conviction took hold that all essential truths had been revealed in the past. This diminished curiosity about the outside world, limited intellectual freedom, and hampered development. What people do with their past—their history—goes a long way toward determining their future.

Review Questions

1. Why did the Renaissance originate in Italy before spreading elsewhere?
2. What is humanism? What medieval ideas did it challenge?
3. What features do the different arts of the Renaissance—sculpture, architecture, and painting—have in common? How do they relate to humanism?
4. How did the Renaissance change as it moved into northern Europe?
5. How did the rise of the Ottoman Empire and the discovery of the New World change the way Europeans thought about themselves?
6. Why did the Muslim and European worlds begin to diverge so dramatically in the late fifteenth century?

Refer to the front of this book for a list of chapter-relevant primary sources available on the CD-ROM.

THE WEST INTERACTIVE

For web-based activities, map explorations, and quizzes related to this chapter, go to *www.prenhall.com/frankforter.*

CHAPTER 13

REFORMATION, RELIGIOUS WARS, AND NATIONAL CONFLICTS

. . . what fools could conceivably be more foolish than those who are overwhelmed by a passion for religion? . . . They value death more than life.

—**Desiderius Erasmus**

Larger Issue: *How do people justify and rally support for wars?*

In 1514, when Erasmus (c. 1466–1536) ridiculed religious passions (as quoted above), he had no way of knowing that an era of religiously motivated warfare was about to begin. Wars are not rare in human history, but a congruence of forces (rivalry among monarchies, the class struggles of a capitalistic economy, opposing belief systems, and a host of other things) made them especially abundant in the sixteenth and seventeenth centuries C.E. People in almost every era have grievances that might lead to war, but they do not always act on their grievances or always find the same issues worth fighting for. If we are to exercise adequate self-control, we need to learn what history can teach us about the motivation for shedding blood. How can it be that a war that seems senseless to some is, to others, worth the sacrifice of life itself?

The Reformation of the sixteenth century C.E. ended the medieval church's monopoly and confronted Europeans with religious pluralism. Thereafter, their armies often professed to fight for different faiths. But sometimes Catholics sided with Protestants against Catholics, and vice versa, and sometimes leaders made suspiciously opportunistic conversions. Wars allegedly fought for reasons of faith obviously also had other causes.

The explanations that people give for their quarrels are not always accurate or sufficient. Because conscience requires us to justify our violent acts, we usually prefer to think that we are fighting for noble causes and that the personal advantages victory brings are only a pleasant by-product of our campaign. The noblest of causes is fidelity to God or, in more secular language, commitment to the defense of ultimate values. The West's major religions, Judaism, Christianity, and Islam, urge people to live together in love and peace, but they have often inspired hatred and slaughter. Is faith (in either a sacred or secular ideal) a cause for war, a pretext for war, a precondition for war, or a preventative for war? Much more than an interpretation of past events depends on understanding what drives people to make war.

TOPICS IN THIS CHAPTER

The Lutheran Reformation • The Swiss Reformation • The Catholic Reformation •
The Habsburg-Valois Wars • England's Ambivalent Reformation • Convergence of Foreign
and Domestic Politics: England, Spain, and France • The Final Religious Upheaval

The Lutheran Reformation

The Renaissance helped make the Reformation possible. Humanist educations whetted appetites for reform by using ancient texts to critique contemporary society and by affirming the dignity of the individual. The Renaissance was, however, confined to an elite segment of society, while the Reformation became a mass movement—something that would not have been possible before the invention of the printing press and the spread of literacy. The Reformation's leaders, like the humanists who headed the Renaissance, believed that ancient wisdom would correct the errors of the recent past. But their enthusiasm was not for paganism's classical culture. It was for the primitive Christianity of the early church.

Luther   Martin Luther (1483–1546) was not rebellious by nature, and for a long time he led a very conventional life. He claimed peasant origins, but his father was an upwardly mobile member of the middle class who could afford to educate his son. Luther completed his arts degree at the University of Erfurt in 1505 and then began to study law. But after a few months, a growing anxiety for the state of his soul led him to drop out of school and enter an Augustinian monastery. He completed the noviate, took monastic vows, and in May 1507 was ordained a priest. He began work on a doctorate in theology, and the Augustinians sent him to lecture at the University of Wittenberg in Saxony.

Luther was thirty-four years old before anything caused him to question his medieval Catholic faith. He had been taught to think of himself as a sinner destined for judgment by a righteous and angry God. Fear of eternal punishment had driven him to become a monk, for the church claimed that this was the surest way to please God. The fasts, prayers, and disciplines of the monastic life failed to bring him assurance of salvation, but sometime after 1512, he had a kind of conversion experience—a burst of insight prompted by reading the letters of the Apostle Paul. Paul, according to the New Testament's Book of Acts, had not wanted to become a Christian and was actively persecuting the church when God suddenly intervened, bestowed faith on him, and made him a Christian. Luther concluded that what had been true for Paul was true for all Christians. They did not earn salvation by doing good works; salvation was a gift God freely gave them while they were still sinners. It could not be earned, and human beings could not comprehend God's motives in bestowing it.

Luther's resolution of his personal crisis of faith did not turn him into a reformer or a critic of the church, for he did not believe that he had discovered anything revolutionary. He had only understood what was plainly laid out for everyone in the Bible. He settled back, therefore, into his routine as a college professor and might never have been heard of had it not been for a chance encounter in 1517 with a Dominican friar named Johann Tetzel (c. 1465–1519).

Albert of Brandenburg, at the age of twenty-three, already controlled two dioceses, but in 1514 he sought to acquire a third: the archdiocese of Mainz, one of Germany's most important sees. Pope Leo X (r. 1513–1521) agreed to sell Albert the office and to license a sale of indulgences in Germany by men like Tetzel to help him raise the money. An indulgence was a dispensation from the need to do penance for one's sins. Church doctrine held that while God freely forgave the guilt of sin, sinners still owed some compensation for the moral damage caused by their sin. Souls that had not fully atoned for their sins in life were sent after death to Purgatory to complete their penances. Originally, indulgences were granted for penances that proved too severe or for crusaders who might die without an opportunity to receive absolution. In 1343, however, the papacy declared that the church possessed an infinite "treasury of merit," a spiritual bank of grace, that it could draw on to pay the debts of individual

Figure 13–1 Martin Luther The Reformation's protagonists were, thanks to the printing press, the first intellectuals in history who could argue their cases in the court of public opinion. The debate made Martin Luther an early media star. This likeness of the reformer is by Lucas Cranach (1472–1553), painter to the court of Luther's protector, Duke Frederick of Saxony.

sinners (both dead and alive). Whenever the church accepted gifts in exchange for this favor, it opened itself to the charge that it was selling salvation.

Johann Tetzel's thoroughly modern marketing campaign created this impression. Tetzel dispatched advance men to whip up customer demand. He organized parades with banners and songs, and composed what may be history's first advertising jingle: "When a coin in my coffer rings, a soul from Purgatory springs!" Luther, who believed that Tetzel was presuming to sell what God freely gave, decided that it was his duty to expose Tetzel as a fraud. Following medieval scholastic tradition, he proposed debating ninety-five propositions relating to indulgences. Tradition holds that he nailed them to the door of his Wittenberg church. If he did, this was not an attack on the church. Church doors served as community bulletin boards, and all sorts of notices could be posted on them. The fact that Luther wrote his ninety-five theses in Latin suggests that they were intended for his fellow scholars and not meant to rouse the populace.

When the debate Luther stirred up hurt sales, Archbishop Albert asked the pope to silence the annoying monk. The pope was willing, but Luther was a subject of Frederick the Wise, the Elector of Saxony (r. 1486–1525), one of the princes who elected the Holy Roman Emperor. Frederick was no proto-Protestant. He had one of the largest collections of holy relics in Europe. He was, however, not about to let the pope intervene in his territories and compromise his power as an independent ruler. He therefore took Luther under his wing.

The Political Context   In June 1519 the election of the Habsburg candidate, Charles V (r. 1519–1556), as Holy Roman Emperor created a situation that gave men like Frederick reason to be protective of their sovereignty. The nineteen-year-old emperor's sprawling domain included Austria, Hungary, Bohemia, the Netherlands, Spain, Sicily, Sardinia, the Kingdom of Naples, and overlordship of Germany and Italy. (See Map 13–1.) Charles posed a threat to every ruler in Europe, and Germany's lords were particularly worried about maintaining their independence. The Reformation provided them with a justification for challenging the authority of the Catholic emperor.

In 1521 Charles summoned Luther to appear before a diet (Germany's equivalent of England's Parliament and France's Estates General) in the city of Worms. Luther had never intended to break with the church, but the series of pamphlets he wrote to explain his position set forth three ideas that ultimately separated Protestants from Catholics: first, that salvation is by faith alone (a gift from God that cannot be earned by human effort; second, that the Bible (not the pope or the tradition of the church) is the only authority a Christian must obey; and third, that every Christian has a direct relationship with God that does not depend on the church and its priests. When the church ordered Luther to recant these beliefs, he refused. To do so, he claimed, would be to violate conscience, the highest court to which each individual is accountable.

The emperor and the diet condemned Luther, but Frederick saved him by spiriting him away to a remote castle. During Luther's absence from the public stage, the Reformation proceeded without him. He passed his time in hiding by translating the New Testament into colloquial German. By taking the position that private conscience and the Bible were the highest authorities to which people were accountable, he had more or less obligated himself to provide ordinary men and women with a version of the Bible they could read for themselves.

Luther's opponents warned that his insistence on the autonomy of each individual's conscience undermined respect for all public authorities and promised to create chaos. Luther feared that they might be right, for while he was in hiding, some of his self-proclaimed followers vandalized churches and monasteries, seized their property, and made radical changes in traditional religious practices. Luther was even more alarmed in 1523, when the leaders of a massive peasant rebellion claimed to be acting on his principles. In 1525 he published a pamphlet, *Against the Robbing and Murdering Hordes of Peasants,* in which he urged the German nobles to "smite, slay, and stab" the peasants—claiming that nothing is more "devilish than a rebellious

Map 13–1
The Empire of Charles V   Charles's empire was the product of a series of carefully plotted dynastic marriages that made the Habsburgs heirs to crucial territories scattered across Europe. ***Question:*** Can an empire consist of scattered states, or must it consolidate its territory in order to survive?

man." Luther was fundamentally conservative. He feared disorder, and there was much about the medieval church that he wanted to preserve. Seeing no other option, he concluded that as part of the state's divinely ordained mission (the maintenance of orderly societies), its head had the right to set up a church and enforce conformity to its practices.

Charles V might have used his power as a head of state to squelch the Reformation had crises on other fronts not distracted him, but a decade passed before Charles could give his full attention to events in Germany. During that time, Lutheranism spread widely, particularly in urban areas. Its empowerment of the individual appealed to humanist scholars and their students at universities, and these men scattered through Germany preaching and leading public discussions of Luther's call to return to the religious practices described in the New Testament. Luther had poetic gifts, and the hymns he composed were marvelous tools for proselytizing the masses. A flood of his pamphlets poured off presses, and woodcut prints and cartoons provided his followers with highly effective and totally novel propaganda. The excuse the Reformation provided for confiscating church property and setting up state-controlled churches also appealed to rulers. In the 1530s the king of Sweden, the dominant Scandinavian monarch, established Lutheranism as his country's official religion, and Denmark and Norway soon followed suit.

In 1530 Charles convened a diet at Augsburg and gave the Lutherans a year in which to return to the Catholic faith. Some of the Lutheran states chose instead to form a military alliance, the Schmalkaldic League (named for the town of Schmalkalden where the allies met). Civil war was averted when Charles was called away to deal with problems elsewhere in his sprawling empire, and he did not return to Germany until 1546. In 1547 he defeated the armies of the Schmalkaldic League, but Catholic France helped the Lutherans recover. Catholic rulers were no more eager for Charles to unite and control Germany than were their Lutheran colleagues.

Charles finally concluded that his huge empire could not be governed by one person. When he retired in 1556, the eastern Habsburg territories were being administered by his brother Ferdinand (r. 1558–1564), and he assigned responsibility for his western possessions, including Spain and the Netherlands, to his son Philip II (r. 1556–1598). In 1555 another diet that met at Augsburg arranged a truce between the Lutherans and Catholics. On the assumption that people of different faiths could not live together, it decreed that each prince could decide for himself whether his state would be Catholic or Lutheran. His subjects would have either to conform or emigrate to a place where their faith was legal. The Peace of Augsburg lasted until 1618, but by polarizing Germany, it created the conditions for one of Europe's most devastating conflicts, the Thirty Years' War (1618–1648).

The Swiss Reformation

Protestants agreed that they should be guided solely by Scripture, but they did not agree on what the Bible said. Luther's conservative practice was to permit traditional customs if they did not contradict Scripture. The Swiss reformers, on the other hand, insisted on wiping the slate clean and restoring only what the Bible mandated. Even this rigorous approach, however, failed to produce consensus.

Zwingli　Ulrich Zwingli (1484–1531), the first of the great Swiss reformers, came to the Reformation via a humanist education that prepared him for the Catholic priesthood. Like the great humanist biblical scholar Erasmus, he believed that the study of the New Testament would sweep away medieval superstition and bring about the moral regeneration of Christian society. Zwingli was a powerful orator, and his gifts served him well when, in 1519, he became preacher at the chief church in the Swiss city of Zurich.

Zwingli used preaching to bring about reform. Because he based his sermons exclusively on biblical texts, he began to question pious customs, such as fasting and priestly celibacy, that had no scriptural basis. He also concluded that churches should be purged of their art and musical instruments, for there was no New Testament precedent for their use. Zwingli denied the Catholic belief that the mass repeated Christ's sacrifice and argued that the Eucharist was not a sacrament but only a symbolic reminder of Christ's work. Luther passionately disagreed, and his opposition to Zwingli endangered the Reformation. In 1529 Philip of Hesse (r. 1509–1567), the leader of the Lutheran princes, arranged a meeting between Luther and Zwingli. Charles V was preparing to attack Germany's Lutherans. (They had begun by then to be called Protestants because of their protestations against Charles's policies.) Philip hoped that a united front would strengthen the Protestant cause, but it was never to be. Luther insisted that Christ's flesh and blood were truly present in the Eucharist, and he was appalled by Zwingli's reduction of the central Christian mystery to a mere symbol. Swiss and German Protestants declined to work together, and in 1531 Zwingli died in a war with Swiss Catholics.

The Anabaptists   Luther considered Zwingli a radical, but some of Zwingli's fellow Swiss did not think that he was radical enough. He convinced them that the Bible was the sole authority in faith, but they were frustrated by his cautious approach to enforcing its precepts. In 1523 they took matters into their own hands and alarmed the authorities by smashing religious art and demanding an immediate end to the Roman mass. When they met resistance, they withdrew from society into communities of their own. They called themselves the Swiss Brethren, but their opponents dubbed them Anabaptists (Rebaptizers). They rebaptized adult converts who had been baptized as children because they considered infant baptism to be unbiblical and therefore invalid. The Anabaptist tent was a broad one, for mainline Protestant establishments tended to associate all dissident Protestant groups with the Anabaptists.

The Anabaptists advocated separating from society and establishing elite communities of "saints" governed solely by Scripture. Their eagerness to recreate biblical societies led some of them to endorse practices, such as polygamy and communal ownership of property, that are in the Bible but that were out of step with the widely held convictions of their contemporaries. A literal reading of the Bible's apocalyptic passages also convinced some Anabaptists that the end of the world was at hand, and this prompted more radical behavior. In 1534 a group of Anabaptists seized the German city of Münster and purged it of everyone who did not profess their faith. Lutherans and Catholics joined forces to retake the city, and the determination of the authorities to suppress the Anabaptist movement moderated its behavior. The Anabaptists gave up hope of mastering the world and retreated to parts of Europe where they could live unmolested. Some (the Mennonites, Hutterites, and Amish) eventually emigrated to North America.

Calvin and the Reform Tradition   Lutheranism did not spread as widely as the brand of Protestantism created by John Calvin (1509–1564), a Frenchman who eventually settled in Geneva. Like Luther, Calvin was the son of a family newly risen to the middle class who was raised a Catholic and educated for the priesthood. At the University of Paris, he made the acquaintance of humanists, but in 1528 his father ordered him to give up his theological studies and enter the law school at the University of Orléans. This legal training shaped Calvin's thought as a reformer.

On May 21, 1534, Calvin, at the age of twenty-five, took a step that radically altered his circumstances. Having been persuaded of the truth of Protestantism by an experience that he described as a burst of insight, he resigned the offices in the Catholic Church that provided his income. His change of mind owed much to humanism, but he did not share the humanists' optimism about human nature. Like Luther, the Apostle Paul, and Augustine of Hippo, he believed that human beings were captive to sin and lost unless God intervened to save them.

Calvin's king, Francis I of France (r. 1515–1547), was a patron of the Renaissance and interested in aspects of humanism, but he had no sympathy with the humanists who called for radical church reform. The papacy had ceded the French king virtual control over the Catholic Church in France, and Francis did not want anyone to interfere with an institution that had become one of the instruments of his power. In October 1534, after militant reformers plastered Paris with posters attacking the mass, the king struck hard at suspected Protestants.

Calvin fled to the Swiss city of Basel, and in August 1535, he published a tightly argued explication of Protestant faith, *The Institutes of the Christian Religion.* The book was immediately popular and immensely influential. Luther was a brilliant polemicist who often dashed off thoughts in response to specific situations. This resulted in some gaps and inconsistencies in his writings that made their interpretation difficult. Calvin, on the other hand, was a systematic thinker who, in lawyerly fashion, developed a complete, succinct, and tightly reasoned case for Protestantism. Catholics, with centuries of scholarship to draw on, were well-prepared for theological debates; Calvin leveled the playing field for Protestants.

Calvin and Luther agreed that the Bible was the sole guide to faith and that salvation was entirely a gift from God. Both endorsed predestination—the idea that humans could not affect God's decision about their ultimate fate. But they differed on the implications of this principle. Luther believed that God's laws were meant to convince people of the depth of their sin and the impossibility of earning salvation by their own efforts. Once they accepted that salvation was God's gift, they were freed from all concern for themselves. Only then were they truly able to devote themselves to serving others. Luther believed that if the church imposed rules governing behavior, people would slip back into thinking that obedience to these rules would earn them salvation. Calvin disagreed. He claimed that God's law was eternally valid. It did not earn anyone salvation, but it was binding on everyone (the damned as well as the saved) simply because it was God's law. It had to be enforced because God is God and we are His creatures.

Catholics insisted that the Protestant doctrine of salvation by faith undercut the motive for moral striving. Why, they asked, bother to be good if good deeds earn you nothing? Calvinist doctrine, however, did not turn people into libertines. Rather, it tended to produce dour moralists and ascetics—people who embraced "the Protestant work ethic," the sober lifestyle of the pleasure-averse laborers who contributed so much to the West's capitalist economy. The Calvinists' behavior made sense psychologically. They believed that the most important decision that could ever be made about their lives had already been made, and they wanted to know what this decision was. Calvin warned that no one could be certain that he or she was among the "elect" whom God had chosen for salvation. But it was reasonable to assume that those whom God had saved would do His will. The Bible taught that "you will know them by their fruits" (Matthew 7:16). The desire to assure themselves that they were saved made Calvinists introspective as well as moralistic and hardworking. By compiling diaries in which they recorded their deeds and analyzed their motives, they hoped to see into their own hearts.

In 1527 the people of Geneva expelled their Catholic bishop, and in 1534 they invited Calvin to reorganize their churches. The rigorous discipline he imposed was not popular, and the town's governing councils refused fully to empower the Consistory, a board of clergy and lay elders that Calvin had set up to police morals. Calvin was dismissed in 1538, but in 1541

Geneva recalled him and submitted to his reform program. With Calvin in charge, Geneva quickly became a haven for Protestant refugees from every corner of Europe. About five thousand of them entered the city between 1549 and 1559—a huge number for a town that originally had about twelve thousand inhabitants. When it was safe for them to go home, the Calvinism they had absorbed in Geneva went with them. John Knox (1513–1572), Scotland's reformer, claimed that Geneva was "the most perfect school of Christ that ever was in the earth since the days of the Apostles."

The lessons people learned in Calvin's "school" extended beyond the practice of faith. Reform (Calvinist) congregations—following what they believed was the custom of the early church—elected presbyters ("elders") to lead them, and they favored some form of representative government. But the emphasis that Calvin placed on the individual conscience did not lead him (any more than Luther) to sanction rebellion against established authorities. He drove those who opposed him from Geneva and even burned a Spanish refugee, Michael Servetus (1511–1553), at the stake for denying the doctrine of the Trinity and the divinity of Christ. When Calvinists were the persecuted rather than the persecutors, however, they could rationalize revolutions—as England and France were soon to learn. (See Map 13–2.)

The Catholic Reformation

At the start of the Reformation, most of Europe's Christians belonged to a church that was literally *catholic* ("universal"). Within a few years of Luther's excommunication, the church headed by Rome's pope was catholic only in name and struggling to defend traditions and institutions that previously had seemed unassailable. Its response has been called the Counter-Reformation. It would, however, be more accurate to call it the Catholic Reformation, for it was more than a reaction to the rise of Protestantism. It owed much to a reform movement that was active within the church before Martin Luther spoke out. In 1517, the year in which Luther attacked indulgences, the Oratory of Divine Love was established in Rome to promote religious renewal among both clergy and laity. Its influential members advocated reform, but they faced a serious obstacle in the Renaissance papacy.

The Renaissance Popes   In the years leading up to the Reformation, the papacy was preoccupied with rebuilding its power. The Great Schism (1378–1417) had lessened respect for popes, and the Conciliarist movement had questioned the basis for their authority (see Chapter 12, "Renaissance and Exploration"). Secular governments were also limiting their right to operate within the boundaries of the stronger nation-sates. The popes responded to these challenges abroad by building up their home territory, the Papal States. Many of the popes were members of the aristocratic families that jockeyed for power in Italy, and they were well-schooled in the use of the tools of Renaissance governments: bribery, deception, assassination, and war. Immersion in Italy's convoluted politics made it difficult to distinguish them from the secular lords with whom they contended.

Popes, like the Renaissance's secular lords, used patronage of the arts to bolster their image as powerful rulers. Pope Nicholas V (r. 1447–1455), the founder of the Vatican library, launched a program for rebuilding Rome that continued for generations. The city filled with buildings designed to bestow majesty on the papacy, but the schemes devised to pay for them earned popes a reputation for greed and worldliness.

The worst popes had few aspirations beyond living like kings and enriching their relatives. Sixtus IV (r. 1471–1484) devoted most of his energies to the wars that raged among the

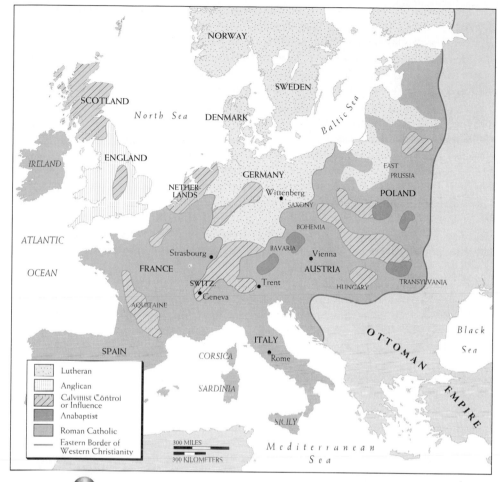

Map 13–2

Religious Diversity in Post-Reformation Europe   By the middle of the sixteenth century C.E., the region that medieval people thought of as Christendom was no longer united in allegiance to a single church. This affected the conduct of the nation-states that were emerging in many parts of the continent. **Question:** Why did Protestantism spread more widely in northern Europe than in the south?

Italian states. He was also implicated in a plot to assassinate the Medici family during mass in Florence's cathedral. Innocent VII (r. 1484–1492) had sixteen children, whom he richly rewarded from the spoils of the papal office. Alexander VI (r. 1492–1503) won the papacy by bribing the cardinals and used the church's wealth to fund wars that he hoped would win an Italian duchy for his son, Cesare Borgia (1476–1507). Julius II (1503–1513) was determined—as he made clear by the name he chose when he became pope—to emulate the conquests of Julius Caesar. He donned armor and personally led troops in battle. He was also a knowledgeable patron of the arts. He commissioned Raphael to decorate the papal apartments and Michelangelo the Sistine Chapel. It fell to a Medici prince, Leo X (r. 1513–1521), to deal with Martin Luther, and, not surprisingly, the aristocratic pope failed to take the ranting of an obscure German monk seriously.

The papacy did not begin to mount a serious offensive against Protestantism until the reign of Paul III (r. 1534–1549). Pope Paul appointed reforming cardinals and a commission to draw up a plan for renewing the church. In 1537 it returned a report that documented the existence of many of the abuses of ecclesiastical authority of which Protestants complained. In 1540 Paul authorized the establishment of the Society of Jesus (the Jesuits), a religious order dedicated to serving the papacy and winning converts for the church. In 1542 he gave the Court of Inquisition authority to hunt down heretics anywhere in Europe, and in 1545 he convened the Council of Trent.

The Jesuits and the Council of Trent were the chief agents of the Catholic Reformation. Ignatius Loyola (1491–1556), a Basque soldier who discovered his spiritual vocation while recuperating from a war injury, founded the Society of Jesus. The Jesuits accepted only the most gifted men, and they subjected candidates for admission to their order to a twelve-year-long course of study and testing that prepared them for the church's toughest assignments. Jesuits reversed gains the Reformation initially made in southern Germany, Poland, and Hungary. They spread the Catholic religion to the Americas, the East Indies, Japan, and China, and they founded hundreds of schools, colleges, and universities to provide Catholics with a firm intellectual grounding in their faith.

The Council of Trent, which met intermittently from 1545 to 1563, set the church on the path that it has (with some adjustments) followed ever since. The council affirmed that faith was based not only on Scripture, as Protestants claimed, but also on the traditions of the church. It rejected the idea that salvation was by faith alone and asserted the importance of good works. It reaffirmed transubstantiation as the explanation for the mystery of the Eucharist and asserted that each mass was an offering of Christ's sacrifice on the cross. The council's decrees were not meant to invite a dialogue leading to reconciliation with Protestants. They were intended to strengthen the Catholic cause by making it perfectly clear where the church stood.

Having decided on its position, the church vigorously defended it. The Inquisition weeded out dissenters, and in 1559 the papacy imposed censorship. It forbade the reading of vernacular translations of the Bible and published an *Index of Prohibited Books*. So strict were the Index's standards that it condemned works by Erasmus, the humanist biblical scholar who had opposed the Reformation.

The success of the Reformation should not be assumed to imply that Catholicism was, by the sixteenth century C.E., a moribund faith. In parts of Europe it was in fact renewing enthusiasm for monastic vocations and a passionate, mystical piety. This was most obvious in Spain, where Ferdinand and Isabella, the "Catholic kings," presided over the last phase in the long Iberian crusade. They crowned their conquest of Islamic Granada by banishing Jews as well as Muslims from Spain and by establishing an Inquisition that mercilessly policed the Catholic orthodoxy of their subjects. Spain's inquisitors were so alert to any whiff of heterodoxy that they briefly incarcerated the Jesuit's founder, Ignatius Loyola, and cast a wary eye on Teresa of Ávila (1515–1582), a Carmelite nun who was the era's leading mystic. Loyola's *Spiritual Exercises* and the works of Teresa and her disciple, John of the Cross (1542–1591), have become classics of Christian mystical literature.

The Habsburg-Valois Wars

The Protestant and Catholic reformers did not work in a social vacuum. Because it was widely assumed that peoples of different faiths could not live together, allegiance to a religion implied support of—or opposition to—a state. Religious motives were often swayed by political realities.

The collapse of the German monarchy that followed the death of Frederick II in 1250 (see Chapter 12, "Renaissance and Exploration") cleared the way for France to move into Italy. Charles of Anjou, brother of Louis IX of France, conquered the Kingdom of Naples and founded a dynasty there that survived until 1435. In 1494 King Charles VIII of France (r. 1483–1498) led an army into Italy to reclaim Naples for France, but a league of Italian states defeated him. In 1499 his successor, Louis XII (r. 1499–1515), occupied the duchy of Milan, but by 1512 the French had once again been forced to retreat from Italy.

The election of Charles V as Holy Roman Emperor in 1519 made the conquest of Italian territory a high priority for Francis I of France (r. 1515–1547). Francis hoped that by winning control over Italy, he could prevent the Habsburg empire from encircling France (see Map 13–1). His first campaign foundered, and Charles captured him in 1525 and held him captive until 1526. No sooner was Francis free, however, than he began a second war that also ended disastrously—particularly for his ally, Pope Clement VII (r. 1523–1534). In May 1527 Charles's imperial army broke out of control and sacked Rome—making the pope a virtual prisoner. Francis still refused to give up. In 1533 he strengthened his ties with the pope, who was eager to get out from under Charles's thumb, by wedding Clement's niece, Catherine de' Medici (1519–1589), to his heir, Henry II (r. 1547–1559). Francis then shocked Europe by establishing diplomatic relations with the Ottoman sultan, Süleyman the Magnificent (r. 1520–1566), who had occupied most of Hungary and assaulted Habsburg Vienna in 1529 with 200,000 men. Süleyman attacked Vienna again in 1532, and Francis wanted him to keep up the pressure on Charles V while the French navy assisted the Turkish fleet against the Habsburgs in the Mediterranean.

Francis began a third war with Charles in 1535. Fighting erupted in Italy, southern France, and the Habsburg Netherlands and dragged on until 1538. A fourth war broke out in 1542. Francis invaded Spain, and Charles thrust into France nearly to the gates of Paris. But by 1544 mutual exhaustion led them to agree to a truce. Both men were dead by the time the Treaty of Câteau-Cambrésis established peace between France and Spain in 1559.

England's Ambivalent Reformation

Apart from the Scandinavian states, England was the only major country to break with the papacy. Its decision to do so owed more to politics than to religion. As nation-states consolidated in the late medieval era, their governments increasingly regarded the papacy as a foreign power whose right to intervene in their affairs was far from certain. In the mid-fourteenth century C.E., the English Parliament limited the pope's authority to fill offices in the English church and hear appeals from English courts. In 1438 the Pragmatic Sanction of Bourges declared that the French clergy (actually their king) would choose the bishops who headed the French church. Even the Inquisition that was established in Spain in 1477 served Ferdinand and Isabella's interests. The decision to make England a nominally Protestant nation was likewise made in the interests of strengthening a nation-state. It was deemed necessary to secure the future of England's Tudor dynasty (1485–1603).

Henry VIII   England's civil war, the War of the Roses, ended in 1485, when Henry Tudor, a Welsh noble, defeated Richard III, the last Plantagenet king, and ascended the throne. England did not yield easily to its new ruler, Henry VII (r. 1485–1509). He spent much of his reign putting down rebellions, but his clemency, intelligent government, and sound fiscal policies laid a solid foundation for his successors, the monarchs of the Tudor dynasty.

Culture in Context: Art as Propaganda, the Vatican

Rome's popes originally resided in the city in a palace attached to the church of St. John Lateran. Only after this burned down in 1308 did they relocate to the Vatican. Their new home took its name, *Mons Vaticanus* ("Hill of Prophecy"), from an ancient Roman shrine dedicated to the goddess Cybele and Attis, her beloved. Attis was a dying-and-rising god, who might have served as a symbol of Christ's resurrection, but that was not what made the Vatican sacred to Christians. The emperor Nero (r. 54–68) had staged the public executions of the Christians accused of setting fire to Rome in 64 C.E. in a stadium on the *Mons Vaticanus,* and it was believed that the Apostle Peter, Rome's first bishop and one of Nero's victims, was buried there.

The emperor Constantine (r. 307–337) built the first church on the Vatican to mark the site of Peter's grave. (Archaeologists have confirmed the existence of a Roman cemetery under the current St. Peter's.) Constantine's church was a great basilica, a large rectangular hall with a flat wooden roof. During the Middle Ages, it was altered, redecorated, and occasionally (as during the papacy's long residency in Avignon) grossly neglected.

It was in such bad shape by the mid-fifteenth century C.E. that Pope Nicholas V proposed replacing it. Julius II, the warrior pope, pulled down most of the old building and on April 18, 1506, laid the cornerstone for a new one. The plan his architect, Donato Bramante, drew up for rebuilding St. Peter's reflected the Renaissance's love of symmetry and classical simplicity. It envisioned a church shaped like a Greek cross (a cross with four equal arms) crowned by a soaring dome. Little construction had been completed by the time of Bramante's death in 1514, and Leo X's architect, the painter Raphael, also died before making much progress. Pope Paul III (r. 1534–1549) resumed work on the project, but by then, thinking about the building had changed. Michelangelo, at the age of 72, was commissioned to redesign it. The Renaissance was yielding to the Baroque period in Western art history. Tastes were changing. The cool rationality of the high Renaissance seemed inadequate to express post-Reformation Catholicism's passionate, mystical faith in the awesome power of Christ's earthly vicar.

Pope Sixtus V's (r. 1585–1590) architect, Giacomo della Porta (1541–1604), erected the Vatican's great dome, and the building was finished by Carlo Maderno (1536–1629) during the reign of Clement VIII (r. 1592–1605). Maderno extended one of the arms of the original Greek-cross plan to create a long nave and designed the building's façade. The impression the Vatican makes on visitors today owes a great deal to the Baroque decoration that Gian Lorenzo Bernini (1598–1680) executed for Pope Urban VIII (r. 1633–1644). Baroque artists used sinuous, twisting, convoluted lines to create exuberant, energetic designs of overwhelming complexity. Their works celebrated the triumphalism of reformed Catholicism—of a faith confidently founded on mysticism, authority, and truths that transcend reason.

Question: Why were Protestant churches so plain and Catholic churches so richly ornamented?

England had long cultivated alliances with the Spanish kingdoms against France, and in 1501 Henry reaffirmed this foreign policy. He obtained the hand of Catherine of Aragon (1485–1536), daughter of Spain's Ferdinand and Isabella, for Arthur (1486–1502), his son and heir. When Arthur died less than six months after the wedding, Henry decided to maintain the tie with Spain by obtaining papal permission for Catherine to wed his new heir, his second son, the future Henry VIII (r. 1509–1547). A dispensation from canon law was required, for a biblical text (Leviticus 20:21) forbade a marriage between a man and his brother's widow.

Catherine endured many pregnancies, but only one of her children survived, a daughter named Mary (Tudor). Henry doubted that England would accept a female heir to his throne and feared that after his death, the country would lapse back into the civil war from which it had recently emerged. He believed that the security of his kingdom depended on his having a son. In 1525, when Catherine, who had not had a pregnancy in seven years, turned forty, Henry, who was thirty-four, decided that his only hope for a son lay in obtaining a younger wife.

Henry hoped that the pope would void his marriage on the principle that God had rendered sterile a marriage that the Bible had forbidden. The church had a long history of finding reasons to dissolve inconvenient marriages for influential people, but Clement VII, the pope to whom Henry appealed, was in no position to oblige England's king. Catherine opposed Henry's petition, and her nephew, Charles V, dominated Italy. (His troops had recently sacked Rome.) The pope prolonged the negotiations to buy time, and Henry turned to Parliament for help in pressuring Rome. It enacted a series of laws that began to sever ties between England and the papacy.

Events came to a head in 1533. Henry had fallen in love with Anne Boleyn (1504–1536), the daughter of one of his courtiers. Anne became pregnant near the close of 1532, and Henry, who was desperate to assure the legitimacy of her child, secretly wed her in January 1533. In May his compliant archbishop of Canterbury, Thomas Cranmer (1489–1556), declared that he had never been validly married to Catherine and that, Anne was therefore his legal wife. To the king's great disappointment, however, Anne bore him another daughter, Elizabeth.

In 1534 the pope came to Catherine's defense and declared her to be Henry's legitimate wife. Parliament responded by passing the Act of Supremacy. It severed ties with the papacy and recognized the king as the head of England's church. The break with Rome did not imply, however, that the king had any sympathy with Protestantism. Henry had made his position clear in 1521 by publishing an attack on Luther. The pope had been so grateful that he had awarded Henry an additional title: "Defender of the Faith."

A few prominent individuals, most famously the humanist Thomas More (the king's former chancellor), refused to swear allegiance to the new church and were executed. Although some modern scholars believe that anticlericalism was on the rise in England, most of Henry's subjects considered themselves to be Catholics. In 1536, when Henry began to suppress England's monasteries and confiscate their vast properties, there was a rebellion (the Pilgrimage of Grace) in the north of England. This was, however, not just a religious protest. It was also a reaction by the numerous tenants who lived on monastic estates to Henry's disruption of their lives. The strongest support for reforming England's church came from the merchant class, which had commercial ties with those parts of Europe where Protestantism thrived. This segment of English society was well represented when Parliaments met in 1536, 1537, 1538, 1539, and 1543 to draw up regulations for the new church, but apart from endorsing the use of vernacular Scriptures, Henry made few concessions to Protestantism. The Anglican Church was to be an English Catholic church—an institution ruled by bishops (whom the king appointed), staffed by a celibate clergy, affirming seven sacraments, and continuing most medieval liturgical practices.

The king had risked much to marry Anne, and when her second pregnancy miscarried, he lost patience with her. He accused her of adultery, beheaded her, and took a third wife, Jane Seymour (1509–1537). On October 12, 1537, she died not long after producing the long-sought male heir Prince Edward. Henry's next bride, a German Lutheran named Anne of Cleves (1515–1557), was chosen to forge an alliance with Germany's Lutheran princes. Thomas Cromwell (c. 1485–1540), Henry's chief minister, believed that this would dissuade France and Spain from heeding the pope's call for a crusade against England. Henry, however, disliked Anne, and the marriage was annulled. In 1540 he wed Catherine Howard, the sprightly young niece of the duke of Norfolk. Her flagrant promiscuity with young men at court prompted her execution in 1542. A few months later, Henry married his sixth wife, Catherine Parr (1512–1548), a sensible widow with strong Protestant sympathies. She provided her aging husband with domestic comforts and took charge of the education of his children.

The Tudor Succession   When Henry died in January 1547, his nine-year-old-son became England's king, Edward VI (r. 1547–1553). Edward was afflicted with chronic ill health but was intellectually precocious, and thanks to his stepmother and the Lutheran tutors she provided, a sincere Protestant. The chief monument of his brief reign was a new liturgy for the Anglican Church, *The Book of Common Prayer*. It tried to reconcile the various religious factions that were developing in England by being ambiguous on contentious issues.

The course of the English Reformation was nearly reversed when the young king died. His father's will named his half-sister Mary, Catherine of Aragon's Catholic daughter, next in line to the throne. Edward's Protestant advisors persuaded the dying boy to disinherit Mary, but the English people refused to accept this and rallied to her side.

Mary I (r. 1553–1558) shared her Spanish mother's conservative Catholic faith and was eager to restore England's allegiance to the papacy. She imprisoned some prominent Protestant clergy at the start of her reign but preferred to rid England of Protestants by urging them to re-convert or emigrate. Hundreds fled to the Netherlands, Germany, and Switzerland. There, under the influence of Calvinism, many became Puritans, sober Protestants filled with contempt for Catholic doctrine and ritual.

Mary's first Parliament revoked her brother's religious legislation but balked at rebuilding England's monasteries. This would have required the restoration of their confiscated lands, and these had been purchased by members of Parliament. The thing that alarmed Parliament most about its new queen was her intended marriage. Mary was thirty-seven years old, and she was desperate to bear an heir who would guarantee a Catholic succession to the English throne. The mate she chose was Charles V's son and heir, the future Philip II. Premarital agreements could limit the rights of the queen's husband over her kingdom, but not of their child. When it inherited both their thrones, England, the weaker country, would become a Spanish dependency.

Four months after she became queen, Mary swept Parliament's objections aside and married Philip by proxy. Nine months later Philip arrived in England to meet a bride who was eleven years his senior. With Philip's support, Mary sought formal reconciliation with Rome, and on November 30, 1554, the pope's ambassadors absolved England.

As opposition to Mary's policies mounted, she began to track down and execute Protestants. She may have burned about 280 men and women at the stake. For this, Protestant historians blackened her reputation, but she was actually responsible for fewer deaths than her successor, her Protestant sister Elizabeth.

After less than a year of marriage, Philip left England. He did not give Mary a child, but he did draw her into the Habsburgs' wars with France. This cost England its last continental posses-

Figure 13–2   Elizabeth I of England   Extravagant dress was expected of all monarchs in the sixteenth century C.E., but Elizabeth's jewels and wardrobe were legendary for their splendor. They flaunted what her society believed to be her weakness—her femininity—while cloaking it in a mantel of intimidating majesty.

sion, the French port of Calais. Mary, isolated and disillusioned, lost touch with reality. When she died on November 17, 1558, Elizabeth, her hated half-sister and the daughter of Anne Boleyn, whose marriage to Henry VIII had humiliated Mary and her mother, ascended her throne.

Convergence of Foreign and Domestic Politics: England, Spain, and France

The religious diversity the Reformation created greatly complicated political life in Europe, for almost everyone believed that a state could not survive unless all its citizens shared the same faith. Subjects who differed with the religion of their ruler were suspect as traitors, particularly when wars broke out between Catholic and Protestant states.

Elizabeth's Compromises   In 1558 John Knox (c. 1505–1572), a Protestant exile in Geneva, published *The First Blast of the Trumpet Against the Monstrous Regiment of Women*. Knox blamed the ills of his generation on the women who, contrary (he claimed) to the laws of God and nature, were presuming to govern kingdoms. Mary Tudor had driven him and hundreds of other Protestants from England, and Mary of Guise (1515–1560), a French Catholic, governed his homeland, Scotland, as regent for her daughter, Mary Stuart (1542–1567). What Knox considered a bad situation was destined, from his point of view, to get worse. France soon came under the thumb of its queen mother, Catherine de' Medici, and England's throne passed in 1558 to its second female heir. There were, however, no more blasts from Knox's trumpet. The first was intended to deafen a Protestant enemy, Mary Tudor, but Knox's timing was poor. It grated on the ears of a potential Protestant ally, Mary's sister Elizabeth I (r. 1558–1603).

Elizabeth's succession was legitimate only if the Protestant marriage of her parents was valid, but politicians are sometimes willing to overlook inconvenient facts. Europe's Catholic powers did not immediately attack the new queen. The pope held out hope for her conversion, and Philip II, Mary's widower, considered proposing to her. Elizabeth's position was precarious. England was nearly surrounded by Catholic states, and there was a Catholic claimant to her throne: Mary Stuart, a granddaughter of Henry VIII's sister, who was queen both of Scotland and, by marriage, of France. Religious divisions were also increasing among Elizabeth's subjects. Some opposed her father's Reformation, and some—particularly the Puritans who returned from exile after Mary Tudor's death—believed that it had not gone far enough.

Elizabeth survived by making it difficult for everyone to figure out where she stood. She was adept at depriving potential opponents of clear targets and keeping alive their hopes for reconciliation. She flirted with, but never committed to, the many men who sought her hand in marriage. She endorsed some Catholic practices and some Protestant ideas. Gradually, she eased her country toward a "settlement" of religion: a church with a Catholic hierarchical structure and ritual along with a Protestant theology. This did not end religious conflict in England, but it postponed a showdown until the 1630s.

Philip II and Spain's Golden Age   Elizabeth hoped to maintain England's alliance with Spain against France, but Spain's ruler had other plans. Philip II (r. 1556–1598) inherited the western half of Charles V's empire: Spain, Spain's New World possessions, and the Habsburg Netherlands (modern Belgium, Holland, and Luxembourg). Control of the commercially rich Netherlands and a steady flow of gold and silver from America gave Philip great resources, and he was willing to spend whatever it took to bring more of Europe under his control.

The weakest point in Philip's empire was the Netherlands, a small but highly urbanized and wealthy country whose independent townspeople were notoriously difficult to govern. The Netherlands was a loose collection of culturally diverse provinces. The ten southern provinces were French or Flemish, and the seven northern ones were linked by the Rhine River to Germany and Switzerland. Protestant influences (especially Calvinism) spread to the Netherlands and there, as elsewhere, appealed to urban populations. Townspeople had, throughout the Middle Ages, been predisposed to self-government, and they responded to Luther's defense of the rights of the individual and Calvin's arguments for representative institutions. Philip concluded, therefore, that to confirm his monarchical authority over the provinces, he had to purge them of Protestantism. This only increased the determination of some Netherlanders to resist Spanish domination.

In 1567, after lesser measures had failed, Philip sent an army into the Netherlands to compel conformity to his religious policies. This heavy-handed action roused nationalistic passions, and a resistance movement formed around a native nobleman, William of Orange (1533–1584). William tried to unite all the provinces, but religious disputes doomed his efforts. In 1579 the largely Franco-Catholic southern provinces sided with Spain, while the north's more easily defended Dutch-speaking provinces formed a Protestant alliance (the United Provinces) and continued the fight for independence. Because the United Provinces received help from England's Protestant queen, Philip concluded that to defeat them he had also to defeat England. Developments seemed to favor his success. William of Orange was assassinated in 1584. A pro-Spanish faction won ascendancy at the French court, and a plot unfolded in England to place Mary Stuart on Elizabeth's throne.

Henry VIII had hoped to win Mary's hand for his son, Edward, but the Scots wed her instead to King Francis II (r. 1559–1560) of France. An alliance with France helped Scotland maintain its independence from England, and the regent who ruled Scotland for Mary was her mother (also named Mary), a member of the powerful French family of Guise. The Scots, however, did not want to be dominated by France any more than by England, and in 1559 a cadre of nobles overthrew Mary of Guise. Their motives were religious as well as political, and they called a native son, John Knox, home from exile in Geneva to reform Scotland's church. A year later, Francis II died, and his young widow, Mary Stuart (r. 1542–1567), returned to govern a Scotland she had not seen since early childhood. The queen, who had been raised and educated at the elegant French court, was ill-prepared for life in a much poorer and less sophisticated society. Her manner offended men like Knox, and she was soon at odds with her court. She was suspected of adultery and accused of helping to murder her second husband, a great-grandson of England's Henry VII whom she wed in 1565. When she began an affair with (and ultimately married) the man suspected of killing her husband, the Scots had enough. They forced her to abdicate in the name of her infant son, James, and in the summer of 1568 she fled to England. For some inexplicable reason, she believed that Elizabeth, for whose throne she was a competitor, would help her. Elizabeth was uncertain what to do and kept Mary in luxurious confinement for twenty years. Finally, evidence of Mary's involvement with Philip II's plots against England persuaded Elizabeth to order Mary's beheading (1587).

By then Philip's plan for overthrowing Elizabeth was nearing completion. It involved sending a great fleet and army to the Netherlands to pick up additional troops and ferry them across the channel to England. Various setbacks delayed the departure of Philip's Spanish Armada until the summer of 1588, and then the expedition was undone by a combination of bad planning and worse weather. Philip continued to threaten England, but his resources were diminishing and his problems multiplying. The struggle in the Netherlands continued, and in 1589 he attacked France. The English also discovered an effective way to fight him. Privateers (government-licensed, privately funded pirates) raided Spanish shipping. The queen herself invested in these highly profitable ventures, over a hundred of which sailed in some years. England did not yet have a navy, but it was becoming a major sea power.

After Philip's death in 1598, Spain began to decline. The gold and silver that Spain had imported from the Americas had not been invested in building up the country's economy. Instead, it had flowed through Spain to fund Philip's numerous wars. The church controlled about half the land in Spain and supported a huge number of clergy. Most of the rest of the country was in the hands of an entrenched aristocracy that clung to its feudal prerogatives. The portraits the artist El Greco (c. 1541–1614) painted of Spain's grandees proclaim their sense of entitlement, and the paintings by Velázquez (1599–1660), a generation later, suggest a royal court that had drifted into the realm of fantasy. The era of Spain's fading glory produced its greatest writer: Miguel de Cervantes Saavedra (1547–1616). Cervantes' groundbreaking novel, *Don Quixote,* affectionately lampooned his countrymen's romantic devotion to an archaic, medieval way of life that was dooming them to irrelevance.

France's Wars of Religion   Spain was not Elizabeth's only concern. A war between Catholic and Protestant factions raged in France for much of her reign and complicated her foreign policy. France's Protestants were Calvinists called Huguenots. (Scholars are unsure of the derivation of their name.) In France, as elsewhere, the Reformation attracted people who were critical of established authority and who saw religious change as part of a broader program of reforms. Many of these came from the professional and middle classes and the lower nobility—educated people who chafed under the restraints of institutions that they regarded as outmoded.

For most of the sixteenth century C.E., France's royal government left much to be desired. Francis I used the French Catholic church as a source of political patronage and squandered his country's resources in futile wars with his Habsburg rival, Charles V. Francis's son, Henry II (r. 1547–1559) achieved little before a tournament accident ended his life and delivered France into the hands of his Italian wife, Catherine de' Medici (1519–1589). Catherine was the power behind a throne that passed in succession to three of their sons. Francis II (1559–1560) survived his father for only a year. He was succeeded by his ten-year-old brother, Charles IX (r.1560–1574). The third brother, Henry III (r. 1574–1589), was an adult when he became king, but his preoccupation with the delights of debauchery subverted his effectiveness as a ruler.

It was all that Catherine could do simply to preserve the Valois dynasty, for France was less a unified kingdom than a league of powerful feudal principalities. Whenever its kings were weak, aristocratic factions led by great noblemen fought for dominance at court. For much of the sixteenth century C.E., religious differences defined the opposing camps. The Catholic party was led by the dukes and cardinals of the Guise family and the Protestants by the Bourbons, a cadet branch of the royal house. In 1562 the duke of Guise began a war with the Protestants by slaughtering seventy Huguenot who had met for worship. Ten years later, Catherine's attempt to reconcile France's Catholic and Protestant factions culminated in an act of genocide that shocked Europe and drove the two parties even farther apart. When the French aristocracy gathered in Paris in August 1572 for the wedding of Catherine's daughter, Margaret, to Henry of Navarre, the Bourbon head of the Huguenot faction, someone tried to assassinate one of the Huguenot leaders. Fear of Protestant reprisals prompted the crown to act quickly and with great force. Early on the morning of August 24, the feast of St. Bartholomew, the king's army fell on the unsuspecting Huguenots. The slaughter spread to other cities, and some seventy thousand Protestants may have perished before the purge ended. The St. Bartholomew's Day Massacre poisoned relationships between Protestants and Catholics throughout Europe and diminished hope that the faiths could coexist peacefully.

The civil war that followed weakened France—to the advantage of Spain and England, whose governments provided aid to the combatants. In 1589 a monk extinguished the Valois dynasty by assassinating Henry III. This opened the way to the throne for the Bourbon heir, the Protestant Henry of Navarre, who became France's Henry IV (r. 1589–1610). After a prolonged struggle, Henry concluded that his largely Catholic France would not accept a Protestant king, and he converted (allegedly quipping, "Paris is worth a Mass"). Henry IV, a nominal Catholic with Protestant credentials, had enough credibility with both sides to end France's religious wars. In 1598 he issued the Edict of Nantes, which declared France a Catholic country but designated places where Huguenots could worship and ceded some towns to their control. Since 1555, a similar arrangement (the Peace of Augsburg) had maintained order in Germany, but events there were about to demonstrate that religious segregation was not a permanent solution.

The Final Religious Upheavals

By the end of Elizabeth's reign (1603), a lull was developing in Europe's conflicts. England was fairly secure. Spain's struggles in the Netherlands were winding down, and France was recovering from its long internal bloodletting. There were, however, problems on the horizon. Despite all the killing, Europe's population had increased by about forty percent during the sixteenth century. The gold and silver that had flooded in from the New World had caused inflation to soar, and poverty was inspiring riots and rebellions. Governments strained to control their subjects, and some failed conspicuously.

The Thirty Years' War   By separating Germany's Lutherans and Catholics, the Peace of Augsburg diminished opportunities for the two faith communities to learn to trust one an-

People in Context: William Shakespeare (1564–1616)

Literature flourished in Elizabethan England as never before, and the period's greatest author was, as one of his contemporaries put it, "not of an age, but for all time." He might have added "and for all cultures," for William Shakespeare's plays have been translated into many tongues, staged as operas and Broadway musicals, and produced as commercially successful films. Given their fame, it is surprising that we know so little about their author.

Shakespeare, for all his talent, seems to have been a conventional man. John Shakespeare, his father, was a glove maker, money lender, and commodity trader in the town of Stratford-on-Avon. He and his wife, Mary Arden, had eight children. Will, the eldest of their four sons, was born in a dreadful year in which about 250 of Stratford's eight hundred inhabitants died of the plague. John served a term as mayor of Stratford and applied for a coat-of-arms to confirm his rising social status. But by the time Will was eleven, his father was suffering serious financial reverses and could do little to help his son make a start in life.

Shakespeare's only formal education was in Stratford's free school. His plays testify to his familiarity with the major classic authors (Ovid, Plutarch, Seneca, etc.) but do not suggest that he was unusually well read. He never attended a university. At the age of eighteen he married Anne Hathaway, a woman eight years his senior. Six months after the wedding, their daughter Susanna was baptized, and three years later they had twins—a boy and a girl.

No one knows how young Shakespeare supported his family or what drew him to London in the late 1580s and to the theater. Somehow he learned to act and write plays, and by 1592, his work was attracting envious notice from his competitors. By 1597, he was rich enough to purchase the second largest house in Stratford, and by 1599, he was part owner of a new London theater called "The Globe." Shakespeare's family may have secretly clung to the old Catholic faith, but Shakespeare was no propagandist or passionate advocate for a cause. He was a professional playwright whose goal was to please his audiences and avoid trouble with his monarch. He wrote to make a living, and when he could afford to (in 1613), he laid down his pen and devoted the rest of his life to managing his business interests.

Shakespeare wrote exclusively for his own company at the rate of about two plays a year. Scholars credit him with 154 sonnets, several longer poems, and about forty plays. The authorship of some items is disputed, for Shakespeare gave no thought to preserving his work for posterity. He died on April 23, 1616, and seven years passed before a group of admirers gathered up his scattered plays and edited them for publication.

Question: Does Shakespeare's work support the theory that artists reflect the dominant values and concerns of the eras in which they live?

---

other. Some people were also determined to undermine Augsburg's arrangements. The Jesuits reclaimed much of southern Germany for the Catholics, and the Calvinists, Protestant rivals of the Lutherans who were not recognized as a legal faith by the Augsburg agreement, were equally aggressive in their recruiting. In 1608 the Calvinist ruler of the Palatinate, Frederick IV (r. 1592–1610), established the Protestant Union, an alliance of Protestant states. Duke Maximilian of Bavaria (1573–1651) countered by recruiting members for what was called the Catholic League. France, England, and Holland supported Frederick, and the Habsburgs—both Spanish and Austrian—backed Maximilian.

The only additional thing required for a war was an incident to trigger hostilities, and Bohemia provided one. In 1618 Archduke Ferdinand (1578–1637), the Catholic heir (Ferdinand II) to the Holy Roman Empire, became king of Bohemia. Bohemia had a tradition of religious heterodoxy that dated back to the early fifteenth century C.E.. It had provided refuge for Anabaptists, and Calvinism had spread among its aristocrats. Despite this, the Jesuit-educated Ferdinand was determined to impose Catholicism on the Bohemians. When he tried, the Bohemian nobles responded by literally ejecting his agents—they hurled them out a window onto a dung heap. Ferdinand considered this "Defenestration of Prague" a declaration of war and prepared to invade Bohemia. The Bohemians turned to Frederick IV's son and successor, Frederick V (r. 1610–1632) for help, but when the German states chose sides, they did not allow religion to stand in the way of political advantage. Some Lutherans, who despised Calvinists, supported Ferdinand, and some Catholics, who did not want the Catholic Habsburgs to grow stronger, sided with Frederick.

In the first phase of the war, the Catholic forces swept through Germany and routed Frederick, but that did not end the conflict. The possibility of a Germany united under a Catholic monarch so alarmed Germany's neighbors that they intervened on the Protestant side. Denmark was the first to attack, but its campaign only prompted the Catholics to seize some ports on the Baltic. That, however, brought Sweden into the fray. In 1630 Sweden's great warrior king, Gustavus Adolphus (r. 1611–1632), forced Ferdinand to retreat from northern Germany. Catholic France then allied with Lutheran Sweden, and after Gustavus Adolphus was killed in battle, France directed the course of the war. France was governed by Cardinal Richelieu (1585–1642), chief minister for Henry IV's son, Louis XIII (r. 1610–1643). Richelieu was a sincere Catholic, but he put the interests of his country above those of his church. The last thing France wanted was a unified Habsburg Germany on its eastern border, so Richelieu gave Germany's Protestants the aid they needed to fend off their emperor. The intervention of foreign powers turned Germany into an international killing ground. By the time the war ended, battles, raids, plagues, massacres, and famines had ended the lives of about eight million people, about forty percent of Germany's population.

The Peace of Westphalia that concluded the war in 1648 ensured that Germany would remain an impotent collection of hundreds of tiny states and that the Holy Roman Empire would be an empire only in name. The victors rewarded themselves with bits of German territory, and the Habsburg defeat cleared the way for the Swiss cantons and the Dutch Republic to be recognized as independent states. Germany's collapse and Spain's humiliation also meant that France now had a chance to dominate the continent. (See Map 13–3.)

England's Civil War   By the time Westphalia brought the continent's religious wars to an end, a conflict between Puritans and Anglicans was raging in England. England's religious factions had different political visions for their country. The Puritans wanted self-governing congregations overseen by a national synod to which they elected representatives. The secular complement for such a church was a Puritan monarch and Parliament. Elizabeth and her successors understood this, and they insisted on preserving the Catholic hierarchical system (that is, bishops appointed by the crown) for the Anglican Church as a support for the monarchy.

Elizabeth's heir, James I (r. 1603–1625), was Mary Stuart's son, Scotland's King James VI. James's experience with Scotland's Presbyterians left him with no affection for Protestantism or representative government. In 1598 he published a book, *A True Law of Free Monarchies,* that clarified his stance. It asserted that God appointed kings and that kings were accountable only to God. This was out of step with recent trends in English history. The Tudor dynasty had

Chronology: Leaders of the Reformations and the Wars of Religion

RELIGIOUS LEADERS	POLITICAL LEADERS	EVENTS
Luther (1483–1546)	Charles V (r. 1519–1556)	Diet of Worms (1521)
Leo X (r. 1513–1521)	Francis I (r. 1515–1547)	Habsburg-Valois Wars
Zwingli (1484–1531)	Henry VIII (r. 1509–1547)	(1521–1544)
Clement VII (r. 1523–1534)	Catherine of Aragon	English Reformation (1534)
Calvin (1509–1564)	(1485–1536)	Geneva reformed (1541)
Ignatius Loyola (1491–1556)	Edward VI (r. 1547–1553)	Peace of Augsburg (1555)
Paul III (r. 1534–1549)	Mary Tudor (r. 1553–1558)	Council of Trent (1545–1563)
Knox (1505–1572)	Philip II (r. 1556–1598)	Scotland reformed (1559)
Theresa of Avila (1515–1582)	Süleyman (r. 1520–1566)	Spanish Armada (1588)
	Elizabeth I (r. 1558–1603)	French Wars of Religion
	Catherine de' Medici	(1562–1589)
	(1485–1536)	Edict of Nantes (1598)
	Mary Stuart (r. 1542–1567)	Thirty Years' War
	Henry IV (r. 1594–1610)	(1618–1648)
	James I (r. 1603–1625)	English Civil War
	Frederick V (1596–1632)	(1642–1646)
	Ferdinand II (1578–1637)	English Republic (1649–1660)
	Gustavus Adophus	
	(r. 1611–1632)	
	Richelieu (1585–1642)	
	Charles I (r. 1625–1649)	
	Cromwell (1599–1658)	

needed Parliament's help to effect the Reformation and manage its consequences, and Parliament had come to think of itself as a partner with the monarch in governing England.

Parliament met only when the monarch called it, and what kept its tradition alive was its control of taxation. England's kings could not levy taxes without parliamentary approval. To avoid calling a Parliament that might try to limit his authority, a king had to meet the expenses of government from his permanent sources of income. James enhanced these by imposing customs duties, selling titles of nobility, and doing everything he could think of to fill the royal coffers without resorting to Parliament. He had no sympathy with any aspect of Puritanism and even designed a national campaign to encourage the recreations, games, and sports that the Puritans opposed. His major concession was to commission a new vernacular translation of the Scriptures. The result was the eloquent text popularly known as the "King James Version" of the Bible.

James's policies and dissolute court were so offensive to Puritans that some of them gave up hope for England's reformation and decided to make fresh starts elsewhere. In 1593 a small group of radical Puritan separatists left London for the Netherlands, and in 1620 they moved on to establish a colony called Plymouth in North America. They were the vanguard of a much larger migration that eventually brought thousands of more mainstream Puritans to New England and the islands of the West Indies. Those who left were, however, somewhat premature in predicting the decline of Puritan power in their homeland.

James's son and successor, Charles I (r. 1625–1649), shared his father's belief in the autocratic nature of monarchy, and for eleven years (1629–1640) he avoided convening Parliament. He was much less willing than his father to compromise with Puritanism, and the Puritans suspected him of being a Catholic at heart. What ultimately brought him down was his determination to impose an Anglo-Catholic liturgy on his kingdoms. In 1637 Charles ordered Scotland's Presbyterian clergy to use England's prayer book. The Scots promptly rebelled, forcing Charles to call a Parliament. He quickly dissolved this "Short Parliament" when it presented him with a list of demands for reforming his government. A few months later, when the Scots invaded England, the king had no choice but to reconvene what came to be known as the "Long Parliament." Relations between Charles and Parliament quickly soured, and when Charles tried to use force to break Parliament up, it raised an army to fight the king (1642).

A brilliant military leader named Oliver Cromwell (1599–1658) emerged from the ranks of the country gentry to command this army, and in 1646 he captured the king. Cromwell purged his opponents from Parliament, and in 1649 it voted to abolish the monarchy and establish the House of Commons as England's government. The king was given a show trial and then beheaded on January 30, 1649. The state church became Puritan, and England was declared a republic.

Cromwell led armies more successfully than governments. He conquered Scotland and Ireland but could not keep the disparate elements in Parliament working together. In April 1653, with the support of the army, he disbanded Parliament and drew up a new constitution. It vested power in regional military governors who reported to Cromwell, the republic's "Lord Protector." Cromwell continued to experiment with governmental reforms, but he failed to establish a stable system of popular government. After he died in 1658, his subordinates tried to carry on for another year, but the country had lost faith in the Puritan

Figure 13–3 The Four Horsemen of the Apocalypse Although the German artist Albrecht Dürer created this famous print at the end of the fifteenth century C.E., it serves to illustrate the devastation that later befell his country during the Thirty Years' War. The image of four horsemen (representing pestilence, war, famine, and death), whose appearance heralds the end of the world, comes from the Bible's Book of Revelation.

Map 13–3

Europe after the Peace of Westphalia The Treaty of Westphalia redrew the map of Europe. France and Sweden acquired additional territory. The United Provinces and the Swiss cantons were recognized as independent states, and Germany's continuing fragmentation was assured. *Question:* What proved strongest in Europe—the forces of unification or fragmentation?

experiment. It finally invited the heir to its throne, Charles I's son Charles II (r. 1660–1685), to return from exile in France and restore the monarchy and the Anglican Church. The Puritan revolution, however, had not been a complete failure. England's kings moderated claims to absolute authority and conceded Parliament a role in their governments.

Larger Issue Revisited

The Reformation ended the ecclesiastical monopoly of the medieval church and confronted Europeans with religious pluralism. The result was an era characterized by strife within and among nations. Combatants claimed to champion different faiths, but their quarrels had multiple causes, and they ignored religious differences when it was to their advantage. The determination of the German princes to defend their separate sovereignties had much to do with their decisions to embrace or combat the Reformation. In France, religion organized the aristocracy into opposing camps that struggled for ascendancy at court and control of the nation. In England, most openly of all, political motives and perceived national interests lay behind the decision to break with the papacy.

Europe was, in the sixteenth and seventeenth centuries C.E., working to resolve numerous power struggles. There were tugs of war between regional and centralized governments. Nobles resisted the growing power of kings. Social and economic classes and rural and urban areas were in conflict. The emerging nation-states were competing for territory and European dominance. Religious convictions, both sincere and opportunistic, provided moral justification for the morally troubling decision to shed blood that was going to be shed anyway.

Religion did, however, have a logical link with politics, for it affected how people thought about authority. The sovereignty that Protestantism claimed for individual conscience predisposed Protestants (particularly Calvinists) to favor some form of popular government. Catholics were inclined to the traditional belief that authority was a gift God bestowed on rulers of His choice. Partisans from both camps faced the same temptation: to equate the defense of a political system with loyalty to transcendent principles. When that connection is made, any war can seem worth fighting.

Review Questions

1. What key beliefs forced Luther to separate from the Catholic Church?
2. How were Calvinists different from Lutherans? From Anabaptists?
3. Was the English Reformation a reformation or a revolution?
4. What effect did the Reformation have on Catholicism and the power of the papacy?
5. Was religion the cause of, or the excuse for, the wars of the sixteenth and seventeenth centuries C.E.?
6. What were the political implications of the Protestant and Catholic theologies of the Reformation era?

Refer to the front of this book for a list of chapter-relevant primary sources available on the CD-ROM.

THE WEST INTERACTIVE

For web-based activities, map explorations, and quizzes related to this chapter, go to *www.prenhall.com/frankforter.*

THE WEST AND THE WORLD

West is a slippery term whose meaning changes with its context. Dictionaries define *west* as the direction that is opposite to that of Earth's rotation. *West*, however, often designates a place more than a direction. The word's Indo European root (*wespero*), which means "evening," associates the West with the setting sun. Etymologically, therefore, the specific lands that an individual thinks of as western are determined by the place from which he or she views the sun.

West is, however, more than a geographical term. It also has cultural associations and uses that reflect historical experiences. For the ancient Egyptians, the West was the place of death; the desert west of the Nile where the dead were interred on the first stage of their journey along the path that the sun daily blazed into the underworld. For medieval peoples, the West was the Latin Christian homeland tucked up in the northwestern corner of what they assumed to be the inhabited world. For European explorers of the 15th and 16th centuries, the West was the "New World." Their cartographers, who thought of Earth as stationary, divided the globe into halves, into "eastern" and "western" hemispheres. From the perspective of the Europeans who settled in North America, the West was (at first) the unexplored territory beyond the Allegheny Mountains. But as this land came under the plow, the West retreated across the Mississippi River.

The West has had many locations on maps, and its geopolitical meaning has also varied. During the Cold War, the term implied a distinction between democratic and communist lands. Since the fall of the major communist states, however, the West has taken on the meaning of the "First World" as opposed to the "Developing World." These uses of the term ignore the facts of geography and history. Russia, the leading communist power, has strong historical links with Europe's "western" civilization, and the economic divisions that characterize the current global situation are better described as a split between north and south than east and west. The modern world has often been described as a "global village," an image that suggests that its people are growing closer together and that terms such as East and West should be losing their significance. It seems, however, that the members of the global village are willing to go to ever more extreme lengths to defend their separate cultural identities.

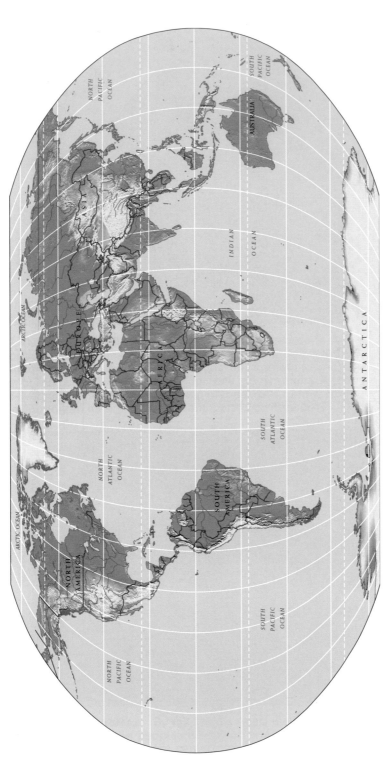

Map 4: The West, circa 2000 c.e. With the end of the Cold War and the subsequent collapse of the Soviet Union, the nations of Eastern Europe regained their political autonomy while new states were created in the former Soviet empire. Definitions of the West have changed in the aftermath of the Cold War, especially in terms of identifying areas of the globe that have been influenced by the West. For example, regions of European settlement and independent nations that were once under European colonial rule are often included in contemporary definitions. In terms of geographical sweep, it may be useful to think of the West in terms of America and Europe, but if one includes cultural and material influence, then large portions of the globe have been exposed to Western civilization.

Photo Credits

Part One: NASA Headquarters

Chapter 1: Archivo Iconografico, S.A./CORBIS BETT-MANN/(c) Archivo Iconografico, S.A./CORBIS; The Granger Collection, New York

Chapter 2: The Metropolitan Museum of Art/The Metropolitan Museum of Art.; The Metropolitan Museum of Art/Photograph, The Metropolitan Museum of Art.; Library of Congress/Courtesy of the Library of Congress

Part Two: Scala/Art Resource, N.Y.

Chapter 3: Gianni Dagli Orti/CORBIS BETTMANN; Joe Cornish/Dorling Kindersley Media Library; The Metropolitan Museum of Art/The Metropolitan Museum of Art, Rogers Fund, 1906. (06.1021.117)

Chapter 4: George Grigoriou/Getty Images Inc.—Stone Allstock; Araldo de Luca/CORBIS BETTMANN/(c) Araldo de Luca/CORBIS; The Metropolitan Museum of Art/The Metropolitan Museum of Art, Rogers Fund, 1907. (07.286.86); Getty Images Inc.—Image Bank; Laurence King Publishing Ltd./Laurence King Publishing, Ltd

Chapter 5: CORBIS BETTMANN; Scala/Art Resource, N.Y.; Warner Forman/Art Resource, N.Y.

Chapter 6: Alinari/Art Resource, N.Y.; Sami Sarkis/Getty Images, Inc.- Photodisc.; SuperStock, Inc./Capitoline Museums, Rome, Italy/Canali PhotoBank, Milan/SuperStock.

Part Three: German Information Center

Chapter 7: SuperStock, Inc,; Turkish Tourism and Information Office; Library of Congress/Courtesy of the Library of Congress

Chapter 8: Trinity College Library/The Board of Trinity College Dublin; Ann Munchow/Ann Munchow Fotografin; The New York Public Library/Art Resource/Picture Collection, The Branch Libraries, The New York Public Library, Astor, Lenox and Tilden Foundations

Chapter 9: Universitetet Oldsaksamling Oslo/(c) University Museum of Cultural Heritage-University of Oslo, Norway; Art Resource, N.Y./Bildarchiv Foto Marburg/Art Resource; Picture Desk, Inc./Kobal Collection/Picture Desk/The Art Archive/Dagli Orti

Chapter 10: French Government Tourist Office; John Sanford/Photo Network

Part Four: Digital Vision Ltd.

Chapter 11: CORBIS BETTMANN; Steve Vidler/eStock Photography LLC; Réunion des Musées Nationaux/Art Resource, New York

Chapter 12: ROGER ANTROBUS/Getty Images, Inc.—Taxi; John Heseltine/San Lorenzo Basilica; Library of Congress/Courtesy of the Library of Congress

Chapter 13: The Metropolitan Museum of Art/The Metropolitan Museum of Art, Gift of Robert Lehman, 1955. (55.220.2); SuperStock, Inc./National Portrait Gallery, London/SuperStock.; Fogg Art Museum/Harvard University Art Museums/Courtesy of the Fogg Art Museum, Harvard University Art Museums, Gift of Paul J. Sachs

Suggested Resources

Introduction

Scientific research into the origins of human beings and their societies is of fairly recent origin. It tends to be controversial, for some people believe that it strays into areas that belong to faith and religious tradition. The following materials sample some of the major approaches to the subject.

R. Ardrey, *The Territorial Imperative: A Personal Inquiry into the Animal Origins of Property and Nations* (1997); J. Cartwright, *Evolution and Human Behavior: Darwinian Perspectives on Human Nature* (2000); A. Cherry, *The Socializing Instincts: Individual, Family, and Social Bonds* (1994); E. Delson, et al., *Encyclopedia of Human Evolution and Prehistory* (2000); J. Diamond, *Guns, Germs, and Steel: The Fates of Human Societies* (1997); P. H. Gouyon, *Gene Avatars: The Neo-Darwinian Theory of Evolution* (2002); D. Lambert, *Encyclopedia of Prehistory (2002)*; A. Montagu, *The Nature of Human Aggression* (1976); S. Pinker, *The Language Instinct: How the Mind Creates Language* (1995); S. Sanderson, *Then Evolution of Human Sociality: A Darwinian Conflict Perspective* (2001); R. J. Werke, *Prehistory: Humankind's First Three Million Years* (1999).

For a discussion of the history of the development of evolutionary theory see:
http://www.ucmp.berkeley.edu/history/evolution.html
For an illustrated narrative description of one theory of human evolution see:
http://www.becominghuman.org

Chapter 1

Scholars who study the transition from the prehistorical to the historical eras must infer a great deal from scanty evidence. Archaeologists have made some lucky discoveries at widely scattered sites, but only a few key locales have been intensively explored. Anthropological studies of modern tribal peoples have suggested theoretical models that might shed light on the remote past, and these have been of particular interest to students of gender roles. The dramatic progress that ecologists have been making in uncovering information about Earth's climate cycles has also yielded valuable information about the environments to which early human cultures adapted. The following list of titles offers only a partial introduction to some of the work that has been done in these fields.

M. N. Cohen, *The Food Crisis in Prehistory: Overpopulation and the Origins of Agriculture* (1977); M. Ehrenberg, *Women in Prehistory* (1989); H. Frankfort, et al., *The Intellectual Adventure of Ancient Man* (1946); C. Freeman, *Egypt, Greece, and Rome* (1996); M. Gimbutas, *The Goddesses and Gods of Old Europe* (1982); N. Grimal, *A History of Ancient Egypt* (1988); D. O. Henry, *From Foraging to Agriculture* (1989); M. Isler, *Sticks, Stones, and Shadows: Building the Egyptian Pyramids* (2001); S. N. Kramer, *History Begins at Sumer* (1959); S. Lloyd, *The Archaeology of Mesopotamia* (1984); S. Pollock, *Ancient Mesopotamia: The Eden That Never Was* (1999); J. N. Postgate, *Early Mesopotamia* (1992); R. Rudgley, *The Lost Civilizations of the Stone Age* (2000); E. R. Service, *Origins of the State and Civilization: The Process of Cultural Evolution* (1975); H. W. F. Saggs, *Civilization Before Greece and Rome* (1989); D. C. Snell, *Life in the Ancient Near East* (1997); A. J. Spencer, *Early Egypt: The Rise of Civilization in the Nile Valley* (1993).

For textual and visual information on ancient Sumer go to:
http://www.ragz-international.com/sumer.html
http://www.edu/art/arth100/monumentality/Sumer/sumer.html
To explore Egypt's Old Kingdom and the pyramids useful links will be found at:
http://www.art-and-archaeology.com/timelines/egypt/old.html

Chapter 2

The invention of writing made it possible for human beings to document their lives in unprecedented detail. Ancient peoples produced both intentional and unintentional records—that is, public monuments that they expected to survive and incidental jottings whose survival has been totally fortuitous. From these things it is possible, for the first time, to infer something about the intellectual lives and thought processes of human beings. The works listed below survey some of this intriguing work.

B. Brier, *The Murder of Tutankhamen* (1998); H. Frankfort, et al. *The Intellectual Adventure of Ancient Man* (1946); N. Grimal, *A History of Ancient Egypt* (1988); O. R. Gurney, *The Hittites* (1954/81); A. Kuhrt, *The Ancient Near East, c. 3000–330 B.C.* (1995); S. Moscati, *Ancient Semitic Civilizations* (1960); K. R. Nemet-Nejat, *Daily Life in Ancient Mesopotamia* (1998); H. W. F. Saggs, *Babylonians* (1995); J. & D. Oates, *Nimrud: An Assyrian City Revealed* (2001); J. B. Pritchard, *The Ancient Near East: An Anthology of Texts and Pictures* (1958); D. Redford, *Akhenaten* (1987); G. Robbins, *Women in Ancient Egypt* (1993); N. Sanders, *The Sea Peoples: Warriors of the Ancient Mediterranean* (1978).

For information on Egypt's Amarna era and New Kingdom see:
http://publish.uwo.ca/~charring/egypt/17nouemp.htm
http://www.friesian.com/tombs.htm
http://www.nationalgeographic.com/egypt

For links to sources on ancient Israel see:
http://www.fordham.edu/halsall/ancient/asbook06.html
For links to sites on ancient Assyria see:
http://www.aina.org/aol/nimrud

Chapter 3

The classical Greek civilization that arose in the Aegean was incredibly inventive and potent. It permanently changed life in the West, and its influence continues to be felt today. Scholars divide, however, on the issue of its sources. Some emphasize its originality and others stress its indebtedness to other cultures. The works listed below provide a starting point for investigating this issue.

A. Andrews, *Greek Tyrants* (1963); J. Boardman, *The Greeks Overseas*, rev. ed. (1980); W. Bernal, *Black Athena: The Afroasiatic Roots of Classical Civilization* (1987); J. Boardman, J. Griffin, and O. Murray, *Greece and the Hellenistic World* (1988); A. C. Brackman, *The Dream of Troy* (1974); F. Braudel, *Memory and the Mediterranean* (2002); A. R. Burn, *Persia and the Greeks: The Defense of the West*, rev. ed. (1984); J. M. Camp, *The Archaeology of Athens* (2002); J. Chadwick, *The Mycenaean World* (1976); O. Dickinson, *The Aegean Bronze Age* (1994); R. Drews, *The Coming of the Greeks: Indo-European Conquests in the Aegean and Near East* (1988); R. Drews, *The End of the Bronze Age: Changes in Warfare and Catastrophes, ca. 1200 B.C.* (1993); M. I. Finley, *The World of Odysseus*, rev. ed. (1979); J. Griffin, *Homer* (1980); V. D. Hanson, *The Western Way of War* (1989); W. Forrest, *A History of Sparta, 950–121 B.C.*, 2nd ed.(1980); L. G. Mitchell and P. J. Rhodes, eds., *The Development of the Polis in Archaic Greece* (1997); R. Osborne, *Demos* (1985); S. B. Pomeroy, S. M. Burstein, W. Donlan, J. T. Roberts, *Ancient Greece: A Political, Social, and Cultural History* (1999).

For images of Minoan and Mycenaean art an architecture see:
http://employees.oneonta.edu/farberas/arth/ARTH209/minoan_mycenaean.html
http://okanagan.bc.ca/hist/hist110/Greece/Bronze
For sources on ancient Sparta see:
http://www.csun.edu/~hcfll004/sparta.html
For ancient Athens see:
http://www.indiana.edu/~kglowack/Athens

Chapter 4

The artistic and literary monuments of classical Greek civilization were created over the span of only a few generations–and against a background of frequent military activity. Wars tested Greece's institutions and prompted its intellectuals to think deeply about the phenomena of the natural world and the mysteries of human self-awareness. This produced a body of philosophical, scientific, and artistic work of unsurpassed importance. The sources listed below provide an introduction to this material and to the context in which it evolved.

J. Boardman, *Greek Art* (1985); J. Boardman et al., *Greece and the Hellenistic World*(1988); W. Burkert, *Greek Religion* (1985); A. Burn, *Persia and the Greeks: The Defense of the West*, 2nd ed. (1984); J. K. Davies, *Democracy and Classical Greece* (1993); K. J. Dover, *Greek Homosexuality* (1978); C. W. Fornara & L. J. Samons, *Athens from Cleisthenes to Pericles* (1991); Y. Garlan, *Slavery in Ancient Greece* (1988), M. Grant, *The Ancient Historians* (1970); W. K. Guthrie, *History of Greek Philosophy* (1962–1981); E. Hamilton, *The Greek Way* (1930); M. M. Henry, *Prisoner of History: Aspasia of Miletus and Her Biographical Tradition* (1995); D. Kagan, *Pericles of Athens and the Birth of Athenian Democracy* (1991); G. E. R. Lloyd, *Early Greek Science* (1970); R. Meigs, *The Athenian Empire* (1972); J. J. Pollitt, *Art and Experience in Classical Greece* (1972); S. B. Pomeroy et al., *Ancient Greece: A Political, Social and Cultural History* (1999); J. D. Romilly, *A Short History of Greek Literature* (1985); A. Shapiro, *Women in the Classical World* (1994); I. F. Stone, *The Trial of Socrates* (1989).

For views of Athens' Acropolis and the Acropolis museum see:
http://www.grisel.net/acropolis_museum.htm
http://www.sonic.net/~hellenik/index.html
For images of classical art see:
http://arthist.cla.umn.edu/art/htm/ancient/gcl_hell.htlml
http://www.metmuseum.org/collections/department.asp?dep=13

Chapter 5

Roman civilization was a Hellenistic civilization. That is, Rome adopted and adapted the cosmopolitan Greek culture that spread throughout the West in the wake of Alexander the Great's conquests. The Romans were, however, also innovators and pioneers–particularly in the arena of law and politics. America's "founding fathers" were greatly attracted to the study of Roman history, and their idealized visions of ancient Rome influenced the formation of the early American republic. Roman successes were the result of lessons learned through a painful process of trial and error. The following works provide an introduction to the Romans' legacy from the Greeks and to the experiences that helped the Romans structure their unique institutions.

G. Alföldy, *The Social History of Rome* (1985); N. Bagnall, *The Punic Wars* (1990); R. A. Bauman, *Women and Politics in Ancient Rome* (1992); J. Boardman et al., *The Roman World* (1990); E. N. Borza, *In the Shadow of Olympus: The Emergence of Macedon* (1990); A. B. Bosworth, *Conquest and Empire: The Reign of Alexander the Great* (1988); T. J. Cornell, *The Be-*

ginnings of Rome: Italy and Rome from the Bronze Age to the Punic Wars (1995); M. H. Crawford, *The Roman Republic,* 2nd ed. (1993); R. M. Errington, *The Dawn of Empire: Rome's Rise to World Power* (1971); P. M. Fraser, *Ptolemaic Alexandria* (1972); M. Grant, *Cleopatra* (1972); P. Green, *Alexander of Macedon* (1991); E. S. Gruen, *The Hellenistic World and the Coming of Rome* (1984); N. G. L. Hammond & F. W. Walbank, *A History of Macedonia* (1988); P. Horden & N. Purcell, *The Corlrupting Sea: A study of Mediterranean History* (2000); A. D. Long, *Hellenistic Philosophy: Stoics, Epicureans, Skeptics,* 2nd ed. (1986); R. E. Mitchell, *Patricians and Plebeians: The Origin of the Roman State* (1990); M. Pallottino, *The Etruscans* (1975); J. J. Pollitt, *Art in the Hellenistic Age* (1986); H. H. Scullard, *A History of the Roman World, 753–146 B.C.E.* 4th ed. (1980); R. Syme, *The Roman Revolution* (1960); F. W. Walbank, *The Hellenistic World* (1993); B. H.. Warmington, *Carthage,* 2nd ed. (1969).

For information on Alexander the Great see:
http://www.geocites.com/Athens/1358
http://www.makedonija.info/alex.html
For information on the Persian Empire and views of its capital, Persepolis see:
http://tehran.stanford.edu/imagemap/persepolis.html
For sources and images from ancient Rome see:
http://www.fordham.edu/halsall/ancient/asbook09.html
http://www.geocities.com/Athens/Forum/6946/rome.html

Chapter 6

The Roman empire was a remarkably successful and long-lived institution. It maintained order and stability throughout the entire western world for over two centuries, a record that no subsequent government has equaled. The empire was not, however, sustained by a single set of unchanging institutions. To preserve the empire, Rome's leaders had to constantly adapt and reorganize it. Eventually, it changed so much that its core identity was threatened. The works listed below are only a few of the many important studies of stages in this intriguing process.

T. Barnes, *The New Empire of Diocletian and Constantine* (1982); H. C. Boren, *Roman Society,* 2nd ed. (1992); B. Campbell, *The Emperor and the Roman Army* (1984); R. Duncan-Jones, *The Economy of the Roman Empire* (1982); A. Ferrill, *Caligula: Emperor of Rome* (1991); K. Galinsky, *Augustan Culture* (1996); M. Grant, *The Roman Emperors* (1985); E. N. Luttwak, *The Grand Strategy of the Roman Empire* (1976); P. MacKendrick, *The Mute Stones Speak: The Story of Archeology in Italy,* 2nd ed. (1983); F. G. B. Millar, *The Emperor in the Roman World, 31 B.C.–A.D. 337* (1977); R. P. Saller, *The Roman Empire: Economy, Society and Culture* (1987); E. T. Salmon, *A History of the Roman World, 30 B.C. to A.D. 138* (1968); D. Shotter, *Augustus Caesar* (1991); R. Syme, *The Roman Revolution* (1960); T. Wiedemann, *Emperors and Gladiators* (1992).

For information and images related to Rome's emperors see:
http://etext.lib.virginia.edu/users/morford/augimape.html
http://www.roman-emperors.org
To explore Pompeii see:
http://pompeii.virginia.edu
For images of major Roman buildings see:
http://www.greatbuildings.com/buildings/Roman

Chapter 7

As the Roman empire declined, its eastern and western halves separated. This foreshadowed the split that has emerged between the Christian "west" and the Muslim "east." During the Middle Ages, however, the civilization that spread through Europe was transformed by a surge of influences from the Middle East. The most significant of these was, of course, Christianity. But the brilliant Byzantine and Islamic cultures that arose in the Middle East were also instrumental in helping Europe emerge from its Dark Age and restore its civilized institutions. The works listed below provide an introduction to key elements in this process.

K. Armstrong, *Muhammad: A Biography of the Prophet* (1992); T. Barnes, *The New Empire of Diocletian and Constantine* (1982); P. Brown, *Augustine of Hippo* (1967); P. Brown, *The World of Late Antiquity, C.E. 150–750* (1971); R. Browning, *The Byzantine Empire* (1992); W. Goffart, *Barbarians and Romans, A.D. 418–584: The Techniques of Accommodation* (1980); M. Grant, *The Fall of the Roman Empire* (1990); P. J. Heather, *Goths and Romans, 332–489* (1991); A. H. Hourani, *A History of the Arab Peoples* (1992); C. H. Lawrence, *Medieval Monasticism,* 2nd ed. (1989); J. Morehead, *Justinian* 1995); H. St.L. B. Moss, *The Birth of the Middle Ages, 395–814,* 2nd ed. (1972); G. Ostrogosky, *History of the Byzantine State,* 2nd ed. (1969); F. E. Peters, *Muhammad and the Origins of Islam* (1994); A. Schimmel, *Islam: An Introduction* (1992).

For information on the Emperor Constantine and the origin of Byzantium see:
http://www.newadvent.org/cathen/04295c.htm
http://www.metmuseum.ord/explore/byzantium/by2_2.html
http://www.greatbuildinigs.com/buildings/Hagia_Sophia.htm
For links to sites relating to the Huns and Germans see:
http://hsiungnu.chat.ru/
http://www.archaeolink.com/germanic_tribes.htm
There are numerous sites relating to the history and practice of Islam, some of which take strongly partisan positions. As is the case with all web materials, students need to exercise judgment in evaluating their reliability:
http://www.al-islam.org/lifeprophet/

Chapter 8

Early medieval Europe was characterized by a diversity of peoples and cultures. Several attempts were made to overcome its political fragmentation and restore the unity it had enjoyed during the Roman era, but none succeeded for very long. The result was a period in history about which it is difficult to generalize with any accuracy. The following works offer a brief introduction to the mix of peoples and movements that contributed to Europe's reorganization and its gradual emergence as an original and influential civilization.

L. Bitel, *Isle of the Saints: Monastic Settlement and Christian Community in Early Ireland* (1990); P. H. Blair, *The World of Bede* (1970); J. Boussard, *The Civilization of Charlemagne* (1971); O. Chadwick, *The Making of the Benedictine Ideal* (1981); N. Christie, *The Lombards, the Ancient Longobards* (1995); R. Collins, *Early Medieval Spain: Unity in Diversity, 400–1000* (1983); G. Duby, *Rural Economy and Country Life in the Medieval West* (1968); P. J. Geary, *Before France and Germany: The Creation and Transformation of the Merovingian World* (1988); F. D. Logan, *The Vikings in History*, 2nd ed. (1991); H. R. Loyn, *The Governance of Anglo-Saxon England, 500–1087* (1984); R. W. Mathisen, *Roman Aristocrats in Barbarian Gaul: Strategies for Survival in an Age of Transition* (1993); R. McKitterick, *The Frankish Kingdoms under the Carolingians, 751–98/* (1983); R. McKitterick, *Carolingian Culture: Emulation and Innovation* (1994); J. P. Ply & E. Bournazel, *The Feudal Transformation, 900–1200* (1991); J. D. Randers-Pherson, *Barbarians and Romans: The Birth Struggle of Europe, A.D. 400–700* (1983); S. Reynolds, *Fiefs and Vassals* (1994); J. Richards, *The Popes and the Papacy in the Early Middle Ages, 476–752* (1979); L. White, *Medieval Technology and Social Change* (1972); I. N. Wood, *The Merovingian Kingdoms, 450–751* (1994).

For sources on feudalism and manorialism see:
http://www.fordham.edu/halsall/sbook1i.html
http://www.historyguide.org/ancient/feudalism.html
http://www.learner.org/exhibits/middleages/feudal.html
For a description of Charlemagne's church at Aachen see:
http://www.jfks.de/slife/classtrips/france2000/aachencathedral.html

Chapter 9

Europe entered the Middle Ages as the weakest of the Mediterranean world's three civilizations. Its Byzantine and Muslim neighbors were far more advanced intellectually and had richer economies and more thriving urban institutions. Not surprisingly, therefore, Europe languished on the defensive, struggling with successive waves of invasion and migration. By the 11th century, however, European societies had begun to stabilize, and Europeans were able to reverse course and take the offensive. The wars of conquest, which they inaugurated—the crusades, both signaled and promoted the revival of European civilization, but these wars have left a legacy of hate that continues to the present day. The following works provide an introduction to major developments in a period of Western history that has special contemporary significance.

K. Armstrong, *Holy War: The Crusades and Their Impact on Today's World*, rev. ed. (2001); G. Barraclough, *The Crucible of Europe, the Ninth and Tenth Centuries in European History* (1976); R. Bartlett, *The Making of Europe: Conquest, Colonization and Cultural Change, 950–1350* (1993); U. R. Blumenthal, *The Investiture Controversy: Church and Monarchy from the Ninth to the Twelfth Century* (1988); M. Brett, *The Rise of the Fatimids: The World of the Mediterranean and the Middle East in the 4th Century of the Hijra, 10th Century C.E.* (2001); D. Crouch, *The Reign of King Stephen, 1135–1154* (2000); D.C. Douglas, *William the Conqueror: The Norman Impact Upon England* (1964); E. Ennen, *The Medieval Town* (1979); J. Haldon, *Byzantium: A History* (2000); E. M. Hallam, *Capetian France, 987–1328* (1980); C. Hillenbrand, *The Crusades: Islamic Perspectives* (1999); R. Jenkins, *Byzantium: The Imperial Centuries, 610–1071* (1969); R. Hodges, *Towns and Trade in the Age of Charlemagne* (2000); H. Kennedy, *The Prophet and the Age of the Caliphates: The Islamic Near East from the Sixth to the Eleventh Century* (1986); R. S. Lopez, *The Commercial Revolution of the Middle Ages, 950–1350* (1971); G. A. Loud, *The Age of Robert Guiscard: Southern Italy and the Norman Conquest* (2000); R. I. Moore, *The First European Revolution* (2000); S. Reynolds, *Fiefs and Vassals* (1994); S. Reynolds, *Kingdoms and Communities in Western Europe, 900–1300* (1984); J. Riley-Smith, *The First Crusaders, 1095–1131* (1997); J. Riley-Smith, ed., *The Oxford Illustrated History of the Crusades* (1997); W. Roesener, *Peasants in the Middle Ages* (1992); S. Runciman, *A History of the Crusades* (1964); J. R. Strayer, *Feudalism* (1985); W. Treadgold, *The Byzantine Revival, 780–842* (1988); D. Webb, *Pilgrims and Pilgrimage in the Medieval West* (1999).

For illustrations and information relating to Constantinople, the capital of the Byzantine Empire see:
http://www.fordham.edu/halsall/byzantium/images.html#ex3
http://w4u.eexi.gr/~ippotis/consten.html
For images from the Bayeux tapestry go to:
http://www.sjolander.com/viking/museum/bt/bt.html
For sources on the crusades to the Holy Land see:
http://www.fordham.edu/halsall/sbook1k.html
For links to sites with information about medieval towns see:
http://www.trytel.com/~tristan/towns/towns.html

Chapter 10

During the High Middle Ages, the contours of some of Europe's major nation states began to appear on the map and strides were made toward the development of their characteristic political and cultural institutions. This was also a period of intellectual and artistic inventiveness. Great cathedrals—wonders of engineering and architectural vision—were erected.

Universities appeared. Literacy spread, and Europeans engaged in lively (often contentious) debates that produced break-throughs in philosophy and science. The works listed below provide an introduction to some of the key developments in one of the most vibrant periods in European intellectual history.

D. Abulafia, *Frederick II: A Medieval Emperor* (1988); J. B. Baldwin, *The Government of Philip Augustus: Foundations of French Royal Power in the Middle Ages* (1986); J. W. Baldwin, *The Scholastic Culture of the Middle Ages, 1000–1300* (1971); M. Barber, *The Cathars: Dualist Heretics in Languedoc in the High Middle Ages* (2000); R. Bartlett, *England under the Norman and Angevin Kings, 1075–1225* (2000); C. H. Berman, *The Cistercian Evolution: The Invention of a Religious Order in Twelfth-Century Europe* (2000); J. Bony, *French Gothic Architectgure of the Twelfth and Thirteenth Centuries* (1983); M. T. Clanchy, *Abelard: A Medieval Life* (1997); K. J. Conant, *Carolingian and Romanesque Architecture, 800–1200*, 2nd ed. (1979); S. C. Ferruolo, *The Origins of the University* (1985); J. Gillingham, *Richard I* (1999); L. B. Glick, *Abraham's Heirs: Jews and Christians in Medieval Europe* (1999); W. C. Jordan, *Louis IX and the Challenge of the Crusade: A Study in Rulership* (1979); C. H. Lawrence, *The Friars: The Impact of the Early Mendicant Movement on Western Society* (1994); J. Marenbon, *Later Medieval Philosophy (1150–1350): An Introduction* (1987); M. R. Menocal, *The Arabic Role in Medieval Literary History: A Forgotten Heritage* (1987); P. Munz, *Frederick Barbarossa: A Study in Medieval Politics* (1969); S. Reynolds, *Kingdoms and Communities in Western Europe, 900–1300* (1984); H. de Ridder-Symoens, ed., *Universities in the Middle Ages* (1992); H. Schulze, *States, Nations and Nationalism* (1994); W. S. Stoddard, *Art and Architecture in Medieval France* (1990); J. R. Strayer, *On the Medieval Origins of the Modern State* (1970); W. L. Warren, *Henry II* (1973).

For information of Scholasticism see:
http://www.nd/Departments/Maritain/etext/scholas1.htm
For images from medieval illuminated manuscripts of various periods go to:
http://www.columbia.edu/cu/libraries/indiv/rare/images/date.html
For examples of Romanesque and Gothic architecture see:
http://www.bc.edu/be_prg/aup/cas/fnart/arch/gothic_arch.html
http://www.owlnet.rice.edu/~hart205/Cathedrals/Plan/plan.html

Chapter 11

The late medieval world was tested in many ways, and, over all, it confronted its challenges successfully. Despite failures of leadership and what was sometimes an all-consuming preoccupation with the struggle to survive, Europe's cultural creativity was undiminished. Europeans weathered their crises, restored their institutions, and emerged from their trials prepared for a new era of invention and expansion. The following works may have special contemporary significance, for they illustrate how the West has responded in the past when it perceived threats to its survival.

C. Allmand, *The Hundred Years War: England and France at War* (1988); T. S. R. Boase, *Death in the Middle Ages: Mortality, Judgment, and Remembrance* (1972); R. Brown-Grant, *Christine de Pizan and the Moral Defense of Women: Reading Beyond Gender* (1999); J. H. Burns, ed., *The Cambridge History of Medieval Political Thought* (1988); N. Cantor, *In the Wake of the Plague: The Black Death and the World It Made* (2001); A. Curry, *The Hundred Years War* (1993); K. Fowler, *Medieval Mercenaries*, vol. 1: *The Great Companies* (2001); R. Frame, *The Political Development of the British Isles, 1100–1400* (1995); R. Gottfried, *The Black Death: Natural and Human Disaster in Medieval Europe* (1983); D. Herlihy, *The Black Death and the Transformation of the West* (1997); W. C. Jordan, *The Great Famine: Northern Europe in the Early Fourteenth Century* (1996); J. Larner, *Marco Polo and the Discovery of the World* (1999); J. P. Morrall, *Political Thought in Medieval Times* (1962); F. Oakley, *The Western Church in the Later Middle Ages* (1979); Y. Renouard, *The Avignon Papacy, 1305–1403* (1970); J. Schatazmiller, *Jews, Medicine, and Medieval Society* (1994); J. R. Strayer, *The Reign of Philip the Fair* (1980); M. G. A. Vale, *War and Chivalry: Warfare and Aristocratic Culture in England, France, and Burgundy at the End of the Middle Ages* (1981); N. W. Warner, *Joan of Arc: The Image of Female Heroism* (1981).

For information on medieval climate and environment see:
http://www2.sunysuffolk.edu/mandias/lia/little_ice_age.html
http://www.carleton.ca/~tpatters/teaching/climatechange/climateawareness/aware28a.html
For links to sites that deal with the medieval plagues see:
http://jefferson.village.virginia.edu/osheim/intro.html
http://www.byu.edu/ipt/projects/middleages/LifeTimes/Plague.html
For information on the crises of the late medieval church see:
http://www.beyond.fr/villages/avignonpopes.html
http://www.fordham.edu/halsall/source/grtschism1:html
For medieval manuscript illuminations inspired by the Hundred Years' War see:
http://www.bnk.fr/enluminures/themes/t_1/st_1_02/2102.html

Chapter 12

Europe's Renaissance and Age of Exploration mark a turning point in global history. Many of the key developments that have shaped life in the modern world can be traced to this era: mass literacy, global exchanges of goods and cultures, widening divergence of Christian and Muslim peoples, and the resurgence of the humanistic element in Western civilization. The works listed are only a few of the many studies that have explored the transition from the medieval to the early modern eras.

H. Beinart, *The Expulsion of the Jews from Spain* (2002); S. Bemrose, *A New Life Of Dante* (2000); P. Burke, *The European Renaissance: Centers and Peripheries* (1998); A. W. Crosby, *The Biological Expansion of Europe* (1986); E. L. Eisenstein, *The Printing Press as an Agent of Change* (1978); F. Fernandez-Armesto, *Columbus* (1991); M. Greene, *A Shared World: Christians and Muslims in the Early Modern Mediterranean* (2000); J. Hale, *The Civilization of Europe in the Renaissance* (1994); J. N. Hillgarth, *The Spanish Kingdoms, 1250–1516* (1978); G. Holmes, *Renaissance* (1996); J. Huizinga, *The Autumn of the Middle Ages* (1924/1996); H. Inalcik, *The Ottoman Empire: The Classical Age, 1300–1600* (1973); L. Jardine, *Worldly Goods: A New History of the Renaissance* (1996); P. Johnson, *The Renaissance: A Short History* (2000); M. L. King, *Women of the Renaissance* (1991); B. G. Kohl and A. A. Smith, *Major Problems in the History of the Italian Renaissance* (1995); G. Leff, *The Dissolution of the Medieval Outlook, an Essay on Intellectual and Spiritual Change in the Fourteenth Century* (1976); B. Lewis, *Istanbul and the Civilization of the Ottoman Empire* (1963); B. Lewis, *What Went Wrong? Western Impact and Middle Eastern Response* (2002); L. Martins, *Power and Imagination: City-States in Renaissance Italy* (1989); C. G. Nauert, *Humanism and the Culture of the Renaissance* (1995); P. Russell, *Prince Henry "the Navigator": A Life* (2000); G. V. Scammell, *The First Imperial Age: European Overseas Expansion, c. 1400–1715* (1989); B. Thompson, *Humanists and Reformers* (1996); D. Waley, *The Italian City Republics* (1969).

For links to images and information relating to the Italian and Northern Renaissances see:

http://www.ibiblio.orgwm/paint/tl/it-ren/
http://www.abcgallery.com/index.html
http://sunsite.ord.uk/wm/paint/tl/north-ren/

For links to information about Ottoman civilization see:

http://www.exploreturkey.com/exptur.phtml?id=274

For a site relating to the early history of trans-Atlantic cultural contacts see:

http://muweb.millersville.edu/~winthrop/atlantic.html

Chapter 13

Despite the confident predictions of many secularists, religion has not faded as a significant factor influencing the behavior of modern peoples and states. The history of the era of Europe's reformation and religious wars may, therefore, be of special interest to students of current world affairs. It is also important for the study of American history, for the religious ideologies that emerged at this time were transplanted to America and shaped the American way of life. The works listed provide only a brief introduction to the vast body of scholarship inspired by this rich, complex era.

R. Ashton, *Counter-Revolution: The Second Civil War and Its Origin, 1646–1648* (1995); R. Bonney, *The European Dynastic States, 1494–1660* (1991); W. J. Bouwsma, *John Calvin: A Sixteenth-Century Portrait* (1988); F. Braudel, *The Mediterranean and the Mediterranean World in the Age of Philip II*, 2 vols. (1976); E. Cameron, *The European Reformation* (1991); P. Caravan, *Ignatius Loyola: A Biography of the Founder of the Jesuits* (1990); P. Collinson, *The Religion of Protestants: The Church in English Society, 1559–1625* (1982); A. G. Dickens, *The English Reformation*, 2nd ed. (1989); R. S. Dunn, *The Age of Religious Wars, 1559–1715*, 2nd ed. (1979); P. Gay and R. K. Webb, *Modern Europe to 1815* (1973); P. Gaunt, *Oliver Cromwell* (1996); S. Greenblatt, ed. *The Norton Shakespeare* (1997); C. Haigh, *Elizabeth I*, 2nd ed. (1998); M. P. Holt, *The French Wars of Religion, 1562–1629* (1995); H. Kamen, *Spain 1469–1714: A Society of Conflict*, 2nd ed. (1991); R. J. Knechy, *Catherine de' Medici* (1998); S. J. Lee, *The Thirty Years' War* (1991); C. Lindberg, *The European Reformations* (1996); J. McConica, *Erasmus* (1991); A. McGrath, *A Life of John Calvin: A Study in the Shaping of Western Culture* (1990); A. McGrath, *Reformation Thought: An Introduction*, 2nd ed. (1993); H. A. Oberman, *Luther* (1992); M. R. O'Connell, *The Counter Reformation, 1559–1610* (1974); S. Ozment, *The Age of Reform, 1250–1550: An Intellectual and Religious History of Late Medieval and Reformation Europe* (1980); S. Ozment, *Protestants: The Birth of a Revolution* (1992); G. Parker, *Philip II*, 3rd ed. (1995); J. M. Roberts, *The Penguin History of Europe* (1996); W. P. Stephens, *Zwingli* (1994); B. Thompson, *Humanists and Reformers: A History of Renaissance and Reformation* (1996); G. H. Williams, *The Radical Reformation*, 2nd ed. (1992); J. Wormald, *Mary Queen of Scots: A Study in Failure* (1991).

For links to source materials and images relating the Protestant and Catholic Reformations see:

http://history.hanover.edu/early/prot.htm
http://history.hanover.edu/early/cath.htm
http://www.martinluther.de/english/homef.htm

For information on Elizabethan England and Shakespeare see:

http://www.bardweb.net/england.html

For links to information on the religious wars see:

http://www.lukehistory.com/resources/ecwpubs.html

For information on the culture of Spain's Golden Age see:

http://www.kfki.hu/~arthp/tours/spain/p_17.html

INDEX

Note: Page numbers ending in "f" refer to figures. Page numbers ending in "m" refer to maps. Page numbers ending in "t" refer to tables.

SINGLE PC LICENSE AGREEMENT AND LIMITED WARRANTY

READ THIS LICENSE CAREFULLY BEFORE OPENING THIS PACKAGE. BY OPENING THIS PACKAGE, YOU ARE AGREEING TO THE TERMS AND CONDITIONS OF THIS LICENSE. IF YOU DO NOT AGREE, DO NOT OPEN THE PACKAGE. PROMPTLY RETURN THE UNOPENED PACKAGE AND ALL ACCOMPANYING ITEMS TO THE PLACE YOU OBTAINED THEM [[FOR A FULL REFUND OF ANY SUMS YOU HAVE PAID FOR THE SOFTWARE]]. *THESE TERMS APPLY TO ALL LICENSED SOFTWARE ON THE DISK EXCEPT THAT THE TERMS FOR USE OF ANY SHAREWARE OR FREEWARE ON THE DISKETTES ARE AS SET FORTH IN THE ELECTRONIC LICENSE LOCATED ON THE DISK:*

1. GRANT OF LICENSE and OWNERSHIP: The enclosed computer programs <<and data>> ("Software") are licensed, not sold, to you by Pearson Education, Inc. publishing as Prentice Hall. ("We" or the "Company") in consideration of your purchase or adoption of the accompanying Company textbooks and your agreement to these terms. We reserve any rights not granted to you. You own only the disk(s) but we and/or our licensors own the Software itself. This license allows you to use and display your copy of the Software on a single computer (i.e., with a single CPU) at a single location for <u>academic</u> use only, so long as you comply with the terms of this Agreement. You may make one copy for back up, or transfer your copy to another CPU, provided that the Software is usable on only one computer.

2. RESTRICTIONS: You may <u>not</u> transfer or distribute the Software or documentation to anyone else. Except for backup, you may <u>not</u> copy the documentation or the Software. You may <u>not</u> network the Software or otherwise use it on more than one computer or computer terminal at the same time. You may <u>not</u> reverse engineer, disassemble, decompile, modify, adapt, translate, or create derivative works based on the Software or the Documentation. You may be held legally responsible for any copying or copyright infringement that is caused by your failure to abide by the terms of these restrictions.

3. TERMINATION: This license is effective until terminated. This license will terminate automatically without notice from the Company if you fail to comply with any provisions or limitations of this license. Upon termination, you shall destroy the Documentation and all copies of the Software. All provisions of this Agreement as to limitation and disclaimer of warranties, limitation of liability, remedies or damages, and our ownership rights shall survive termination.

4. LIMITED WARRANTY AND DISCLAIMER OF WARRANTY: Company warrants that for a period of 60 days from the date you purchase this SOFTWARE (or purchase or adopt the accompanying textbook), the Software, when properly installed and used in accordance with the Documentation, will operate in substantial conformity with the description of the Software set forth in the Documentation, and that for a period of 30 days the disk(s) on which the Software is delivered shall be free from defects in materials and workmanship under normal use. The Company does <u>not</u> warrant that the Software will meet your requirements or that the operation of the Software will be uninterrupted or error-free. Your only remedy and the Company's only obligation under these limited warranties is, at the Company's option, return of the disk for a refund of any amounts paid for it by you or replacement of the disk. THIS LIMITED WARRANTY IS THE ONLY WARRANTY PROVIDED BY THE COMPANY AND ITS LICENSORS, AND THE COMPANY AND ITS LICENSORS DISCLAIM ALL OTHER WARRANTIES, EXPRESS OR IMPLIED, INCLUDING WITHOUT LIMITATION, THE IMPLIED WARRANTIES OF MERCHANTABILITY AND FITNESS FOR A PARTICULAR PURPOSE. THE COMPANY DOES NOT WARRANT, GUARANTEE OR MAKE ANY REPRESENTATION REGARDING THE ACCURACY, RELIABILITY, CURRENTNESS, USE, OR RESULTS OF USE, OF THE SOFTWARE.

5. LIMITATION OF REMEDIES AND DAMAGES: IN NO EVENT, SHALL THE COMPANY OR ITS EMPLOYEES, AGENTS, LICENSORS, OR CONTRACTORS BE LIABLE FOR ANY INCIDENTAL, INDIRECT, SPECIAL, OR CONSEQUENTIAL DAMAGES ARISING OUT OF OR IN CONNECTION WITH THIS LICENSE OR THE SOFTWARE, INCLUDING FOR LOSS OF USE, LOSS OF DATA, LOSS OF INCOME OR PROFIT, OR OTHER LOSSES, SUSTAINED AS A RESULT OF INJURY TO ANY PERSON, OR LOSS OF OR DAMAGE TO PROPERTY, OR CLAIMS OF THIRD PARTIES, EVEN IF THE COMPANY OR AN AUTHORIZED REPRESENTATIVE OF THE COMPANY HAS BEEN ADVISED OF THE POSSIBILITY OF SUCH DAMAGES. IN NO EVENT SHALL THE LIABILITY OF THE COMPANY FOR DAMAGES WITH RESPECT TO THE SOFTWARE EXCEED THE AMOUNTS ACTUALLY PAID BY YOU, IF ANY, FOR THE SOFTWARE OR THE ACCOMPANYING TEXTBOOK. BECAUSE SOME JURISDICTIONS DO NOT ALLOW THE LIMITATION OF LIABILITY IN CERTAIN CIRCUMSTANCES, THE ABOVE LIMITATIONS MAY NOT ALWAYS APPLY TO YOU.

6. GENERAL: THIS AGREEMENT SHALL BE CONSTRUED IN ACCORDANCE WITH THE LAWS OF THE UNITED STATES OF AMERICA AND THE STATE OF NEW YORK, APPLICABLE TO CONTRACTS MADE IN NEW YORK, AND SHALL BENEFIT THE COMPANY, ITS AFFILIATES AND ASSIGNEES. HIS AGREEMENT IS THE COMPLETE AND EXCLUSIVE STATEMENT OF THE AGREEMENT BETWEEN YOU AND THE COMPANY AND SUPERSEDES ALL PROPOSALS OR PRIOR AGREEMENTS, ORAL, OR WRITTEN, AND ANY OTHER COMMUNICATIONS BETWEEN YOU AND THE COMPANY OR ANY REPRESENTATIVE OF THE COMPANY RELATING TO THE SUBJECT MATTER OF THIS AGREEMENT. If you are a U.S. Government user, this Software is licensed with "restricted rights" as set forth in subparagraphs (a)-(d) of the Commercial Computer-Restricted Rights clause at FAR 52.227-19 or in subparagraphs (c)(1)(ii) of the Rights in Technical Data and Computer Software clause at DFARS 252.227-7013, and similar clauses, as applicable.

Should you have any questions concerning this agreement or if you wish to contact the Company for any reason, please contact in writing: Prentice Hall, One Lake Street, Upper Saddle River, NJ 07458.